PROTESTANTISM, CAPITALISM, AND
NATURE IN AMERICA

MARK STOLL

Protestantism, Capitalism, and Nature in America

✝ ✝ ✝

University of New Mexico Press Albuquerque

Library of Congress Cataloging-in-Publication Data

Stoll, Mark, 1954–

    Protestantism, capitalism, and nature in America / by Mark Stoll. — 1st ed.

    p.   cm.

    Includes bibliographical references and index.

    ISBN 0-8263-1780-4 (cl) 0-8263-1781-2 (pbk.)

    1. Nature — Religious aspects — Christianity.   2. Human ecology — Religious

aspects — Protestant churches.   3. Protestant churches — United States — Doctrines.

4. Capitalism — Religious aspects — Christianity.   I. Title.

BT695.5.S75   1997

261.8'362'0973 — dc20   96-25351

                                              CIP

For Lyn

Contents

Preface

Why has the United States been the world's leader in reducing pollution, establishing parks, and protecting wilderness? Why does the United States have the world's largest and most powerful environmentalist movement? And why does this active environmentalism occur in the world's most powerful industrial economy? A reader of the standard historical accounts would surely come away believing that the environmental movement and the environmental or ecological ethic are a century old, at most, and have no roots deeper than Emerson or Thoreau, or perhaps Gilbert White of Selborne, England. In fact, it is difficult to discern much of an intellectual genealogy at all for what we call modern environmentalism. The enormous impact of religion — specifically Christianity and particularly Protestantism — on American ideas about nature, both positive and negative, is least acknowledged of all.

Protestantism has been the fireman at the boiler, the switchman on the tracks, giving momentum and direction to American ideas about nature. It is a curious fact of American history that the people who dominated the early, formative years of both capitalism and environmentalism grew up with the same cultural and religious values. The source of those values for most of them was the most fanatically religious area of colonial British America, New England.

The connection between Protestantism, capitalism, and nature continues today. Protestantism has continued to refresh itself and readjust its values through periodic eras of revival, like the one currently in the United States. The closest contemporary parallel we have to those early Puritan settlers, in theology, ethic, and self-assuredness, are the conservative Prot-

estant churches. Those churches continue to produce the foremost advocates of both resource development and wilderness preservation: witness
James G. Watt and Dave Foreman.

This book describes two similar but different things: how people's religious thinking about nature, and how people's religious thinking, have
affected the natural world. The former has an explicit and the latter an
implicit effect upon nature. The book treats religion not as something that
goes on within the four walls of a church but as something that cannot be
contained within walls or even within a creed, a force in society that in-
trudes into all aspects of life. Likewise, it does not deal with capitalism as a
system (if it is a system) but rather as an entrepreneurial spirit, eager to
organize and rationalize for long-term profit, eager to build and act and
extract and produce and distribute and trade, and jealous of any power that
seeks to impede such activity.

When Protestants withdrew from the Church of Rome in the sixteenth
century, they put together a body of doctrine that was to have rather different effects on nature in different contexts. On the one hand, this doctrine
helped produce the forms of rational law and bureaucracy that allowed
liberal capitalism to arise, and promulgated a work ethic whose spirit animated liberal capitalism's new types of entrepreneurs and workers. This
rationalized world with a busy, productive populace in a growing economy
led to increasing exploitation of natural resources. On the other hand,
Protestantism disseminated the ideals and motivations that created a militant sympathetic attitude toward the natural world, an attitude that engen-
dered the unique forms of environmental activity in such Protestant nations as Germany, Britain, and the United States. One might say that green
and Green — money and ecology, capitalist development and environmental protection — are Protestantism's double legacy.

Protestantism, Capitalism and Nature is divided into two parts. Book One
describes the explicit and implicit ways in which Protestant doctrine bears
upon nature. As the theoretical grounding for Book Two, it lays the theological foundation for the thought and action of Protestants in relation to
the natural world. The first chapter shows how Protestants think of the
world in specifically religious terms. Chapter 2 describes how Protestantism has guided the lives and ethics of its advocates and its children. It
explores the often unconscious workings of this powerful belief system and
follows the subtler ways it shadows people throughout their lives long after
either conversion or apostasy.

Book Two examines ways in which Protestants have acted upon nature in
history, concentrating especially on people influenced by the Calvinist and

Puritan traditions. Although this focus distorts the total picture of Americans and their relationship to nature, it uncovers most clearly the tracks of Protestantism's influence on the development of the industrial exploitation and transformation of nature alongside the development of an ideology of love and protection of nature, themes which more often than not bypass Southern Protestants, black Protestants, Catholics, and Jews. (Jefferson makes an appearance in Book Two because of his influential expression of the American agrarian ideal, but also because he represents some of the reasons Southern traditions produced no indigenous environmental movement.)

Biography best tells the story in Book Two. The traces of youthful religion in adult lives, often disguised or transformed, are easier to see in a portrait than a mural. The subjects of the biographies have been chosen because they show the development of a group of ideas and attitudes of special significance with regard to Americans' use of and respect for nature. Yet — and this is particularly true of the last half century — a work of this size and scope can only begin to map the variety of paths the Protestant tradition has led to. The final chapter, consequently, looks at several recent individuals whose lives suggest some of the more important of the many roads Protestants have trod.

Caveat lector: I by no means intend my thesis on Protestantism's contribution to industrial capitalism and the environmental movement to be a monocausal explanation for them. Church walls cannot keep religion in, and just as certainly they cannot keep the wide world out. Many factors motivate the affairs of humankind, and other writers have ably chronicled how a number of them have affected Americans and nature. I do, however, wish to shed light on this persistent blind spot.

I want to thank several people for their assistance and advice. Foremost, I wish to express my gratitude to William H. Goetzmann, who not only read and commented upon each chapter of the original dissertation, but helped from the beginning in the conceptualization and organization of the whole. With his help I discovered a topic broad enough to include my interests in religion and nature as well as allow me to range across different fields and times, from religion to railroads and from Puritans to preservationists. Consequently it has been great fun to plan, research, and write this work.

I also wish to thank Robert Abzug, Robin Doughty, Aaron Forsberg, Michael G. Hall, Howard Miller, Don Palm, and Don Worster, who each read and commented on the whole book. Jim Bradley, Ed Brannon of Grey Towers National Historical Landmark, and Char Miller were generous with their time and knowledge of Gifford Pinchot. Betsy Stoll located material at the Missouri Historical Society in St. Louis. I owe a debt of gratitude to Durwood Ball, my editor at the University of New Mexico Press, for his enthusiasm for the book. If my prose reads well, it is partly due to the fact that he and copyeditor Ruth Steinberg have made crooked places smooth and the rough places plain. Although I have benefited from the best advice, responsibility for the text and for any errors in it is of course mine.

Finally, and most of all, I must thank my wife, Lyn, and my children, Alex and Erin, for all their support and encouragement.

The Lumbermen
of Eden

It is November 1850 in Maine. From tall, ancient timber, autumn leaves fall. Southbound gray geese call overhead. Moose move nearby. Frost will soon cover the log piles and ice will block the streams and lakes. Not until March will rains finally melt the ice and spring floods carry logs to the mills to be cut by water or steam power. The crystal waters of the Ambijejis stretch broad and clear. Deer browse among the dark pines of Millnoket's ridges. The Penobscot flows through lakes and rocky canyons and over waterfalls. Mount Katahdin's rugged sides appear through breaks in the clouds. An Indian traps in the warm sunshine below while a snowstorm covers the peak.

On a carpet of moss, amidst the scents of leaves, beneath the music of the pines, the lumbermen make their winter camp. While fires of pine knot and beech illumine the long evenings, and jokes and songs lighten duty, the men think of sisters, wives, and daughters, angels of their homes, whose hearths burns brighter for their work. Even if they lack the village sounds of Sunday church bells and choir voices, they do not miss them. They work in the old, majestic temple of God, walled by pines and domed by the sky. They hear his voice in the breeze as it sounded in Eden, and their spirits kneel as they swing their axes. Far from falsehood, they hear truth speak. To God, their labor is an offering equal to that on any altar.

The lumbermen work on, knowing that ships wait to take their loads of lumber to distant shores and exchange them for exotic cargo for the return voyage. In peace, the men labor and bare the shaded earth to the sun and sky. Close behind them they sense the advance of coming ages, in which smiths and farmers will fill the virgin earth and cover it with wheat and corn. Still, they gladly leave behind the cities and plains to live and work in the wild, rocky forests of Maine, close to the heart of Nature, a rugged nurse and sturdy mother to them. There, where no man is a slave, freedom and labor walk hand in hand. As fiery sunrise breaks over Katahdin, they are up and doing, ruggedly hewing their way through the world.

These scenes came from the imagination of John Greenleaf Whittier as he expressed them in his poem "The Lumbermen." As one of the leading American literary figures of his day, he enjoyed an established reputation when he published it in *Songs of Labor, and Other Poems* in 1850. This cycle of poems praised labor as a dignified, sanctified pillar in the temple of freedom and republican virtue. In the precincts of this temple, the free laborer was blessed, and none was enslaved but machinery and nature. A forgotten work written in treacly mid-Victorian style, "The Lumbermen" nevertheless compressed in a few stanzas a whole gamut of mid-nineteenth-century attitudes toward nature.

Within "The Lumbermen" a number of themes emerged. Labor sancti-fied the man, and entry into God's creation uplifted his thoughts. Because men's activity in the world took place in the amoral sphere of economic endeavor and public life, they needed these sanctifying influences. The products of their labor made up the raw materials for manufacturing and worldwide commerce, linking them with international industrial capital-ism. The vanguard of civilization, lumbermen replaced the Indians, whose lives were little more than another part of nature, and tamed the wild north woods for the world of farmers and artisans. As they placed the natural landscape progressively under human control, they sent the fallen trees to mills. The mills in turn operated through enslaving water and steam, the forces of nature.

Women, children, and ministers remained at home, marginal to this world of economic activity, for they were angels already and needed no uplift or purification. They engaged in no economic endeavors but lifted their voices in Sabbath choirs while keeping the hearth warm for the men's return after six months. Yet the lumbermen were not really removed from angelic feminine influence, for Nature, a nurse and mother, conferred her blessing upon those who worshipped and worked close to her.

Whittier and his readers missed the irony in this scenario. In their view, labor was good and idleness sinful; commercial civilization was a bless-ing and wilderness unproductive. Therefore, every swing of the axe was a prayer to God. On the other hand, Nature was a nurturing, sustaining mother, and Creation untouched by man was a temple built by the hand of God. The lumbermen who were uncovering the virgin earth so that others might make her fruitful were at the same time worshiping God by cutting down his temple. Where would humanity go to restore virtue and morality essential to the Republic, when Mother Earth had been made barren and God's temples all laid low? Hardly audible at mid-century, this question would grow ever more insistent in the next decades.

A Quaker abolitionist, Whittier possessed a long New England Puritan pedigree. The themes he used in his poem to lumbermen in the Maine woods were as much a product of the Protestant tradition as Whittier himself. His self-contradictory treatment of nature exemplified the complex legacy that religion left to the United States. He believed strongly in the moral virtue of labor, and that material progress accompanied and supported moral progress. Thus, he praised the development of the country and opposed labor unions. Yet he felt a mystical call from nature, which connected him with other New Englanders like the Romantic, William Cullen Bryant, or the Transcendentalist, Ralph Waldo Emerson.

The complexity of the Christian point of view about nature has made it difficult to identify its historical influence. Since the late 1960s scholars and writers like Lynn White, Jr., William Leiss, Frederick Turner, and Peter Marshall have popularized the claim that Christianity propagated an arrogant attitude toward the natural environment, and shaped the Western endeavor to control the natural world. They lay the blame for polluted air, water, and earth, for radiation and deadly chemicals, and for ravaged forest, field, and mountain directly upon Christian anthropocentrism — arrogance and hubris toward non-human creation. They emphasize the Christian doctrine that teaches that humans must subdue and have dominion over creation and that God made the world for man.[1]

This point of view downplays or ignores Christianity's other face. As a creation religion, Christianity has proclaimed that God created a world that clearly manifested his goodness and wisdom, and sustained it with his daily providence. It has declared that God, the great Artisan of the universe, designed each and every creature for its own purpose in the divine scheme. Christians have professed that man, lord of creation, must prepare for the day when his own Lord would return and require an accounting from his manager (man) of his property (the world). The Biblical injunction to conquer nature was balanced by the need to regard God's creation with wonder, love, reverence, and care.

The onus that critics have placed upon Christianity in general they lay more heavily on Latin than on Greek Christianity, and more heavily still on Protestantism than on Catholicism. In their perception, Christianity *caused* the ecological crisis, through a worldview that devalued the natural world in itself and promoted a utilitarian and antagonistic attitude toward non-human creation. It is true that Christianity, as well as Judaism, contains elements, such as dualism and anthropocentrism, that have supported such a worldview. It is not true that these elements have monopolized Christian thought about nature. St. Francis of Assisi is probably the most famous example of a Christian who preached the brotherhood of creation rather than human dominion over it. Historical attitudes towards nature derive from countless factors, including physical factors, such as climate and geography; social factors, such as gender, economics and class; and intellectual factors, such as science and religion. As a number of more recent writers have noted, with its wide spectrum of nature teachings, Christianity is less to blame for the ecological crisis than some of the uses to which it has been put.

The complement to the viewpoint that Christianity is hostile to nature is the idea that other religions and traditions, especially those of the Third World, specifically value nature.[2] As a consequence of their doctrines of transmigration of souls between animals and humans, Hinduism, Jainism, and Buddhism have tended to cherish all life. Taoism teaches unity, continuity, change, and flow in the human as well as non-human world. Shintoism, animism, and American Indian religions see the invisible and visible worlds in close cooperation. By contrast, in the major religions of the West — Judaism, Christianity and Islam — rank humanity above a created world that contains no nature spirits or divine beings, at least in official dogma.

This perspective suffers from oversimplicity. For example, in the Hindu epic, *Mahabharata*, Krishna and Arjuna prepare for founding the city Indraprastha by setting fire to the forest Khandavaprastha. The rise of Chinese civilization brought deforestation and ravaging floods. Hawaiian priests paid for just one of their spectacular feathered capes with the lives of 80,000 birds. For millennia before Europeans arrived, American Indians hunted buffalo by driving whole herds off cliffs, and transformed the landscape of North America by regularly setting fires. Non-Western spirituality has provided no guarantee against major, often deleterious, human environmental impact.[3]

The anti-Western perspective would logically imply that many of the peoples of the world would forgo or modify Western technology, rather than harm nature in violation of religious precepts. There are innumerable instances that demonstrate that this supposed religious barrier is at best a weak one. Around the world, developing nations have followed the Western path to industrial development. The worst contemporary industrial pollution problems are not in Protestant countries, but in Eastern Europe and the former Soviet Union, around the Mediterranean, and in India and China. If not for Western nations, the Japanese might have blithely exterminated species of whales. The precepts of ecology and environmentalism originated in the Christian West and have followed, not preceded, the spread of industrialism.

Evidence in fact suggests that an empirical perception of scarcity, far more than an ecological worldview or ethic, creates effective conservation consciousness. Much vaunted for a life and religion in harmony with nature, American Indians, for example, varied a great deal in their ecological consciousness, which (logically enough) reflected the relative ecological fragility of their immediate environment.[4] Early administrators of the British Empire instituted major conservation measures in their regions in order to preserve threatened commodity agriculture in the Caribbean and prevent famine and resulting social unrest in India.[5] Existing or impending scarcity prompted America's first conservation laws and led Gifford Pinchot to promulgate America's first conservation ideology.

Preindustrial cultures often appear environmentally benign because the power of religious belief to change the natural environment is limited or magnified by technological capacity. During the Middle Ages in northwestern Europe, peasants or serfs not only had to clear the thick northern Europe forest in order to plant their crops, they also constantly had to prevent nature from reclaiming what they had already cleared. To them, the Biblical idea of human dominion over nature formed more a goal than an achievement. Particularly in subsistence economies, it is not dominion over nature but competition with nature that characterizes the human relationship with the environment. Peasants do not look with a kindly eye upon the insects, birds, mice, rats, rabbits, moles, polecats, foxes, weasels, and other beasts who wish to share their bounty, or the weeds which try to share their land. Farmers the world over have adopted pesticides and modern farm technology the moment they have become available to them. Competition quickly changes to dominion with better technology. Give guns and metal implements to a hunter-gatherer society, or farm equipment and chemical fertilizers and pesticides to an agrarian one, and human impact upon the environment increases dramatically.[6]

Humans depend upon active manipulation of nature for food, shelter, and clothing, which then gives rise to technology, however simple, to achieve these ends. At the same time, humans have recognized the impact, both benign and malign, of uncontrollable natural forces. Religion, then, must allow for both beneficial human change of the natural environment and preservation of beneficial natural forces. Experience in combination with religious values channels practice. Religions with the greatest affect on action must balance the needs of active and passive relations to nature. Ethics that enjoin too much passivity, like Buddhism or especially Jainism, that cannot be strictly followed by the average believer but only by a few monks or holy men, have less power over everyday behavior. Jainism so reveres life that its holy men wear no clothes, except for a mask over the mouth and nose to prevent the accidental inhalation and death of insects and germs. Yet Jains as a group form one of India's entrepreneurial classes. Tata, one of the largest industrial companies of India, is owned by a Jain family.

Thus, like other religions, Christianity bears an ambiguous relationship to the natural world. Its Biblical and theological roots lie in the pastures of Palestine, the irrigated fields of Mesopotamia, and the agricultural and urban landscapes of Greece and Rome. Distinct religious attitudes toward nature arose in each of these places and then mixed and interacted during the rise and fall of the ancient Mesopotamian and Mediterranean empires. Already in place by the fall of the Roman Empire were most of the religious elements that Whittier would draw upon in the nineteenth century when he urged his lumbermen to conquer nature while worshipping in it.

Protestantism, the focus of this book, has been the dominant religious force in the formation of attitudes toward nature in the United States. For centuries, Protestants ruled this country and thought of it as a Protestant nation. Since World War II, vehement anti-Catholicism and anti-Semitism have waned and Catholics and Jews have taken ever more prominent roles in public affairs, but until comparatively recently Protestants completely dominated mainstream American intellectual and cultural life. Their tale is the saga of the rise of industrialism and environmentalism in America. Their doctrines and values shape its central and essential themes.

Drawn from theology developed over millennia, American Protestant views of the natural world were founded on Jewish and Classical concepts preserved in the Bible and early Church dogma; they were built from the doctrinal selection and modification of the Reformation of the sixteenth and seventeenth centuries; and they were adapted to the experience of Christians in a quickly developing society on the edge of a vast wilderness. The American continent called forth a variety of responses, grounded generally or specifically in Christian faith and ethic. Some Protestants found faith from the evidence of God in the goodness and wisdom of creation. Others envisioned a transformation of the wilderness into a new Eden for the Second Coming of Christ. The dogma that the earth was made for man became a popular justification for both use and abuse of nature. Many believed in the conquest and control of nature for the benefit of humanity. Still others saw the mountains and forests as sacred places where mankind might find mystical experiences or moral renewal.

Throughout the centuries, religion has impelled Americans toward many different lives, with many different relationships with the natural world. This is the story of some of those lives, and of how Americans conquered a continent while they praised God in its groves.

Book I

Protestantism, Capitalism, and Nature

☩ ☩ ☩

ONE

Beauty and Wonder, Dominion and Stewardship

For the beauty of the earth,
For the beauty of the skies,
For the love which from our birth
Over and around us lies,
Lord of all, to Thee we raise
This our hymn of grateful praise.

For the wonder of each hour
Of the day and of the night,
Hill and vale, and tree and flower,
Sun and moon, and stars of light,
Lord of all, to Thee we raise
This our hymn of grateful praise.

—FOLLIOTT S. PIERPOINT (1864)

"I believe in Providence," said he. "Our fathers came into these valleys before us. They got the richest of them. They won't yield anything now. But the Lord foresaw this and prepared something for us & what is it. Why he meant us to bust open these copper mines and then we will have money to buy the corn that we cannot raise."

—NORTH CAROLINA MOUNTAIN DWELLER,
RECORDED IN THE JOURNAL OF JOHN MUIR (1867)

Moreover, that this economy and this diligence, with respect to those good things which God has given us to enjoy, may flourish among us; let every one regard himself as the steward of God in all things which he possesses. Then he will neither conduct himself dissolutely, nor corrupt by abuse those things which God requires to be preserved.

—JOHN CALVIN, *COMMENTARIES ON THE*
FIRST BOOK OF MOSES CALLED GENESIS (1554)

The common coin of contemporary intellectual exchange stills bears the marks of Christianity's stamp. Understanding Protestantism's influence on the environmental debate begins with understanding the roots of Protestant doctrines of nature. Although these doctrines are common to nearly all Christians, history has given them an importance and emphasis unique to Protestants. Before the invention of movable type and before the Reformation, the Catholic Church enjoyed a near-monopoly on the sources and distribution of knowledge. Printing and Protestantism broke the Church's ability to control information. At the same time, they disseminated Christian doctrines more widely and pervasively than before, and surviving pre-Christian ideas and attitudes of folk culture retreated before the advancing implications of doctrine.[1]

If the new Protestant temple of faith rested on the twin pillars of Biblical literacy and godly reform, its foundation was the Truth of the Bible. The Reformation accentuated the Bible's importance and centrality, because having rejected obedience to the Catholic Church hierarchy, Protestants invested authority in Scripture alone. In America, immigration cut people off from both folk tradition and traditional sources of authority and inflated the importance of the Bible in Protestant American culture even more.

Nevertheless, because the Bible comprised a collection of corrupt texts in ancient languages, Protestants still relied on translators and exegetes to clarify the waters of truth. The task was complicated by internal tensions and contradictions accumulated during the long, slow process by which Christian canon and theology grew. The Bible itself preserved changing perspectives, needs, and cultural and natural environments from the centuries it took for it to be written. The Hebrews, a minor Near Eastern people, borrowed cultural and religious elements from neighboring nations and from the dominant cultural centers in Mesopotamia, Egypt, and Greece. Syncretic tendencies increased markedly when early Christianity spread throughout the Roman Empire. To Gentiles, Christianity was now the borrowed tradition, and they added many more-or-less compatible elements of pagan philosophy, attitudes, and traditions. If all this contradictory material presented Protestants with problems to solve, it also made available a multitude of traditions to enrich their understanding of God, the world, and their place in it.

For Protestants and indeed all Christians and Jews, understanding nature is fundamental to understanding God. Of course, the central concern of Judaism and Christianity is the relation between God and humanity. As creation religions, though, they are grounded in the natural world in ways basic to that relationship. The creation stories of Genesis defined the relationships between God, nature, and humanity and laid out the major Biblical and theological themes. In no place is nature more prominent and important than in these passages. The Bible begins with the creation of the world, and twenty-five verses pass without a human in them.

If the first three chapters of Genesis defined the divine order, generations of expositors have uncovered multiple meanings in Genesis seminal to American Protestant thought about nature. Positive themes tending to value nature in itself fall into three categories: God manifesting his wisdom, power and glory in creation, and creation in turn glorifying him; the vision of a regained Eden; and dominion interpreted as stewardship. Treatments tending to devalue the world in its "natural" state extolled man's dominion over nature or depicted fallen nature. The most important concepts added to these core ideas came during the crucial early years of Christianity when early church leaders, the "Church Fathers," attached to them dominant philosophical and scientific ideas of the time. Crucial ideas which the Fathers adapted to Christian doctrine included the order and harmony of nature, the teleology of nature (especially the assumption that the world was made for man), God the artisan deity, and the God-in-nature mysticism of neo-Platonism.[2] In one mode or another, this doctrinal nucleus underlies all American Protestant–based religious and spiritual thought about nature.

Creator and Creation

The most significant aspect of Christian doctrine about nature is its understanding of God as the creator and sustainer of the universe. The world is both manifestation and medium of divine power, glory, and goodness. The primary passages which express this view are found in Genesis, in the magisterial opening words of the six days of the creation of the heavens and the earth and all the things and beings which fill them. The Bible's initial chapter presents a powerful, transcendent God who makes the universe come into being with his word. In the next chapter, a more anthropomorphic God molds man and animals out of clay, breathes life into them, plants a garden, and thus demonstrates an intimate concern for and involvement in earthly creation. Nearly every step during the six days of creation God proclaims "good." The stately, measured prose and imagery of Genesis 1 present a structured and ordered cosmos crafted according to divine will and have long elicited awe and wonder at the cosmos and its divine origins.

In many memorable and oft-repeated verses and figures, other Biblical passages expanded upon these themes of God's power over and in his world and praise the plan of creation. As its creator, God regards the world like a sovereign or landlord. Psalm 24 proclaimed, "The earth is the Lord's, and the fullness thereof; the world, and they that dwell therein." Wisdom of Solomon 11:20 declared, "Thou hast ordered all things in measure, and number, and weight." Isaiah compared God to a potter fashioning man out of clay.[3]

God's care extends to the smallest part of his domain. Psalm 104 described with beauty and grandeur the providence of God in all of creation and affirmed that the sustenance and care of every creature comes from God's special providence, without which life cannot exist. The psalmist described how God in his wisdom gave appropriate food and shelter to every creature (a notion bearing the implication of the ecological interconnectedness of things).[4] In a well-known reaffirmation of God's special providence, Jesus commented in Matthew 10:29 and Luke 12:6 that even a sparrow "shall not fall on the ground without your Father."

A momentous implication of Genesis 1 was that God's wisdom and power are clearly evident in creation. Psalm 19 asserted, "The heavens declare the glory of God; and the firmament sheweth his handywork." Because nature thus reveals aspects of God and his plan, worldly beauty and goodness leads humankind to him, said Wisdom 13:1–7.[5] The most powerful and influential expression of this concept that man can understand God through created things appears in St. Paul's letter to the Romans 1:20: "For the invisible things of him from the creation of the world are clearly seen, being understood by the things that are made, even his eternal power and Godhead. . . ." This verse provided the primary basis for the natural theology tradition in Christianity.[6]

Psalms 8, 33, and 148 urged the worship of and praise for the deity responsible for creating this well-structured universe. Very popular among Protestants, Psalm 148 depicts God's works glorifying and praising him. It recapitulates the first chapter of Genesis and enjoins all of creation to praise God. The heavens, angels, sun, moon and stars, the dragons of the deep, weather and the elements, mountains, trees, animals, birds, kings and princes, and all people—all join in his praise. Psalm 148 inspired Milton, who paraphrased it for Adam and Eve's morning hymn in *Paradise Lost*. It begins: "These are Thy glorious works, Parent of good, / Almighty! Thine this universal frame, / Thus wondrous fair: Thyself how wondrous then! / Unspeakable, who sitt'st above these heavens / To us invisible, or dimly seen / In these thy lowest works; yet these declare / Thy goodness beyond thought, and power divine." Such disparate figures as Benjamin Franklin and John Muir admired this hymn.[7]

Christian Neo-Platonism

Early Roman Christians found it relatively easy to conflate the Hebrew deity of a good, ordered, providential creation with the pagan creator deity variously conceived as the Good, the One, the divine artisan or architect, or the Prime Mover. In *Timaeus* and the tenth book of *Laws*, for example, Plato advanced the idea that an intelligent, good, reasoning, and divine artisan (like Isaiah's God the potter) created the cosmos and sustains it with his providence. Order implied design to the Greeks, who originated three arguments for a designed universe that still retained their persuasive power to Protestants of the nineteenth century: physiology, especially the examples of the eye and hand; cosmic order, particularly in the heavens; and the earth as a fit environment for human and other life. As in the Bible, not scientific curiosity about nature but wonder at it and admiration for cosmic wholeness and unity marked the design theory. Nevertheless, the passionate Biblical God of history was never comfortable in the toga, masquerading as the indifferent, faceless Hellenistic deity of order.[8]

Of immense consequence for American Protestantism was the third-century adaptation of Plato known as neo-Platonism. The work of Plotinus and his followers, neo-Platonism mystically spiritualized a conception of the organic unity of nature. Neo-Platonists imagined the universe in terms of emanation from and return to a totally transcendent divinity immanent in the processes of the world. They envisioned a triune God divided into the One, Mind, and Soul. The One, also called the Good, was an indescribable, transcendent, absolute, unchangeable entity that was the source of all being. From it, Mind emanated like light from a candle. Mind contained the eternal forms or patterns according to which the changeable world is formed, the way a human mind contains ideas and designs. From Mind, the Universal Soul emanated. Finally, from Soul emanated the mutable material world in all its diversity. The cosmos formed a unity like the unity of body and soul of a living organism. Because the One was Good and emanation was a necessary act of that goodness, neo-Platonists regarded the world as good and as lacking nothing that was good. Evil arose from matter, which was at the opposite end of the chain of being from the Good.[9]

Neo-Platonists were mystics who yearned for union with the One, which had contradictory implications for their attitude toward the physical world. On the one hand, they viewed the beauty of the world as a trap for the material-minded, a distraction from the goal of union with God. On the other hand, in worldly beauty also lay the beginning of the soul's ascent to God. The first step of this ascent was contemplation of beauty with the

rational mind, which formed an idea of beauty. Turning inward, away from
the world's beauty, which after all represented only "copies, vestiges, shadows" of the idea of Beauty in the Divine Mind, intuition led the soul to Pure
Beauty in the Divine Mind, and thence to the ecstasy of mystical union with
the One. Plotinus felt that the artist was closest to union with the One
because he both was attuned to beauty and mirrored the creative process of
God in the artistic process of creation from ideas in his mind.[10]

Christianized by many Church Fathers, especially St. Augustine (an im-
mensely influential figure in Western and especially Protestant Christianity,
which began in large part as an Augustinian revival), neo-Platonism augmented Biblical themes in critical new ways. Like the God of Genesis 1, the
One created a good universe. Yet the One's totally transcendent otherness
together with its immanence in the world and its processes gave new dimen-
sions to the active, passionate God of the Bible. Like Genesis and Psalm
104, neo-Platonism described a universe dependent upon God for its existence, and like Psalm 148 it urged creation to turn back toward its source
and recognize its creator. Yet it prescribed a retreat inward, where in passive
contemplation the soul might reunite with God. This mystical element,
foreign to original Christianity, provided the source for Christian mysticism
and Western nature mysticism in general. Its dualism and low regard for
matter as furthest from the Good could lead to a *contemptus mundi* due to the
need of spirit to ascend to God. Yet the idea of the universe as an abundant
emanation from the Goodness and Wisdom of the divine, the notion of the
world's unity in diversity, and the use of nature and its beauty as a ladder to
higher contemplation and union with the One, reinforced Christian praise
of and interest in the creation of God. Moreover, as Christianity displaced
old pagan nature gods, Christian neo-Platonism put God back into nature
and its processes.[11] A revived neo-Platonism, transmitted by Puritans, pu-
rified by Transcendentalists, and disseminated by such nineteenth-century
nature writers as Thoreau, John Muir, and John Burroughs, added a crucial
spiritual element to the early environmental movement.

Neo-Platonic influence on Western thought about nature is remarkable
in its range and scope. St. Augustine, St. Francis, St. Bonaventure, Meister
Eckart, and many Western mystics accepted the idea of the earth's creatures
as good and contemplation of them as the first step on the mystical road to
God. To Renaissance neo-Platonists, Romantic scientists such as Alexander
von Humboldt, and supporters of the recent Gaia hypothesis, the earth is a
unity, an organism. Hegel, nineteenth-century evolutionists like Robert
Chambers, Ernst Haeckel, and the American Lamarckians, and twentieth-
century process philosophers like Alfred North Whitehead and Charles

Hartshorne elaborated the notion that immanent divinity expresses itself creatively in the process of cosmic change. Augustine, Puritan theologian Jonathan Edwards, and Transcendentalist Ralph Waldo Emerson viewed earthly beauty as the door to spiritual awareness; Augustine and Emerson regarded the artist as closest to the divine mind. Kant, Coleridge, and Emerson emphasized the use of reason and intuition in discerning the ultimate reality of idealism. Many others, including Spinoza, the Cambridge Platonists, Leibniz, the German idealists, the Romantics, Henri Bergson, and Teilhard du Chardin, trace the roots of their ideas about God, nature, and mankind to Plotinus and his followers.[12]

Natural Theology

The search for evidences of God in nature supported not only Christian neo-Platonism but also a second long and exceedingly influential Christian tradition, natural theology. Enlisting reason, not mysticism, to support Christianity, natural theology rested on Biblical passages like those in Wisdom and St. Paul's epistles, reinforced by concepts from Hellenistic philosophy.[13] Up to the seventeenth century, it inspired a vast "hexameral" genre of immense tomes that sought to reconcile and illustrate the six days of Genesis with contemporary science. After the early seventeenth century, natural theology grew quite significant in Protestant thought and produced popular volumes by John Ray, William Derham, and William Paley in England and Christian Wolff in Germany. In the first half of the nineteenth century natural theology evolved into the "footprints of the creator" literature that strove to harmonize science, especially geology, with Christianity, and was best represented by the works of Scottish geologist Hugh Miller. In nineteenth-century Britain and America, natural theology thoroughly infused scientific interest in nature with the sense that science was a holy or moral pursuit, and strengthened Romantic and Transcendental belief that through nature the soul found spirit. Since then, its influence has waned, although it is still alive in such works as British philosopher Richard Swinburne's 1979 *The Existence of God.*[14]

The Church Fathers formulated many key natural theological concepts. St. Augustine achieved great eloquence on the evidence of God visible in creation and the divinely ordered chain of being which brought him to know God and his attributes.[15] St. John Chrysostom, added a significant metaphor when he said that God had given humankind his Word in his book of revelation, the Bible, which however was written in obscure languages that only a tiny elite could read. Alongside this book God had placed the "book" of nature, which was clear, unfalsifiable, and available to all.[16]

The attractive idea that the books of nature and revelation complemented each other held hidden dangers because it did not allow for the possibility the two might conflict. Medieval thinkers realized conflicts could only be solved by granting supremacy to one book or the other.[17] By the Renaissance, many believed that in differences between the Bible and science, between the books of revelation and nature, science should be preferred as less speculative. This view found an extreme expression in *Theologia Naturalis sive Liber Creaturarum*, a sixteenth-century book by the Spanish scholar, Raymond of Sebonde (or Ramon Sibiude). According to Raymond, the baptized could obtain from nature all the essential knowledge of religion. God wrote the book of nature with his own finger, tracing in each creature the letters spelling wisdom and knowledge. Needing no authorities, either Scripture or teachers, science confirmed revelation and enabled belief, and thus preceded Scripture. Raymond lauded the book of nature so highly, nearly making revelation superfluous, that the Catholic Church placed its Prologue on its Index of prohibited books in 1595. The dangers that the Church guarded against by this act arose instead in Protestant Britain and America, where the next logical step, Deism, dispensed with revelation altogether and depended entirely upon nature and reason.[18]

In its rejection of scholastic authority, its confidence in science and its ability to understand creation, and its certainty that science supported religion, natural theology became one of the mainstays of Protestant thought. When Protestants had rejected the ecclesiastical and theological authority of the Catholic church, the authority and importance of both the Bible and nature as sources of truth and authority increased dramatically. Moreover, in such missteps as its condemnation of Galileo, the Catholic church promoted Protestants' view of themselves as free seekers of truth as written in both of God's "books." Calvinists, in particular, stressed the measureless power of sovereign God and saw an aid to faith in its manifestation in nature.[19] In their 1648 creed, the Westminster Confession, Calvinist British Puritans paraphrased Romans 1:20 in the opening sentence, devoted Chapter IV of the confession entirely to creation, and in Chapter V affirmed God's providence for all creatures, "to the glory of His wisdom, power, justice, goodness, and mercy."

By the latter half of the seventeenth century, neo-Platonism began to mix more strongly with natural theology. A group of English neo-Platonist philosophers, the Cambridge Platonists, disseminated new arguments for natural theology in works such as Ralph Cudworth's *The True Intellectual*

System of the Universe and Henry More's *An Antidote Against Atheism*. More produced a veritable encyclopedia of nature's evidence for the existence of God.[20] Because natural theologians must look so selectively at nature to see goodness, harmony, and the workings of providence, More's list of evidence became tiresomely familiar as succeeding authors cribbed from him.[21]

British scientists and churchmen seized on this new synthesis of mysticism and science and produced two books, long influential in the English-speaking world, the 1691 *The Wisdom of God Manifested in the Works of the Creation* by naturalist John Ray, and the 1713 *Physico-Theology* by Anglican William Derham. Archdeacon William Paley wrote the crowning and most popular work of this tradition, *Natural Theology; or, Evidences of the Existence and Attributes of the Deity Collected from the Appearances of Nature* (1803), for decades a standard university textbook. Here, Paley collected and organized every argument and example of natural theology he could find. The strength and weakness of his book, and natural theology generally, can be seen in his famous watch analogy, which opens the first chapter. Paley described crossing a heath and striking his foot against a stone; no one, he thought, would think it absurd to believe that the stone had lain there forever. But had he found a watch upon the ground, he would have concluded differently.

> When we come to inspect the watch, we perceive — what we could not discover in the stone — that its several parts are framed and put together for a purpose. . . . This mechanism being observed . . . and understood, the inference we think is inevitable, that the watch must have had a maker — that there must have existed, at some time and at some place or other, an artificer or artificers who formed it for the purpose which we find it actually to answer, who comprehended its construction and designed its use.

Thus, by analogy, a Maker must have formed the universe for a purpose and "designed its use."[22] The weakness here was that the stone did not imply a maker, which after all was the point of his argument. It was only as part of a larger *system* that the stone became significant. Systemic thinking is generally more productive of the emotion of religious awe than particularistic study and tends to lead to spirit-in-the-system conceptions like neo-Platonism.

In the thirteenth century the seventh general of the Franciscan order, St. Bonaventure, added another persistent metaphor, that of God's vestiges or footprints in creation. In his mystical tract *The Mind's Road to God*, Bonaventure explained a six-step path to God, a version of neo-Platonism that began with sense and ascended through reason and intuition to achieve illumination of conscience. Thus, the evidences of God in nature led "into the way of God." Bonaventure concluded with a ringing affirmation of the presence of God in nature.[23]

Paley was popular if quickly obsolete. An emerging "footprints of the creator" literature abandoned a strict reliance on the Mosaic account of creation but nevertheless felt constrained to affirm the general agreement between the Bible and the developing sciences of geology and paleontology. The "footprint" metaphor dated back to the thirteenth-century mysticism of Franciscan St. Bonaventure, whose *The Mind's Road to God* traced a path to neo-Platonic union with God that began with the "vestiges" or "footprints" (*vestigia*) of God in creation. But in the midst of this agreeable harmony sung by divines and natural scientists, there suddenly appeared a discordant note in the form of Robert Chambers's *Vestiges of the Natural History of Creation*, printed anonymously in 1844. Chambers's apparent folly was to imply that the changes in the fossil record were the result of the incremental evolution of life, a step at a time from microscopic animals to man to a future being superior to man. Chambers felt this was easily reconciled with Genesis if creation came through God's will and not his acts. That is, if God *willed* a change, it might happen over time; if he *acted*, the change would be discontinuous. Intended as a work of natural theology, *Vestiges of Creation* instead stirred nearly every scientist and cleric in England to attack.[24] Nonetheless, this pre-Darwinian work foreshadows post-Darwinian harmonizations of evolution and Christianity.

A self-taught geologist and writer of popular science, Scotsman Hugh Miller, replied to Chambers in his 1847 *Footprints of the Creator; or, The Asterolepis of Stromness*, the era's best-written and best-known reconciliation of science and Christianity. Miller's objection to Chambers's evolutionary point of view was that it undermined the basic assumptions of Christianity. The impossibility of the incremental evolution of an immortal soul unacceptably implied that either animals had souls or mankind did not. Miller continued to insist that the books of revelation and nature agreed, which he proved using the new understanding of the six "days" of creation as representative of a geologic ages.[25]

Miller was one of the last great scientists who was a religious popular writer. As science developed and professionalized in the nineteenth and twentieth centuries, its emphasis on the particular and measurable increased and on first causes and teleology decreased. In this century, the idea that the world manifests the nature, attributes, and purposes of God, or that it is capable of only one interpretation, has nearly collapsed. For their part, late nineteenth-century American liberal religious leaders, amateur naturalists, natural scientists, and others — like Reverend Henry Ward Beecher, theologians Eugene W. Lyman and Henry Nelson Wieman, philosopher John Fiske, naturalists John Muir and John Burroughs, and geologist Joseph LeConte — followed more and more the neo-Platonic path blazed by the Cambridge Platonists, the Romantics, and Transcendentalist Unitarians and stressed God's immanence in the world and its processes.[26] The feeling that nature yields spiritual and moral benefits still remains a compelling force in American religion and environmentalism, but rarely in science.

Fallen Nature

Christianity's view of nature has a dark side that counterbalances the bright doctrines of the glory and goodness of God in nature. The Bible and Christian theology portrayed nature as an instrument of divine will. God gave his blessings and his curses through natural forces, in which his will thus was manifest. Traditionally, natural disaster has told of God's displeasure with and chastisement of his people.[27] The Old Testament is replete with examples. In the bleak vision of Isaiah 34, animals and plants return to live in barren Idumea (Edom) after God wreaks his vengeance there. Jeremiah in his twelfth chapter describes God's punishment in terms of ecological disaster, perhaps a prolonged drought.[28] God's providence may well sustain all creation, telling of his glory, but he can also withhold his blessings, telling of his wrath.

In God's first act of punishment in Genesis 3:14–19, God curses the serpent, Eve, Adam, and all nature as well — "cursed is the ground for thy sake." Old Testament writers did not develop the concept of the fall of nature implicit in God's curse in Genesis 3:17–19, although sometimes authors expressed related ideas of nature's decline, such as when Psalm 102:25–26 mentions that the earth grows old and senescent. The Church Fathers did not generally emphasize the fallenness of nature because it conflicted with both creation's goodness and purpose in all things.[29] Yet many Christians have found in the Fall an explanation for the reality of the human relationship with animals. As a result of the Fall man retained only partial dominion over creatures, although he retained full use of the creatures genuinely required for life. On the other hand, the results of human sin, which brought animals under the curse as well, required them to serve mankind.[30] The idea of the fall of nature also produced popular explanations for unpleasant or dangerous natural events, plants, or animals.

Christianity counterbalanced the doctrine of the fall of nature with anticipation of God's restoration of Eden. The Bible looked back on the idyllic days before the Fall of Adam when humans, God, and nature lived together in peace and harmony, and in eschatological moods looked forward to God's creation of a new paradise. Certainly the most famous passage expressing this is Isaiah 11:6–9, in which "The wolf also shall dwell with the lamb," and "They shall not hurt nor destroy in all my holy mountain: for the earth shall be full of the knowledge of the Lord, as the waters cover the sea." Isaiah in 55:12–13 foretells the return of fertility to the wastes, making the mountains and hills sing and the trees clap their hands, and in 66:17 (echoed in the New Testament) God promises "new heavens and a new earth."[31] St. Paul in Romans 8:19–21 believed that fallen creation would join in the restoration of things in the millennium, inspiring many Christians to look for a re-creation of Eden or the recovery of dominion at the end of time.

Excitement over the seemingly real possibility of creating a new Eden has often run high. The dramatic events of world discovery coincided with the equally dramatic course of the Reformation, and together produced among Protestant nations recurring millennial fever and visions of paradise regained. Francis Bacon inspired many generations of English Protestant scientists with his prediction that science and discovery would hasten the last days and create a new Eden. The New England Puritans were certain that Christ's return was near and took pride in creating the prophesied new Eden in the American wilderness. Mormons sought to make the Utah desert bloom in anticipation of Christ's imminent return and renewal of the earth. Today, American millennialism remains vigorous, but since the mid-nineteenth century the realities of urban industrial life have tarnished the vision of creating a paradise in America for Christ's return.

Human Dominion

The Bible also enjoined human will over nature. God's injunction to make the earth an instrument of human will was the very first of his commands. The story of the six days of creation climaxed with fateful words of Genesis 1:26–28:

And God said, Let us make man in our image, after our likeness: and let them have dominion over the fish of the sea, and over the fowl of the air, and over the cattle, and over all the earth, and over every creeping thing that creepeth upon the earth. So God created man in his own image, in the image of God created he him; male and female created he them. And God blessed them, and God said unto them, Be fruitful, and multiply, and replenish [fill] the earth, and subdue it: and have dominion over the fish of the sea, and over the fowl of the air, and over every living thing that moveth upon the earth.

To most commentators, the second chapter of Genesis elaborated on human power over animals when it described both the creation of animals to help man keep the garden of Eden and Adam's act of naming of them.

In Genesis 9:1–3, after the Flood, God renewed and amplified his command to have dominion, saying he "delivered" animals "into your hand," to have fear and dread of man. In the Hebrew text, "subdue" and "dominion" clearly imply military conquest and rule and perhaps even enslavement of nature. In antiquity, the vanquished in war (nature, in this case) must obey the new masters, and moreover, war in the ancient world bestowed the right of victors to enslave the vanquished. Christian writers even explicitly made Adam's act of naming the animals in Genesis 2:19, "like a master giving names to slaves in his service," a symbol of his dominion.[32]

With another reference to subjugation and rule, the well-known cadences of the eighth Psalm sing the praises of dominion and man's exalted position in creation, placing him "a little lower than the angels" and making "him to have dominion over the works of thy hands" by putting "all things under his feet."[33] This psalm also was compatible with the Great Chain of Being, the hierarchical, interlocking design of the universe with humanity midway on the chain between material creation and God. Both the Chain of Being and dominion reinforced Christianity's belief in human distinction from and superiority over the beasts and all creation.

The same verse in Genesis that conferred dominion upon man described how God made man in his image and likeness. More than anything else, the creation of humans in the image of God set them apart from all of creation and amplified human superiority in the doctrines of the earth made for man, the chain of being, and human dominion over the earth. Influenced by Hellenistic body-soul dualism, Church Fathers rejected "image" as physical resemblance to God, since physically humans betrayed too much affinity to animals, and located God's image and likeness in the human soul. Be-

cause the soul was divine and the body it ruled was bestial, and because God
mentioned image and dominion in the same Genesis command, Christians
often thought it was the soul that gave man the power of dominion. The
human combination of divine soul and bestial body proved as well humanity's place on the chain of being just below the angels yet above the animals,
giving rise to the pejorative import of words like "brutish," "beastly," and
"bestial."[34]

The infusion of Platonic and Aristotelian philosophy into Christianity
gave a huge boost to the Biblical idea of teleology in nature, that is, the idea
of purpose in and for the world, and that, moreover, that purpose was the
benefit of the crown of creation, humans.[35] "The heaven, even the heavens,
are the Lord's," said Psalm 115:16: "but the earth hath he given to the
children of men." In light of the doctrine of dominion and the notion that
God created Eden for Adam and Eve, early Christians easily assimilated the
Greek belief that because the world had design it had purpose, and that that
purpose was man.[36] Mankind's changes of the earth were consistent with
this concept because cultivation served humanity's role as caretakers of the
earth, just as Adam had been charged to "dress" and "keep" Eden. Man
brought order to nature where he went, and his activity in the landscape
helped finish creation.

In the seventeenth century, the followers of Francis Bacon came to regard science and technology as the means of regaining lost dominion over
nature: mankind's recovery of dominion, they believed, would bring the
millennial redemption of man and nature. Their impact was far-reaching,
because Bacon's ideas dominated the scientific ideology of the English-
speaking world for more than two centuries. Bacon took science away from
philosophers and theologians, whose deductions produced nothing but endless wrangling, and based it on the more reliable principle of induction
from observation of natural phenomena. In answer to the charge that science without religion led to atheism, Bacon replied that science and religion supported each other. Holy work that strengthened faith and defended it against superstition and atheistical philosophy, science would help
humanity regain the paradise of Eden and the powers lost in the Fall: "For
man, by the fall, lost at once his state of innocence, and his empire over
creation, both of which can be partially recovered even in this life, the first
by religion and faith, the second by the arts and sciences."[37]

Seventeenth-century Puritans seized upon Bacon's millennial vision and
actively promoted and participated in the science of their day. Protestants
of the Enlightenment period and the nineteenth century also saw Baconian
science as the first defense against the doubts, speculation and attacks of

skeptical *philosophes* of the Continent, among whom irreligion was common. Although even in Bacon's day science and religion were beginning to go their separate ways, ironically aided by Bacon's strict separation of the two, through the nineteenth century and often into the twentieth, English-speaking Protestants insisted that science supported religion, and that, properly viewed, the two stood in harmony.[38]

Bacon stood at a historical crossroads. After him, the physical sciences and technology followed one road, while the natural sciences and natural theology took another. Ironically, the physical sciences emphasized just what Bacon had railed against, as they strongly preferred not induction but deduction from logical premises, as for example in the works of Descartes or Newton's *Principia*. The abstract approach of physical science treated the world as a mechanism driven by calculable, knowable forces. Inspired by the search for the evidences of God's design, natural science kept close to the phenomena at hand and observed the adaptations and interrelationships of creatures. Although deservedly prominent in the history of science, proponents of the mechanistic physical sciences formed but a small elite. The works of natural science, on the other hand, were far more popular, and many amateurs, including a large number of curates and divines, made important contributions to its progress. Thus, much of the popular science of the seventeenth, eighteenth, and nineteenth centuries bore a strong religious stamp.

Stewardship

Dominion baldly stated could have doleful implications for the natural world, created for man and wholly given to his power. The classical assumption that the world was made for man, the Genesis command to subdue and have dominion over the earth, as well as interpretations that Eden was made for man's enjoyment and nature was cursed for man's punishment, enhanced the anthropocentrism inherent in Christian dogma and soteriology. Until very recently, Christians have generally assumed that man always played center stage in the terrestrial drama.[39] Yet one of the most important implications of the doctrine of dominion is human stewardship of the earth, which combines the theme of dominion in the first chapter of Genesis with man's purpose of dressing and keeping Eden in the second. John Calvin, for example, strongly endorsed stewardship (relating it in the process to the Calvinist ethics of work and moderation).[40] Aside from Wisdom 9:2–3, no Biblical passage explicitly developed this idea, but some Christians subsequently emphasized it, based on Jesus' three parables of stewardship in the Synoptic Gospels.[41] As humanity's control over nature has increased in the last two centuries, the principle of stewardship of the earth has become more important and more explicit among Protestant denominations. In the last twenty years stewardship has allowed even the most conservative denominations to promote an environmental ethic. Ambiguous as "stewardship" may be, and too anthropocentric for many activists, it nevertheless encourages responsibility.[42]

The Role of Wilderness

The Bible contained one further theme related to nature, which, apart from the medieval establishment of monasteries in wild areas, received little emphasis until the European discovery and settlement of America: the theme of wilderness.[43] Wilderness played its most prominent part in the exodus of the nation of Israel from Egypt. The time when Moses led his people through the wilderness was remembered as a terrible time of hunger and thirst, a time when God tested his people before allowing them to enter and take Canaan, the land flowing with milk and honey. Wilderness was a place of God's presence, where sacrifice to God should take place (Exodus 3:18, 5:1), where the mountain of God stood (Exodus 4:27, 18:5), where God gave Moses the tablets of the law. Wilderness played another role in the Bible as a host or refuge, for example for Hagar or more often for God's leaders and prophets: Moses tending sheep near Horeb, David defending his flock against predators, Elijah being fed by ravens, John the Baptist preaching and baptizing, and Jesus preparing for his ministry and facing the three temptations of the Devil. In America, a wilderness to European eyes if ever there was one, those who, like the Puritans and Mormons, went into the wilderness the more perfectly to be a people of God, found these passages to be a great comfort and inspiration.

Finally, wilderness had an eschatological part to play. The twelfth chapter of Revelations went beyond Isaiah's prediction of the renewal of the wilderness[44] to grant wilderness a specific role in the last times. In it, a woman (the church), persecuted by a dragon (Satan), flees into the wilderness, where she finds refuge until the time when "the dragon was wroth with the woman, and went to make war with the remnant of her seed, which keep the commandments of God, and have the testimony of Jesus Christ." New England Puritans, for example, believed that they were living out the words of this prophecy, persecuted as they were in England and surrounded as they thought by Satan's minions (the Indians and French).

Nature in Protestant Theology

These various Christian concepts of nature yield not a single, imposing conviction, but a spectrum of possible points of view. The best-known Biblical passage concerning human relations with nature — to subdue and have dominion over the earth — had an ambiguous historical effect. In itself essentially sterile, it cannot be held solely responsible for any specific action. God's injunction is so vague that it is permissive rather than prescriptive. Its basic sense is that nature must be made an extension of human will, analogous to the relationships ("dominion") between God and creation, king and subjects, master and slave, husband and wife, parent and child. God "delivered" creation into human power — yet for what specific purpose and with what specific treatment the Bible is virtually silent.

Once taken from Genesis by the church and given to common people, the injunction to subdue the earth and have dominion over it was elastic and plastic, shaped and used in response to the desires and needs from whatever social, economic, political, or religious source. Combined with the capitalist work ethic, with an Enlightenment heritage of exaggerated Cartesian dualism, and with a psychology of aggressiveness, it produced, especially in nineteenth-century America, a powerful rationale for the subjugation of the American wilderness.

The concept of dominion was a realistic recognition of human power over nature, over both animals and agriculture, a power without parallel on earth. Responsibility is implicit in traditional concepts of power, whether of king, master, husband or parent. Stewardship, which itself is an analogy from human managers of kingdoms, property, or dependents, thus associates itself naturally with dominion. As human power over nature continues to grow, stewardship becomes one of the most useful concepts for balancing the needs of people and nature. Although it has long been associated with conservationism, only in the past decade or so have most American churches come to emphasize stewardship as a Christian response to the ecological crisis. (The Mormons are an exception, for whom stewardship was an essential tenet from the start.) Stewardship opens the broadest doorway through which Christian doctrine can contribute to and reinforce environmental action.

Long ago, Jewish and Christian monotheism drove out the nature spirits that infused the ancient world and "desacralized" nature. Yet, the doctrine of immanence, particularly as elaborated in neo-Platonic thought, has kept spirit in nature. A tree no longer contained a spirit, but it composed an artifact of God, infused by God's spirit, the soul of the universe. Even science, outwardly so cool and rational, retained a heavily religious motivation far into the nineteenth century, particularly in Protestant countries.

In contrast to dominion over nature, Christianity's neo-Platonic element, containing concepts of immanence, providence, and the book of nature, proved extremely fertile for positive action on behalf of nature. Reinforced by moralism and moral activism, it promoted nature study, nature mysticism, and a love of nature and the creatures that culminated in the American preservationist movement. It taught the proto-ecological idea of the harmony of creation and interrelationship of all things and the proto-evolutionary idea of the world as Becoming (not static Being) whose diversity and change constituted its beauty. Neo-Platonism certainly had its elements of illusionism and world denial, yet these never attained the dominance they had in Indian mysticism, with its doctrines of *maya* (the world as illusion) and total abnegation of the world.

Finally, the concept of Eden, a time when man and nature lived in harmony, benevolence, and peace, and which will one day be restored, underlies much in the history of Western relation to the natural world. Not only have specific religious movements like Puritanism, Mormonism, and even Jim Jones's ill-fated Guyana community tried to build a godly society in a new Eden, but such environmental ideas as national parks and wilderness preservation contain implications of the preservation of Edens from fallen mankind's corruption and malice.

Thus, a rich and powerful mixture of ideas about nature came with the English when they first arrived on American shores: dominion, which would help them conquer a continent; anthropocentrism, which would render the wilderness a storehouse for human use; dualism, which would despiritualize objects and places; millennialism and Biblical traditions of wilderness, which would give them a sense of place in sacred history and space; Augustinian piety, with its intense devotion and neo-Platonism; and natural theology, which would heighten interest in study of the natural world. The wild landscape would long dominate human activity on the American continent. When in the latter nineteenth century Americans finally began to dominate the wilderness, they would argue over the fate of nature using ideas first conceived more than a millennium and a half before.

TWO

Capitalists and Militants, Rationalists and Ascetics

The Perswading of the European *Powers, to shake off the Chains of* Popery. *This Argument; There is no* Popish Nation, *but what by Embracing the* Protestant Religion, *would* ipso facto, *not only assert themselves into a Glorious* Liberty, *but also* Double their Wealth *immediately; 'Tis Marvellous, that it is no more yet hearkened unto! Sirs, Prosecute it, with more of* Demonstration. *One showes, That the Abolishing of Popery in* England, *is worth at Least Eight Millions of Pounds yearly to the Nation. Let the Argument be tried with other Nations; the Argument,* Ab Utili.

— COTTON MATHER (1710)

Once to every man and nation
Comes the moment to decide,
In the strife of truth and falsehood,
For the good or evil side;
Some great cause, some new decision,
Offering each the bloom or blight,
And the choice goes by forever
'Twixt that darkness and that light.

—JAMES RUSSELL LOWELL (1845)

In the midst of civil war, great and learned divines from the kingdoms of England and Scotland gathered in Westminster, their black Geneva gowns flapping like the wings of a council of ravens. They came to perfect a great instrument a century in the making: the Calvinist Westminster Confession of Faith. They produced a work that was black as a Bible, ponderous and powerful, now reverently and quietly bearing its earthly burdens, now hissing and shrieking like a demon caged. Behind it, dissolving into the shadows of the past, stood a fantastic crowd: splendid popes, ragged friars, bishops with their croziers, serfs with their hoes, lords amid their retainers, "cunning women" amongst their physics and charms, monks vowing poverty, ladies doing penance — inhabitants of an organic and structured world suffused with magic and mystery. Advancing from the shadows of the past into the light of the present marched citizens of a brave new world: capitalists, workers, businessmen with their ledgers, farmers with their harvesters, preachers at their pulpits, politicians on their stumps, reformers seeing visions, suffragettes joining demonstrations — residents of an atomized and unbounded environment infused with rationality and moralism.

The Westminster Confession found its place at the axis of British-American Calvinism, and Calvinism gave intensity to the Puritan impulse. But in spite of the best work of the Westminster divines, their achievement disintegrated in the next century or two, and was abandoned at last, rusted and forgotten. Its echoes, though, can still be heard. They are heard in the roar of a bulldozer as it clearcuts timber. They are heard in the click of a lock as an Earth First! activist chains himself to a tree. Calvinism is now feeble, but the momentum of the Puritan impulse still moves American enterprises and crusades.

When Protestants preached either dominion over nature or wonder at God's artisanship in it, they spoke in terms that Catholics and indeed most Christians shared. Yet nature suffered a peculiar fate in the hands of Protestants. It was in Protestant-dominated countries — England, Germany, the United States — that the factory system of modern industrial capitalism with its worldwide systems of natural resource exploitation arose most forcefully.[1] Paradoxically, an ardent love of nature flourished in these nations alongside the rising factory system. Romanticism flowered especially brightly on the fertile soils of Germany, Britain, and America. Germans invented the science of ecology in 1866 and created the first ecological political party, the Greens. Britons first extended humanitarian ideals to the natural world with the Society for the Prevention of Cruelty to Animals. And Americans gave the world its first national parks and its most vigorous environmental movement. Though the industrial revolution has arrived in many other countries, in no other climate of the world have the contradictory notions of resource exploitation and environmental protection thrived with the vigor that they have in these three Protestant nations.[2]

None of the Protestant denominations of the nineteenth century explicitly bid the lumberman to destroy the forest or, for that matter, the woodsman to spare the tree. Nonetheless, the forms that Protestant doctrine took, especially among Calvinists and their heirs, encouraged lumbermen and woodsmen to exactly those acts. In their teachings, if idleness was sin, then work was blessed, and if work was godly, then productiveness was sanctified, and if production was sanctified, then resource exploitation was religious duty. At the same time, if the invisible things of God could be seen in creation, then creation was an abode of the spiritual, and if creation was filled with sacred precincts, then from nature's bosom flowed piety and virtue, and if nature taught virtue to humanity, then exploitation of her holiest places for profit was desecration.

Indeed, Protestant religious values encouraged the exploitation of nature in many ways. Protestantism's work ethic resulted in production of goods and demand for raw materials. Its reaction to Catholic "superstition" — the Protestant label for Catholic ceremonies, prayer to saints, and other non-Biblical magical or semi-magical practices — removed many obstacles to exploitation of man and nature. Its anti-authoritarianism encouraged limitation of government's power not only over conscience but over economic action, social relations, and property rights.

Countervailing values in the Protestant tradition inspired early environmental organizations and animated their supporters. Particularly in Calvinism, Protestantism's "worldly asceticism" created a motivation upon which environmentalists have relied to promote their program. Its strong rationalism lent support to nature preservationism and the science of ecology. Its principles of evangelism and moral activism gave birth to the vital spirit within ecological militancy.

The Protestant Ethic and the Spirit of Capitalism

If there is a primary cause of the ecological crisis, it is the industrial revolution. The Protestant blessing to rational, orderly capitalistic activity set it apart from the world's other religions. In Europe before the Reformation, the medieval mind erected a variety of barriers to an ethic of work as a moral duty and to notions of ever-expanding production and consumption. Saints' days proliferated throughout the calendar and repeatedly interrupted regular day-to-day work rhythms. The Catholic Church frowned upon activities that contradicted its elevation of the common good above the private and created regulations affecting usury, finance, acquisition for its own sake, economic competition, daily transactions, poor relief, and social mobility. As church strictures weighed on the consciences of the wealthy, the rich gave and bequeathed their "ill-gotten" gains to acquire merit and shorten their stays in purgatory, in the process handing the Church much of Western Europe's wealth.[3]

The leaders of the Reformation did not intend to disturb the social and economic ethic of the medieval church, but the logic of their theology drew Protestants further and further from the blueprints of medieval society and helped prepare the plans for the modern age, with its work ethic, capitalist production, and market economy. Even to their contemporaries, Protestant businessmen projected the image of humorless devotion to constant work, a devotion which had no parallel before the sixteenth century.[4]

Protestants did not invent the work ethic. The Greeks and Romans had condemned indolence and early Christians put work into a religious context. "*Qui laborat*," said St. Augustine, "*orat*" — he who works, prays. The founder of the Western monastic tradition, St. Benedict, made work a basis of his order. Early and medieval Christian thinkers noted that God created man to work in Eden, to dress and keep it, not to lie idle in the midst of plenty.[5]

The work ethic emerged as a salient component of Protestantism because work was ordained by God, it was associated with asceticism, and it was useful to society, whereas idleness offended God, tended toward vice, and burdened society with useless mouths to feed. John Calvin thought that "men were created for activity," and preached, "We are born to work . . . ."[6] English Puritans frequently cited St. Paul's admonition in II Thessalonians 3:10, "If any would not work, neither should he eat." To Puritan writer William Perkins work was one of the four aspects of the dignity of man.[7] The Puritan minister John Cotton taught that God blessed only the most diligent.[8] A corollary to the Puritan work ethic was that poverty was a moral failing and idleness a sin. When the Puritan Long Parliament set about revising the poor laws, it favored the workhouse over alms. Work had become a duty — to oneself, to others, and to God.

Around 1600 Puritans began to elaborate the concept of the two callings, which overlapped and reinforced the work ethic: the "general calling," God's call to the believer to be a Christian, and the "particular calling," his station in life.[9] When Puritans like Perkins claimed the particular calling was "ordained and imposed on man by God, for the common good," when they decried sloth and negligence as offenses against the order God had set in the world — they merely rehearsed medieval thinking. However, when Perkins connected success in one's calling with evidence of salvation, he introduced a novel idea: the faithful might construe diligence and success in business as a sign of election. Perkins enjoyed immense popularity among Puritans, and his theory was widely influential.[10]

In books that found places on Protestant bookshelves well into the nineteenth century, Restoration-era Puritan Richard Baxter perpetuated and expanded the work ethic. Themes of diligence and labor, idleness and sloth, and the shortness of time pervaded his texts. An hour of relaxation was not only a temptation to sin, but it was an hour lost to labor for the glory of God. The "saints' everlasting rest" (as he entitled a book) was in heaven, not here on earth. In his *Christian Directory*, Baxter preached the virtues of continuous hard work to both rich and poor and its benefits to the community. Wealth was not an evil in itself, but a sign of God's favor. Time spent away from work was time wasted, failure to make the best profit was poor stewardship, and profit was God's gift. Yet work was not an end in itself, but for the common good and the glory of God. With wealth came duty, not repose or pleasure.[11]

After the New England revivals of the 1730s and '40s known as the Great Awakening, the Puritan synthesis of the general and personal callings disintegrated. Churches split into factions for and against the revivals. Evangelical factions emphasized the call to Christ of the general calling, while their opponents, fearful of emotional excess and zealotry, stressed the conservative virtues of the personal calling and the work ethic. Afterwards, evangelicals tended to concentrate on the state of believers' souls and rightness with God, while religious liberals focused on behavior in this world and the probity of the Protestant ethic. Religion's association with the work ethic continues today.[12]

Also, as Calvinism has lost its force, industry and frugality have become more general virtues, rather than specifically religious injunctions.[13] From Benjamin Franklin to William Graham Sumner, secularized New Englanders, for secular reasons, perpetuated the work ethic. These Puritan-derived traits — a compulsion to keep busy, a general suspicion of idleness and pleasure for its own sake, and a sense of the social obligation of the rich — have come to be characteristic of American life. A huge proportion of the men who built American industry had roots in New England and many, like C.P. Huntington of the Southern Pacific, devoted their lives to piling up wealth, not enjoying it. Devout Baptist John Rockefeller felt God had given him his money. Born in Calvinistic Scotland, industrialist Andrew Carnegie believed himself to be a steward of his wealth and dedicated it to the common good.

Ceaseless activity contributed to an expanding economy and increasing productivity, and to rising per capita income and growing consumption. Calvinism thus accelerated natural resource use, generated air and water pollution, and glutted landfills. The old injunctions to work hard in one's calling, to order one's business rationally as a steward of the Lord, and to make money but not to enjoy it accelerated the industrial revolution, which demanded the rational exploitation of coal, wood, iron, cotton, and much else, and which in turn has meant industrial pollution, scarred landscapes, and deforestation. The Puritan road to sanctification was paid for by ecological degradation.

Yet because the obligation to earn wealth but not take pleasure in it was a religious duty, Puritans preserved the self-denial component of the work ethic, asceticism, in a secular setting and eventually asceticism came to be seen as a secular virtue. To Puritans and their descendants, self-indulgence meant giving in to self-love and selfishness, while self-denial meant devoting one's wealth or talents to purer and more worthy purposes. "The Sum of all your Religion or saving Grace is these three, *Faith*, *Self-Denial*, and *the Love of God*," wrote Baxter, and "*Public Service* is Gods *greatest Service*."[14] Self-denial was godly, but at its most virtuous it benefited the common good.

Today, environmentalism has taken up the cause of asceticism and preaches this facet of the Protestant ethic far more than most churches. Virtuous environmentalists forego plastic, artificial fabrics, and "non-organic" food, though it costs them more money. They create for themselves inconvenience by buying non-disposable and recyclable articles.[15] In poor countries, everything is recycled through necessity; in rich ones, recycling is voluntary and must rely on an ascetic impulse to get people to go out of their way to take the extra steps necessary to recycle paper, glass, plastic, and cans, as well as to use less and re-use more. Voluntary self-denial, a descendant of the self-imposed asceticism of the Puritans, forms an essential part of contemporary ecological consciousness.

Individualism

Puritanism not only transmitted a vigorous work ethic — the backbone of industrial capitalism — it also supplied the principles of individualism and anti-authoritarianism that later generations used to justify laissez-faire capitalism and inhibit government regulation of private action, including environmental regulations. Certainly Baxter and other Puritans did not desire to encourage economic individualism. Although they knew their advice would often lead to the accumulation of riches, their emphasis lay on the Christian's duty to God as steward of his property and on his usefulness to society. Their challenge was to forestall worldly problems raised by the Protestant ethic.

This challenge was exacerbated by the atomistic implications of Protestantism itself. The Reformation eliminated the mediation of the church and placed primary importance on the direct relationship between God and man. Protestant ministers played a far smaller role in parishioners' spiritual lives than Catholic priests, through whom God channeled grace and forgiveness by means of the sacraments and confession. They could only assist members of their congregations to seek in themselves the signs of grace and salvation. Puritan theology and devotional literature promoted self-examination and self-criticism to search out evidence of election and eliminate sin.[16]

Generally speaking, the more uncompromising the variety of Protestantism was, the weaker was the authority of the institutional church. Often without ready institutional resources like ecclesiastical courts to suppress individualism, Calvinists and Puritans bolstered ministers' authority and control over their congregations by setting up sentinels of conscience to guard against both material and spiritual self-absorption and self-sufficiency. They condemned in strongest terms self-centered sins like pride and selfishness and inculcated the needs of God's plan and of the common good ahead of their own.[17] It was an old strategy used for new purposes; suspicious of individualism and concerned for hierarchy and institutional order, Catholic theologians had used the common-good ideal to support the necessity of cooperation for shared objectives and to prescribe normative rules for society.[18]

By the middle of the eighteenth century, this emphasis on the common good had evolved into forms unimaginable to earlier Puritan divines. Adam Smith, professor of moral philosophy at Edinburgh in Calvinistic Scotland, felt no qualms of conscience when he wrote *The Wealth of Nations*, the founding document of economic liberalism and laissez faire. When he proposed to unleash the economic activities of individuals and allow them to pursue their own interests, he did not intend to set men at each other's throats and allow them to destroy Christian civilization. He proposed to let men gain *personal* wealth so that they could thereby enrich the *common*-wealth. Adam Smith was saying that government economic regulation impaired the common good, which was served better by the invisible hand of innumerable decisions made for purely private gain.

The Christian religious ideal of the common good descended from medieval antecedents through the Puritans and Adam Smith to wind up permutated as the Benthamite Utilitarians' definition of the common good as greatest good for the greatest number. After Bentham, Utilitarianism split into two variants: J. S. Mill and others, who favored government intervention in society and the economy, and Herbert Spencer and the Social Darwinists, who favored laissez faire.[19] Those are still the basic terms of the current American argument over how much the government need involve itself in social and economic affairs to best serve the public welfare.

Unlike Continental economic thinkers, Adam Smith and British and American liberals inherited not only the ideal of the common good, but the Protestant tradition of anti-authoritarianism as well. From the time of Martin Luther, Protestants had resisted the idea of earthly religious authority. Two of their principles encouraged this. The first, the priesthood of all believers, denied the Catholic church's elevation of the spiritual office of the priest above his flock and proclaimed the spiritual equality of all believers. The second was the principle that the Bible, open to all and understandable to all, contained a complete revelation of God's word to humanity. Catholics explicitly repudiated these positions in the sixteenth-century Council of Trent's decree that both revelation and tradition were essential to salvation and required the interpretation of the Catholic hierarchy. If obedience to Scripture and conscience characterized Protestant thought, obedience to authority became a hallmark of Catholic doctrine. St. Ignatius of Loyola, in Calvin's day founder of the Jesuits, taught his order to be ready to believe that white was black if the hierarchy of the church defined it so.[20]

In contrast, Protestant theology contained a latent individualism. The Reformation released the uncontrollable genie of dissent by conferring legitimacy on dissenters to whom their local minister, church, nation, or the world were not sanctified enough. To Luther's dismay, Anabaptists, millenarians, and fanatics appeared almost as soon as the Diet of Worms adjourned. In the Netherlands, Britain, and America, dissent and sectarianism persisted to such a degree and became so powerful that toleration and finally pluralism became inevitable. Protestant ecclesiology reflected this suspicion of religious authority. Presbyterians replaced bishops with presbyteries and assemblies made up of ministers and laymen. New England Puritans so feared religious authority that they created a congregational polity with no central authority at all. (Horrified by a peasant revolt, Luther rejected the social and political implications of his anti-authoritarian doctrine, threw his support behind centralized secular authority, and helped send Germany down a different path.)

Rejection of human authority also changed the relationship between religion and nature. During the English Civil War, when the power of the Church of England dissolved, instead of the hoped-for unity based on the word of God in the Bible, the nation split into religious factions, including a number of very visible radical sects. The Restoration in 1660 could not repair the damage to Anglican prestige and authority, yet reliance upon the Bible alone had produced fanaticism and division. With these two sources of religious authority discredited, many people turned to a third, which they imagined spoke with an infallible and uniform voice.

That source was the book of nature — the natural world as interpreted by the rational mind. After 1660, everyone from Puritan to Deist, from Cotton Mather to Thomas Jefferson, was studying nature to discern divine truths. On the one hand, this heightened interest in nature gave impetus to the sciences, and on the other, it reinforced the Christian tradition which looked for spiritual experience in the natural world. It was no coincidence that in the late seventeenth century the Royal Society and neo-Platonism (revived by the Cambridge Platonists) flourished at the same moment. Science benefited in important ways from Protestant anti-authoritarianism. Rejection of religious authority and confidence in human ability to discern truth in Scripture reinforced the growing trend which rejected the accepted wisdom of medieval, deductive Aristotelian science and whose outcome was the triumph of empirical, inductive Baconian science. The Catholic hierarchy's repression of Galilean theory long impaired the progress of science in Catholic countries and alienated Catholic scientists. In contrast with Britain and America, French science came to ally itself with skepticism and anticlericalism.[21]

Suspicion of authority was hard to keep within bounds. In England, religious dissent accentuated and extended the decentralization of power that already existed in its constitutional arrangement of king in Parliament (in contrast to the absolute kings of Continental kingdoms). Opposition based on conscience arose in both religion and politics at the same time. The seventeenth- and eighteenth-century political groupings that were ancestors to modern political parties were associated with religious factions: Tories with king and bishops, Whigs with opposition and dissent. Eighteenth-century thinkers applied the logic of anti-authoritarianism to other fields of learning like political economy. If authoritarianism was harmful in politics and religion, it might well be harmful to the wealth of nations, as Adam Smith concluded. The fruit of economic liberty fell from the trees of political and religious liberty.[22]

The connection between Protestantism and laissez-faire capitalist theory received further strength when revolutionaries and government opponents in Britain and America married Protestantism to defense of property rights. In the Puritan Revolution, Protestants, defending the Reformation against a "papist" monarch, allied themselves with cloth manufacturers, small and medium urban merchants, common lawyers, and independent small farm-

ers. These groups were frustrated by the government's favoritist, conservative, and monopolistic economic policy.[23] The Glorious Revolution of 1688
ousted James II both because of his Catholicism and because of the threat
he posed to property rights. After 1763 American colonists were primed to
resist any British legislation that seemed to threaten religion and property.
Beginning with the Sugar and Stamp Acts, Americans feared for their property rights, and in the bishop controversy and the Quebec Act they feared
for their religion. Colonists looked back at both revolutions as forerunners
of the Spirit of 1776; especially in Puritan New England, defense of property and religion became one cause.[24]

Thus, by the early nineteenth century, religion had provided or reinforced many of the ideas which fenced in the perceived legitimate functions
of government, especially in the United States. Guarantees of property
rights went into the Constitution and Bill of Rights and helped insulate
property from government action (although the early Supreme Court affirmed the power of the government to subject property to some demands
for the common good, as in the Charles River Bridge case). Southerners
and Westerners resented infringement of the freedom of owners to use (or
abuse) their property as they saw fit. Americans' suspicion of government
interference in the economy weakened Henry Clay's "American System"
and killed the Second Bank of the United States. During the Jacksonian era,
anti-authoritarianism exploded in American religious, economic, and political life and transformed the country into a nation of sectarianism, free
banking, and open democracy. In Jacksonianism the vineyards of individualism and anti-authoritarianism planted in the Reformation produced one
of their most intoxicating vintages.

Hence, Protestantism directly and indirectly placed many hurdles in
the way of government action in behalf of the natural environment. Anti-
authoritarianism, individualism, and property rights made it extremely difficult for the American government to justify intervention to prevent or
regulate private behavior on private property that did ecological damage.
For example, after the government established Yellowstone National Park
in 1872, congressmen tried for years to make its resources available for
private exploitation.[25]

Only in the late nineteenth century, and especially during the Progressive Era of the early twentieth century, could the government finally begin
to take its first steps to implement conservation measures proposed as much
as a half-century before. The common-good ideal had grown equal to the
anti-authoritarian principle. In the twentieth century, every two steps forward taken by environmentally minded administrations has been followed

by one backward step taken by laissez-faire administrations. After the advances of Progressivism, the New Deal, and Great Society liberalism came the retreats of the 1920s, 1950s, and 1980s and 1990s. Must government defend the common interest in the environment against private profiteering, or has the government hurt the public good by preserving nature? The debate continues whether the common good is better left in private or government hands.[26]

Rationalization

Protestantism transformed the way people think about nature by transforming the way people think. Protestants passionately demanded that all aspects of daily life, society, and government conform to the divine plan contained in the Bible and Christian belief. Unbiblical beliefs and practices, from transubstantiation and relics to talismans and village magic, found condemnation as superstition. The ungodly found no safety in pedigree and traditional loyalties, as Archbishop Laud and King Charles I discovered to their sorrow. The ascetic Protestantism of the Puritans and the sects furthered rationalization because, compared to Catholic religious culture, it intensified the religious control and regulation of life.[27] A product of a long and complex history, the Catholic Church was too messy, self-contradictory, and compromised with the world. Although rationality has long been a major component of Western culture, as just the examples of Aristotle and St. Thomas Aquinas could demonstrate, never had a movement arisen with as far-reaching implications as the Protestant blueprint for a new world.[28]

Erasing the distinction between religious and secular, Protestants projected their Biblical and godly order over the world, both human and natural. In depersonalizing the former and disenchanting the latter, they helped turn the page on medieval traditional culture of magic and fealty and opened the chapter on the modern rational world of science and contracts. Rationalization of the cosmos and society ultimately led to industrial exploitation of both nature and people. As its implications worked themselves out, they led to the modern state, with its professional administration, specialized officialdom, and law based on the concept of citizenship; to a rational law, codified and rationally interpreted and applied; to modern science; to a contractual economy based on the market principle; and to a religious-based ethic for the conduct of life whose logical consequence was explicit rationalism.[29]

Puritans and sectarians accomplished this by relentlessly applying the logic of their theology to their lives and constantly pressing for a rational social order measured against the yardsticks of morality and piety. The strict and unwavering theology of Calvinism answered the need for order in a disorderly world.[30] Protestants repudiated Catholic "magical" ceremonies and "superstitious" beliefs, attacked the popular magic, superstition, and traditions derived from paganism or folklore, and "disenchanted" the medieval world. The unmediated relation between God and man and the absolute individualism of predestination encouraged the breakdown of an ethic of brotherly love, which in turn reinforced individualism. Closing the monasteries, Protestants insisted on a "worldly asceticism" which required the godly live in the world but not of it. Worldly asceticism had no brotherly implications. Loyalty to God transcended earthly loyalties and dissolved connection to family, friends, locality, country, and nature. If necessary, the elect, like Christian leaving his family in Bunyan's *Pilgrim's Progress*, turned their backs on kith and kin to search for their own salvation and make themselves instruments of divine will.

Ascetic Protestantism transformed people, transformed nations, and transformed history because it valued godly activity, emphasized individual activism and responsibility, and weakened the power of authority with a direct relationship to the sacred and sacred traditions. In this new world without magic or mysticism, new men felt the scales of superstition fall from their eyes, shook loose the chains of tradition, and went forth to master and order their world. Then, when they crossed the seas, they found wilderness full of wild animals and wild peoples and set to work to subdue and order them, to bring them within the bounds of rational civilization, rational Christianity, rational government, rational capitalism, rational science.[31]

Rationalization became both scourge and succor for the natural world. Rationality in the business world motivated the search for greater efficiency, greater productivity, and faster and more thorough exploitation of resources, which in turn has led to huge economies of scale and dramatic increases in resource extraction and use. Yet, modern conservationism stemmed from the desire for the rational (or "scientific") management of resources. Environmentalists base the management of wildlife upon ecology, the demystified, systematic, rational study of the interconnectedness of things. An important, rationalistic segment of the modern environmental program is the desire to order and manage even the waste products of civilization through recycling and pollution "control" (a synonym for mastery), and a primary goal has been the passage of laws and creation of agencies to rationally regulate industry and individuals in the interest of "clean" or "pure" food, water, air, and landscape. Rationalization remains in the service of order and purity, if no longer godliness.

Rationalization has led people to believe that they can solve environmental problems with arbitrary lines on a map: on one side lies recreational "use," on the other commercial agriculture; on the one side lies "green-belt," on the other, side streets, cars, homes, offices, and factories; on the one side lies "pristine" wilderness, on the other side civilization. It is much like the Calvinist intent to divide the world into the godly and the ungodly, into the saved and the damned. It is the impulse to wall-in the holy city, the New Jerusalem, to build what New England Puritans called "the Hedge,"[32] with the Chosen within, Nehemiah on the wall, and, outside, Satan scheming to get in. The rationalistic need to divide and separate the forces of good and evil, stasis and change, and spirituality and materialism has given American history many Nehemiahs, from George Catlin proposing a park for Indians and buffalo to roam forever unhindered by white civilization, to John Muir fighting an unholy dam in God's own Yosemite National Park, to the Sierra Club's David Brower blocking a dam in the Grand Canyon. Yet "something there is that doesn't love a wall": the rationalist moral masons are never idle, and seem never weary.

Moral Marginality

By the early twentieth century, the defense of natural scenery against exploitation for profit had become intensely moral, with New England leading all other regions in its devotion to the cause. Yet, less than a century before, Americans had nearly unanimously urged the conquest of wilderness. The reasons for this shift are many, including disappearance of wild places and animals and the growth of cities. The *moral* fervor evoked in nature's defense, however, could not have had just secular sources.[33] In the interval, middle-class Protestantism had evolved a strong emphasis on morality, while the scope of its moral concern had gradually broadened to take in even some of the natural world. The origins of this moralism and newly ethical attitude toward nature lay in Puritanism, the Christian tradition, and Western concepts of masculinity and femininity.

The story has its beginning in the mid-seventeenth century, when the Puritan movement failed in its very moment of triumph. Following the Civil War and execution of Charles I, the Puritan commonwealth faltered and Charles II was restored to the throne in 1660. The country was ready for respite from strife and intolerance and turned from the hot intolerant zeal of Calvinist Puritanism to the cooler ecumenical devotion to reason and benevolence, the reflections within of the divine light and moral purity. Reason and benevolence also avoided the doctrinal rigidity of Calvinism and preserved its moral intensity and contempt for the material world. So pervasive did this turn away from divisive creeds and doctrine to benevolence and good deeds become that when Massachusetts Puritan Cotton Mather penned his popular *Essays to do Good*, a quintessential Deist like Benjamin Franklin could find it inspirational.[34]

The emphasis on benevolence led to the nineteenth-century middle-class conviction that morality was the central characteristic of Christianity and indeed of any superior civilization. To distinguish godly from ungodly, Christian from heathen, civilized from uncivilized, human from bestial, Americans looked for signs of moral feeling, a sensitivity for "higher" things, and an appreciation for "uplifting" literature, art, music, emotions, and experience.

But moral feelings cannot be exercised without objects of moral concern, and Protestants developed very strong sentiments about who legitimately "deserved" solicitude, in the process laying the foundations for modern humanitarianism. During the eighteenth and nineteenth centuries, the circle of humanitarian concern gradually extended to include groups of increasing diversity: first the poor (the "deserving," not "vicious" poor), then heathens, slaves, women, children, criminals, Indians, and lower classes. Humanitarianism even extended to ever larger portions of the natural world: first, domesticated animals, and, finally, wild nature — or at least portions of it. There are no Societies for the Prevention of Cruelty to Fish or the Gypsy Moth, or for the Preservation of Poison Ivy or Vacant Lots. The question is, then, how humanitarians came to feel pity not only for unfortunate Christians, but for forests and mountains, buffalo and birds, whales and wolves. Moreover, what criteria determine inclusion or exclusion from concern, and why would any part of nature attract ethical concern at all?

The common thread that links the objects for which Christians feel pity and compassion and on whose behalf they act benevolently is a quality that might be called "moral marginality." "Moral marginals," be they people, animals, or things, are all marginal to the mainstream of society, particularly to public life in its material and non-spiritual aspects. More importantly, they must be marginalized (willingly or not) because of their salient *virtue*. If something or someone — a miser, drunk, or outlaw, for example — is socially marginalized for immoral or amoral characteristics, Christians exempt him from benevolence, even treat him with contempt. Although insofar as such a person is conceived of as a victim, for example of bad parents or evil but impersonal social forces, he might become the legitimate object of humanitarian feelings and action.

The principles of "moral marginality" were first defined in the Old Testament when God set off the descendants of Abraham from the rest of the world as his chosen people. Many things marked the Hebrews as a unique people: monotheism, an invisible deity, divinely instituted law, a sacred history, and a physical mark, circumcision, differentiating them from all others. They set themselves apart from and made themselves marginal to the other peoples of the Middle East while believing in the centrality of their religion and sacred history and in the marginality of other peoples and religions. Properly interpreted, all events, whether disaster or prosperity, supported their self-conception because it indicated God's testing, chastisement, or favor for themselves (for example, in Isaiah 10:5–6 or Psalm 78) or punishment of their enemies (for example, in Isaiah 13:17–22). Self-marginalization of religious groups is self-validating. Jewish experience has provided a model for Christian groups who find themselves on the margin of society — outsiders partly by ostracism, partly by deliberate separation from a sinful world — and who interpret their marginality as a mark of their favor in God's eyes. Moreover, for Christians, adversity comes from the Devil, thought to be especially enraged against communities of God's people, which reinforces their self-identity as a people doing God's will against allied evil powers visible and invisible.

Prophets attained special status by marginality within the Hebrew community itself. These men (Judaism neglected female prophets) achieved holy status not simply by separating themselves from the regular community, which would of itself not raise status but lose it, but by adopting standard means which the community recognized as religiously virtuous, including visions, preaching, and sometimes bizarre behavior.[35] Standing on the margins of society, apart both from everyday life and from ordinary religious and priestly organizations, prophets could free themselves from social constraints and perceive and condemn social ills and religious transgressions.

The New Testament brought an important new factor to moral marginality, what might be called religious feminization, or symbolic emasculation. Jesus and his followers emphasized traditionally feminine traits — passivity and non-aggression, compassion, lovingness, receptivity, as well as economic and political marginality — and explicitly linked them to the marginality of the prophets. This is clearly delineated in the central statement

of the Christian ethic, the Sermon on the Mount, in which Jesus invoked
the religious status of prophets to bless the forgotten, hopeless believers, all
of whom he placed in passive and victimized categories: the poor in spirit,
the mourners, the meek, the merciful, the pure, the peacemakers, the persecuted (Matthew 5:3–5, 7–12). Jesus had no words to bless the rich, the
powerful, the mighty, the warriors, the landowners and moneylenders,
the authorities of state and religion. Indeed, he very nearly denied them the
possibility of salvation at all (Matthew 19:23–24). Moreover, Jesus bade
his followers to suppress such masculine urges as lusting after women,
dominating others, resisting aggression, hating enemies, seeking glory and
honor, and accumulating wealth: "Ye cannot serve God and mammon"
(Matthew 5:28, 39–42, 44, 6:2–4, 19–20, 24).

Other elements of the New Testament reinforce this feminized piety. No
figures display their masculinity in fights, war, lust, wealth, or power — no
Joshua, no Samson, no David, no Solomon. Most, like Jesus, are unmarried
and childless, and marriage itself seems reluctantly accepted (I Corinthi-
ans 7:7–9). Jesus went so far as to praise emasculation (Matthew 19:12),
prompting one early Father, Origen, to castrate himself.[36]

Early church leaders reinforced Christian feminized spirituality, avoid-
ing activities like commerce, government, war, sex, and parenthood, asso-
ciating them with the sinful world, and established traditions of monasti-
cism and celibacy. Ironically, the feminization of spirituality made it more
difficult for women to find a place in the church. If holiness was a measure
of the adoption of feminine traits, how could women attain holiness? Their
solution to this problem was to protect their pure femininity from assault or
corruption, like the female saints, or to avoid the pollution of unspiritual
masculine touch altogether, like the Virgin Mary or nuns.

Remasculinization of piety formed a major theme of the Reformation
and gave the world the Protestant ethic. Protestants repudiated monasti-
cism and celibacy and pushed the godly into the public world of commerce
and politics — in the world but not of it. Their standard of private piety
remained unmasculine: quiet reflection, sobriety, restraint. While Calvinists allowed their sober piety to be the mark of chosenness, radical sectarians, like the Jews, often adopted a severer code of marginality in a more
exaggerated group identity and withdrawal from the corruption of the
world. Some, like Quakers, adopted peculiar modes of speech, dress, and
action to set themselves further apart from the worldly and accentuate their
own sense of holiness.

In the eighteenth century, when benevolence began to assume its position
as the mark of a true Christian, feminized piety and marginality permeated

its concepts. First, ministers preached that the emotions, especially those associated with women, such as compassion, pity, and sorrow, distinguished true benevolence from hypocrisy because they demonstrated unfeigned spiritual feeling. Secondly, unlike Catholic almsgiving, which bestowed charity on the basis of need, but like Puritan almsgiving, benevolence took into account the moral worthiness of recipients. Benevolence combined traditional compassion for devout unfortunates with Protestant respect for the masculine piety of the righteous active in the world. These "virtuous" poor were victims — of famine, misfortune, or malevolence — but exhibited the masculine traits of activity, diligence, and industry. "Vicious" poor deserved their fate: their marginality resulted from moral failings like idleness or evil propensities, and not adversity in spite of virtue.[37]

The feminine aspect of moral marginality expanded throughout the nineteenth century. The doctrine of male and female "spheres" took hold in middle-class Britain and America, strictly defining sex roles and separating masculine and feminine forms of piety. As a typical document put it in 1897,

> . . . Men are ordained to govern in all forceful and material matters, *because they are men*, physically and intellectually strong, virile, aggressive; while women, by the same decree of God and nature, are equally fitted to bear rule in a higher and more spiritual realm, where the strong frame and the weighty brain count for less, but the finer fibre of the woman's body and the spiritual uplift of her affection and her soul are the indications of a power not less than that of a man, and even more necessary to the progress and elevation of the race.[38]

Women's sphere contained home, children, and religion; men's contained work, commerce, and politics. Passive, tender, nurturing, and spiritual, women tended to home and church, withdrawn from public life; active, aggressive, domineering, and physical, men lived in a dirty, dangerous, wicked world. Civilization was supposedly guided by the higher impulses that found their source in the feminine. Men without feminine influence would relapse into barbarism.

The female sphere grew to encompass those pursuits which were or were perceived to be marginal to public and economic life. These pursuits, generally described together as "higher" or "uplifting," included art, literature, poetry, music, the life sciences, philosophy, and religion. (Physical science was based on the "masculine" traits of reason, rationality, and calculability, while life sciences relied on less precise and less "logical" description and dealt with such more feminine subjects like plants and flowers. Note, too, that religious feeling remained prominent in the works of life scientists long after it had disappeared from the works of physicists and chemists.) The Victorians expected women to interest themselves in these areas and to bring them into the home to instruct, instill, and inspire their husbands and children. Women and their organizations became the mainstays of the denominations. As Western civilization in the nineteenth century became increasingly masculine, aggressive, and materialistic, "feminine" aspects and activities lost influence even as they rose in status (partly, one suspects, as a salve to conscience).[39]

Western concepts of masculinity and femininity combined with Christian-based moralism and humanitarianism to create the essential moral framework for the defense of nature. The natural world was seen in two contrary ways, as "wilderness" and "nature." Wilderness was masculine: wild, threatening, dangerous, an abode of uncivilized peoples, an adversary against which a man could test himself and attempt to conquer. Nature was feminine: a goddess like Natura or Gaia, smiling, beautiful, bountiful, life-giving, nurturing, spiritual, a home, a sanctuary. Wilderness was an "it"; nature was a "she." Interpretation of activity in the natural world was reflected in the genderized vocabulary used to express it. Men "conquered" or "tamed" wilderness, but with a change of metaphor they "ravished" or "raped" nature.

Masculine enterprise penetrated ever further into the virgin continent, and many in the middle classes saw in nature a feminized victim of amoral and immoral materialistic forces. Men were sacrificing nature for money, desecrating her majestic primeval temples in the service of mammon. By 1900, just as the marginalized elements of America's culture and conscience were beginning to reassert their influence, nature had attained true moral marginality in the eyes of many. Women and men from "less manly" categories — botanists, naturalists, nature-lovers, and women's clubmembers — rose in nature's defense and for the first time raised effective barriers to economic exploitation of the land.

The psychological element of the evangelical temperament was at work here as well. Alienated sons of evangelical families often turned from masculine piety and activity and toward the more feminized and marginal "higher" pursuits like art, poetry and literature (Romantic especially), life science, the ministry, or teaching. Emerson, who remembered his father with resentment and who grew up close to his mother and aunt, confessed his ineptitude in practical matters in his essay "Prudence." Associated in the "Transcendental Club" with such Victorian marginals as Unitarian ministers and unmarried women intellectuals, Emerson taught the inferiority of material pursuits to scholarship, art, and religion, and saw in nature the doorway to spiritual and moral understanding.

Alienation from the masculine sphere could express itself in hostility to the aggressive, dominating aspects of Western civilization and sympathy for the moral marginals, the victims of Western masculine domination.[40] In this way, advocacy for nature, ecology, environmentalism, wilderness, wild rivers, wild animals, and just about "wild" anything was usually linked with hostility to one or another facet of mainstream capitalist culture. Rebellious sons also left the city for nature because there they might find refuge from anxiety, guilt, and conflict which could accompany the act of rebellion. Psychologically, this could heighten their perceptions of nature as a place of safety, nurture, and love where they could escape or overcome those feelings.[41] Thoreau self-righteously separated himself from town life to live on nearby Walden Pond and preached to others to do the same. Alienated from his father, after quitting a machine-shop job Muir escaped into the Sierras, where he lived for several years. Replete with domestic and maternal metaphor, his writings consistently regarded wilderness as the moralizing counterpart to money-mad civilization, humanity's true home, and a place to be nurtured and healed.

The Protestant revival of interest in the prophets also resulted in revival of the tradition of vatic marginality, the withdrawal from society (often, both Biblically and recently, to the wilderness) to decry the nation's sins. Combined with the Protestant evangelical heritage, it has produced a powerful line of moral environmental radicals from John Muir to Dave Foreman.

The Protestant Temperament

Ironically, the capture of religion by the Victorian feminine sphere of home, church, and family could channel masculine activity against nature. In the South, where male culture had traditionally encouraged combativeness, confrontation, and aggressiveness, the steady rise of evangelical religion all through the nineteenth century gradually suppressed long-time masculine outlets like fighting, drinking, gambling, and horse racing. One masculine activity left untouched, however, was hunting. Sport hunting (as opposed to subsistence hunting), rising in popularity in parallel with evangelicalism, allowed men to safely vaunt their prowess far from the female sphere of family, home, and church.

Protestant childraising techniques exacerbated the increasing direction of violence against nature. Parents regarded it as their religious duty to "beat the devil" out of their children, that is, to use physical punishment to suppress the child's will (which, due to the sin of Adam, inclined toward evil) and instill obedience to God and parents. Denied the right to express any anger or resentment, children, particularly boys, often matured full of bottled anger, rage, resistance, and rebellion toward self, parents, and the world. Reformation theology thus encouraged the suppression of natural emotion but left it with no legitimate outlet. Historian Philip Greven has called the resultant personality the "Protestant temperament."

This anger had to go somewhere, and usually ended up being "displaced," in the Freudian term: applied to another target. Boys vented their anger and resentment in painful or cruel childhood games, taunting weak or unusual children, and bullying. They also commonly tormented animals, for example by tying objects to the tails of dogs, dropping cats in wells, catching and blinding birds, and in countless other ways. In adulthood, supported by numerous Biblical passages as well as by law and custom, family "patriarchs" directed pent-up wrath at the errors and disobedience of wives, children, and domestic animals. The advance of evangelical culture in nineteenth-century America increased the severity of corporal punishment and caused many men to repress emotions and suppress aggressive activities; the most socially harmless safety valve left was hunting and killing game.[42]

Southern natural abundance encouraged a self-indulgent trend toward binge killing (shooting as much as one could of whatever game was within range) as a measure of male pride. A merchant in Louisiana, for example, recorded fifty-three hunting trips in nine months in 1883–84, during which he bagged 518 animals. Men frequently kept tally of the size of their day's kill — 34 birds, 24 night hawks, and so forth — and local newspapers often proudly reported exceptional hunting feats. This overkill drastically reduced game in the South, but it also accelerated acceptance there of conservation ideas after the turn of the century, when the evangelical tone of many conservation ordinances indicated that evangelicals now regarded even hunting and fishing as activities of masculine intemperance that needed to be curbed.[43] The feminization of American religion in the nineteenth century thus first encouraged and then restrained the Southern male passion for hunting.

If as an adult, the child, particularly the son, identified with his father, the pattern would likely reproduce itself and the cycle of violence would continue. A son might, however, identify instead with the victims of his father's wrath, particularly his mother, the figure of loving pious mildness in an evangelical household, and break free of the cycle. Alienated from the masculine values preached in the Protestant ethic, such sons might tend toward the ministry, scholarship, or other non-economic pursuit, or in the nineteenth century toward a Romantic outlook[44] or devotion, not to the vengeful Old Testament God, but to the loving, indwelling New Testament or neo-Platonic Father.

Having broken from the cycle of violence, sympathetic to victims of aggression and injustice, disaffected with the Protestant ethic world of work and profit, and self-righteous to counter guilt over rebellion against parental authority, sons join or lead crusades for maternal nature and against heartless mammon. Sons displace their anger at their fathers, criticizing not the parents themselves but the "masculine" economic or "corrupt" features of society, rightful targets of moral criticism since the time of the prophets. Full of pious rage and speaking like prophets and evangelists, men like Muir and Foreman fulminate against materialist society in defense of the mountains or the earth.

Moral Activism

The moral urgency that animates the environmental movement is also a direct legacy of Calvinism and Puritanism. John Calvin began the powerful tradition of moral activism and civil disobedience that has driven most American reform movements. The activist wing of environmentalism traces its roots through the Puritans directly to God's holy self-appointed instruments, the committed Calvinists.

Calvin taught that disorder and sin were offenses to God and that saints must dedicate their lives to restoring godly order. Sin led to lethargy, sloth, and impotence; righteousness brought energy, activity, and strength from God. Saints acted, and acted as instruments of God's will.[45] This search for order led to Calvin's doctrine of the magistracy, which enjoined obedience to the magistrate who by the very fact of his civil position had been placed in charge by God to oversee orderly society.

However, because rulers were obliged to govern justly, sometimes God "raises up some of his servants as public avengers, and arms them with his commission to punish unrighteous domination, and to deliver from their distressing calamities a people who have been unjustly oppressed. . . ."[46] In what turned out to be a wide loophole indeed to his requirement of total submission to civil authority, Calvin made "one exception" to the obedience due evil magistrates:

The Lord, therefore, is the King of kings; who, when he has opened his sacred mouth, is to be heard alone, above all, for all, and before all; in the next place, we are subject to those men who preside over us; but no otherwise than in him. If they command any thing against him, it ought not to have the least attention. . . . But since this edict has been proclaimed by that celestial herald, Peter, "We ought to obey God rather than men," [Acts 5:29] — let us console ourselves with this thought, that we truly perform the obedience which God requires of us, when we suffer any thing rather than deviate from piety.[47]

Calvin supported his arguments for resistance to ungodly magistrates mainly with examples from the history of the Hebrews and the experiences of the prophets. Along with Protestants of all sorts, Calvin had rediscovered the prophets, long neglected in Christian thought. As they searched the Bible for precedents and justification for resistance to Catholic ecclesiastical and civil powers, Protestants revived the prophetic tradition of condemnation of kings and nations who neglected God's ordinances. Because the Hebrews had first become a nation as the chosen people of God by making an eternal covenant with him, kings and princes who violated the covenant lost their right to rule. As the prophets reminded them repeatedly, kings must obey God in order to justifiably expect the obedience of God's people. Protestants demanded no less of their own kings and rulers.[48]

Together, godly activity and the renewed prophetic tradition produced the inflammable mixture of moral activism. When the summons came to build God's kingdom or call kings to account, English Puritans performed prodigies. In America, they established a flourishing "Bible Commonwealth." In England, they overthrew a "popish" king and his corrupt church. Puritans, though, found out quickly that moral activism was a two-edged sword. Sectarians arose in both England and America who strove to build a holier church and commonwealth than even Puritans dreamed.[49] During the Great Awakening of the 1740s in New England, revivalists forced good Puritan ministers to fend off accusations that they were cold and unconverted, and unworthy of their office.

Moral activism did not go to the grave with the last Puritan. The children of the Puritans did not cease to reproach the unrighteous who failed to heed holy law. In New England, colonial Puritan ministers had railed against the sins of their congregations lest the Bible Commonwealth wither and die. Driven by a vision that was by turns millennial, evangelical, and utopian, their spiritual heirs — Congregationalists, Presbyterians, and Unitarians — worked resolutely to make the world a godly place.

By the mid-nineteenth century, civil disobedience lost its Calvinist moorings and attached itself to a vague "higher law," a phrase Senator William Seward made famous in an 1850 slavery debate. The interpreters of higher law were no longer the ministers of the Bible commonwealth but rather those sentinels of conscience they had placed in each Puritan heart. In Thoreau's classic 1849 defense of civil disobedience, he wrote,

> Must the citizen ever for a moment, or in the least degree, resign his conscience to the legislator? Why has every man a conscience, then? . . . Those who know of no purer sources of truth, who have traced up its stream no higher, stand, and wisely stand, by the Bible and the Constitution, and drink at it there with reverence and humility; but they who behold where it comes trickling into this lake or that pool, gird up their loins once more, and continue their pilgrimage toward its fountain-head.[50]

Prophets for a new age, oracles of the higher pools of truth, Seward and Thoreau carried on the tradition of holding civil government answerable to something greater.

Beginning in the nineteenth century, Americans in great numbers answered the call of conscience and higher law and organized themselves on behalf of many reforms and moral causes—temperance, abolition, the Social Gospel, and then conservation—to call government and society to account. The moral tenor of the rhetoric of the early Sierra Club, founded in 1892, is unmistakable. In the environmental movement before the 1960s, civil disobedience was rare, but activists called upon government to defend nature from conscienceless greed. The activist wing of the ecologically pure-in-heart has steadily grown with time and today constitutes a visible and influential element. In the words of one Sierra Club member, responding to the question the club magazine put to its readership, "Would you ever break the law in support of an environmental goal?":

> Of course! There is a higher law that governs the universe and the natural systems inside it. That is the law to be obeyed. Civil disobedience and monkeywrenching are acceptable. These methods have been called radical. I consider the unchecked destruction of a delicate ecosystem that supports so many to be radical. Hell, I'm a conservative.[51]

"Conservative" the respondent may be, but almost certainly not Calvinist, and possibly even atheist. The environmental movement today rarely evinces any real religious orthodoxy, although vague moral and spiritual values frequently appear. Yet environmentalists betray their Calvinistic moral and activist roots. Protection of nature is now the higher law, "an ethic and conscience in everything we do, whatever our field of endeavor," in the words of David Brower. "We are in a kind of religion, an ethic with regard to terrain. . . ."[52] Prompted by moral resolve, environmentalists rally in defense of virtuous nature against the amoral forces who let themselves be overcome by greed or who drink from a lower pool of truth. Environmental leaders from John Muir to David Brower have described themselves in religious and prophetic and evangelical terms.[53] They are determined that the righteous shall yet prevail.

Modern society displays everywhere unintended consequences of the doctrines laid down by John Calvin, William Perkins, Richard Baxter, and scores of Calvinist and Puritan men of the cloth. Contemporary capitalist theory and practice owe them a debt. The environmental movement's moral outrage, activism, and appeal to government intervention draw on the same account. The world has been transformed with new answers that are often only old ones rephrased.

Book Two

Protestants, Capitalists, and Nature

✠ ✠ ✠

THREE

God, Nature,
and the Puritans

You, sinful Crew, have not been true
unto the Light of Nature,
Nor done the good you understood,
nor owned your Creator.

— MICHAEL WIGGLESWORTH, "DAY OF DOOM" (1662)

Besids, what could they see but a hidious & desolate wildernes, full of wild beasts &
willd men? and what multituds ther might be of them they knew not. Nether
could they, as it were, goe up to the tope of Pisgah to vew from this willdernes a
more goodly cuntrie to feed their hops; for which way soever they turnd their eys
(save upward to the heavens) they could have litle solace or content in respecte of
any outward objects. For summer being done, all things stand upon them with a
wetherbeaten face; and the whole countrie, full of woods & thickets, represented a
wild and savage hew.

— WILLIAM BRADFORD, *OF PLYMOUTH PLANTATION,*
ON THE ARRIVAL OF THE SEPARATISTS IN MASSACHUSETTS IN 1620

No other English colony — for that matter, no other place in the world —
was quite like New England. It flourished and grew on some of the poorest
soil in the Empire, dissenters ran the established church, and a ministry
with little official power dominated lay life. Yet, in that little-regarded
corner of the British Empire the inhabitants nursed a fervent and zealous
Calvinism. When in the nineteenth century their descendants rushed forth
across the American continent, they brought with them a mentality molded
and fired in a Puritan land. The power of that mentality soon propelled
them disproportionately not only into the boardrooms of industry but
also into the ranks of reform societies and of nature stewardship and pres-

ervation groups. Particularly after the Civil War, New Englanders dominated national economic, intellectual, and cultural life. By then, what the
Calvinist and Puritan traditions had to say about nature mattered a great
deal.

Europeans first contemplated the wild shores of America much like a
painter gazes at a blank canvas. To them, America had no past, no history —
it was a continent in future tense. With the colors available to them, how
should they paint what they saw? Some filled their canvas with the wilderness of Sinai, where dangers and demons threatened Christian settlers.
Others depicted a Canaan flowing with milk and honey, beckoning Europeans away from Egyptian slavery. Was America an Eden where fallen men
struggled for redemption? Or were the colonists to follow God's plan and
restore the howling wilderness to paradise? Upon this bare canvas poured
the visions and dreams (and nightmares) of the European soul.

In the seventeenth century, the English often referred to their new settlements in America and elsewhere not as "colonies" but "plantations." They
crossed the seas and "planted" new communities. The Puritans "planted"
the Gospel in a heathen wilderness. The English also planted the beliefs,
viewpoints, and intellectual traditions that would shape the landscape of the
American mind. The first two centuries of English presence on the American continent was a seedtime of ideas and attitudes from European stock.
Although European ideas adapted to their new environment, colonial
American contributors to the arts and sciences depended upon the Old
World for model, style, and conception. Self-conscious of their location on
the fringes of Western civilization, educated Americans longed to participate in European learned life.

Of the varieties of attitudes toward nature planted with the first generations of Puritans, three stand out for their lasting influence. The educated elite blended Calvinism with more secular literary and philosophical trends to produce that sense of nature's purity and man's vileness.
Most Puritans fixated more narrowly on the Bible, whose concepts and
phrases they combined with the Calvinist ethic of work and activity to
generate compelling rationales for the transformation of the wilderness
into which they had ventured. Finally, many Puritans struggled to overcome their remoteness to keep abreast of European developments, particularly in natural science, to which they made their own contributions in
the service of man and God. These three perspectives on nature clearly
manifested themselves in the works of Anne Bradstreet, Edward Johnson,
and Cotton Mather.

Paradise Lost: Anne Bradstreet

In 1662 Michael Wigglesworth published "God's Controversy with New-England," in which he described America as "A waste and howling wilderness, / Where none inhabited / But hellish fiends, and brutish men / That Devils worshipped."[1] That image of a howling wasteland full of demons and devil-worshippers forms the common portrayal of the attitude of early New England Puritans toward the natural world.[2] Themes of hostility toward and exploitation of nature, grounded in Biblical types and imagery, did dominate such accounts as William Bradford's *Plymouth Plantation*, Edward Johnson's *Wonder-Working Providence of Sions Saviour, in New England*, and Cotton Mather's histories of New England. New Englanders' high literacy rates and intense Protestantism combined with their concentration on the Bible as the source of religious truth meant that the Bible above all else gave their colony meaning and purpose: a persecuted remnant of the righteous driven from Babylon to seek refuge in wilderness where Satan had heretofore ruled unchallenged.

However united in mission and motive, not all New Englanders saw their new land with the same eyes. Deeply impressed with the arguments of natural theology, many found more divinity than deviltry there.[3] Then, too, the unusually large proportion of New Englanders who had received higher education and brought their libraries to this edge of European civilization brought a more cosmopolitan understanding of nature and its relation to God and humanity. These educated Puritans supplemented the biblical and theological conceptions of nature with a third, the nature of Renaissance poetry and philosophy, replete with ideas and conventions drawn from classical antiquity.

From this eclectic mix of sacred and secular learning, seventeenth-century Puritans constructed and bequeathed a powerful, enduring religious understanding of man and nature: paradise lost. Mixing Calvinism, natural theology, and pastoralism, this tradition conceived of mankind as fallen, justly damned except for the chosen few, and of nature as Arcadian, groaning under human sinfulness, yet springing directly from and thus telling of the power and glory of God. While, in England, John Milton produced the classic exemplar of the genre, in America, this cosmopolitan Puritan mixture of Biblicism, natural theology, and classical antiquity found its most eloquent expression in the poetry of Anne Bradstreet. Bradstreet's poetry consistently depicted nature as Edenic if impermanent, and man as fallen but elected for eternity. She best conveyed these themes in two major poems from the beginning and end of her life, the Quaternions and "Contemplations."

When the first Puritans arrived in Massachusetts Bay aboard the *Arbella* in 1630, a newly married woman of about seventeen years was with them. Even though Anne Bradstreet was a dedicated Puritan from a family of dedicated Puritans, she voyaged to the New World with reluctance. As she remembered it from old age, "I . . . came into this Covntry, where I fovnd a new world and new manners at wch my heart rose. But after I was convinced it was ye way of God, I submitted to it & joined to ye chh. at Boston."[4] Soon she helped to found the new "plantacion" of Ipswich, on the sea thirty miles by Indian trails from Boston, where she lived for about a decade. Then again she helped plant a new settlement, this time at Andover, a beautiful inland location on the banks of the Merrimac River. There she raised her eight children and lived out her life, dying in 1672.

Bradstreet read a good deal and wrote poetry, which, quite unusually for a woman, was published, in *The Tenth Muse Lately sprung up in America. Or Several Poems, compiled with great variety of Wit and Learning, full of delight* (London, 1650). Conventional in style and diction, if clever and lively, these early poems relied heavily on bookish knowledge from the Old World, clear evidence that she continued to resist the "manners" of this new country. Little more than the title hinted that the author lived at the farthest edge of European civilization and the nearest edge of a measureless forest. Still, from Spenser's *Shepheards Calender* to Sidney's *Arcadia* to du Bartas's hexameron,[5] the pastoral, philosophical, and theological works that most clearly influenced Bradstreet's thought and poetry focused on nature, showing her enduring interest in the agreeable aspects of nature.

Possessing surprisingly muted spiritual themes for a committed Puritan,[6] Bradstreet's four Quaternions (which are sets of four poems) describe four debates for priority between the Aristotelian four elements of nature, the four humors, the four ages of man, and the four seasons, all personified as sixteen sisters. Influenced by Renaissance scientific and alchemical thought, Bradstreet associates each element with a humor, age, and season: Fire with Choler, Middle Age, and Summer; Earth with Melancholy, Old Age, and Autumn; Water with Phlegm, Childhood, and Winter; and Air with Sanguine, Youth, and Spring.

Here as elsewhere in her poetry, Bradstreet treats nature and humanity differently: poetry of nature is secular and classical, poetry of man moral and Biblical. Partly, her treatment of nature reflected a contemporary fashion for pastoral poetry, but partly, one suspects, it indicated a paucity of sufficiently sympathetic Biblical portrayals of nature. Indeed, three quaternions are almost completely classical, with only scattered Biblical allusions. The seasons, for example, compare their forces and bounty, strongly evoking the idealized nature of the English pastoral tradition — "swaines . . . with pipes ful glad" frolic, and grapes, lemons, figs, and pomegranates ripen alongside apples and peaches.[7] Only references to the extreme heat and cold of summer and winter suggest the poet's residence in New England instead of England or Greece. Bradstreet describes the warmer months with clear delight and writes extensively of nature's year-round pleasures without a single puritanical caveat about the snares of the senses. Wilderness does not howl and nature displays no effect from the lapsarian curse, although Bradstreet does subscribe to the then-common notion that the Flood marred earthly paradise and, "to this day, impaires [Earth's] beauteous face."[8] The fourth quaternion, "The Four Ages of Man," in contrast, emphasizes that as a consequence of the Fall of Adam man labors under the vanity (in the Scriptural sense of "in vain") of all earthly endeavors.

Another series of personal poems is full of gentle, familiar, and charming references to nature, still, however, based more on literature and learning than the Bible or the wilderness around her. In three poems to her husband absent on business, two liken him to the sun, a symbol of power and masculinity elaborated upon previously in "Fire," in the quaternion of the elements. In the second poem, in her first hint at her interest in natural theology, she tells of God, who

> . . . can tell the starrs or Ocean sand,
> Or all the grass that in the Meads to stand,
> The leaves in th' woods, the hail or drops of rain,
> Or in a corn-field number every grain,
> Or every mote that in the sun-shine hops . . .[9]

—an allusion to Psalm 147. In the third poem, Bradstreet uses several delightful similes of faithful creatures: the "loving Hind that (Hartless) wants her Deer," "the pensive Dove" cooing for her mate, and "the loving Mullet, that true Fish," which supposedly threw itself ashore when its mate was caught.[10] These similes unite the three poems and link them to the quaternions by their use of the creatures of fire (sun), earth (deer), air (doves), and water (fish).

The English Civil War seemed to inspire Bradstreet's Puritan muse to overshadow the classical one. A subordinate theme of the quaternions, the vanity of human existence, now moves to prominence (where it remained for the rest of Bradstreet's career), noticeably in the implicitly millennialist

"The Foure Monarchies" and in "Of the vanity of all worldly creatures."
Note that in spite of its title, "Of the vanity of all worldly creatures" is not a
criticism of nature itself but, inspired by Ecclesiastes and Job 28:7–28,
condemns human attachments to worldly things.

After about 1650, following the end of the Civil War, Bradstreet's poems
changed in purpose, subject, and style, growing more personal and religious. Many late poems and much prose, published in a posthumous second edition of her book or a nineteenth-century volume of her complete
works, concerned illnesses, family deaths, and the burning of her house,
interpreted as lessons of submission, resignation, and the vanity of this
world.[11] Gradually, Bradstreet's natural settings also grew less like Arcadia
and more like New England. If her poems "Contemplations" and "The
Flesh and the Spirit" are any clue, she took meditative walks alone on forest
paths and along the banks of the Merrimac. Bradstreet's acknowledged
masterpiece, "Contemplations" takes the form of a meditation upon nature
while on one such solitary walk, a reflection of the Puritan practices of
"secret" (private) meditation in natural settings and "meditation on the
creatures" (drawing symbolic religious lessons from nature).[12]

"Contemplations" mingles classical learning and Puritan teaching in an
intricately constructed poem which debates the virtues of time and happiness in this world versus the next — the material of the quaternions worked
into the theme of vanity of this world, rather than the other way around.
Although Bradstreet's purpose is to argue heaven's superiority to this world,
"Contemplations" depicts nature so sympathetically that it reminds modern critics of Romantic poetry.[13] Indeed, although Bradstreet's conceptual-
izations look back to the Renaissance, her descriptions of nature and nature's God anticipate later eras.

As in the quaternions, "Contemplations" contains a contest for preemi-
nence between the four elements, fire, earth, water, and air. As Bradstreet
walks through the woods during a colorful autumn sunset and pauses along
a stream rushing over the rocks, she is convinced by each element in turn:
first by the sun (fire), next the trees (earth), then "I once that lov'd the shady
woods so well, / Now thought the rivers did the trees excel" (stanza 21,
water), and finally, upon hearing a nightingale sing, "I judg'd my hearing
better then my sight, / And wisht me wings with her a while to take my
flight" (26, air). In the end, the poet rejects them all and awards preemi-
nence to heaven.

In a fashion reminiscent of the quaternions, Bradstreet places the stanzas
in four groups, the first and third dealing with nature and the second and
fourth with mankind. She compares the virtues of the four elements and

mankind in respect to time and happiness, and concludes that in this world, nature excels miserable humanity in duration and happiness, but in heaven, only man will find eternity and bliss.

The two nature sections, which focus on fire and earth, and water and air, respectively, depict nature in the pastoral tradition, even using classical pagan allusions like Phoebus for the sun, Thetis and Neptune for the sea, and Philomel for a nightingale. Admiring the sun, Bradstreet says she is even tempted like the ancients to make a deity of the sun. Repeatedly the poet speaks of various delights to the senses, and admires the warmth, glory, and strength of the sun, the longevity of the oak, the felicity of the fish, and the mirthful song and carefree flight of the bird.

But in this Eden Bradstreet finds that the only discordant note is her own. Although the beauty, power, and excellence of the sun and earth twice lead her thoughts to the "goodness, wisdome, glory, light" of God the Creator (2, 7), she envies the effortless songs of praise of the grasshopper and cricket. Her "imbecility" or inability, as a sinful mortal, to offer up a better song leads her thoughts from her present Edenic surroundings to a meditation in the second section on the first Eden and the consequences of the fall of Adam. From that time forward, the works of man, a sinner living in a glorious creation, have all been vanity. His consolation is that created things "shall darken, perish, fade and dye, / And when unmade, so ever shall they lye, / But man was made for endless immortality" (20).

That promise receives elaboration in the fourth section. Recalling the elements of water and air from the third section, Bradstreet describes the traditional Christian emblem of the mariner and his vessel seeking haven. The moral is that he who depends on metaphorical smooth seas and fair winds for happiness will find no security. She concludes that time turns all things to rust and dust, "But he whose name is grav'd in the white stone [Rev. 2:17, a symbol of salvation] / Shall last and shine when all of these are gone."

Essentially, "Contemplations" is also Bradstreet's restatement of Ecclesiastes, expanded with material from the quaternions. Once before she had paraphrased Ecclesiastes, in "Of the vanity of all worldly creatures," and in "Contemplations" she overlays the same reference with related Biblical and classical material. Ecclesiastes 1:2–7 contains every dominant motif of the poem: the vanity of earthly endeavors, time and eternity, and the four elements:

Vanity of vanities, saith the Preacher, vanity of vanities; all is vanity.
What profit hath a man of all his labour which he taketh under the

sun? One generation passeth away, and another generation cometh·
but the *earth* abideth for ever [cp. stanza 18]. The *sun* also ariseth, and
the sun goeth down, and hasteth to his place where he arose. The *wind*
goeth toward the south, and turneth about unto the north; it whirleth
about continually, and the wind returneth again according to his cir-
cuits. All the *rivers* run into the sea; yet the sea is not full; unto the
place from whence the rivers come, thither they return again. [Em-
phasis added.]

All is "vanity and vexation [a word Bradstreet uses twice (29, 30)]" (Ecclesiastes 2:11), and the final passage concludes that since all is vanity, it is the
whole duty of man simply to fear God and keep his commandments.

The poem "The Flesh and the Spirit" follows "Contemplations" and
functions as its postscript. It begins, "In secret place where once I stood /
Close by the Banks of *Lacrim* flood" — as if to take up the argument on the
very spot where we left the poet at the end of "Contemplations." She
overhears two sisters, Flesh and Spirit, debate the merits of the themes of
"Contemplations." Flesh inquires, "What[?] liv'st thou on / Nothing but
Meditation? / Doth Contemplation feed thee so / Regardlessly to let earth
goe?" The bulk of the poem is taken up by Spirit's rejoinder, which para-
phrases the description of the New Jerusalem in Revelation 21:10–22:5 and
concludes, "This City pure is not for thee, / For things unclean there shall
not be: / If I of Heaven may have my fill, / Take thou the world, and all
that will."

"This City" here spoken of also evokes the *City of God* of St. Augustine, a
book often cited for devaluing nature and accentuating the otherworldli-
ness of Christianity, and clearly echoed in Bradstreet's theme of the vanity
of worldly things. Bradstreet's sudden recollection of Genesis amidst her
rapture at earthly beauty ("Contemplations" 11) recalls Petrarch's ascent of
Mount Ventoux in 1336. Upon gaining the summit, Petrarch had been
overwhelmed by the spectacular view. He opened Augustine's *Confessions*,
which he was wont to carry with him, and, chastised by Augustine's insistence on valuing heavenly things above earthly, grimly turned from the
beauty of the landscape and descended the mountain.[14] One can visualize
Bradstreet, like Petrarch, admiring a New England autumn sunset and
opening her Bible to the story of Eden, only to be reminded of the danger
of attachment to this world.

Yet, Bradstreet and her Puritan readers accepted Petrarch's logic in attenuated form. Her sympathetic use of pastoral and pagan references, albeit
heavily leavened with Biblical allusions and symbols, yields mild, affection-

ate descriptions of nature, especially when contrasted with fallen man. While Bradstreet was writing "Contemplations," another Puritan poet, Milton, was picturing a similarly pastoral Eden in *Paradise Lost*.[15] Lacking Bradstreet's postlapsarian "imbecility," Milton's Adam and Eve join creation in praising the Creator in an extended paraphrase of Psalm 148 (Bk. V, ll. 153 ff.). Themes of human sinfulness did not preclude beautiful nature passages in the poetry of either Puritan.

Furthermore, as the first section of "Contemplations" demonstrates, nature for Bradstreet as for Milton (compare Bk. V, ll. 507–12) is almost a sacrament in itself, a way to faith. Central to Bradstreet's faith was the knowledge of divinity that nature and its beauty yielded. In a testimonial for her children to be read after her death, she discussed the doubts that troubled her throughout her life — doubts about the veracity of the Bible, about miracles, about the truth of Protestantism and the falseness of Catholicism, about the very existence of God. Neither learning, nor Bible, nor sermons had brought her back to faith: Anne Bradstreet had found God in nature.

> That there is a God my Reason would soon tell me by the wondrovs workes that I see, the vast frame of ye Heaven + ye Earth, the order of all things night and day, Summer & Winter, Spring and Autvmne, the dayly providing for this great hovshold vpon ye Earth, ye p^{r}serving + directing of All to its proper End. . . .[16]

From the evidence of God in nature she would reason her way back to Puritan orthodoxy. Indeed, so much did natural theology mean to her that she wrote a poem praising the natural theologian du Bartas.[17]

Thus, Bradstreet challenges the standard understanding of Puritan attitudes toward nature. Almost never did she dwell on nature's negative aspects.[18] This wilderness poet neither hated nature nor feared it nor calculated its value. And certainly Anne Bradstreet was a wilderness poet. Three times she moved with her family to rough new settlements in the forest. Bradstreet unapologetically intermingled Biblical and classical, moral and pastoral, in effective statements of Puritan subjects.

Anne Bradstreet's attitudes were not unusual among Puritans. Prominent Puritans praised her in print during her life and after her death. Edward Taylor owned *The Tenth Muse*, Cotton Mather lauded her, and others attested to her continued popularity. Demand was great enough to produce a third edition of her poems in 1758.[19] Bradstreet was the daughter of a Puritan governor, the wife of a Puritan magistrate, and the mother and mother-in-law of Puritan ministers. The books that inspired her came out of a Puritan's library. She wrote in Puritan New England, was published in Puritan England, and was read by Puritans for decades. Her pastoral Puritanism was as legitimately Puritan as the familiar "howling wilderness." Bradstreet's poetry is evidence that already the New England elite in its wilderness Jerusalem was thinking in terms of the redemption of fallen man in his wilderness paradise. A future New England elite group, the Transcendentalists, would think along similar lines.

The New Jerusalem in the Wilderness: Edward Johnson

A passionate interpretation of American wilderness and their place in it moved Massachusetts Puritans as a people to transform the natural landscape for the greater glory of God. This dream of a renewed world grew stronger with each new boatload of godly immigrants, until by 1640 the vision of working in unison to build a literal new Jerusalem fired nearly every soul. This confident faith in the possibility of establishing a godly nation on American soil developed into one of the most enduring elements of the Puritan legacy: the final restoration of Eden and God's kingdom on earth.

Aboard the *Arbella* with Anne Bradstreet in 1630 was Edward Johnson, a 31-year-old joiner. Johnson's heart did not rise when he arrived in America, nor did he ever have to "submit" to the way of the New England churches. Johnson was a dedicated and enthusiastic captain in the Lord's army ready to begin His great work. Johnson went back to England to retrieve his wife and seven children and returned in 1636 to dedicate his energies to the colony. One of the founders of Woburn, he became captain of the militia, town clerk, and deputy to the General Court.

Events after 1636 increasingly worried New Englanders like Johnson. Anne Hutchinson stirred up religious discord in the colony. Some New Englanders seemed more tempted by personal profit than determined to enjoy the freedom of Christ's ordinances in their purity. By the 1640s, many fellow English Puritans criticized the "New England Way" for doctrinal and ecclesiological inflexibility. Some New Englanders murmured about lack of liberty and religious toleration. In 1648 rising defensiveness and self-justification led a New England synod to define orthodoxy and prompted several prominent ministers to publish defenses of New England.[20]

Soon after, Johnson began his own account of God's purpose in New England and compiled the first history of the Puritan settlements, known by its running title, *Wonder-working Providence of Sions Saviour, in New En-*

gland, published in London in 1654. No member of the well-educated elite, Johnson was simply a convinced and active believer who wanted to defend and support the cause. Since ministers and a few magistrates dominated the published discourse of the time, Johnson's book provides a rare window into the fervent zeal of a soldier in the Puritan vanguard in the American wilderness. As a sort of ideal type himself, Johnson echoed in a more rustic form the typology, tropes, and Biblical allusions that proliferated throughout more sophisticated Puritan texts. In contrast to Bradstreet's sophisticated poetry, his honest and heartfelt expression of the Puritan common cause in New England rested almost solely on the Bible.[21]

Wonder-working Providence reinterpreted the Puritan mission in light of the circumstances of 1650. In 1630, with Protestants on the retreat on the Continent in the Thirty Years' War and Puritans under Anglican persecution, the first Puritan settlers came to America seeking a refuge where Protestantism might wait out the attacks of the "Antichrist" before returning to Europe, and where "they might enjoy Christ and his Ordinances in their primitive purity."[22] In the next decade, the arrival of perhaps 20,000 people produced an accelerating sense that something marvelous was taking place in New England. Johnson's account captured the feeling of energy, accomplishment, and united purpose of the time. The outbreak of civil war in Britain heightened the New England conviction that their removal to the wilderness was part of the divine design, probably presaging the millennium. Full of expectation of the imminent Second Coming of Christ, *Wonder-working Providence* transformed the series of small providences of the pioneer days into a providential history proving that New England "is the place where the Lord will create a new Heaven, and a new Earth in, new Churches, and a new Common-wealth together. . . ."[23] No cosmopolite, Johnson represented that stratum of Puritans to whom the Bible was sufficient. With never a mention of sweetly singing Philomels or New England autumn sunsets, his book ignored pagan antiquity and earthly beauty. Interestingly, few specifically New England scenes of nature appear in the work of either Bradstreet or Johnson. While Bradstreet's nature was the nature of European classical pastoral literature, Johnson saw nature in terms of biblical parallels or divine providence.

To Johnson, the location of the Puritan colony in the wilderness was rich in Scriptural meaning. Particularly in Book I, the words "wildernesse," "wast[e]," or "desart" appear on practically every page, with various import in different contexts. Wilderness to Johnson first of all provided a refuge for Christ's church from the Antichrist, a gathering and mustering place for his army of saints. Martial metaphor pervaded *Wonder-working Providence*. To be a proper refuge and gathering place, the wilderness must be conquered for Puritan use. The Puritans from the beginning took as part of their purpose to fulfill the command of Genesis to multiply, and replenish and subdue the wilderness, and took pains provisioning their ships, "filling them with the seede of man and beast to sow this yet untilled Wilderness withall. . . ." In all of *Wonder-working Providence*, Johnson praised only a single woman by name, because she excelled in multiplying and replenishing (she had lots of children), "a certaine signe of the Lords intent to people this vast Wildernesse."[24]

Johnson's Puritans saw Biblical wilderness recreated in American wilderness. Puritans used a system called "typology" to recognize in current events an exact replay of Old Testament episodes. The Hebrews' exodus from Egypt, forty years in the wilderness, and arrival in Canaan, the Promised Land flowing with milk and honey, prefigured the Puritan's progress. Every Biblical parallel they found strengthened their self-conception as the elect of God, his chosen people, and invested "the great straites this Wildernesse people were in" with divine significance. Both Israelite and Puritan fled persecution from unjust rulers, underwent testing and trial in the wilderness, and by the Providence of God arrived in the Promised Land. In the wilderness, both Hebrews and Puritans received the tutelage and correction of God, who would "awaken, rouze up, and quicken them with the rod of his power" if they strayed.[25]

While wilderness formed a sacred setting, nature itself was God's medium for goodness or discipline. Every natural feature or event to Johnson was God's provision for his chosen or providential aid for planting Christ's churches in the wilderness. The beaver trade providentially prepared the country for their presence by attracting early colonists. God dealt with the problem of numerous hostile natives by sending a plague among them which "not onely made roome for his people to plant; but also tamed the hard and cruell hearts of these barbarous *Indians*. . . ." God changed the weather for his people, sending an unusual abundance of rain, which astonished "the Heathen."[26]

Despite their trials, the book of Exodus assured the Puritans that God "had not saved their lives from the raging Seas to slay them in the Wilderness with Famine." The first settlers, sick with scurvy and weak from hunger and unable to raise much food, were "perswaded that Christ will rather raine bread from Heaven [that is, manna], then his people should want, . . . and the Lord (who hath the Cattell of thousand Hills, and the Corne of ten thousand Vallies, the whole Earth, and fulnesse of it) did now raise up fresh supplies to be added to these both of men and provision of food. . . ." By these "labour and wants accompanying a Desert, and terrible Wildernesse," God wanted to force the colonists to acknowledge their need of providence. Johnson also thought the story of their wants and deliverance would be an example and comfort to God's people worldwide.[27]

If the typology of Exodus helped explain the struggles and afflictions of their early years, by 1650 no Puritan could see New England as a merely temporary refuge or only a Sinai testing ground. That they no longer lived in a wilderness but in a permanent settlement within a wilderness called forth new Biblical and eschatological interpretations. God, the world's landlord, had placed the Puritans in charge of his business in America. New Englanders proclaimed that all along they had been following Christ's purpose in spreading the Gospel to the ends of the earth "and promoting his glorious Kingdom, who is now taking the heathen for his inheritance, and the utmost ends of the earth for his possession. . . ." Because "The Earth is the Lords, and the fulness of it," Puritans were acting as his stewards in spending their wealth to bring the Gospel to the wilderness.[28]

To this godly end, Johnson said, the Lord had sent the Puritans from corrupt and doomed England, the "Babylon" of Revelations, to a "heathen desart land" to be "the living stones" for the building of the New Jerusalem and the consecration of Christ's new Temple, both foretold in prophecy for the Last Days. The most important Biblical type for this Temple work was Nehemiah, who had led the remnant of Israel out of Babylon to reconsecrate the Temple of Jerusalem and to rebuild its walls, spears at the ready for fear of sudden attack from their enemies.[29]

And enemies they had, for their labors had attracted Satan's attention, and he sent his servants to stop them. In England, Puritan armies put the bishops to flight, while in America, another Puritan army defended the new Sion against the American "Devils," the Indians. The "couragious Souldiers" of the Lord executed "vengeance upon the heathen" by decimating the Pequot tribe in 1637 in a victory for God against Satan. Even so, Johnson condemned only "proud" and "contentious" Indian tribes. With other tribes, he urged conciliation and conversion, and praised John Eliot's Christianization efforts.[30]

One of the most important themes of *Wonder-working Providence* is that Satan had sent internal enemies (sectaries) to disrupt God's work in New England. If they could be evicted, Isaiah's vision might be fulfilled and the wolf lie down with the lamb, Edenic peace be recovered, and the world be prepared for Christ's return. ". . . Therefore," warned Johnson, "be sure there be none to hurt or destroy in all his holy Mountaine," none to disturb Isaiah's prophecy that "the earth shall be full of the knowledge of the Lord." Toleration could only nurture serpents in the new Garden.[31]

Johnson employed pastoral nature imagery, but only in Biblical and not classical allusions. Using analogies of the minister as defender of God's vineyard or sheep from natural enemies, Johnson elaborated the Puritan self-conception as God's people laboring in his vineyard on a hill or mountain surrounded by a wall or hedge, a Biblical metaphor for Israel under God's protection, while surrounded by enemies in the wilderness.[32] Johnson's most common pastoral analogy for the ministry was of shepherds who had followed Christ to feed "his bannisht flock," keep them "in desert land," and defend them from "devouring Wolves." This alluded to the image of Christ the shepherd and his injunction to his followers to "feed my sheep," as well as to the Old Testament promise to gather the scattered sheep, reject their wayward shepherds, and provide a godly shepherd to feed and protect them in the wilderness.[33] Johnson's metaphorical walls or hedges reflected New England's chosenness, as well as its conviction that the outside world, New and Old, natural and human, was the dangerous, threatening domain of Satan.

All around him, in two decades of changes in the land, Johnson beheld the fulfillment of God's plan to create a new Eden in anticipation of Christ's imminent return. As Johnson proudly pointed out, the "Churches of *Christ*, began with a small number in a desolate and barren Wildernesse, which the Lord in his wonderfull mercy hath turned to fruitful Fields," and "in the roome of dismall Swampes and tearing Bushes, they have very goodly Fruit-trees, fruitfull Fields and Gardens." In Boston, "the hideous Thickets . . . were such, that Wolfes and Beares nurst up their young from the eyes of all beholders, in those very places where the streets are full of Girles and Boys sporting up and downe, with a continued concourse of people."[34]

Johnson's vision of Eden resembled an improved version of England, with a similar landscape but with godly government, church, morals and beliefs. He proudly contrasted the former and present state of New England, this

remote, rocky, barren, bushy, wild-woody wilderness, a receptacle for Lions, Wolves, Bears, Foxes, Rockoones, Bags, Bevers, Otters, and all kind of wild creatures, a place that never afforded the Natives better than the flesh of a few wild creatures and parch't Indian corn incht out with Chestnuts and bitter Acorns, now through the mercy of Christ become a second *England* for fertilness in so short a space, that it is indeed the wonder of the world. . . . Thus hath the Lord been pleased to turn one of the most hideous, boundless, and unknown Wildernesses in the world in an instant, as 'twere (in comparison of other work) to a well-ordered Commonwealth, and all to serve his Churches. . . ."[35]

Johnson included economic activity as a sign that New Englanders were making a garden of the wilderness and noted that, far from the fears of the first settlers that New England would suffer from lack of a staple commodity, "every thing in the country proved a staple-commodity, wheat, rye, oats, peas, barley, beef, pork, fish, butter, cheese, timber, mast, tar, sope, plank-board frames of houses, clabbord, and pipestaves, iron and lead is like to be also." Colonists who formerly had to import all necessities from England now "have not only fed their Elder Sisters, Virginia, Barbadoes, and many of the Summer Islands that were prefer'd before her for fruitfulness, but also the Grandmother of us all, even the firtil Isle of Great Britain" as well as Portugal and Spain. Johnson marveled "that this Wilderness should turn a mart for Merchants in so short a space."[36]

Johnson extolled the industry that produced a new England in New England, yet fretted over the temptations of Mammon. The early arrivals had worked together in harmony under the common "penury of Wildernesse." God had rewarded them, but only so long as "plenty and liberty marre not their prosperity." He remarked on the frequent departures from the tight-knit seaboard Puritan communities for Connecticut or "the backside of this Desert" and decried the tendency of new inland towns "to grasp more into their hands then they could afterward possibly hold" due to greed for meadowland. Worst were vintners and merchants, who advocated religious toleration in order to attract settlers and increase their incomes.[37] With nature as his instrument of punishment in New England as in the Bible, God prepared the rod to keep his children upon the way they should go. Johnson noted with satisfaction that a plague of caterpillars had reminded the Puritans of their purpose, especially the farmers who had moved far inland in pursuit of profits. He prayed fervently for the departure of base selfishness and the return of purity of heart and purpose.[38]

Edward Johnson's world was filled with sacred meaning. The earth was truly the Lord's in his vision, and nothing in it happened by chance or escaped from his divine purpose. By 1650 the wilderness and the Puritans' place in it had taken on cosmic importance and now meant many things — a refuge, a gathering place of an army of saints, a place of testing, the means of God's providence, a haven for the Devil's minions, the site of the New Jerusalem, and the new Eden.

Present but not explicit in Johnson's book was another meaning of wilderness: a place of no history and no authorities — unlike other possible refuges for the Puritans such as Holland — where Puritans were completely free to create their own unique vision of a godly nation.[39] Whether Catholic or Protestant, colonizing Europeans of the day hoped to start society over again and established utopian communities in the wilderness from Montreal to Mexico. This hope has remained a tradition among Americans long after it disappeared elsewhere, and still inspires people to see wild nature as a place where all things are possible.

The Puritans' accomplishment was real. Johnson was right in contrasting all other colonizing efforts with the Puritans' orderly and speedy erection of a European-style commonwealth where none existed before. Euphoric zeal and common purpose, combined with increasing immigration comprising high numbers of talented and educated people, produced what was indeed a wonder of the world. In the wild nature of the vast American continent, God's people prospered and prepared for the last days. Yet nature was also the flaw in Johnson's vision. The very prosperity and trade that sprang from the planting of a new Eden also generated the lust for private gain that profaned the precincts within which God meant to work his will. Thus, Johnson's book, the first printed celebration of New England's history, became New England's first jeremiad, a summons to the faithful to recall and return to their purpose.

Wonder-working Providence expressed the myths central to New England Puritans' understanding of themselves. From John Winthrop the governor to Johnson the artisan, Puritans believed in the millennial transformation of man and nature, the refuge in the wilderness, the duty to subdue nature and replenish the earth, the work of spreading the Gospel and raising a new church, the need to put religion before profits, the testing of the Puritan Israel in the American Sinai.[40] In following generations this unified vision would fragment and its elements reappear in recombinations throughout American history.

In broader perspective, Johnson's work exemplified the ability of Western Christians of all creeds to justify their global colonization efforts. Clearing land, introducing foreign plants and animals, expanding agriculture, developing trade, and conquering, converting, expelling, or exterminating aborigines — in sum, the wholesale transformation of entire ecosystems — all received blessing as God's work. Yet everywhere as well, the voice of Christian conscience — here in a whisper, there in a shout — limited or shaped European activities. Johnson, for instance, never weakened his demands for continued self-sacrifice and dedication to a higher cause, for stewardship of the earth, and for conversion of the Indians when possible. Christian ideology about nature arrived in the wilderness of the New World as a promise wrapped in a threat.

Evangelical Science: Cotton Mather

As an intensely devout, prominent Puritan minister, both son and grandson of prominent Puritan ministers, Cotton Mather assumed the heavy responsibility of carrying the New England Puritan tradition into the eighteenth century. He lived in an era of great change in science, theology, politics, and society — the age of Boyle, Newton, Ray and Derham, and Locke, of the Cambridge Platonists, Deists, and German Pietists, and of the Glorious Revolution. Mather saw decline of ministerial authority and the rise of an increasingly prosperous, materialistic, and religiously liberal colonial upper class. Still, he carried on the old traditions well, and accommodated them to current intellectual trends. Puritans of Mather's day were eagerly accommodating nature in the Bible to the nature of science and philosophy. Extremely proud of both his doctorate in divinity from Calvinist Glasgow University and his election as a fellow of the Royal Society, Mather could write passages of millennialist fervor next to digests of the latest in natural philosophy (science) or natural theology.[41]

Calvinist and Puritan religious intensity derived from the insistent principle that no aspect of life or experience lay outside the realm of religion. In this respect, Mather's universe was identical with Johnson's. However, in language and conception it evolved steadily in new directions. In his early career, Mather's concept of the Puritans' place in the wilderness echoed the metaphors and world view of Johnson's generation. But by the turn of the century the old terms and concepts were fading from Mather's books, never repudiated but supplanted by the new outlook of an age of rationalism and science.

Mather's 1694 *Short History of New England* defended old notions of a covenanted people in a new context of secular governors and religious toleration. In it, with the Salem trials still fresh in people's minds, he warned how the Hedge, which in the traditional conception protected the Puritan community, was endangered more from within than without. From covetousness to witchcraft, sinfulness was in effect creating gaps in the Hedge through which the devil could enter, a danger heightened by their situation in a wilderness. He called for a Nehemiah to come forth in the tradition of the governors of the commonwealth to help rebuild the gaps in the walls of the New England Jerusalem.[42]

Like Johnson, Mather described the interior of the hedge in Biblical agrarian or pastoral terms, as a garden or vineyard planted by God and protected from *"Wild-Beasts"* by ministers — the living hedges — or as the flocks of God's people to be guarded from wolves. Harvard was the nursery or "seminary" (from Latin *seminarium*, "seed-bed") which would supply new plants to keep the hedge around God's people strong. Like Johnson, who condemned those who moved to the "backside" of the wilderness, Mather worried about those "Swarming into New Settlements" on "the *Wrong side of the Hedge"* where they would *"Perish for Lack of Vision."*[43]

Both in his *Short History of New-England* and *Magnalia Christi Americana*, Mather brought out the meaning of the Puritan wilderness in ways similar to Johnson. He described the first generation of Puritans leaving their pleasant homes, crossing a vast ocean, and settling in a terrible wilderness solely for *"The Pure Enjoyment of all [God's] Ordinances."* America's *"Indian Wilderness"* was ready to receive God's people and his Gospel, and, indeed, for this purpose God had arranged for America to be discovered before the Reformation so that it might serve as a refuge for Protestants. Mather noted the opportunity in America to reestablish the model of the pure primitive church, a city upon a hill.[44] Mather also believed that God intended to gather an army of saints in New England, and described the Puritans' wars against both internal dissent and the Indians. To both Johnson and Mather, the wilderness meant temptation, testing, and tutelage, as it had for the Israelites under Moses or Jesus. Mather also echoed Johnson's view that the trials of wilderness were designed to force people to rely upon God's providence, through which they were not only sustained with food but their enemies (the Indians) smitten with pox.[45]

The Puritans had not neglected their other purpose in coming, that of converting an *"Indian Wilderness"* to Christianity. Like Johnson, Mather devoted a chapter to the Christianization of the Indians (Book VI, Chapter VI). Christianization of the wilderness also meant its transformation into a new England. Like Johnson, he celebrated how "an *Howling Wilderness* in a few Years became a *Pleasant Land.* . . ."[46] But, unlike Johnson, Mather had no illusions that New England had become either a new Eden or a New Jerusalem. At the outset of *Magnalia Christi Americana*, he only promised

to give unto the *Christian Reader* an *History* of *some feeble Attempts* made in the *American Hemisphere* to anticipate the State of the *New-*

Jerusalem, as far as the unavoidable *Vanity* of *Humane* [human] *Affairs*, and the *Influence* of *Satan* upon them would allow of it. . . .[47]

In *Magnalia Christi Americana* Mather deviated from the typology of *Wonder-working Providence*. Biblical types no longer prefigured the Puritans and their experience; instead, they served as metaphors for them.[48] For example, William Bradford was not the new Moses, he was "a Moses"; John Winthrop was another.[49] Though the New England Puritans may have been God's chosen people in the wilderness, they were not the new Israel but, rather, *like* a new Israel. Seventy years' experience in Massachusetts had lowered Puritans' expectations for their role in religious history. Mather was only too aware of the shortcomings of his fellow colonials.

Similarly, although Mather anticipated the millennium during his life-time — particularly during the 1690s, and again, following William Whiston's prediction, in 1716 — his vision of New England's role in the apocalypse paled in comparison with Johnson's.[50] From a lifetime of listening to jeremiads detailing the sins of his contemporaries, and from a growing understanding that, after Massachusetts's new secular charter of 1691, neither the Hedge against the outside world nor the Puritans' identity as the persecuted remnant could be preserved, Mather concluded that New Englanders had no claim to any special role in the millennium. Downplaying the American wilderness as the stage for the gathering of the saints or God's army, he instead reached across the decaying Hedge, hoping that a reunion of the saints of the world might accelerate the world's end. Although he supported attempts to unite English dissenting groups, his hopes lay not in institutional union but in common principles, particularly Lockean reason (until its deistic and anti-Trinitarian implications alienated him) and German Pietism.

If wilderness and America virtually vanished in Mather's eschatology, nature in general would be renewed. He rejected the common opinion that the New World would escape the universal conflagration of the last days but be an abode of evil whence Gog and Magog would rise and assault the New Jerusalem. Mather believed that the entire world would be destroyed in the general conflagration while God's angels rescued the saints from the flames. After the fires abated, the saints would return to a new earth and, like Adam and Eve, dwell sinless and immortal in a reconstituted Paradise, for (as Paul predicted) nature would be liberated from the servitude and vanity to which it had been subjected since Adam's fall. Saints from past ages would be awakened to live like angels in the City of God in the new heaven, serving God in the administration of his new heavenly kingdom over the new earth.[51] Mather's vision of the millennial future, not of the New England present, promised a new Eden.

Like many other Englishmen, Mather found further support in the advance of science for natural theology. Mather spent much of his life compiling the massive "Biblia Americana,"[52] an up-to-date hexameron like Du Bartas's, which Bradstreet had found so compelling. Sadly, he could not convince the world to publish it. Exhaustive scientific treatises on the first six days had gone out of fashion. So Mather adjusted to his era and, instead of a scientific supplementation of Scripture, he published a spiritualization of science, *The Christian Philosopher*.

Ray and Derham had adapted natural theology to an age when scientific and philosophic developments, led by Newton and Locke, electrified Europe. The New England intelligentsia, of whom the ministry made up the greater part, enthusiastically embraced this new science. John Winthrop, Jr. had been a founding member of the Royal Society, and Mather's father Increase was among the instigators in 1683 of the Boston Philosophical Society, the first scientific association modeled upon the Royal Society.[53] Mather read widely and voraciously in the new science and idolized Newton, Ray, and Derham. In 1712 he began sending contributions to the Royal Society in letters he called "Curiosa Americana," on the basis of which the society elected him a fellow in 1714.

The next year Mather sent to the society a manuscript which he called "The Christian Virtuoso," recalling the title of a book by seventeenth-century Puritan scientist Robert Boyle, whom Mather admired. Both Boyle and Mather hoped to Christianize the concept of the "virtuoso," the ideal of the educated gentleman amateur who participated in all aspects of intellectual life, including science. Published in London in 1720 as *The Christian Philosopher: A Collection of the Best Discoveries in Nature, with Religious Improvements*, this book expressed both Mather's appreciation for the science of his day and his use of it to further religion and piety — "a *Philosophical Religion*: And yet how *Evangelical!*"[54] To Mather as to Francis Bacon, whom he read and quoted, natural philosophy did not lead to atheism but rather to strengthened faith. The world was a temple of God, its architect. Ministers were the "priests of creation," and scientists the employees of God. Citing Chrysostom's notion of God's Books of Nature and Revelation, Mather proclaimed that nature taught truth and that Newton's laws were the laws of God. When Mather expounded on nature as the "Temple of GOD," a phrase from Plutarch, he recalled pagan philosophy even as he anticipated the Romantics.[55]

Science created the skeleton of belief that Mather fleshed out with "religious improvements." He punctuated this précis of recent science with frequent outbursts of praise to God, whose goodness, power, or infinitude science repeatedly demonstrated, or with thoughts on the physical, spiritual, or moral uses of mundane phenomena. For example, interstellar vastness told of the vastness of God; the sun plainly displayed its usefulness to life; rain was an instrument of God's favor or anger; storms were the agents of God's wrath; bees gave mankind the moral example of their cooperative "commonwealth"; the human body revealed the highest example of the divine workmanship; and man's dominion over creatures implied the divine plan.[56]

Although the laws of nature were God's laws, and the universe behaved in a mechanical way, Mather rejected a mechanistic universe. The world was still the theater of God's providence. Gravity was not a property of matter but a mysterious, invisible force which depended upon the immediate work of God to effect it—an opinion which followed Newton. He denied the assertion that animals were machines. Mather thought they exhibited a debased form of reason which was the effect of providence in mindless, soulless nature. To Mather, mechanism was an insufficient model of the universe, which clearly revealed the necessity of God.[57]

Mather built on the old neo-Platonic mystical road to God: natural philosophy not only would lead the mind to God, but speed the coming of the millennium. God had ordained the Great Chain of Being, "a *Scale of Nature*, wherein we pass regularly and proportionably from a *Stone* to a *Man*." By following the "*Footsteps* of a *Deity* in all the Works of Nature," the nature student would "by the *Scale* of *Nature* ascend to the *God* of *Nature*." When contemplation of nature finally banished atheism, universal belief would hasten the restoration of "a desirable *Garden of God*." Christ, by whom all things were created, would restore "ALL THINGS" to the Kingdom.[58] Anne Bradstreet's contemplations had taken her from nature through thoughts of Eden to sober thoughts of human corruption and the promise of heaven; Mather's took him from science to ecstatic visions of the renewed earthly Eden to come.

However much it resembled the world of Edward Johnson or Anne Bradstreet, Mather's universe was different. True, the invisible world still infused the visible: he believed there were devils in the woods and saw angels in his study. Nevertheless, he could be skeptical and insist on proof of supernatural workings. During the Salem witch trials of 1692, he and his father recommended rejection of testimony against witches based solely on "spectral evidence," that is, testimony about spirits who appeared only to the victim. (Unfortunately, their recommendation went unheeded.) Like educated men in England, Mather suspected natural causes were at work in events previously understood to be of supernatural origin.[59] In the smallpox inoculation controversy of 1721, Mather led the crusade by most Massachusetts ministers in support of inoculation. Ironically, one of the charges against the ministers was that they were interfering with divine judgment. Here was the quandary of the age: ministers could not use the divine light of reason to stop impersonal natural forces without staying the punishing hand of the Almighty, which worked through those very forces.

Cotton Mather and most of his learned peers at home and in Britain welcomed the increasing intrusion of the natural into the realm of the supernatural with ever more confident assertions that science and revelation agreed. Yet, this represented a retreat from the pervasively, relentlessly spiritualized universe of New England's founders. The spell of the supernatural had been broken and the seductively rational and orderly Enlightenment was beginning to entrance the Western mind. Perhaps natural causes and not witchcraft caused cows to die or beer not to ferment. Perhaps microscopic "animalcules" and not God's judgment caused disease. (Mather proposed a germ theory of disease, possibly the first to do so.) Reason and natural law seemed to fill so much of the universe that it was all churchmen could do to stuff providence into the interstices. While for a century and a half most Protestants like Mather continued to insist upon the harmony of the books of nature and revelation, the increasing number of discordant notes prompted an ever growing number in the eighteenth century to rely upon the book of nature alone.

FOUR

Nature's God
in the Age of Reason

I kept steady to [Quaker] meetings, spent First Days after noon chiefly in reading the Scriptures and other good books, and was early convinced in my mind that true religion consisted in an inward life, wherein the heart doth love and reverence God the Creator and learn to exercise true justice and goodness, not only toward all men but also toward the brute creatures; that as the mind was moved on an inward principle to love God as an invisible, incomprehensible being, on the same principle it was moved to love him in all his manifestations in the visible world; that as by his breath the flame of life was kindled in all animal and sensitive creatures, to say we love God as unseen and at the same time exercise cruelty toward the least creature moving by his life, or by life derived from him, was a contradiction in itself.

—JOHN WOOLMAN, JOURNAL *(1774)*

But if objects for gratitude and admiration are our desire, do they not present themselves every hour to our eyes? Do we not see a fair creation prepared to receive us the instant we are born—a world furnished to our hands, that cost us nothing? Is it we that light up the sun, that pour down the rain, and fill the earth with abundance? Whether we sleep or wake, the vast machinery of the universe still goes on....

But some, perhaps, will say: Are we to have no Word of God—no revelation? I answer, Yes; there is a Word of God; there is a revelation.

THE WORD OF GOD IS THE CREATION WE BEHOLD *and it is in* this word, *which no human invention can counterfeit or alter, that God speaketh universally to man.*

—THOMAS PAINE, THE AGE OF REASON, PART ONE *(1794)*

In the eighteenth century Puritanism was overtaken by events. The Age of Faith of Luther, Calvin, and Cromwell gave way to the Age of Reason of Newton, Locke, and Linnaeus. With the pejorative term "enthusiasm," many sneered at religious fervor. Reason emerged from the shadows of Calvinist mistrust of that fallen faculty to shine as the beacon of the Enlightenment. Trust of reason led to faith in science, which now endeavored to bare nature's secrets on heaven and earth and even uncover the laws of morality, economics, and politics. As Puritanism lost momentum, many young New Englanders adopted the latest religious fashions arriving practically daily from England, particularly those at the cutting edge of the Enlightenment like Arminianism (which denied predestination), Latitudinarianism (which emphasized morality over creed), Unitarianism (which rejected the divinity of Christ), and Deism (which taught a passive God in a machine-universe). Moreover, New England itself had changed. It had grown too populated, too contentious, too wealthy, and too worldly. Or at least, so it appeared to some.

The situation appalled New England's ministers, whose influence in society continued to wane. Their efforts to revitalize the spirit and theology of the first Puritans generated a religious revival, now known as the Great Awakening of the 1730s and '40s, that shook society to its foundations. Unexpectedly, the Awakening also shattered ministerial and ecclesiological unity by creating factions for and against the revivals. Opposing the revivals emboldened many churches along the urban seaboard to deviate ever further from Puritan orthodoxy. The schism left fervent rural churches closer to the world of Edward Johnson and propelled more cosmopolitan urban churches in new directions that took Anne Bradstreet's universe as their starting point.

The primary events of eighteenth-century America, the Revolution and the creation of a nation, were political rather than religious. The country's dominant leadership during this era came not from New England, aside from the family Adams, but from farther south, particularly Virginia, the oldest, largest, and wealthiest colony. In a general sense this leading colony and state typified America outside New England. In Virginia nature was bounteous and benign, the established church laid on an easy yoke, and the most vigorous churches were the backwoods sects. Reflecting this setting, the state's mentality embraced a much less moral, more practical, and more individualistic approach to both religion and nature.

Paradise Lost: Jonathan Edwards

While the Mather family flourished in Boston, westward in the Connecticut River valley the Stoddard-Edwards family was providing New England with some of its best minds. In 1729 one of those luminaries, Solomon Stoddard, died and was succeeded as Northampton's minister by the man whose brilliance would outshine all other Puritan ministers, his grandson Jonathan Edwards. Intent on revivifying Calvinism, Edwards wedded it with the rising vogue of philosophical idealism. In his works are mixed elements that suggest he was both the last Puritan and the first Transcendentalist.

Born the son of a minister in 1703 in the days of Mather's prime, the precocious Edwards went to Yale at age 13. During his undergraduate and graduate career there, Yale's recently acquired library exposed him to a wide variety of the best Enlightenment scientists and philosophers: Robert Boyle, William Whiston, Derham, Ray, Bacon, Descartes, Locke, Newton, and Cambridge Platonist Henry More, whose works had an early and lasting influence on his ideas. Perhaps prompted by this exposure to science, while at Yale he wrote a few inquiries into natural history, most famously his "Spider" letter of 1723.

After an interlude as pastor of a Presbyterian church in New York City, he returned to Yale as a junior tutor in 1724. The church at Northampton called him in 1726 to assist Stoddard, and upon the latter's death in 1729 he became sole pastor there. In 1735 he instigated a revival in Northampton that first began to fan the low embers of Puritan piety into the flames of the Great Awakening. During the height of revivalist zeal in 1737–42 he was a constant defender of this "shower of grace." By 1748 his stringent Calvinism was bringing him into conflict with his congregation, which dismissed him in 1750. After 1751 he lived in remote Stockbridge as minister to an Indian congregation, from which the College of New Jersey (present-day Princeton) called him to be its president in 1757. Never a robust man, Edwards died in 1758 of a smallpox inoculation.

During his lifetime Edwards published nine major works and several sermons, with others published posthumously. In addition, Edwards's papers included an immense amount of material, much of which has never been published. Although he put his brilliant and creative talents in the service of what even then was a dying tradition, Edwards is widely regarded as America's greatest theologian.[1]

Like many Puritans, Edwards spent much time in and thought a great deal about nature. The prevalence of "secret" or private meditation in a

remote spot had, if anything, increased since the days when Anne Bradstreet walked the Andover woods. In an autobiography penned around
1739, Edwards described how virtually every one of his most intense religious experiences occurred in wild settings. As a boy, he and his school-
mates "built a booth in a swamp, in a very retired spot, for a place of prayer.
And besides, I had particular secret places of my own in the woods, where I
used to retire by myself. . . ." In college, during meditation, he had "sometimes a kind of vision, or fixed ideas and imaginations, of being alone in the
mountains, or some solitary wilderness, far from all mankind, sweetly conversing with Christ, and wrapt and swallowed up in God." After religious
discussions with his father, he would walk in his father's pasture gazing at
the sky and clouds, overcome with "a sense of the glorious majesty and
grace of God." In a telling passage, he recalled how nature inspired him:

> After this my sense of divine things gradually increased, and became
> more and more lovely, and had more of that inward sweetness. The
> appearance of every thing was altered; there seemed to be, as it were, a
> calm, sweet cast or appearance of divine glory, in almost every thing.
> God's excellence, his wisdom, his purity and love, seemed to appear in
> every thing; in the sun, moon, and stars; in the clouds and blue sky; in
> the grass, flowers, trees; in the water and all nature; which used greatly
> to fix my mind. I often used to sit and view the moon for a long time;
> and in the day, spent much time in viewing the clouds and sky, to
> behold the sweet glory of God in these things: In the mean time
> singing forth, with a low voice, my contemplations of the Creator and
> Redeemer. And scarce any thing, among all the works of nature, were
> so sweet to me as thunder and lightning. . . . I felt God . . . at the first
> appearance of a thunderstorm; and used to take the opportunity . . . to
> fix myself in order to view the clouds, and see the lightnings play, and
> hear the majestic and awful voice of God's thunders, . . . leading me to
> sweet contemplations of my great and glorious God.

Edwards also drew on nature for his analogies for the soul's relation to God:
holiness "made the soul like a field or garden of God, with all manner of
pleasant flowers; enjoying a sweet calm, and the gentle vivifying beams of
the sun"; the "sweet and glorious doctrines" of Calvinism were "to my soul
like green pastures"; and an experience of the Holy Spirit pouring itself out
onto his soul "like the sun in its glory, sweetly and pleasantly diffusing light
and life."[2]

These solitary walks and conversations with God continued in New York along the Hudson and when he returned to Connecticut. Others in Edwards's life and experience also sought solitary natural places for prayer and meditation. In a passage describing the religious qualities of his future wife, Sarah Pierpont, he noted, "She loves to be alone, walking in the fields and groves, and seems to have someone invisible always conversing with her." Edwards's biography of fellow minister David Brainerd included similar episodes, including a vision Brainerd twice had of "divine glory and splendor," once while walking "in a dark thick grove" and again at another favorite isolated spot.[3]

Edwards had an overpowering vision of his own in 1737. While out riding for his health, he alighted in a remote spot and began his usual meditative walk. On this walk, however, the person of Christ himself appeared to him in an intense and emotional vision of about an hour, leaving him weeping and exhilarated. While Edwards's autobiography breaks off soon after this point, his "secret" meditations in the woods and along waters were of such clear importance in his life and experience that it is a good assumption they continued the rest of his life.[4]

Edwards reflected other Puritan attitudes toward nature. He frequently mentioned that the wisdom of God was expressed in the glory and harmony of creation, for example in his "Wisdom in the Contrivance of the World." The intricate interconnectedness of all creation awed him: "Perhaps there is not one leaf of a tree, nor spire of grass, but what has effects all over the universe. . . ."[5] Apparently influenced by Mather's *Christian Philosopher*, he accepted the harmony of Newtonian science with evangelical religion.[6] Edwards believed in a determinate universe, one preordained by God in the very arrangement of atoms at creation and running like a clock (even making allowances for miracles) to the inevitable day of judgment.[7]

Although generally Edwards avoided conjecture on the specifics of the millennium, his excitement at the progress of the Great Awakening led him in 1742 to speculate cautiously that it would begin soon in New England.[8] In all other contexts, he avoided such specificity, moving even further than Mather from the first Puritans' vivid expectation of New England's or America's central role in the apocalypse. Edwards lamented the fact that according to Romans 8:19–22 the creatures were forced to labor under man's sinful dominion but would finally be released to a glorious freedom. But Edwards doubted that this earth could be renewed as the site of the eternal abode of the saints. He speculated that the phrase "a new heaven and a new earth" meant that God would whisk the saints away to a distant planet prepared for them, or perhaps that the new earth would be spiritual and not material. Whatever nature's fate, it apparently was not destined to become a renewed Eden.[9]

For all his orthodox Calvinism, Edwards conceived of creation in radically new ways. The restatements of neo-Platonism in the works of Leibniz, Spinoza, and especially the Cambridge Platonists launched a vogue for philosophical idealism that strongly affected New England thinkers of Edwards's time — and Edwards most of all.[10] His position was startlingly close to Bishop Berkeley's, apparently due to similar sources rather than direct influence. For Edwards, "nothing has any existence anywhere else but in consciousness." Perhaps, he thought, the whole physical world existed only in God's mind, who communicated all our perceptions and ideas to our minds.[11]

Edwards's understanding of the process of the universe was thoroughly neo-Platonic: an interdependent, constantly changing world arranged in the Chain of Being, emanation of the world from God like light from a candle or the sun, and return of the soul to God.

> All dependent existence whatever is in a constant flux, ever passing and returning; renewed every moment, as the colors of bodies every moment renewed by the light that shines upon them; and all is constantly preceding from God, as light from the sun.[12]

Edwards's "Dissertation Concerning the End for which God Created the World" describes in detail how the infinite fullness of God led inevitably to the emanation of excellency, beauty, happiness, and knowledge of himself in the creation of the world and in communication of himself to his creatures. The glory of God was the ultimate end of creation, according to Edwards, who carefully catalogued the fourfold meaning of the word "glory" in Scripture: excellency, shining as from a luminary, the manifestation of excellency to man, and praise. The glory of the universe was the emanation of God's internal glory.

This glory is returned to God in what Edwards termed "remanation": "In the creature's knowing, esteeming, loving, rejoicing in, and praising God, the glory of God is both exhibited and acknowledged; his fullness is received and returned" like light reflected back to the sun. Man's happiness is proportional to his union with God (although Edwards rejected any mystical union with the substance of God, even by the elect in heaven).[13]

To Edwards, the universe was a shadow of God's ultimate glorious reality, like the shadows in Plato's famous allegory of the cave. To the godly mind, these shadows taught divine things; creation was God's means of communicating himself and his qualities to the creatures. "And this is God's manner, to make inferior things shadows of the superior and most excellent, outward things shadows of spiritual, and all other things shadows of those things that are the end of all things and the crown of all things. Thus God glorifies himself and instructs the minds that he has made." Nature was symbol, a language legible to the mind trained and prepared to read it. Edwards recorded the divine meaning of various material objects in an important notebook, first published in this century as *Images or Shadows of Divine Things* (also variously titled by Edwards *The Book of Nature and Common Providence* and *The Language and Lessons of Nature*). He felt "the beauties of nature" — flowery meadows, gentle breezes, great trees, singing birds, "crystal rivers and murmuring streams," "the golden edges of an evening cloud," even "the ragged rocks and the brows of mountains" — "were really emanations, or shadows, of the excellencies of the Son of God," though it "requires a more discerning, feeling mind to perceive it." The key to understanding nature's language lay in the Bible, especially in the Puritan system of typology by which the New Testament was understood as symbolically restating the Old. In other words, the book of revelation revealed the meaning of the book of nature.[14]

Edwards carried on the Puritan tradition, Anne Bradstreet–style. Humanity labored in the "paradise lost" scenario, cursed since the Fall yet surrounded by the glorious creation of God. Earth would be an Eden but for humanity. As his most famous sermon, "Sinners in the Hands of an Angry God," exemplifies, Edwards was pessimistic about the majority of his fellow men. God regarded them as loathsome creatures justly to be condemned to eternal damnation. As the last great Puritan, Jonathan Edwards fought a rearguard action defending Calvinism and the Puritan way. But as a proto-Transcendentalist, he thought of nature as flowing continuously from the mind of God and telling of divine things. In spite of Edwards, idealism could not resuscitate Calvinism, which in the next century would fade away while idealism took the nation.

The Protestant Ethic: Benjamin Franklin

The Age of Reason had long waited in the wings of the Age of Faith. On the shelves of Cotton Mather's study sat a 1635 German edition of Raymond of Sebonde's *Theologia Naturalis*.[15] The preface of Sebonde's book had been the first to state that not only did nature reveal God, it contained all one needed for salvation, a thesis which earned it a place on the Catholic Church's Index of prohibited books. Protestants treated it more sanguinely, yet it contained the kernel of that troublesome creed of reason, Deism, which in Mather's time had only just begun to take root within the Puritan Hedge, but which within decades of his death was blossoming everywhere.

Deism arose alongside an increasing faith in human ability to understand and control the world. Isaac Newton's spectacular success in discerning the orderly laws of the universe added momentum to the new trust in reason. To John Locke, reason took precedence over religious experience. Early deists, Lord Herbert of Cherbury and John Toland, went further — still concluding, though, that Christianity and the Bible contained nothing contrary to reason.[16] As reason became the measure of things, nature became the standard by which reason was calibrated. Enlightenment thinkers used nature to prove and expound religion.

The decline in interest in religious experience and revelation drained God from the natural world. The universe and all that was in it looked like a machine, obeying natural laws mechanically. Newton's triumphs heightened interest in nature, for at last mankind was uncovering her secrets. The Enlightenment began the great age of scientific exploration.[17] From the American colonies, where John and William Bartram were botanizing and producing widely admired books, to the Pacific Islands, where Captain James Cook's scientific expedition was exploring, Europeans were engrossed in the study of the natural world. Enlightenment scientists explained nature by means of reason.

As men went to and fro over the earth and knowledge was increased, Francis Bacon's reputation climbed. The advance of science seemed to presage the subjugation of nature under human dominion, the control of nature for human benefit, and the transformation of nature into an instrument of human will. Science was most valuable when it was most useful and applicable to the good of mankind. Thus, scientists and inventors like Franklin and Jefferson sought to honor Bacon and disseminate their inventions and improvements as widely as possible.

Amidst all this reason and science, basic perspectives of Protestantism lived on. Natural theology, which reasoned from timeless nature to God, accorded well with the Age of Reason. Dogma proved easier to shed than habits of mind. If, like Franklin, children of Dissenters no longer believed that profits and predestination went hand-in-hand, in them the duty to profit for God in the "Protestant ethic" survived as the duty to profit for business in the "spirit of capitalism." Puritan moralism may have been out of date, but morality and benevolence remained central to the most rational of moral systems. Reason and deism only redirected, and could not replace, the Protestant genesis of belief, capitalism, and virtue.

In Mather's later years, a young Bostonian, Benjamin Franklin, sometimes sat in his congregation. Although Franklin later resented the clergy's sanctimoniousness, power, and influence, Mather's Sabbath expositions of the relationship between religion, science, and service to humanity made a permanent impression on him. Franklin claimed that Mather's *Essays to Do Good* was one of the most influential books he ever read.[18] Moreover, the interest in science which Mather piqued led to the dramatic experiments upon which his fame and influence mostly rested. Thus did one of the most secular Americans of the eighteenth century betray his great debt to the Puritans who preceded him.

Franklin's religious development illustrates how persons raised in a devout household can reject parental creeds but cannot so easily purge habits of mind. Franklin came from a staunchly Protestant lineage. Born in New England in 1706 to an English Presbyterian and a descendant of Massachusetts Puritans, he resisted his parents' fervent faith from an early age. Theological squabbles and the exclusiveness of a creed that damned all non-Calvinists alienated him. He sat impatiently through his father's long daily prayers at home. Yet his father, a chandler, was a practical man, and he raised a practical boy. Franklin absorbed and believed the Boston values of work, diligence, and thrift.

Since Franklin's father had intended him for the ministry, his early reading included religious polemics and the works of John Bunyan. Plutarch, Mather, and Defoe's *Essay on Projects* impressed him with their emphasis on virtue and service to society. When Franklin investigated some books against deism, he found the refutations weaker than the deistic doctrines they argued against, and "soon became a thorough Deist."[19] Where Mather had seen the dangerous direction reliance upon the "reasonableness" of Christianity would lead and pulled up short, Franklin charged onward.

Franklin founded his public career on his misgivings about religion and ministers. His first printed pieces appeared in an anticlerical Boston newspaper as a series of letters under the pseudonym "Silence Dogood," whose name has been taken to be a parody of Mather. During a sojourn in England in the mid-1720s, Franklin wrote and printed a pamphlet called *A Dissertation on Liberty and Necessity, Pleasure and Pain*, his first statement of faith, in which he let his new convictions run to their conclusions. From the Aristotelian-Thomistic concept of the First Mover, he assumed the existence of "God, Maker of the Universe." He argued from God's goodness, wisdom, and omnipotence against the existence of evil or free will. Man was just a machine within the great machine of the universe. This implied a radical equality of all parts of the universe in the sight of God, man included. Both human and animal life was driven solely by desire to avoid pain and experience pleasure. Each creature experienced pain and pleasure in equal measure. He reasoned that since without pain there could be no pleasure, their necessarily equal measure implied that the present life was the happiest possible and that an eternally happy afterlife was impossible.[20]

Franklin soon retreated from this extreme statement. In 1728 he composed a short "Articles of Belief and Acts of Religion," which reinvested God with love for his creatures and humanity with free will, and allowed for Providence in a mechanical universe. Reason as the judge of revelation still remained paramount in Franklin's system. His epigraph declared his principles of natural theology, virtue, and happiness.

> Here will I hold — If there is a Pow'r above us
> (And that there is, all Nature cries aloud,
> Thro' all her Works), He must delight in Virtue
> And that which he delights in must be Happy.[21]

Franklin now denied the equality of creation and confirmed the chain of being, at the top of whose earthly links was man, the rational, worshipping animal. Thus far a conventional statement of natural theology, the "Articles of Belief" now abandoned orthodoxy to propose that between humanity and an infinite, incomprehensibly great God, must be lesser gods, "vastly superior to Man, who can better conceive [God's] Perfections than we, and return him a more rational and glorious praise." Each god was "Author and Owner"[22] of his own solar system with its planets and rational life, and to this god Franklin offered his rational, passionless worship.

In a worship service he wrote to this rational god, Franklin praised his goodness and wisdom as seen in creation. The service included readings that Mather and Edwards might approve: John Ray (who with Derham impressed Franklin, who used them in his 1730 "On the Providence of God in the Government of the World"),[23] Richard Blackmore's poem *Creation*, the Archbishop of Cambray's *Demonstration of the Existence and Attributes of God*, and Milton's restatement of Psalm 148, the hymn to the Creator in *Paradise Lost* (Bk. V, ll. 153 ff.). A petition to God for aid in "eschewing Vice and embracing Virtue" and a thanksgiving for blessings and happiness followed. Aside from the polytheism (supposedly taken from Newton, and apparently for Franklin a brief experiment), this statement of faith represented the foundations of Franklin's lifelong beliefs.[24]

Franklin believed a tree should be judged by its fruit. If a religion produced good for mankind, Franklin felt, it succeeded. Hence, he avoided all sectarian arguments and metaphysical speculations and emphasized that service to man was service to God, but he did accept the superiority of the Christian moral system to all others. He often attended Presbyterian services while in Philadelphia and donated money to religious causes.[25]

Drawing on Puritan moralism and emphasis on dedication to the common good, the example of Mather's various organizations for various good purposes, and Enlightenment programs of benevolence, Franklin's ideas of virtue stressed the common good, and the activities of his life bear this out.[26] His achievements for the public good included Philadelphia's first hospital and the University of Pennsylvania. Franklin gathered a promising group of young artisans called the Junto for the purpose of company, philosophy, and benevolence. The Junto proposed and implemented such beneficial projects as America's first circulating library, a fire department, America's first fire insurance company, a paid nightwatch, and paved and lighted streets.

As prosperity afforded increasing leisure, Franklin's dedication to the common good led to inventions and experiments that would make him famous throughout the world. Combining his artisan's practical disposition with the Baconian goal of useful scientific control of nature, in the 1730s and 1740s Franklin turned his interest to inventions beneficial to mankind. In 1741 he designed an improved version of the cast-iron fireplace, which he called the Pennsylvania fireplace and which, in a later version, became known as the Franklin stove.[27] Other notable inventions included a catheter, the glass harmonica (a musical instrument), bifocals, an instrument for reaching books on high shelves, and the fireplace damper.

By mid-century Franklin was devoting much of his time to the interest in science first kindled in the congregation of Mather's church — although he never showed much interest in investigating nature to discover the mind and attributes of God.[28] Also, like Increase and Cotton Mather, who had established the Boston Philosophical Society in Boston sixty years before, he helped organize the American Philosophical Society in 1743. Franklin explained the society's practical, utilitarian emphasis in "A Proposal for Promoting Useful Knowledge Among the British Plantations in America." "Formed of Virtuosi or ingenious Men" (that is, gentleman amateur scientists) throughout the English colonies, the society's Baconian concerns were "all philosophical Experiments that let Light into the Nature of Things, tend to increase the Power of Man over Matter, and multiply the Conveniencies or Pleasures of Life."[29]

Franklin's famous experiments built on readings in popularizations of Newtonian philosophy. He was never able to understand the sophisticated mathematics of Newton's *Principia*, but the experimental methods and hypotheses of the *Opticks*, which incidentally had also prompted youthful natural history essays by Edwards, were well within his capacity.[30] The mystery of electricity attracted Franklin's attention after seeing a demonstration in Boston of electrical effects. Because electricity had never been observed in nature (aside from yet unprovable speculations about lightning) and no one had been able to establish any scientific laws which governed it, electricity at the time was little more than the subject of parlor tricks. Franklin and friends devised a number of clever experiments from which he deduced several principles basic to electrical science, which he expressed in the terminology of fluids. Among the concepts and terms he coined were the conservation of charge, the "flow" of electricity, electrical "conductors," "positive" or "plus" and "negative" or "minus," and the "battery." With the establishment of these fundamentals, scientists could recognize electricity as a subject for inquiry and explanation. Subsequently, Franklin applied the vocabulary of fluids to heat, contributing the ideas of heat flow and heat conductivity.[31]

Franklin's 1752 kite experiment brought him lasting international fame.[32] With it, he had conquered lightning, one of the most dangerous and powerful forces of nature. His fame came not only from the scientific implications of his experiments, but even more from lightning rods, that successful leap from laboratory to control of nature for the benefit of mankind. Over a century before, Bacon had predicted that scientific study would lead to control of nature for human benefit, yet before Franklin's day no major example of this prediction had occurred.[33] Franklin seemed to be the fulfillment of prophecy.

Franklin's scientific interests ranged far beyond electricity. In 1742 botanist John Bartram relied upon him to organize and publicize a project to sponsor Bartram's collecting trips. Franklin's fundraising services helped outfit a ship twice sent in search of the Northwest Passage. He helped coordinate American efforts to observe the transit of Mercury across the sun in 1753 and the more important transit of Venus in 1769. As early as 1745 the longer time required for a voyage from Europe to America than the return trip puzzled Franklin and elicited possible solutions. In about 1770 he learned about the Gulf Stream from a sea captain and published the first chart of it. On subsequent voyages across the Atlantic, he carried out experiments measuring the Gulf Stream's temperature, breadth, and depth. Other scientific subjects that stimulated his thinking included the weather, waterspouts, why water dissolves salt, what makes seawater sometimes luminous, Philadelphia mortality rates, population growth in America, the origins of fossils, the reasons for the earth's magnetism, and the cause of earthquakes. Franklin's methodical, common-sense approach, combined with an exceptionally lucid writing style, made him one of the age's outstanding "virtuosi."

Throughout his life Franklin publicized his revised version of the authorized Puritan morality and ethic for society, grounded now upon very pragmatic bases. The practical, business-minded middle and northern colonies saw the sense of his sentiment and made a great success of his mouthpiece, *Poor Richard's Almanack*. Franklin's 1758 essay collecting Poor Richard's sayings, "Father Abraham's Speech" (later known as "The Way to Wealth") quickly went through numerous editions in America and Europe. This essay, together with "Advice to a Young Tradesman" (1748), expressed the secularized Protestant ethic in classic form with the twin concepts "Time is Money," and "the Way to Wealth . . . depends chiefly on two Words, INDUSTRY and FRUGALITY."[34] Although Franklin had "heard it remarked that the Poor in Protestant Countries on the Continent or Europe, are generally more industrious than those of Popish Countries,"[35] his deist leanings brought him to divorce the ethic from theological underpinnings and ground it solely upon practicality and common morality. The benefits he saw might be both personal and social, both moral and pecuniary, but in no way indicated salvation. The archetypal American entrepreneur who rose from humble origins to wealth, fame, and influence, Franklin was the best advertisement for his own ethic.

The implications of Franklin's thought about nature were enormous. Although a contemporary of the early Romantics, Franklin never wrote about scenery. The word "sublime" never escaped his pen. Without any intrinsic value, nature was an object for rational, down-to-earth inquiry, not mystical or rapturous contemplation. Man the rational, superior being must find out nature's secrets and put natural processes under control. Franklin's relationship with nature was active, part of an active life. Nature was the object of action. He sent kites in the sky and put electricity in bottles, and plumbed the sea and charted the Gulf Stream. He was a doer — a successful businessman, assemblyman, scientist, government official, delegate, and diplomat. In the end, his interest in nature only extended to the degree that it "let Light into the Nature of Things, tend to increase the Power of Man over Matter, and multiply the Conveniencies or Pleasures of Life."[36]

Franklin's promotion of dispassionate investigation and human control

of nature left room for paradox. His ethic of industry and frugality promoted an ethic of production, which a century later would power the rise of
industrial capitalism and the expansion of exploitation of natural resources
to feed its factories. (Although he favored laissez-faire economic policies,
Franklin was no proto-industrialist. He thought the only honest way to
wealth was farming.)[37] In Franklin's world of science and business there was
no place for a romanticized or mysticized nature. Yet Franklin believed in
pursuing science, invention, and business for humanitarian purposes. He
was not a wanton exploiter of man or of nature. The true crown of his
scientific achievements was not his discovery that lightning was electricity,
but his invention of the lightning rod. He believed that a life well lived
benefited everyone. The modern efforts through voluntary societies to deal
with environmental problems by means of science and technology constitute at least as much of his heritage as the exploitative, polluting capitalist
endeavors they seek to restrain.

God's Chosen People in Paradise: Thomas Jefferson

Among those Americans whom deism influenced profoundly was Thomas
Jefferson. But if Jefferson arrived at similar conclusions about virtue, benevolence, and the power of reason as others in the Enlightenment, he
expressed them with a distinctly Southern voice. Raised in a world very
different from that of New Englanders like Franklin, one without the Puritan moral and ethical grounding, Jefferson's view of nature had implications more characteristic of the South than the North. Jefferson wrote no
classic expressions of the "spirit of capitalism" which might lead to industrial production, and he asserted a profound individualist suspicion of government and power which left little room for the growth of a conservationist or preservationist ethic. Insofar as nature had any moral purpose at all, it
was to preserve the virtue of the independent yeoman farmer.

In Virginia, religion did not dominate life to the extent it did in New
England. In contrast to the Puritan colonies, Virginia had grown from an
almost purely business venture. Soon after its establishment its culture
revolved around growing tobacco for export. Born in 1743 into a gentry
founded on tobacco and slavery, Jefferson grew up on or near the frontier
and attended Anglican services. At church he surely never heard jeremiads
lamenting Virginia's moral decline from its founding standards, or allusions
to Moses and Virginia's chosenness, or to Nehemiah and a New Jerusalem
in the wilderness. Rather, Virginia's gentry-controlled Anglican church

served as a moral support for a deferential and commercial agrarian society. Broad in its theology, it was a comfortable church for a colonial gentleman. Throughout his life Jefferson attended Anglican services and retained affection for Anglican liturgy and the Psalms.[38]

Yet Jefferson's birth into the ranks of the gentry did not endow him with love of hierarchy and authority. Instead, a powerful anti-authoritarian prejudice colored his thought. In religion, politics, science, morals, and most other aspects of life, he rejected the unexamined authority of individual, institution, tradition, and history. To a great extent this bias grew out of the history and environment of his native colony. Like New England, Virginia had been a land of possibility, a place of no history, tradition, or hierarchy. Unlike the Puritans, early Virginia settlers sought wealth more in this world than the next. According to historian T. H. Breen, Virginia promotional literature emphasized chances of wealth and attracted an "extraordinarily individualistic, fiercely competitive, and highly materialistic" population. "By establishing economic privatism as the colony's central value, the Virginia Company of London spawned an aberrant society, a subculture of excessively individualistic men. . . ."[39] With the discovery of a staple commodity, tobacco, the colony settled more or less permanently into a boomtown, frontier condition — rough, grasping, competitive, individualistic. This relatively open and fluid society, within which fortunes might be made, bred habitual disdain for church and governmental authority. Due to the demands of tobacco planting, Virginians did not live in towns but on scattered farms and plantations and often reluctantly performed communal duties, like militia service, which might reduce time spent on growing tobacco and hence cut profits.

Competitiveness and profit-mindedness produced an exploitative attitude toward labor and land. This culminated in a slave society, which in turn reinforced a resistance to "slavish" obedience to authority. Southerners felt no need to be stewards of the land. Virginia's mild climate and fertile soils encouraged heedless exploitation. On the other hand, Virginians did not pursue a millennial transformation of the landscape, in part because it was so Edenic already.

Jefferson's attitudes reflected this milieu. Jefferson spoke of his youth, "a time of life when I was bold in the pursuit of knowledge, never fearing to follow truth and reason to whatever results they led, and bearding every authority which stood in their way." To him, "freedom" and "liberty" often connoted freedom from taxes, from enforced duty to the community, from government regulation and interference of all sorts, and from established religion. The word "duty" rarely appeared in Jefferson's discourse, and then not as a positive obligation to the common good (other than the duty to live a life useful to society or to follow the moral teachings of Jesus) but as one's duty to preserve life, liberty, and pursuit of happiness. His disdain for the past and its customs and traditions reflected Virginia's own lack of mythic origins and Virginians' belief in the possibilities of the present and future.[40]

Thus for Jefferson human authority could not be the source of absolute truth. He reasoned with Locke that because human understanding was limited and fallible, established authorities might sometimes support truth, but at other times they inevitably gave error the force of law and inhibited progress of science and philosophy. Mankind's ultimate authority could only be God, the author of truth.

Man could find this truth in two places. The first was within each human being, in the innate faculties of morality and reason which God had implanted. Jefferson denied that ethics could only be understood by the educated: "He who made us would have been a pitiful bungler if he had made the rules of our moral conduct a matter of science. For one man of science, there are thousands who are not. What would have become of them?" Although this was Chrysostom's idea of God's democratic Book of Nature applied to morality, Jefferson's concept of the innate moral sense came from his readings of Scottish philosophy, particularly Common Sense Realism. Jefferson was something of a rationalist antinomian. "We should all then, like the quakers, live without an order of priests, moralise for ourselves, follow the oracle of conscience, and say nothing about what no man can understand [like the Trinity], nor therefore believe; for I suppose belief to be the assent of the mind to an intelligible proposition."[41]

Every moral notion arose from the innate moral faculty to be tested and proved by the faculty of reason. Reason was the measure and judge of all things, and especially so in religion, in which people must "unlearn the lesson that reason is an unlawful guide to religion" because "reason and free enquiry are the only effectual agents against error." Everything must be questioned, from the existence of God to the authority of the Bible. Reason and the evidence of the senses, for example, implied that immaterial entities had no existence, and that God and spirit had to be material beings (not an unusual position during the Enlightenment).[42]

The classical, moral, rationalist, and deistic authors who inclined Jefferson to skepticism included Lord Kame, Helvetius, Locke, Bolingbroke, Hume, and Voltaire. Yet other writers helped Jefferson construct belief: "... I have read [Priestley's] Corruptions of Christianity, and Early opinions of Jesus, over and over again; and I rest on them, and on Middleton's writings . . . as the basis of my own faith." Man's moral and reasoning faculties help him distinguish truth from error, while also proving the moral and rational nature of God, who had written them in man's nature.[43]

As intent as Puritans and other Protestants on stripping away centuries of human additions to the pure core of Christianity as practiced in the primitive church, Jefferson wanted to go much further than most Christians thought necessary and discover Christianity as it came from the lips of "the personage" Jesus, not as interpreted, augmented (especially with Greek and Platonic philosophy), and distorted by Paul and others. With the removal of those historical distortions and encrustations, "there will be found remaining the most sublime and benevolent code of morals which has ever been offered to man." Unitarianism came closest to primitive Christianity, and he hoped it might become the general religion of his country.[44]

The second place where truth could be discovered was nature, because nature clearly came directly from the hand and mind of God. Founding his creed on natural theology, Jefferson could not look at the universe in whole or in its parts, at the motion of the heavens, or at the distribution, interrelationship, generation, and uses of terrestrial phenomena, and not

> believe that there is, in all this, design, cause and effect, up to an ultimate cause, a fabricator of all things from matter and motion, their preserver and regulator while permitted to exist in their present forms, and their regenerator into new and other forms.[45]

Jefferson expressed the Enlightenment belief that, since all nations had "knoledge [*sic*] of the existence of a god"[46] from their observation of nature, there was a natural religion which lay at the center of all religions. Christianity's superiority lay in its highly developed moral system, not its revelation.

Jefferson appealed over and over to the authority of nature. So strongly were creation and creator connected in his mind that in some passages he slipped so unconsciously from "nature" to "creator" as to make them synonymous. It is difficult to find a page from his hand which does not use the words "nature" or "natural" or a synonym. For Jefferson, as for Raymond of Sebonde, nature was all one knows, and all one needs to know. Reasoning from nature, the ground behind and beyond all human thought and activity, he could overleap history, revelation, tradition, law, institutions, and political, economic, social, and religious authority of all kinds.

Jefferson never systematized his concept of nature, nor did he seem aware that appeals to nature could justify contrary propositions.[47] In effect, nature could speak only with the voice he gave it. He used "nature" as needed as an elastic concept to justify his rejection of human authority.

Jefferson agreed with the Biblical tenet that the things that are made teach the invisible attributes of God. Just as human moral and reasoning faculties must have come from a moral and rational God, so creation demonstrated the power and mind of the creator.[48] The order and reasonableness of nature and its evident design fascinated Jefferson. Typically for his age, he thought of this order in terms of the "economy of nature," a proto-ecological elaboration of the idea of the chain of being which implied the intricate and balanced interrelationship of all life. Science, then, was the process of "cooperating with nature in her ordinary economy." Extinction was inconceivable to an Enlightenment thinker like Jefferson because he assumed both a steady-state universe and God's creation of a perfect and complete cosmos. Jefferson insisted that mammoths must yet roam somewhere in the interior of America: "Such is the economy of nature, that no instance can be produced, of her having permitted any race of her animals to become extinct; of her having formed any link in her great work so weak as to be broken." In his wisdom God had preordained the nature and habitat for every beast, in this case the tropics for elephants and the polar regions for their mammoth cousins. Late in life, perhaps as a result of the futile search for the mammoth, Jefferson acknowledged that species could become extinct.[49]

To Jefferson the highest goal was to understand the order and reasonableness of the world in order to use it for the benefit of humanity. Consequently, it is no surprise that he placed Bacon alongside Newton and Locke in "my trinity of the three greatest men the world had ever produced." Their portraits hung in Monticello.[50] Under the added influence of predominantly Scottish theories of moralism and benevolence, he believed the human purpose was to learn about creation in order to understand its manifold uses to mankind.

Jefferson was a "zealous amateur" in science, which he viewed as the rational, empirical method to search out the laws of nature, which were the laws of God. He made no fundamental discoveries on the level of Franklin's, but he was an inveterate collector and notetaker, who loved to measure and calculate. His wide-ranging curiosity led to notable contributions in archeology, Indian anthropology, paleontology, meteorology, agriculture, and natural science, especially his *Notes on Virginia*, an important argument for the worldwide uniformity of natural processes.[51]

If Jefferson exemplified the Southern preference for descriptive science

in nature over experimental science in a laboratory like Franklin's, his emphasis on utility led him, like Franklin, to make his results public. On his
plantation he experimented regularly to improve Southern agricultural
methods. Jefferson investigated crop rotation, fertilization, new virtues of
plants, better plowing methods like contour plowing, and new farm machinery. Typical of his desire to serve mankind was his most celebrated
invention, the moldboard plow, whose design he published widely.[52]

For all his materialism, Jefferson did not believe that God had created a
mechanical universe that ran without divine guidance or miraculous interference. On the contrary, he saw "evident proofs of the necessity of a super-
intending power to maintain the Universe in it's [*sic*] course and order."
Jefferson's feeling for the author of nature was not grounded solely on reason; he also loved the hymn to the creator contained in the 148th Psalm.
God also acted in human affairs through his "over-ruling Providence,
which by all its dispensations proves that it delights in the happiness of man
here and his greater happiness hereafter. . . ." God did not solely act to
provide prosperity and goodness, for he could also work his will through
epidemics and war, and could punish in his wrath, as Jefferson once predicted would be the fate of slaveowners. It is indeed striking that a man so
immersed in the science and rational spirit of his age should yet see the
hand of God in epidemics (which even Cotton Mather had ascribed to
natural causes) and human events.[53]

Jefferson rarely thought of nature in consciously Biblical terms. One of
the more surprising analogies he did borrow was the Exodus from Egypt
through the wilderness to the Promised Land. God, he said, "led our fore-
fathers, as Israel of old, from their native land, and planted them in a
country flowing with all the necessaries and comforts of life" and "has
covered our infancy with his providence, and our riper years with his wisdom and power. . . ." An early proposal for the design of the seal of the
United States (before his famous pyramid-and-eye design) portrayed the
children of Israel on one side.[54]

Jefferson did not, like the Puritans, believe that Americans were the new
Israel, God's Chosen, because of their devotion to the divine law and covenant. Instead, he proclaimed,

Those who labor in the earth are the chosen people of God, if ever He
had a chosen people, whose breasts He has made His peculiar deposit
for substantial and genuine virtue. It is the focus in which he keeps
alive that sacred fire, which otherwise might escape from the face of
the earth. Corruption of morals in the mass of cultivators is a phenom-

enon of which no age nor nation has furnished an example. It is the mark set on those, who, not looking up to heaven, to their own soil and industry, as does the husbandman, for their own subsistence, depend for it on casualties and caprice of customers.[55]

Not God or covenants but nature itself bestowed chosenness from daily contact with the earth (which gave its bounty according to soil and industry) and from awareness of heaven (whence came providential rain and sunshine). America was "a chosen country," rich and fertile like Canaan, "with room enough for our descendants to the hundredth and thousandth generation."[56] The idea of the farmer drawing his virtue from the soil remained popular in America, long a nation of farmers, and would be prominent in such doctrines as Manifest Destiny and Progressivism.

A firm believer in progress and mankind's rise from savagery to civilization, Jefferson saw no advantage to living in nature, as the Indians lived. As President, he attempted to change Indians into ideal yeoman farmers, "that state of society, which to bodily comforts adds the improvements of the mind and morals." Yet he felt thwarted by "interested and crafty individuals among them" who "inculcate a sanctimonious reverence for the customs of their ancestors; that whatsoever they did, must be done through all time; that reason is a false guide, and to advance under its counsel, in their physical, moral, or political condition, is perilous innovation; that their duty is to remain as their Creator made them, ignorance being safety, and knowledge full of danger. . . ." There were few men less prepared than Jefferson to understand an attachment to the past or resistance to the "dictates" of reason. Nor did he see any advantage to living "as the Creator made them." While the state of nature meant ignorance, modern city life endangered morals. The only safely enlightened and virtuous people were independent farmers.[57]

Several of Jefferson's ideas echoed Christian attitudes about nature without explicitly recognizing their provenance. His ideas on the expansion of agriculture across the United States and the Americas recalled the Genesis command to be fruitful, multiply, fill the earth and subdue it. Foreshadowing the enthusiasms of advocates of Manifest Destiny, Jefferson even envisioned his country expanding into and filling both North and South America. He often implied that the earth was created for mankind's benefit. Providence, or God's hand in nature, for example, appeared in his writings only in connection with human action, never for any lower animal's sake. Even the earth's oblate-spheroid shape was the result not of natural causes but of God's design because this shape was best planned to prevent drifting of the poles, which would cause the earth's depopulation.[58]

Thomas Jefferson's basic understanding of nature itself did not stray very far from the paths of the Puritans. His and Anne Bradstreet's faiths started from the same point — the evidence of God's design of nature. Both Puritan and Virginian inhabited a world made for man and blessed by providence. They both rejected human invention and authority in religion and sought the purest springs of truth. They both saw the hand of God in the deliverance of English colonists to America from the corruptions of the Old World. Like Edward Johnson, Jefferson welcomed the spread of agriculture and the increase of population. Yet, if he shared much with the Puritans, Jefferson's shifts in emphasis centered attention more on this world than the next. Bradstreet followed nature to God and orthodoxy; Jefferson reasoned from nature to man and society. America was not an Eden inhabited by fallen men awaiting the promise of heaven, but a promised land of virtuous farmers reaping abundance in the present.

Although his world was not nearly as infused with sacred meaning as the Puritan cosmos, Jefferson brought God and nature so close that they were nearly one. Like Enlightenment thinkers from the time of Newton, he saw a static universe, not an evolving one, a universe which God had ordered and whose laws he had laid down at creation. Not laws of human invention but God's eternal laws implanted in nature and in the innate moral faculty guided mankind. God endowed mankind with reasoning intelligence to discover those laws. Enlightened rational contemplation and investigation of nature guarded religion, morality, virtue, and liberty. Contact with nature kept civilization from atheism, corruption, tyranny, and immorality. God blessed those who lived by the light of these principles, and to Jefferson the English-speaking people of America were the last hope to keep the fire aglow. There, providence blessed God's chosen people with abundance from a chosen land.

Like his New England cousins, Jefferson advocated the spread of white civilization across the wilderness, even as he looked to nature for divine instruction. Unlike them, he left behind no legacy that later generations could use to preserve or defend wild nature. He and most other Southerners admired the empirical and the utilitarian and preferred the logic of natural theology to the mysticism of neo-Platonism. Jefferson detested the effect of mystical Platonism on Christianity and disliked Paul, Augustine, and Calvin. Rare would be the Southern theologian influenced by post-Kantian German idealist mysticism. Transcendentalism had virtually no impact in the South, where religious men continued to trust the empirical common-sense approaches of Locke, Thomas Reid, and Paley. Natural theology could lead to scientific understanding of ecological relationships, but it could not produce such spiritual fervor as animated the Muir wing of the preservationist movement. When twentieth-century conservation came to the South, it did so in an evangelical culture, not a rationalist one.[59]

While the Puritans established traditions of communal responsibility and government involvement for the common good which their descendants could rely upon to restrain private exploitation of natural resources, the Southern ethic entailed individual freedom of action and weak powers of authority. Fellow Southerners shared Jefferson's profound suspicion of authority. Unfortunately, Southerners did not share Jefferson's concern for careful agricultural methods. Aside from a few fellow rationalists like Edwin Ruffin, most Southerners yielded to the temptation of cheap, plentiful, fecund Southern land, exploited the soil, and then abandoned the eroded, exhausted fields.[60] If the South and North shared a regard for the divine in nature, it would nevertheless be no accident that the first parks and nature preserves would appear outside the South and under the auspices of the Northern-dominated Republican Party, and that New Englanders and Northerners filled the ranks of conservation and preservationist organizations.

FIVE

Conquest and Contemplation

America is a very fine country, of an immense, almost of an incalculable extent, embracing every climate in which the sugar cane, and lofty pine, receive their growth and acquire their maturity. The far greater portion of her domains remain still in a state of primitive nature, uncultivated and unprofitable, where the foot of the husbandman has never yet trod, although a land that invites the hand of the labourer, whose industry would make her flourish with every abundance desirable by man; a land that would give support and happiness to millions and millions of families to the latest posterity.

This gift, this bounty, this felicity to the human race, rest at the disposal of the United States of America: it is a deposit from Providence confided to their hands for the benefit of mankind; and it is the duty of America to discharge this trust with care, with activity, and with integrity.

— COLONEL JAMES SWAN, AN ADDRESS TO THE SENATE
AND HOUSE OF REPRESENTATIVES OF THE UNITED STATES,
ON THE QUESTION FOR THE INQUIRY INTO
THE STATE OF AGRICULTURE, MANUFACTURES AND COMMERCE (1817)

> *The groves were God's first temples. Ere man learned*
> *To hew the shaft, and lay the architrave,*
> *And spread the roof above them — ere he framed*
> *The lofty vault, to gather and roll back*
> *The sound of anthems; in the darkling wood,*
> *Amid the cool and silence, he knelt down*
> *And offered to the Mightiest solemn thanks*
> *And supplication. For his simple heart*
> *Might not resist the sacred influence*
> *Which, from the stilly twilight of the place,*
> *And from the gray old trunks that high in heaven*
> *Mingled their mossy boughs, and from the sound*
> *Of the invisible breath that swayed at once*

All their green tops, stole over him, and bowed
His spirit with the thought of boundless power
And inaccessible majesty. Ah, why
Should we, in the world's riper years, neglect
God's ancient sanctuaries, and adore
Only among the crowd, and under roofs
That our frail hands have raised? . . .

— WILLIAM CULLEN BRYANT, "A FOREST HYMN" (1832)

The nineteenth century was a critical, if contradictory, time for American attitudes toward nature. Time and again pioneers, soldiers, clergymen, businessmen, land speculators, and visitors of all sorts ventured to the edge of their civilization and gazed upon the wilderness, half musing on the sublimity and beauty of the scenery and half calculating how much it was worth as farmland, mines, water power, or future cities. In this era of Romanticism, Americans infused landscape with the power to uplift the poetic soul toward moral and religious thoughts. In this age of expansion, the nation felt the exhilaration of building an empire of liberty and Christian civilization. By the end of the century, the escalating conflicts between the two views and uses of nature polarized the contemplators and the builders into opposition. Yet for a time, at the height of the Romantic Era, people accepted both and celebrated the divinely ordained conquest of a divinely blessed continent.

The vast uncivilized territory to the west excited America's imagination. In the nineteenth century, no less than in the seventeenth, the wilderness was a place of possibility, an Eden before the Fall, a land where dreams could come true, mankind could be redeemed, and people could build a new society without the problems of the old. So much nature direct from the hand of God inspired an American mysticism, the New England Transcendentalists' appropriation of the neo-Platonic pathway from the earthly to the heavenly. Yet, elsewhere after 1800, mounting flames of evangelical Protestantism repeatedly swept the country — especially intensely between 1815 and 1840 in the "burnt-over district" of upper New York State — and inspired new Bible-based dramas as Mormons and other utopians relived the exodus from Babylon to the New Jerusalem in the wilderness. A continent inspired dreams of dominion, as the Manifest Destiny expansionists envisioned empire, gleaming rails across the land, and an industrial–

agrarian paradise. Westward went mystics, utopians, and subduers of the earth, pursuing their dreams of heaven.

Paradise Lost: Ralph Waldo Emerson

Oliver Wendell Holmes, in a famous remark, called Ralph Waldo Emerson's "The American Scholar" "our intellectual Declaration of Independence."[1] How much Emerson, in that or any other work, really broke from Europe is debatable. Unquestionably, however, Emerson declared independence from both the sectarian Biblicism of the evangelical wing of the Puritan tradition and the Enlightenment assumptions of the rationalist wing to which he belonged. Since the Great Awakening, New England's rural, Calvinist churches had concentrated on gathering the saved, while the urban, now Unitarian churches accommodated themselves to the world and the Age of Reason. It was Emerson's nineteenth-century version of the "Puritan dilemma," how to be in the world but not of it. Emerson was a man who treasured the Puritan moral and intellectual tradition into which he was born, yet who lived in what to him was a crass and commercial age. He hoped to revive it by transforming it: to infuse spiritual inspiration into a morally and intellectually respectable religion, to be an Anne Bradstreet without resignation and submission, a Cotton Mather without Biblicism, or a Jonathan Edwards without terror and predestination.

In the early nineteenth century, pure-minded idealists like Emerson found the dilemma sharpened as the rough and aggressive political and economic world of Jacksonian America relegated them to the sidelines. While admitting a certain admiration for the sphere of politics and economics, Emerson and the idealists posited a higher, invisible world beyond, a world accessible though the portals of nature's beauty. The American in the wilderness was still a fallen Adam in Eden, but now, for the first time, Emerson and the Romantics invested nature itself with redemptive power. A man in tune with nature was in harmony with God and thereby hastened the millennium, the new Eden. Emerson's powerful prose carried his Transcendentalist love of natural beauty out of the narrow confines of his tiny Unitarian denomination and made it a dominant American intellectual movement, later to have a huge impact on the history of environmental thought.[2]

Although thus far bearing no famous names, like the Mather and Edwards families, the Emerson family tree too was heavy with Geneva gowns.[3] Emerson's father, William, was pastor of Boston's First Church, which had moved well along the path from Congregationalism to Unitarianism, William died in 1811 just before Emerson's eighth birthday, leaving his devout and more orthodox mother and aunt to raise the family. After the failure of an older brother to enter the ministry—his study of German higher criticism, which treated the Bible like any other ancient text, had created a crisis of faith—Emerson entered Harvard Divinity School to carry on the family ministerial tradition. A bout of near blindness prompted a convalescent trip in Charleston, South Carolina and St. Augustine, Florida for the winter of 1827, which he spent in contemplation and self-examination. (This illness, as much as his neo-Platonism, was responsible for his later love of metaphors of vision.) Two years later Emerson took a job as junior pastor of Boston's Second Church, "Old North," the church of Increase and Cotton Mather.

Emerson's 1832 resignation from the ministry was a crucial moment. The outward conformity of his life as a Unitarian minister now ended and the unconventional beliefs upon which he long had brooded came to the surface. With the publication of *Nature* in 1836, he began to spread his message. Fame from his 1837 Harvard Phi Beta Kappa Address, "The American Scholar," mixed with notoriety from the repudiation of Harvard Divinity School Unitarianism in his 1838 "Divinity School Address." In 1836 he joined six friends, who had all been reading University of Vermont President James Marsh's edition of and essay on Coleridge's *Aids to Reflection*, and formed the Transcendental Club, which lent its name to a new movement. From 1840 to 1844 he advised, contributed to, then edited the Transcendentalist publication *Dial*. The trajectory of Emerson's idealist thought was by now well established, although now his focus began to move away from idealist abstractions to the issues of living in the world.[4]

With the way prepared by eighteenth-century New Englanders like Edwards, Emerson modernized neo-Platonism for the nineteenth century. (Emerson's comment that nature "is a great shadow pointing always to the sun behind us," for example, recalled Edwards's "shadows of divine things.") Like a comet orbiting round the sun, Emerson's wide-ranging readings repeatedly returned to the neo-Platonic tradition, be it embodied in the American, English, and German Romantics, German idealists, Cambridge Platonist Ralph Cudworth, or Plato and Plotinus themselves.

Idealism also filled a personal need in Emerson's youthful period of rebelliousness. His avid readings of eighteenth-century skeptic David Hume helped him break with the "corpse-cold Unitarianism" of his parents and teachers. Yet Humean skepticism left him with a hunger for belief. Emerson rebuilt faith upon the assertion that intuition brought knowledge that transcended mere sense data.[5] Idealist philosophy's contention that ultimate reality was spiritual not physical, also justified Emerson's attraction to the contemplative life of the scholar-philosopher-poet and alienation from the aggressive, grasping, expansive spirit of his times. Idealism raised the status of certain neglected values and groups above the "selfish," "mean," "low," "sensual" materialists who dominated American society. He and other "beautiful souls" could commune with Beauty, Truth, and Divine Unity above the "splendid labyrinth of . . . perceptions" wherein the rest of benighted humanity "wander[ed] without end."[6]

In the language of Victorian gender ideology, the doctrine of the "spheres," Emerson and the Transcendentalists explicitly and implicitly condemned the activities of the male sphere and approved those of the female, rejecting the pursuit of worldly wealth and power as materialistic and amoral. Let the scholar and poet "be a cænobite, a pauper, and if need be, celibate also," Emerson wrote; poverty was virtue's "ornament." It was better to "die for Beauty, than live for bread." The male sphere, which included all "the lucrative professions and practices of man," was merely "selfish and sensual," "the effect of the mercenary impulse."

Emerson's attraction to moral marginality and the moral and spiritual virtues of the female sphere paralleled his personality and upbringing: his close relationship with his mother and aunt, bitterness toward his father, and a gentle, almost "womanly" personality (according to several contemporaries). Aware of being marginalized along with women by antebellum society, Emerson noted that men spoke to clergymen as they spoke to women, in "mincing and diluted speech," and scholars found themselves popularly classed with women and children. It was not that Emerson resisted the doctrine of the spheres, for he agreed with conventional wisdom that civilization's "higher" activities reflected female influence. Yet Emerson protested that the world had its priorities inverted. Passive contemplation of Truth and Beauty was a "manly" activity. Pursuit of "land and money, place and name" caused "the man in you" to die, while "silence, seclusion, austerity" brought "the noble, manlike, just thought."[7]

Natural theology had always infused nature with divine qualities; Emerson's generation now for the first time imbued it with moral ones. With its facilitative role in neo-Platonism, its frequent personification as a goddess (sometimes a virgin, other times a mother), its unmediated relation to the Creator, and its innocent state apart from the activities of man, nature filled the leading role in Emerson's philosophy. Locating nature firmly within the "higher" female sphere, Transcendentalists cherished nature as a symbol of the divine, wellspring of morality, and refuge from materialism. Implicitly for now, exploitation of nature for profit became the lowest form of attack upon divinity, femininity, and domesticity.

Hence, Emerson turned to nature in his search for reason and faith. Desiring a living faith that acknowledged the active power of God in the present world, he discarded the accumulated dead doctrines of other ages. "No facts to me are sacred; none are profane; I simply experiment, an endless seeker, with no Past at my back." He admired Quakers, who sought truth individually, within themselves. But most especially, Emerson turned from doctrines and creeds to read the unfalsifiable, eternal words of God as he wrote them in the book of nature.[8]

The discovery of truth began in solitude, looking up in reverence at the stars, where natural theology had always begun, but in the context of the Puritan tradition of solitary meditation in nature. Emerson habitually walked the country roads and fields around his home in Concord Village, and spoke of exhilarating spiritual experiences while crossing a bare common, walking in the woods, or standing on Mt. Auburn in Cambridge. If "the mind is open to their influence," all natural objects made a similar impact on the reverent mind, although more when in unity of the landscape as a whole than as individual objects.

Corrupt, materialistic man was blind to this constant revelation around him, which, however, was clear to the marginal people of society: children, idiots, Indians, unschooled farm boys, "babes and even brutes." Likewise, country-dwellers were superior to city-dwellers, who tended toward corruption. (No stickler for "consistency," Emerson was perfectly capable of praising progress and condemning the Indian's "childish illusions" and the "nonsense of his wigwam.") Nature was man's hope, for in the woods, "the plantations of God," he was "always a child." There, alone, passive almost to invisibility (a "transparent eye-ball"), he became sensible of the universal soul. Passivity of the soul was essential for insight, according to Emerson. Nature was not spiritual or divine in herself. The power to produce delight resided not in nature but in man, "or in a harmony of both." Nature reflected the mood of the observer, wearing "the colors of the spirit."[9]

Perhaps it was his Puritan background that led Emerson to think of nature in terms of her purpose and utility. She (Nature was feminine) was made for man, and without him she was "waste and worthless." Nature's "uses" ranged along a scale, each "higher" and "nobler" than the previous, a ladder to the divine. Nature's lowest use, of course, was as a commodity to be bought and sold and nourish man's physical wants. But this "steady and prodigal provision that has been made for [man's] support and delight" did not imply that man might live idly. Emerson firmly supported the Protestant work ethic. Man must work, yet remain on guard against entrapment in the material world.[10]

Nature's second use fulfilled "a nobler want of man, . . . namely, the love of Beauty." To Emerson, as to Plotinus, "The world thus exists to the soul to satisfy the desire of beauty."[11] Yet, because beauty was external to the soul, Nature had yet higher uses.

Nature's third use was as symbol. Similarly to the Puritan emblematic and typological tradition and Edwards's theology, natural facts symbolized spiritual facts and moral laws corresponded to physical laws. The world corresponded to the spiritual because it was an emanation of the spirit. All mankind recognized such connections between the physical and the spiritual as the "universal soul within or behind his individual life" embodying "Justice, Truth, Love, Freedom," and a creating soul in nature called Spirit and denoted "the FATHER."[12]

In the Book of Nature, physical "words" were symbols telling of the spiritual reality behind the illusion of the material world. Written in a universal language, it lay open to all men, not just scientists or scholars. "A life in harmony with nature, the love of truth and virtue, will purge the eyes to understand her text," so that by degrees "the world shall be to us an open book." Yet, only if men exercised their intuition of the moral sentiment, which all possessed, could they read and understand the Book of Nature. For the Transcendentalist Emerson, as for the Calvinist Edwards, though the book was open democratically to all, it was comprehended only by the spiritual elite.[13]

The highest "use of the world" comprised all the preceding uses. This use educated the rational and intuitive faculties and led them to God. The material world teaches the rational mind. Intuition "transfers all these lessons into its own world of thought, by perceiving the analogy that marries Matter and Mind."[14] The first of these lessons was a revised version of the Puritan dream of the millennium, but brought about by the exercise of human will over the world and employment of the powers granted to mankind in Genesis. The world, said Emerson,

> is made to serve. It receives the dominion of man as meekly as the ass on which the Savior rode. . . . More and more, with every thought, does his kingdom stretch over things, until the world becomes, at last, only a realized will, — the double of man.[15]

Emerson had once avidly read Bacon and here his vision of the extension of man's dominion led clearly to the Baconian millennium, the new Eden brought about by scientific control of nature. Emerson's love of nature lacked sympathy for wilderness, and he looked forward to the day when the country would be transformed into farms and gardens, a renewed paradise, a refutation of Malthus and Ricardo.[16]

The greatest lesson nature taught man was that all nature taught religion and morality: "Therefore is nature ever the ally of Religion. . . . This ethical character so penetrates the bone and marrow of nature, as to seem the end for which it was made." This uniform, pervasive morality was the clearest evidence of the universe's essential unity in its variety. Unity in variety, expressed in the poem "Each and All," formed a central tenet of both neo-Platonism and Romanticism and underlay the development of ecological thinking in Europe (especially Germany) and America. Emerson, for example, rejected science which only "separates and classifies things" in favor of science which saw the world as one, and spoke of the "continuity of this web of God." In his essay, "The Method of Nature," Emerson described nature as flowing, growing, and changing.[16]

In ways that recalled the "paradise lost" theme of Milton (a favorite poet of Emerson and the Romantics) as well as his Puritan heritage, Emerson thought of the human relation to nature in terms of sin, salvation, and the millennium. ". . . We are as much strangers in nature, as we are alien from God." "Man is fallen," barred from the Garden and the presence of God, out of touch with the spirit behind the material world. All men bear the consequences of original sin, for "we are all entitled to beauty, should have been beautiful if our ancestors had kept the laws. . . ." Because mankind violated and violates natural, intellectual, and moral laws, humanity lives in misery. Nature's "ferocity" in war, plague, cholera, and famine are caused by human "crime" and paid for by "human suffering. Unhappily, no man exists who has not in his own person become, to some amount, a stockholder in the sin, and so made himself liable to a share in the expiation."[18]

For the rising generations of the nineteenth century, the Calvinist scheme of fall and redemption was dead. Transcendentalists proposed a radical further revision of the Christian formula: Nature, not Christ, offered salvation. Unpredestined, an individual undergoes a conversion experience "the moment the mind opens, and reveals the laws which traverse the universe." Teachers and preachers who instructed only the rational faculty (the unregenerate, in a sense) could not help, but the poet or artist, who used his intuition to realize Art (the elect, in a sense), could provoke the receptive soul. The soul then intuited the moral sentiment and achieved "an insight of the perfection of the laws of the soul." Itself now redeemed, the soul would redeem the world and restore its "original and eternal beauty." The millennium was at hand, for "when a faithful thinker . . . shall . . . kindle science with the fire of the holiest affections, then will God go forth anew into the creation." With the rational faculty in harmony with intuition at last, mankind would enter "the kingdom of man over nature, which cometh not with observation, — a dominion such as now is beyond his dream of God. . . ."[19]

Throughout Transcendentalist thought about nature run many quite conventional strands: a world made for man, who stands at the top of the earthly great chain of being; the inferiority of animals and man's animal nature; the benefits moral and material of man's expanding dominion over nature; nature's design and goodness as proof of a wise, benevolent deity; creation as the embodiment of the truths of morality and religion; the harmony of the books of nature and revelation and of science and religion. For two centuries, Americans had expressed similar sentiments. Emerson and Transcendentalism, however, represented something new and important for Americans and nature. While Jefferson's God had been primarily the transcendent ruler of an ordered universe, Emerson's was an immanent soul in an unfolding cosmos. Jefferson's relation to nature was intellectual; Emerson's was intuitional and mystical. To Emerson, the proper attitude of man toward the universe was wonder and joy.[20]

Emerson was also the first major American figure to relink the passive nature mysticism of neo-Platonism with similar doctrines in Eastern religion and philosophy. Especially in this century, Americans interested in both nature and spiritual matters — from Supreme Court Justice William O. Douglas to poet Gary Snyder — have shown a marked affinity for Eastern spirituality ever since. The attraction of neo-Platonists for Indian mysticism is no coincidence. Since the establishment of Greek trading routes with India in the sixth century B.C., Greek philosophers had been aware of Indian thought. Indian parallels in the philosophies of Heraclitus, Plato, and Plotinus are unmistakable, while both Plato and Plotinus were interested in Indian philosophy.[21]

Although Emerson himself did not incline to scientific study of nature — the view from a distance sufficed for him most of the time — he made a close relationship with nature a high and noble occupation. He very importantly was the first major figure amidst the materialist and commercial spirit of nineteenth-century America to link morality with love of nature. Thus, he directly inspired Thoreau, Burroughs, Muir, and many others to spend their lives communing with, investigating, writing about, defending, and, in effect, preaching about nature, and convinced them they were answering a holy calling.

Yet, on the other hand, Emerson's powerful idealist division between the self and nature, between the "Me" and "Not-Me," separated lovers of nature from direct interaction with her. The Transcendentalist was in but not of nature. Workmen in the landscape distracted Emerson. This passive, distanced relation to nature would tend to support preservation and condemn use or development of natural places. Therefore can Emerson be considered the font of environmentalist moralism.

The New Jerusalem in the Wilderness: Joseph Smith

Although Emerson and the Transcendentalists pushed ahead on many of the paths marked out by their New England forebears, German higher criticism had cut them off from the literal Biblicism of early New Englanders. But just as the sophisticated outlook of Anne Bradstreet had coexisted with the plebeian enthusiasms of Edward Johnson, Transcendentalism's cosmopolitan world ran parallel to a universe of plain folk in which Biblical literalism mixed with popularized Enlightenment ideas. The early Christian synthesis of philosophy and the Bible had come undone: while Bostonians sought intimations of a Greek ethereal transcendent reality, the farmers of the hinterland obeyed the stern commands of the God of Israel. Emerson, scion of a Boston ministerial first family, had updated idealism for the nineteenth century. Son of a frontier hardscrabble farmer, Joseph Smith revitalized the vision of a New Jerusalem in the wilderness.

Smith's life and thought ran on a less-exalted parallel to Emerson's. Smith, too, was born to a long New England pedigree and lived at the margins of American life. After a youthful period of skepticism, he saw a vision in the woods, where he returned to reason and faith. He then embarked on a career teaching that revelation had not ended with the early Christian church but was available to all. His rejection of churchly learning, doctrine, and history has compelled one commentator to call the Book of Mormon "America's religious declaration of independence."[22] Denying his marginality, he preached that the worldly and carnally-minded were the outsiders, while believers were at the true center of things. He preserved the work ethic and the drive to conquer nature for religious purposes. He felt that mankind must prepare for the millennial restoration of man and nature. Smith built his own world far more dramatically than any contemporary, and the huge world, or much of it, did come round to him — at present, six million share it. The Church of Jesus Christ of Latter-day Saints is the lengthened shadow of this one astonishing man.

The many parallels between Emerson and Smith arose from the fact that both were descendants of Puritans, living in the same materialistic world — in it, but not of it. However, they took from the Puritans very different inheritances. Smith incorporated many elements of New England culture that the sophisticated Unitarians of eastern New England had long left behind, like Biblical literalism and village magic. A clear continuity with the outlook of the first settlers flowed through Mormonism. In Smith's ideal of restoring the true form of the Christian church; in his strict division between saints and outsiders; in his determination to build a literal New Jerusalem as a refuge for the gathering of the saints in the Last Days; in his explicit millennial role for America; in the renewal of Eden; and in his growing realization that he must move to the remote wilderness to accomplish his mission; in all these he closely resembled the carpenter of Woburn, Edward Johnson.[23]

Smith's vision, like Johnson's, reflected the religious needs and imagination of the common people of New England and is a window on their attitudes toward nature. Early Mormonism appealed to the lost, the poor, and the economically and religiously dispossessed, and promised a kingdom of God wherein the first would be last and the last would be first. This religion of practical Yankee farmers and artisans regarded nature with an unsentimental, empirical eye. Like Johnson, Smith had a practical and transformative perspective on nature, not contemplative and passive. Mormonism's activist orientation included a nature ethic combining dominion and stewardship. In contrast to the Bible's ambiguity, the Book of Mormon explicitly stated that God created the world for mankind to replenish and use. It quite strongly reaffirmed that his power and providence influenced natural events. This emphasis on the action of God through nature and of saints on nature obstructed the sentimentalization of nature (and ignored Mormon references to "mother earth").[24]

Smith's attitude toward wilderness also recalled Johnson's in many ways. Wilderness formed a refuge for God's people, the Saints. It harbored the Devil's disciples, the Indians (now called "Lamanites"), whom the Saints must work to redeem. Wilderness was an adversary which must be tamed to build the City of Zion and restore paradise in anticipation of the millennium. Smith also shared Johnson's fondness for the vineyard and shepherd metaphors, strengthened with the affirmation of the Jeffersonian republican tradition of the yeoman farmer. When the Mormons arrived in Utah, the religious ethic prepared for them by their ancestors had well prepared them to "make the solitary places to bud and to blossom, and to bring forth in abundance," and they transformed the land, people, and ecology of Utah.[25]

The extremely idiosyncratic faith which inspired this work came from the mind and imagination of Joseph Smith. Born in Vermont to a family of hard-luck farmers, Smith grew up amidst wide religious diversity.[26] His paternal and maternal grandfathers were a Universalist and a Deist. Both his parents were seekers of religious truth. His father remained aloof from organized religion but had a number of religious visions and dreams. His mother, though, yearned for a church. The family moved to the "burnt-over district" of New York, and during one of the area's frequent revivals she joined the Calvinist Presbyterian church. These early influences— Universalism, Deism, Calvinism, and visions—colored one or another aspect of Mormonism.

Doubts about denominations, religion, and even the existence of God disturbed Smith as a teenager. He brought himself back to faith through Bible readings and the usual evidences of God in nature. As he recalled later,

> For I learned in the scriptures that God was the same yesterday, to day, and forever. That he was no respecter to persons, for he was God. For I looked upon the sun, the glorious luminary of the earth. And also the moon rolling in their magesty through the heavens. Also the stars, shining in their courses. And the earth also upon which I stood. And the beast of the field and the fowls of heaven and the fish of the waters. And also man walking forth upon the face of the earth in magesty and in the strength of beauty whose power and intiligence in governing the things which are so exceding great and marvilous even in the likeness of him who created them.
>   . . . My heart exclaimed, "All these bear testimony and bespeak an omnipotent and omnipreasant power. A being who makith Laws and decreeeth and bindeth all things in their bounds."[27]

Sometime in his mid-teens, in a troubled state of mind, he went in Puritan style to a cleared spot in the woods to meditate alone. In a vision reminiscent of Edwards's, God and Jesus appeared to him in a shaft of light and told him to join no church, for they were all false. The era's fervent revivalism was making visions practically commonplace, but Smith's attracted public ridicule, so he kept it to himself and his family.[28]

Quite uncommon, however, were the yearly visits, from 1823 to 1827, of the angel Moroni, who assured Smith of salvation and gave him a mission. Moroni told him of golden plates upon which the history of Jews in ancient America was inscribed and which were buried nearby with special seer stones. (Smith was locally known for his use of seer stones to find treasure.) He also informed Smith that the last days were approaching and that he must prepare for Christ's return. In 1830 Smith had five thousand copies of his translation of the plates printed as the Book of Mormon and organized the church that became the Church of Jesus Christ of Latter-day Saints.

The purported history of lost Jewish tribes, the Book of Mormon relocated sacred Christian history in the wilderness of America. After departure from Jerusalem for America around 600 B.C., the Jews divided into two factions, the evil Lamanites and the righteous Nephites. Christ appeared in America following his resurrection and taught the Lamanites and Nephites. Obedient to his instruction, the American Jews lived for a time in peace and harmony. Then the Lamanites abandoned religion and agriculture, lived as hunters, and, cursed by God with dark skin, became the ancestors of present-day American Indians. Soon so effete and irreligious that they could not resist the onslaught of the Lamanites, the Nephites died out in A.D. 421.

Over the years, a number of further revelations and divinely inspired documents supplemented the Book of Mormon and partly revised and partly added radically new elements to the Christian tradition. Smith located the Garden of Eden in the New World, again giving America a role in sacred history. The Fall had been necessary in order to bring man's agency, that is, his freedom to do good or evil, into the world, and in a scene comparable to Milton, Satan and his allies had been cast out of heaven for arguing against human agency. Adam and Eve lived after their expulsion in the land of Adam-ondi-Ahman, a green and gently rolling place in present-day Daviess County, Missouri. In a remnant of seventeenth-century theory preserved in the amber of popular culture, Smith described earth before the Fall as green and rolling, with no mountains or valleys, a single undivided continent surrounded by water. The division of the continents, the creation of climatic zones, and the appearance of mountains occurred at the expulsion from the Garden or at the time of Christ's crucifixion. The present landscape is a fallen landscape. The Saints' mission was to redeem the fallen earth and recreate Eden. Smith looked forward to the day in the Second Coming when "the earth will be renewed and receive its paradisiacal glory," "looking forth . . . for the valleys to be exalted, and for the mountains to be made low, and for the rough places to become smooth — all this when the angel shall sound his trumpet."[29]

Implicitly compensating his lower-class Saints with exaltation in the next world above the people who had power over them in this one, Smith envisioned a vivid, elaborate other world that in effect dramatically accentuated the dualism of nature and spirit. In stark contrast to Emerson's nature mysticism, concentration on the spirit world devalued nature, leaving it little more than inert matter. In a curious twist, Mormon dualism insisted that all things were material, even the persons of the Trinity, who were three distinct Gods, although of one purpose, mind, and glory.[30]

Co-eternal with matter and other "intelligences," God created the world, not from nothing, but from operation upon inchoate matter. God had not authored natural laws but rather learned to understand and control them, including the natural laws, presently unknown to humans, governing miracles. God was not immutable, but evolved: what God had been, men now were; what God was, men could become. In what Smith termed their "exaltation," humans advanced to become gods in the afterlife. Smith posited an infinity of worlds inhabited by "intelligences" more advanced than humans. God himself resided with the angels "on a globe like a sea of glass and fire" near the star "Kolob."[31]

With three levels of heaven and a hell for the enemies of God, Mormon doctrine envisioned the most complex afterlife since Dante. Because the Christian church had apostatized in its first century, Mormon baptism of the dead gave a second chance to Christian souls from this millennium-and-a-half of apostasy to accept the true church. Life in heaven resembled life on earth, including wives and children. God himself had wives to help him create spirit children to people the earth. Because without embodiment these spirit children could not advance toward exaltation, siring a large family of earthly children not only replenished the earth but was a good deed which earned the parent reward in heaven (and justified plural marriage). Non-believers and the childless would be mere servant angels in heaven. Because physical form is a necessary stage to exaltation, the devil and his cohorts try to possess people or animals, an explanation for the Biblical casting out of demons.[32]

In this world, the Saints had much more to do than simply replenish the earth. They must subdue and transform it, for they expected the Kingdom of God at any time. The imminence of the millennium required Mormonism to be a total religion, involving every aspect of life — religious, social, economic, and political — a revival of the Puritan Bible Commonwealth. Smith's vision of the millennium concentrated on gathering the Jews and Saints (who were technically adopted Jews) out of "Babylon" and into a literal Zion where they would find refuge and safety until the time Christ returned and the earth would be renewed.[33]

The ordeal of coming out of Babylon, enduring many trials, establishing the New Jerusalem in the American wilderness, and redeeming the earth recapitulated the Puritan experience of persecution, separation and removal, ordeal, and building. As failure and persecution drove the Mormons from a succession of New Zions—from New York to Ohio, from Ohio to Missouri, from Missouri to Illinois, where Smith was murdered in 1844—they understood at last that their only solution was removal to the remote and isolated wilderness of Utah's Great Basin. Only this isolation enabled the Mormons to create their political, economic, and religious kingdom of God on earth. Like the Puritans, they finally could find peace only by leaving their neighbors far behind and settling in a distant wilderness, a place of no history where all seemed possible.[34]

The Mormons, like their New England ancestors but without typological theory, saw themselves living anew the Exodus flight from Egypt. The Mormon Moses, Brigham Young, their leader after Smith's death, led his people across the Mississippi without getting wet (it froze just prior to their departure), just as the Hebrews had crossed the Red Sea. Small providences like the miracle of the quail and "manna" provided for the "Camp of Israel" as it crossed the wilderness and arrived in the Promised Land.

With a more effective union of church and state than the Puritans had had, the Mormons redeemed the earth in ways that Johnson and Winthrop would have recognized. As in Massachusetts, the church began the orderly planting of New England–style villages across the land, each with meeting house, village, fields, and commons. Certain Puritan doctrines received heightened emphasis in Utah. Stewardship was a central tenet, which, under the firm hand of church direction, resulted in such policies as central control and conservation of water, timber, and minerals. The Mormon goal of total separation from Babylon for a self-sufficient Kingdom reinforced frugality and industry. The need to speed preparation for Christ's return further spurred the Protestant work ethic. (Still today, Utah's nickname is the "Beehive State," and its motto is "Industry.") Even in heaven everyone was busy getting ready for that great day. The Puritan Baxter had promised the saints everlasting rest, but Mormons had no rest in this life or the next.[35]

That the Mormons moved to a desert disdained by Spaniards, Mexicans, Americans, and most Indians brought them far greater afflictions than the Puritans ever endured. Unreliable rainfall (from drought to destructive floods), occasional severe killing winters, late frosts, and devastating grasshopper and cricket plagues struck them, not to mention Indian wars and federal invasions. Yet each test, seen as God's punishment, strengthened faith and discipline, and remarkably few Mormons left, and remarkably many immigrants continued to arrive.[36]

The Mormons did not, like Edward Johnson, rejoice to see their Kingdom "turn a mart." Nevertheless, whereas they did not at first develop an export economy, they cheerfully took profits from outsiders within range, selling to the Forty-Niners and working on railroads and in mines, which brought in enough capital to save their Kingdom from economic collapse. Their insularity and resistance to inclusion in a market economy delayed the exploitation of their rich mineral resources and their transformation into a colony of the East, postponing environmental effects.

With their exceptionally singular religious beliefs, Mormons maintained a far greater unity, coherence, homogeneity, and unified purpose than had the Puritans. Reacting against the power of the religious hierarchy of the Anglican Church, the decentralized Puritan congregations could not restrain centrifugal social and economic forces. Mormons reacted instead against a chaotic religious scene and created a centralized authority in the Mormon church which acted as a centripetal force, which for decades cemented the Kingdom together. A strong Mormon doctrine of economic equality and cooperation made irrigated desert farming possible, and conversely, living in a desert strengthened the community because cooperation was necessary. Few left to join the California Gold Rush, although many worked in the new mines of Nevada and Colorado in the 1860s. Like the Puritans, Mormons could take pride in the orderly erection of a commonwealth that contrasted with the disorderly development and greater colonial dependency of surrounding regions.[37]

The Puritan commonwealth and the Mormon Kingdom followed similar paths of decline, with the result that the wider market economy had a growing environmental impact. Both Zions lasted in their purest forms for about a generation. In both cases, the dream and the community began to fray and fragment during the second generation. Johnson decried the movement away from the towns into the "backside of the wilderness" and the rise of merchant influence at cross purposes with the religious vision. In Utah, there were no mining, river, or railroad towns for twenty years. But mines appeared, in the 1860s outside the borders (the Puritan "Hedge") of the Kingdom, and later, within them, drawing Mormon workers. The railroad came in 1867, bringing an end to isolation and the beginnings of "Gentile" invasion and economic control of the colonial type. The Homestead Act drew the fast-growing Mormon population out of their New England–style villages, settled them along section lines in "string settlements," and, in the long term, encouraged speculation, commercial farming, and ranching.[38] Both Puritan and Mormon finally yielded their dreams to the forceful imposition of control by a distant, hostile, secular central government.

Settled in harsher country than the Puritans, the Mormons overburdened the land in spite of their efforts at stewardship. Those who settled in the more fragile mountain canyons ultimately left them scarred and eroded. Overgrazing of the originally grassy floor of the valley left it permanently covered in sage and weeds. Elsewhere, overgrazing wreaked havoc on irrigation systems and dams, as erosion silted up ponds and channels. The celebrated success of Mormon irrigation should not overshadow the impact of a large population on an arid country.[39]

In spite of that, Mormons did believe that if God gave the earth to the care of humans, they must use it wisely.[40] Particularly in the first generation, Mormons pursued not exploitation of nature for profit, but rather irrigation and environmental modification for sustained use. The Mormon church today teaches an environmentalist ethic based upon the premise that God gave the world to our care and humans must use it wisely. Mormon history demonstrates that a utilitarian nature ethic — dominion over disenchanted nature — which has in some hands justified environmental exploitation has in others left a heritage of conservation. Indeed, in their centralized control over development, their protection of watersheds, and their cooperative irrigation districts, Mormons blazed the trail that the nationwide Progressive conservation movement would follow half a century later.

God's Chosen People in Paradise: William Gilpin

Most Americans did not, like Emerson, wander through the woods listening to what the pine tree sayeth, nor did they, like Mormons, join in communal efforts to transform man and nature for the millennium. Especially in the North, Americans gloried in the expansive, commercial mood that dominated their nation between the War of 1812 and the Civil War. Settlers moving West, traders setting up shop in new towns, businessmen building banks and railroads, merchants sending their ships to China, all saw themselves as part of a great historical moment ordained by Almighty God. White Americans had a divine mission to fulfill. They called this task of continental conquest "Manifest Destiny."[41]

Manifest Destiny was a new form for an old idea of American mission. To Puritans, America was a city upon a hill, an example for the peoples of the Old World. The revolutionaries of Jefferson's time, watching the lights of liberty winking out all over the world, felt a sacred duty to keep the fire of liberty aglow in America as a beacon to the oppressed of the earth. By the 1840s, the experience of half a century of an advancing frontier, of adding new stars to the flag, and of regular saltatory extensions of the national boundary had again refashioned Americans' understanding of their mission.

America's divinely foreordained destiny, said the advocates of Manifest Destiny, lay in spreading the empire of freedom and democracy by admitting self-governing neighboring states to the protection of the Union. No one knew the limit of growth; it might be the Pacific, or Darien, or, as even Jefferson had once predicted, Tierra del Fuego. Rapidly advancing technology like railroads and telegraphs kept expanding the bounds of possible expansion. Devotees of Manifest Destiny were mainly young Jacksonian Democrats living in the North or border states. Their impatience with the pace of expansion increased roughly with proximity to the frontier. One of the great visionaries of Manifest Destiny was the soldier, explorer, politician, and tireless promoter of the West, William Gilpin.[42]

Born in 1813 or 1815 into a wealthy, cultured, and well-connected family of Pennsylvania-Delaware Quakers, Gilpin's imagination went West before he did. Gilpin descended from one of Cromwell's officers who turned Quaker and joined William Penn's experiment in Pennsylvania. His grandfather Thomas was a friend of Franklin and member of the American Philosophical Society; his father Joshua a canal-builder, paper-mill founder, poet and writer; his uncle Thomas an inventor, scientist, and mechanic; and his brother Henry a prominent and active Jacksonian, editor of Madison's papers, host to Alexis de Toqueville, magazine editor, member of the American Philosophical Society, and associate in various capacities with many educational and cultural institutions. William's family connections not only stood him in good stead on several occasions, but resembled the cultured trans-Atlantic background of the best-known prophet of Manifest Destiny, John L. O'Sullivan.[43]

Restless and somewhat indulged as a child, Gilpin matured into a restless and, certainly for a Quaker, rather self-indulgent adulthood as a slave-owning military man.[44] West Point had proved boring, and he quickly got out of it the way he got in — with his father's government connections. When the Second Seminole War erupted in 1836, he hastened to join up. Gilpin saw a little action and a lot of the United States, spending eighteen months recruiting through Missouri and Kentucky. When his episodic military career picked up again during the Mexican War, he saw action against Indians and in the battles of El Brazito and Sacramento. After the war, he organized and led volunteers to subdue Indians harassing traffic along the Santa Fe Trail. His last military glory was as Civil War governor of Colorado, when he organized the Colorado volunteers who turned back the Confederate invasion of New Mexico.

Drawn to St. Louis between wars, Gilpin gave strong support to the Democratic Party and expansionist Senator Thomas Hart Benton. In 1839 his political involvement won him editorship of the St. Louis Democratic newspaper and a vehicle for his Western boosterism. Using information gleaned from friendships with such mountain men as William Ashley and William Sublette, he publicized Oregon. In 1841 Gilpin moved to Independence, Missouri, the terminus of both the Oregon and Santa Fe Trails, to be close to the migrations West. There, he met most of the great frontier figures — Kit Carson, the Bents, the Sublettes, Captain John C. Frémont, and Marcus Whitman. He joined Frémont's 1843 expedition to Oregon and, before returning to Missouri, helped in the effort of American settlers there to organize a provisional state government.

In the decade before the Civil War, as Benton and his Jacksonian allies went down in defeat to the rising faction of pro-slavery Democrats, Gilpin's political activity waned for a time. He came back to politics to work for the Republican Party after 1859 and against secession in 1861. His political friendships won him appointment as governor of Colorado Territory for a short and controversial tenure. Gregarious, garrulous, nervous, and visionary, he was not well fitted temperamentally for the job. Gilpin stayed in Denver and after the war returned to boosting the West and railroads. A string of failures in land speculation ended with spectacular success in Colorado's San Luis Valley, and he lived out his life a wealthy man — although, with his late and stormy marriage, not a contented one.

Gilpin's fame rested on his visionary promotion of the West. Seeing the West and the frontier for the first time as a recruiter in 1836 changed his life. Already letters home at the time outlined many of his lifelong interests: the beauty of the scenery, the land's potential for growth and development, and the temptations of land speculation (for which he always seemed to have too little capital — and the wrong instincts).[45] As a newspaper editor and especially after his Oregon journey, he tirelessly took his message to the public, becoming a major spokesman for Manifest Destiny. Insisting on American possession of all of Oregon up to 54°40′, he presented his case in Washington to President James K. Polk, the secretary of state, and both Missouri senators, and wrote statistic-laden statements to be read in both houses of Congress. His grand strategy was to set up the United States as a channel of trade between Europe and Asia. Beyond these commercial considerations, Gilpin grandiosely proclaimed the continental destiny of the American people.

Gilpin became a constant champion of western development, transcontinental railroads, and Rocky Mountain gold. He denied the negative name, "Great American Desert," for the prairie west of Missouri, and popularized instead the benign-sounding "Great Plains." He recognized the site of Kansas City as the location of a future great city. His promotion of the gold potential of Colorado won him respect as a sort of seer after its discovery in the 1850s. His 1860 book of geopolitics, *The Central Gold Region*, had a wide impact. Slightly rearranged, and with additional speeches and tracts re-printed in the appendix, it reappeared in 1874 more accurately entitled *Mission of the North American People, Geographical, Social, and Political*.

Although divine intent played a central role in his vision of Manifest Destiny, Gilpin never explicitly revealed his religious beliefs, which appar-ently paralleled those of such secularized thinkers as Jefferson. He had grown up in a rather relaxed religious atmosphere. His father, Joshua, was a strong enough Quaker to marry a Quaker, and to complain about the poor example older brother Henry's non-Quaker lifestyle made for William, yet he freely used his connections to get his son into West Point and the army.

In his attitude toward nature, Gilpin, like his father, mixed the Romantic sensibility of his day with practical good sense. His prose frequently re-peated such phrases as "sublime" (a term which for Romantics implied the spiritually uplifting effect of beautiful and awesome landscape) and "ro-mantic beauty," both of which terms popped up even in the most utilitarian passages. Gilpin claimed, for example, that the Rockies possessed "precious and base metals, precious stones, coal, marbles, earth, thermal and medici-nal streams and fountains; and all of these adorned by scenery forever varying, fascinating, and sublime."[46]

This combination of sublimity and bounty gave Gilpin a pronounced predilection to imagine the West as a paradise or Eden of unending abun-dance and fertility. In the Rockies, he effused,

> indigenous grasses, fruits, and vegetables abound; it swarms with ani-mal life and aboriginal cattle; food of grazing and carnivorous animals, fowls and fish, are everywhere found; the forests and flora are superla-tive; the immense dimensions of nature render accessibility universal. An atmosphere of intense brilliancy and tonic tone overflows and em-balms all nature; health and longevity are the lot of man.[47]

Within the Rockies lay a series of small mountain-bounded basins he called "parcs" — "the paradise of the aboriginal herds, with which they swarm at all seasons, and are the favorite retreat of the Indians." Just as Edenic, Gilpin insisted, were the Great Plains. Far from being "a great North

American desert," the plains were "the PASTORAL GARDEN of the world," "supremely, indeed, the most magnificent dwelling-place marked out by God for man's abode."[48] In both parcs and plains, the weather, in a favorite Gilpinism, was perpetually "vernal."

This western paradise, a place of plenitude, purity, and perfect health, lay waiting for the fulfillment of America's predestined greatness. God when he designed the earth plainly indicated America's future. The West was replete with signs of the "sublime order of Creation" and "the supreme engineering of God." (In the Bible, God was a potter, in Greek philosophy an artisan, in the Enlightenment an architect or mason, but in Gilpin's machine-age metaphor, God was an engineer.) This "supreme engineering of the Creator" manifested itself in the very structure of the continent: a great bowl (the Mississippi valley) bounded east and west by mountain ranges and maritime coasts, like ears on a head. Everywhere Gilpin turned, he saw "the sublime order and symmetry" that pervaded the American landscape. Manifest Destiny was foreordained by the shape of North America and the unbounded fertility of its "calcareous plains."[49]

Gilpin did not search the Bible for keys to America's destined role; he rested his predictions on what he believed to be the firm bedrock of science, especially the work of German geographer Alexander von Humboldt. From Humboldt's concepts Gilpin devised a worldwide system to explain how Manifest Destiny followed the design of God (or "Nature" — like Jefferson, Gilpin used the two words interchangeably). A line of equal average temperature called the "isothermal axis" circled the globe. This axis passed through China, India, the Middle East, the Mediterranean, France, and across the American continent via Boston, New York, St. Louis and Denver, and back to the Pacific at the Oregon coast.

For 30° to 35° on either side of this axis was a belt, the "isothermal zone," the key to God's design of the earth and America's divine destiny. For millennia, the great empires of the past had arisen and declined in this zone in a sun-following sequence, beginning with China and passing through India, Mesopotamia, Rome, and western Europe. Next in line was North America, whose "auspicious architecture" gave it its great historical advantage: it was so situated that it could contain the entire isothermal band from north to south, and thus would produce the first perfect civilization. This westward tendency of civilization "has reached the Plateau of America, up which it will ascend to plant the sacred fires over its expanse and shine upon the world with renewed effulgence."[50] Bright with the sacred fires of liberty, a city on a hill cannot be hid.

Gilpin did not trust to theology or philosophy to reveal destiny to mankind. His faith was Baconian: science was the key that would unlock the mysteries of the universe. Because it could "penetrate the deep designs of Providence," science brought man into harmony with God and Nature and lifted him out of barbarism. "Science . . . reveals to the world this shining fact, that along [the isothermal axis] civilization has traveled, as by an inevitable instinct of nature, since creation's dawn."[51] On this new, perfectly designed continent, the progress of civilization would culminate in the American nation.

> The American realizes that "Progress is God." He clearly recognizes and accepts the *continental* mission of his country and his people. His faith is impregnably fortified by this vision of power, unity, and forward motion. . . . Rescued from the quicksands of the past, *democratic-republican power*, rightly understanding itself, has here set and perpetuated in the world its own indestructible foundations.[52]

Gilpin, along with his fellow Democrat, Benton, never tired of excoriating the Old World, especially Britain, whose empire rested on base motives and tended to make the least useful employment of conquered lands, that is, exploiting them colonially rather than making them available to the virtuous land-hungry farmer. Like Jefferson, Gilpin gloried in the pastlessness of the New World that freed Americans from the encumbrances of history so they could see divine purposes clearly. ". . . *American* society is fresh, pliant, and ductile," he proclaimed. "It commences its career upon a foundation of truths, discovered and accepted from nature."[53]

The democratic American people were peculiarly suited to carry out God's plan. The wild, untamed continent, said this veteran of many wars, had to be conquered for civilization, and Americans' strength, discipline, freedom, rectitude, and wisdom "invest them with a supreme conquering power." Universal male suffrage, literacy, Christianity, access to resources, and unified language, all of them "stupendous forces of civilization," brought "peace and progress." "The pioneer people . . . occupied the foreground of progress, and clear open the track of empire." "Pushed onward by the hand of God," this

> grand pioneer army . . . advances with miraculous celerity, order, and self-discipline. Incredible conquests are achieved. In number, two millions strong, self-governed, self-fed, self-armed, self-commanded, it plants empire in the wilderness by a system of colonization at once perfect and inscrutable.[54]

No Eden in these passages, the wilderness was an enemy of civilization to be vanquished. Each family was a platoon, making a farm "on the outer edge of the settlements." "As individuals fall out from the front rank, or fix themselves permanently, others rush from behind, press to the front, and assail the wilderness in their turn." Thus, a "tidal wave of population" defeats "the glebe, the savages, and the wild beasts of the wilderness, scaling mountains and debouching down upon the seaboard.[55]

Gilpin believed that American divine destiny would not be fulfilled by whites alone. The continent would see a meeting and mixing of the great cultures of the world — (white) American, Mexican, and Oriental. Moving in from a different direction, each would provide its best aspects and give rise to a republican millennium, "a new and grand order in human affairs."

> The civilized masses of the world meet — they mutually explain and understand one another — they are mutually enlightened, and fraternize to reconstitute human relations and institutions in harmony with nature and with God.

This conception of the West as a meeting and blending of civilizations tempered the racism of Gilpin's frequent references to the white races and to Anglo-Saxons. Nevertheless, Indians and blacks did not fit into his scheme. He either treated them as an obstacle to be removed, or as if they were virtually invisible. Hence he could remark on "an uninhabited, Indian country" when it could hardly be both.[56]

Although Gilpin frequently emphasized the pastoral rather than agricultural character of the civilization to be erected on the Great Plains and the Great Basin, in his millennial vision *"the People occupied in the wilderness"* would bring forth "the *industrial* conquest of the world." They would accomplish this through railroads, industrial organization, and the liberal minting of gold coin from the inexhaustible reserves contained in the mountains of the American West. *"Machine forces* emanate from *free* intellect. . . . They unify and fuse mankind. . . . They exalt civilization. . . . They give lustre to the reinvigorated Labor and Industry of the world, with unlimited triumphs and conquests." They produce democracy, equality, peace, and abundance.

Gilpin's vision was not of great sooty cities or vast smokestack industries, but of small industry integrated with the rural economy, something of a virtuous, steam-powered Jeffersonian arcadia. "Rural intelligence and moderation resist successfully urban rapacity." "Room is discovered for industrial virtue and industrial power. . . . Labor and industry construct their own empire" under "the ameliorating graces of commerce." Commerce itself would have to be "rescued from the despotic monopoly" of Eastern cities, which were corrupted by contact with the senescent, enervated, and degenerate Old World.[57]

> Behold, then, rising now and in the future, the empire which industry and self-government create. The growth of half a century, hewed out of the wilderness — its weapons the axe and plow; its tactics, labor and energy; its soldiers, free and equal citizens.
>
> Behold the oracular goal to which our eagles march, and whither the phalanx of our States and people moves harmoniously on, to plant a *hundred States* and consummate their *civic* greatness.
>
> . . . It is *here* that the pre-eminently divine gifts, vouchsafed to the AMERICAN PEOPLE by God *through Nature*, speak out and enforce from every heart a pious prayer of thanksgiving.
>
> *Here* are united, in special magnitude, a variety of *new powers* and *fresh forces*. All of these combine to dictate, and are auspicious to, the structure of a political society of vast dimensions, upon the highest level attainable by energetic intelligence, — order and mental culture.[58]

America after 1860 did not live up to Manifest Destiny. Expansion stopped, the democratic republic descended into bloody civil war, and the growth of cities, industry, big business, and widespread political corruption ended Jeffersonian dreams of a virtuous agrarian republic. Four years before his death in 1894, Gilpin's last book, *Cosmopolitan Railway*, a scheme for a worldwide railroad network uniting all nations, transferred his utopian dreams to the possibility that railroads could bring the world together in peace and prosperity. (Not long after, E. H. Harriman briefly attempted to create just such a worldwide rail network under American control.)

Although Gilpin's pre-war vision echoed the Puritan and Mormon New Jerusalems, he symbolized a new chapter in the story of the American mission. Zion now stretched across a continent. The army of the "saints" included all frontiersmen and pioneers. The city on a hill proclaimed freedom and democratic-republicanism, not Christianity. Science, replacing the Bible or latter-day prophecy as the oracle of truth and harmony with God and nature, discovered nature's divinely ordained purpose. Industry and technology and not the church unified Gilpin's millennial society.

Gilpin took his secularized millennialism and brought it into the Jeffersonian temple of the yeoman farmer. To both Gilpin and Jefferson, close contact with the soil and with the natural world uplifted society. It preserved virtue, encouraged independence, protected liberty, and supported the democratic republic. For Gilpin as well as Jefferson, if the Indian obstinately and superstitiously refused to be reasonable and adopt the yeoman life, he must be removed from the path of progress.[59]

Perhaps as a consequence of his unexacting religious background, Gilpin took West no specific theology but rather a generalized American Protestant vocabulary which percolated through his often hyperbolic prose. He frequently mentioned God (or "Nature") with a very religious effect, yet his inspecificity excluded any real creed or reference to revelation. Unlike other popularizers of Manifest Destiny, Gilpin did not avail himself of the Biblical edict to subdue the earth and have dominion over it.[60] Nevertheless, in conversation, in speeches, in articles, pamphlets, and books, he urged his "ecstatic vision" (as Henry Nash Smith called it[61]) on his audience with the unfading earnestness of a prophet. Gilpin spoke for many whom the conquest of nature and a continent inspired, and the marks of his popularity remain visible today, from phrases in the poetry of Walt Whitman[62] to the places in the West that bear his name.

Gilpin's secularized Protestantism of God, abundance, expansion, science, industry, and mission fit perfectly the mind and mood of the times and indeed became part of the myth of America. Yet the myth's very popularity was a symptom of future problems. Gilpin premised nearly all his works upon the assumption that American resources were virtually inexhaustible. He believed that the Great Plains had the capacity to hold and support two billion people. This very popular notion of inexhaustibility—built upon the idea of America as a Cornucopia, a Garden, an Eden—constituted the main ingredient in a recipe for ecological disaster such as the Dust Bowl. The pioneer pursuit of the republic of dreams was dashing headlong on a collision course with the limits to expansion and abundance. Even in the early decades of the nineteenth century, many laments sounded the passing of wilderness and of the Indian tribes. The first to perceive the coming collision, in the second half of the century these lamentations progressed to jeremiads.[63]

SIX

Steam and Steel
and Christian Civilization

It is the unrolling of a new map; a revelation of a new empire, the creation of a new civilization.

— ENGLISHMAN SAMUEL BOWLES, AFTER
A RAIL TRIP TO SAN FRANCISCO AND BACK (1870)

What we want is the best possible line, shortest distance, lowest grades and least curvature that we can build. We do not care enough for Rocky Mountain scenery to spend a large sum of money developing it.

—JAMES J. HILL (1890)

In the early and mid-nineteenth century Gilpin and many others declared America's war against the wilderness. But America's "pioneer army" could not continue the battle without advances in technology and transportation to tie them to the developing capitalist economy. An extraordinary generation of Yankee entrepreneurs commanded the assault that brought ultimate victory. Born in the decade beginning around 1815, these men were cradled in the ethic of their Puritan ancestors and raised on a staple diet of Mission and Progress. These restless and energetic sons of New England realized the dream of a continental republic bound together with bands of steel. They threw railroads across the nation, improvising organizations and technology as they went, and built great concerns that by century's end out-produced any other nation, and in some industries any two other nations.

The middle and late nineteenth century was an exciting and inspiring new era of great fortunes made and lost, and made again. America transformed into an industrial giant and the world's breadbasket. Remarkable new inventions revolutionized daily life. At the same time, these years witnessed the defeat of the last free Indians, the disappearance of the buffalo and passenger pigeon, and a conquest of forests and mountains so thorough that ecological ruin threatened from Vermont to California.[1]

This was the age when the Protestant ethic produced many of its most illustrious sons, all bursting with energy, ambition, and the restless urge "to *do* things."[2] Most of America's industrial leaders were of New England or Yankee stock, or from a Calvinist culture — men like Oakes Ames and Charles Francis Adams of the Union Pacific (New England), the "Big Four" of the Central Pacific and Southern Pacific (Yankee), the Vanderbilts of the New York Central (Dutch), James J. Hill of the Great Northern (Scots-Irish), or Andrew Carnegie of the Pennsylvania (Scottish). Industrial leaders of New England extraction or European Calvinist or Pietist heritage disproportionately outnumbered Southerners and Catholics in all major extractive and industrial enterprises. In one study of sixty-one nineteenth-century railroad presidents, thirty were born in New England outright, and a good portion of the rest were only a generation or two removed from New England birth. Northern Pacific President Frederick Billings had so many New Englanders on his board of directors that he was charged with colluding to keep Southerners out. Research from the Harvard Research Center in Entrepreneurial History indicated that this profile accurately portrayed contemporary capitalists in general. These industrial leaders had many common traits and similar backgrounds (often middle class, and rarely agricultural) and disproportionately received high school or college education when both were comparatively uncommon. Imbued with the middle-class mentality of the small shopkeeper and the outlook of a Benjamin Franklin, sober, diligent, thrifty, and talented, they strode out from their Yankee homelands, vanquished the wilderness, and built an industrial power.[3]

But there was more to the lives of these men than just business. This Yankee heritage included varying combinations of religious duty, social conscience, moralism, and even Transcendentalism. Those who called them "robber barons" derided them for always putting personal ambition and greed above the public interest. In their own minds, these "captains of industry" pursued the public interest, which corresponded nicely with private interest. Railroads spread light into a benighted world. They were the avenues by which civilization — Western, Christian civilization — rolled back the forces of barbarism. This mixture of public and private interest brought them not only to invest in the local economies along their tracks, but to fund or support churches, schools, seminaries, Y.M.C.A.'s, and national parks and forests as well.[4]

Hence, a similar background produced not a single type, but a variety of types ranging from the Protestant ethic workaholic to the agent for moral uplift. The lives and careers of the builders of the first transcontinental railroads, Theodore Dehone Judah, Charles Crocker, Collis Potter Huntington, Mark Hopkins, and Leland Stanford of the Central Pacific and Southern Pacific, James J. Hill of the Great Northern, and Jay Cooke and Frederick Billings of the Northern Pacific, clearly illustrate the varied impact of the Calvinist heritage on nature. The railroads these men built very aptly symbolize capitalism's impact on nature in the nineteenth century for several reasons. First, as America's first really large-scale, national enterprises, they pioneered forms of incorporation and corporate organization. Second, they stitched a large country together, bringing raw materials to the factories and products to their markets, and making the American industrial revolution possible. Last, their modification of the landscape, their demand for raw and finished materials, and their opening of otherwise inaccessible wilderness to settlement accelerated the American impact on nature like no other industry.

The Protestant Work Ethic: Judah, Crocker, Huntington, Hopkins, and Hill

Theodore Dehone Judah was an engineer with a vision, a William Gilpin with a practical head on his shoulders. His determination and competence got the transcontinental railroad started long before it might have without him. Born in 1826 in Connecticut and raised in New York, son and son-in-law of churchmen, Judah studied engineering and worked all over New York and New England, quickly becoming one of the best-known railroad engineers of his day. His fame attracted an 1854 invitation to build the first railroad in California, between Sacramento and the Sierra foothill gold country. He leaped at the chance to be "the pioneer railroad engineer of the Pacific Coast!"[5]

Immediately, Judah conceived a purpose far grander than the first local California rail line: a transcontinental railroad. Throughout the 1850s he built local California lines while constantly promoting Pacific and transcontinental railroads. After an 1859 presentation to Congress failed to get money, he returned to California to finish his homework. He scouted out the best route over the Sierras, lined up local investors and began surveying the route. When secession removed congressional supporters of the southern route to the West and made the railroad a war measure, Judah won generous support legislation in 1862, supplemented in 1864 by an even more generous bill.

Judah began arguing with his West Coast backers, who wanted quick construction and profits rather than Judah's quality-built line. Judah was also alarmed at their financial legerdemain when they organized their own construction company and awarded liberal contracts to themselves. Determined to link himself with more responsible investors, Judah went east once again in 1863, hoping to interest the Vanderbilt group. But he contracted yellow fever in Panama and died a week after his arrival in New York City. Sadly, he never saw how his ambition, drive, ability, and salesmanship had found the route, investors, and congressional funding that finally realized the dream of railroads to a transcontinental empire.

Freed from their troublesome chief engineer, the directors continued to build the Central Pacific into the Sierras. Dominating the board were a group of men soon known as the "Big Four": Charles Crocker, Collis Potter Huntington, Mark Hopkins, and Leland Stanford. Unable to sell his plan to San Francisco capitalists, who profited well enough from existing transportation arrangements, Judah had found investors in a successful group of Sacramento merchants, who at the time responded less to the dream of a transcontinental system than to the immediate goal of a transportation monopoly to new silver mines of Nevada. In personality and aptitude they formed a stable (if not always harmonious), complementary set. Moreover, they formed a group portrait of the Protestant ethic as it appeared in the mid-nineteenth century.

Crocker and Huntington were the very embodiment of the work ethic. Born in 1822 in Troy, New York, and raised in Indiana, Crocker from boyhood had the "habit of industry." He once stated, "I never had a nursery period. It was my habit to work day and night."[6] From age ten, he worked and earned and saved, and set up or bought and then sold a series of small businesses. A Forty Niner, he failed at prospecting but found success as partner in a dry goods store in Sacramento.

Politics first brought Crocker together with the rest of the Big Four, all founding members, in 1856, of the California Republican Party (which gave them a political advantage in later dealings with state and national government). When the Central Pacific formed, he oversaw construction, which he learned on the job. The lure of the Nevada silver boom kept decimating his construction crews, so he made the very unpopular decision to bring in Chinese workers, whom he found efficient, uncomplaining, and cheap. Crocker pushed the Central Pacific across the Sierras into Nevada, the most difficult section of the transcontinental line. Except for a short break after completion of the railroad, Crocker worked steadily for the company until his death in 1888.

Biographer Oscar Lewis called Huntington the "grim New Englander" of the group. Personal warmth and social or civic consciousness did not constitute notable parts of his personality. Two values dominated his philosophy: earning and saving money. In his business life, honesty, integrity, and honor all yielded to the demands of profit. Born in 1821 the son of a miserly Connecticut tinker, Huntington grew up believing thrift to be man's highest goal and throughout his life preached and practiced frugality. He later defined his formula for success as poverty + industry + thrift. Sober, chaste, and punctual, he demanded in his early days the same qualities in clerks in his Sacramento business.

Growing up, Huntington was always busy, earning money, investing, peddling, and buying and selling anything that promised a quick return. To Huntington the Gold Rush was a business opportunity. He packed up a cargo of merchandise and headed to California in 1849 by way of Panama. In Sacramento he made a very shrewd merchant, knowing when to buy, when to sell, and charging what the market would bear.

The needs of Central Pacific construction demanded Huntington's presence on the East Coast, which he preferred to California, whose mild climate he thought made men soft and lazy—no place for a man who dedicated his life to business. Despite California's lack of industry and the war's competition for industrial products, his tireless efforts kept supplies coming, money flowing, and Congress happy and generous. Huntington grew to be the most powerful and influential of the Big Four, as well as the most hated for his reputation for ruthlessness. The Central Pacific and the later umbrella organization, the Southern Pacific (which built a transcontinental line of its own), quite successfully cowed, bought, or destroyed potential competitors and achieved an effective monopoly of West Coast transportation which lasted until the election of Progressive Governor Hiram Johnson in 1910. The railroad bought off newspaper editors, politicians, the California legislature, and Congress. In the worst example of ruthlessness, the Mussel Slough incident, it enticed settlers to railroad land in the arid southern Central Valley and, after they had irrigated and improved their lands, violently evicted them as squatters and sold their land plus improvements at a good price.[7]

At Huntington's death in 1900, there was no great public outpouring of grief. Yet his tireless, dedicated work for the railroad had achieved California's not one, but two transcontinental connections, its efficient railroad system under one organization, and indeed a good measure of its prosperity.

As a Sacramento merchant, Huntington's partner Mark Hopkins gave his

firm the needed ballast of the Yankee virtues of steadiness, conscientious-
ness, efficiency, and hatred of waste. Born of New England parentage in
1815, Hopkins was always the quietest and least controversial of the Big
Four. Like Huntington and Crocker, he was wedded to work. Outside his
oversight of the railroad's books and its office, he lived extremely modestly,
considering his wealth. Until his death in 1878 he worked with few breaks
and little concern for his health.[8] Sharing Huntington's concern for the
Puritan virtues of thrift, sobriety, and diligence, Hopkins formed a sort of
alter ego to his aggressive wheeling-and-dealing partner.

These solid, hard-working, calculating captains of industry did not usually waste much time on thoughts that promised no pots of gold at their
end, but they were capable of seeing themselves as part of a larger picture.
As they flung their rail lines across "Indian wilderness," railroadmen hoped
to participate in, as well as profit from, progress and American mission.
Huntington's investments in railroads throughout the world, even if they
brought little or no return, gave him satisfaction that he was helping to
open up the country and promote civilization.[9] James J. Hill, president of
the Great Northern, the last and most solidly built transcontinental, proclaimed that "the History of Commerce, the History of Transportation and
the History of Civilization" followed parallel lines and proceeded from the
same starting place to the same goal, which was the spread of civilization
and Christianity "to the remotest parts of the world."[10]

To be fair, there is more to the story of these men. Most showed at least
some interest in nature and wilderness. Crocker loved being out-of-doors,
and along with Huntington and Stanford gave money toward such public
parks as Golden Gate Park in San Francisco and Lake Merritt Park in
Oakland.[11] Huntington fondly remembered a time during an inspection of
construction work when he had set off on horseback and spent a few nights
under the stars. His favorite modern artist was William Keith, the Scottish
painter of Sierra landscapes. Late in life he bought what became his preferred residence, a log palace called Pine Knott Lodge on Raquette Lake in
the Adirondacks. He even once reproved his stepson for shooting a bird.[12]
Nevertheless, their interest in nature prompted neither Crocker nor Huntington to develop any perceivable desire to preserve or conserve natural
resources.

Utilitarian concerns did turn some railroadmen to conservation. Hill, for
example, became the foremost business spokesman for conservation during
the Progressive Era. His road actively aided development of the Red River
valley, which the Great Northern served, such as funding wetlands drainage, giving low rates to immigrants and their farm equipment, making

available blooded stock and better seed, and pushing for diversification. Because the poor farming practices of the region would lead to declining yields hence result in lower profits, Hill became a convert to conservation. He gave speeches, sent out agents, and supported model farms to spread conservation methods. In his public pronouncements, Hill understood the wider perspective (without losing sight of the bottom line): "If we fail to consider what we possess of wealth available for the uses of mankind, and to what extent we are wasting a national patrimony that can never be restored, we might be likened to the directors of a company who never examine a balance sheet." Hill overoptimistically enticed thousands of immigrants to farms along his line on into Montana, unfortunately well beyond the limit of sustainable dry farming, where they found only dust and broken dreams.

A younger man, Hill (1838–1916) was of the generation of Jay Gould, John D. Rockefeller, John Muir, and John Burroughs. Although Hill firmly asserted the need for a Christian society, which translated into efforts to keep Americans on virtuous farms and out of corrupting cities, he did not necessarily mean that these values should apply to him personally. Despite his Scots-Irish extraction, Hill was not a very religious man and in fact married an Irish-Catholic. Yet the Calvinist ethic left its mark. A liberal philanthropist, he contributed to Protestant, Catholic, and non-religious causes. Like other railroad builders, Hill was a strong believer in an ethic of "work, hard work, intelligent work, and then some more work."[13]

The Protestant Philanthropy Ethic: Stanford, Cooke, and Billings

The last of the Central Pacific's Big Four, Leland Stanford, was of a different type. His Yankee background endowed him with the style and attitudes closer to those of such men as Jay Cooke and Frederick Billings, builders of the Northern Pacific. The alternate sort of Yankee personality they represented emerged from more comfortable childhood circumstances and revealed enduring interest in the common good in education, religion, and philanthropy. Each of these men took pride in his involvement in progress and the advancement of civilization, but had as well a strongly developed social conscience and awareness of public power and responsibility. Each exemplified the Andrew Carnegie "Gospel of Wealth" in action, the theory that the rich were but stewards of their wealth for the public benefit.

Stanford's early interest in education and religion contrasted with his partners' upbringing. Son of an innkeeper, he was born near Albany in 1824. A religious young man in search of education, he enrolled successively in a "manual work school" (part of a popular movement at the time in which students supplemented academic activity with three hours of daily work), a Universalist-run school, and then a Methodist prep school. Stanford's Unitarian-tinged beliefs kept him aloof from the religious revivals which swept the campus. Nevertheless, religious feeling stayed with him throughout his life. In later years Sunday-evening visitors to the Stanford mansion might be invited to join in singing hymns.

Stanford's contact with railroads began early, when he and his brothers cut timber from their father's land to fulfill a contract to supply fuel to a local line. Trained for the law, he went west to Wisconsin looking for his big chance and involved himself in Whig politics. In Sacramento not long after the Gold Rush began, he found the way to wealth in a prosperous grocery store and a lucky investment in a gold mine. Love of politics advanced him in the new Republican Party. His speeches always included a Manifest Destiny-tinged plea for a transcontinental railroad, part of a dream to link Europe and the Orient via the United States. Thus it was no accident that Stanford was a ready investor in Judah's scheme. Stanford's success in politics included two terms as governor in 1862 and 1863 and two as U.S. Senator (cut short by his 1893 death). Stanford's political involvement always helped the Central Pacific, and later the Southern Pacific, and his successful term during the crucial years of the Civil War helped his (and his railroad's) reputation and popularity in later years. He was rarely vilified like Huntington was.[14]

In his later years Stanford professed belief in the doctrines of Social Darwinism and laissez faire. The building of railroads would lead to universal betterment (which government regulation could only hinder). Railroads would unlock the earth's abundance for mankind's benefit.

> The Creator has not given man rational wants without the means of supplying them. He has given us an all-bountiful earth that yields inexhaustible supplies for our use. Men have only to apply their labor intelligently and learn to control the natural forces that surround them to have at their command all the comforts and elegancies of life.[15]

The railroad's influence upon "agriculture, commerce, manufacturers, wealth, and population" would commence "a new era in progress."[16]

Yet, earlier in his career, Stanford supported public and private action for the public benefit, which led him to propose California's earliest conservation laws. He viewed government lands as a valuable public resource. His inaugural gubernatorial address asked for the cession of federal forests to California for two reasons: to speed their development, and to provide revenue for education (a big Stanford concern), charitable works, and internal improvements. Worried about widespread depredation of public timber, he got through the legislature two laws restricting the cutting of timber, never an easy task in development-minded California.[17] Later, he supported the 1890 bill to make a national park of the Yosemite Valley watershed. Although Stanford was never a major influence or actor for conservation, nevertheless, his sense of duty to society prompted action in behalf of nature.

Jay Cooke descended from an old Massachusetts Puritan lineage. Constantly on the move at or near the frontier, his family finally settled in Sandusky in the solidly Yankee Western Reserve in Ohio. Flourishing wildlife there made an impression on the young Cooke, who later recalled the area as "the paradise of the Indians."[18] His father was a lawyer and Whig politician who shared with his son a lifelong devotion to temperance societies.[19] His mother took the family to Methodist services. Always quite religious, Cooke remained a regular churchgoer and Sunday-school teacher in Methodist or Low-Church Episcopal churches. His firm faith in the justice of God as well as his own rightness with God endowed him with perpetual optimism, energy, and dedication. While in charge of selling government bonds during the Civil War, for example, he felt God had chosen him and Lincoln to save the Union.

Religion had a clear effect on Cooke's career. The doctrine of stewardship influenced him early on, and like Carnegie he saw in wealth "the means whereby one can display his social and generous spirit."[20] Throughout his life he gave generously of his wealth, time, and interest, especially to a multitude of religious causes and purposes, but also to colleges, the Academy of Natural Sciences, and the Historical Society of Pennsylvania. In all personal dealings Cooke acted with scrupulous honesty and integrity. (Business dealings, however, were another matter.)[21]

The influence of his pioneer past inclined Cooke to push ahead with development of the wilderness and gave him the instinct to build. Cooke left school early to go to work as a clerk. A series of jobs, first in transportation and then in banking, culminated in the formation of Jay Cooke and Company in 1861, in which he won fortune and fame selling government war bonds. After the war, he speculated in agricultural, lumber, and water-power sites in the upper Missouri and Mississippi area. Visits to these sites reminded him of frontier Sandusky and interested him in building railroads there as the path to development.

Cooke took control of the Northern Pacific Railroad in 1870. Founded and run by New Englanders (mostly Vermonters), the Northern Pacific was to cross the continent from Duluth to the Columbia River but had not made much progress in the time since Congress passed the necessary support legislation in 1864. Under Cooke, construction made great headway. Unfortunately, Cooke's ability to promote Northern Pacific bonds outstripped the line's ability to pay them off, forcing Jay Cooke and Co. to close its doors in 1873 and precipitating a catastrophic national financial panic. Cooke lost control of the line, but in the late 1870s began to recoup his fortune. In 1890 he finally rode the Northern Pacific to Tacoma for the first time, and remarked with satisfaction on his part in its construction:

> My sensations as day after day I passed over this road and through this wonderful country, now so rapidly developing and which now contains six millions of people, where only twenty years ago the Indian and buffalo held full sway, were such as few have ever experienced. It was in a measure the fulfillment of prophecies which I uttered long ago. I felt that I was justified, and those who were so full of doubts long ago now gladly acknowledge that I was right.[22]

Cooke was something of a Jay Gould with a conscience. Both men knew finance, but neither knew much about running good railroads. Cooke got the faltering Northern Pacific moving long enough to enroll his name among those who led the conquest of the wilderness. Yet after the Northern Pacific's fall in 1873 it was up to other men to put it back together again.

Cooke did much more than open the West to settlement; he was present at the creation of the world's first national park, Yellowstone. Along with Northern Pacific public relations man A. R. Nettleton, Cooke jumped at the idea of a national park encompassing the geyser basins around the headwaters of the Yellowstone, a natural tourist magnet near his route in sparsely populated wilderness. The Northern Pacific gave financial support to the Hayden expedition to Yellowstone in 1870, accompanied (at Nettleton's suggestion and with money loaned by Cooke) by artist Thomas Moran. The expedition's report and Moran's paintings, combined with the Northern Pacific's political muscle in Congress, quickly got the bill passed which created Yellowstone National Park in 1872. Promoting itself as the "Yellowstone Park Line," the Northern Pacific was profitably involved in tourism at the park through the middle of this century. In 1899 the Northern Pacific was responsible for the creation of Mt. Rainier National Park as well.[23] Cooke pioneered the idea that corporate self-interest and government preservation of nature for the public benefit could be linked, with profit to both.

Surely the least known of this group of giants, though perhaps the most remarkable, was Frederick Billings, born in 1823 to an orderly and dour Vermont storekeeper. Religion and education were the guiding lights of his youth. Raised in the Baptist Church, he attended an academy which trained young men for leadership in the ministry and whose teachings reinforced his belief in hard work for its own sake. He studied at the University of Vermont, whose former president, the Transcendentalist James Marsh, continued as a stimulating member of the faculty. Billings acquired a good education, a tinge of Transcendentalism, and a strong commitment to temperance. To supplement his income, he taught Sunday school and occasionally filled in for absent preachers. Unlike Stanford, who held aloof from revivalism, Billings interested himself in evangelism and late in life befriended evangelist Dwight L. Moody and donated to his schools.

Intent on making his fortune, Billings entered law with an interest in Whig politics. During the Gold Rush he accompanied relatives to California to look after investments there.[24] While Billings formed a law firm and quickly accumulated a fortune, he found himself drawn to railroads. One of his partners was president of a railroad from San Francisco to San Jose. Billings himself invested in the railroad which brought Judah to California. Billings's life took a turn in 1869, when he moved back East and bought stock in the Northern Pacific, of which he was soon a director. After Cooke's fiasco in 1873 put the Northern Pacific into receivership, Billings came up with a brilliant plan for reorganization which got railroad construction going again and which made him president. He put the Northern Pacific back operating at a profit, but a Wall Street maneuver by a rival railroad forced Billings from the president's chair in 1881, although he continued to work for the road. Billings took advantage of the economic boom the railroad brought and invested heavily in areas like Billings, Montana, to promote economic growth.[25] The Northern Pacific completed its transcontinental line in 1884, only to collapse soon after, due to the new president's mismanagement. Poor health prevented Billings from again taking the helm. Increasing ailments caused him to gradually cut down on his business activity, and he died in 1893.

Strongly philanthropically minded, Billings involved himself deeply in conservation issues. His three constant interests were the place of religion in public life, free public education, and the creation of parks and preservation of scenic landscape. Unlike most people in California, who had come to get rich and return home, and thus cared little about the state's long-term condition, he concerned himself with education, religion, public preserves, orphan asylums, libraries, and continuity. He became San Francisco's foremost philanthropist, investing time and money in innumerable causes. Billings was trustee and later first president of the board of what became the University of California (and originated the name "Berkeley" for its location, in honor of the poet George Berkeley's famous line, "Westward the course of empire"). As the major developer of Billings, Montana, he donated money for schools, churches, and public improvements.

Transcendentalist influences at the University of Vermont may have deepened Billings's appreciation of nature, which continued to develop as his California days brought him into contact with many influences. He read and absorbed Humboldt and renowned Harvard geologist Louis Agassiz, befriending Agassiz on a voyage to California in 1865. He liked San Francisco Unitarian minister Thomas Starr King's Thoreau-style tribute to Vermont, *The White Hills*. He studied and marked the book that turned him into a committed conservationist, the landmark 1864 *Man and Nature* by George Perkins Marsh (cousin of James Marsh). So great an effect did *Man and Nature* have that Billings dedicated his last years to making his Vermont estate — formerly owned by the Marsh family — into a model of conservation as a monument to Marsh and his warnings about human impact on nature.

Billings's interest in nature also deepened with a growing appreciation of Romantic landscapes and art. He began buying the works of such painters of nature as Albert Bierstadt, Asher Durand, John Kensett, William Keith, and Thomas Cole. As a lawyer defending John C. Frémont's Las Mariposas land grant in the 1860s, which included gold mines and a famous grove of sequoias, he met Bierstadt and photographer Carleton Watkins in Frémont's home. He also became acquainted with the estate's manager, Frederick Law Olmsted, designer of New York City's Central Park and later America's foremost public park planner. As Billings's religious understanding of nature grew, he felt God would not forgive those who destroyed his greatest creations. He found appreciation for this viewpoint in the works of John Muir and in his correspondence with James Davie Butler, a family friend who later proposed Glacier National Park.

Billings had a close connection with Yosemite, which he had frequently visited since 1852, the year after whites rediscovered it. Around 1860, Billings's firm commissioned Watkins to make a series of photographs of Las Mariposas to try to interest investors in the mines. Watkins returned in 1861 to take a series of pictures of Yosemite and the Calaveras sequoia grove and in 1863 published the Yosemite shots in an album. Billings sent a copy to Agassiz, who was inspired to give his support for a proposed reserve. Other copies of the album circulated through Washington and helped win support for the milestone 1864 bill giving Yosemite to California to preserve as a park for the enjoyment of the people. Olmsted was made chairman of the commission in charge of the park. Billings continued to support Watkins's subsequent photographic work in Washington, Oregon, and Yellowstone.

In 1865 Billings spoke out for the first time for the need to protect not only Yosemite but other natural landscapes in California. That same year he and Yosemite commissioner William Ashburner met Olmsted in the office of the mayor of San Francisco and encouraged him to design a great boulevard and public park for the city. Later, as president of the Northern Pacific, Billings promoted an alliance of business, tourism, and conservation. He told work crews to spare any landscape with scenic value. He had trees planted as wind- and snowbreaks across the barren prairies of the Dakotas, and his Land Department encouraged farmers to plant others. Billings encouraged the first Northern Pacific guidebooks and photographs to publicize the Dakota Badlands and the Yellowstone Valley and National Park. The pictures by the photographer he engaged, F. Jay Haynes, soon came to be the standard views.[26] Builder of railroads, developer of the West, conserver of natural resources, preserver of natural beauty, Billings's extraordinary career exemplified the inherent ambiguities of the Yankee in the wilderness.

In many cases, it was not railroad leaders but company men who involved themselves in conservation and preservation, with the general good of the railroad still in the back of their minds. The Southern Pacific, for example, kept a close eye on the fate of Yosemite Park and the Sierras, tied up as they were not only with tourism and public relations, but also with the prosperity of the areas through which its lines ran and upon which its fortunes were founded. Many of the Southern Pacific's leaders involved themselves in conservation, both in their employer's cause and privately. Notable among them were its chief land agents William H. Mills, Benjamin B. Redding, and B. A. McAllaster, and chief counsels W. W. Stow and William F. Herrin, who was also vice-president and the hand behind the Southern Pacific political machine. Passenger department managers like James

Horsburgh, Jr., and E. O. McCormick worked to create new local and national parks, and the department booster periodical, *Sunset Magazine*, contained many articles on conservation, preservationism, and forestry.

As early as the 1860s, the Southern Pacific had sent writers, artists, and photographers into Yosemite to publicize it, and had printed pamphlets and posters. Officials gave free passes and other assistance to John Muir, Yosemite's most famous "citizen." Mills was part-owner with the Southern Pacific of the *Sacramento Record-Union*, in which he continually defended conservation. In the 1870s and 1880s Mills waged a newspaper war against hydraulic mining in the Sierras, which increased flooding and siltation for farmers in the Valley. As longtime Yosemite Valley Commissioner he fought (frequently in vain) to protect the park from various special interests.

Mills's frustration in Yosemite probably prompted the Southern Pacific to have the 1890 bill introduced in Congress that would make a national park out of the watershed surrounding the Valley, which alone had been included in the 1864 state park boundaries. Muir drew the new boundaries and with R. U. Johnson, editor of *Century Magazine*, gave it wide publicity. The combined power of Muir, Johnson, Senator Stanford, the Southern Pacific lobbyists, and chief Southern Pacific attorney Stow battled the California interests who wanted use of the same federal lands. When these interests stymied the bill, Southern Pacific district land agent Daniel K. Zumwalt managed not only to enlarge the park's boundaries and to double the size of the proposed Sequoia National Park introduced earlier with the support of the Southern Pacific, but to sneak them through Congress with practically no debate in the last frenzied days of the session.

During the next few years, the Southern Pacific supported the establishment of the huge Sierra National Forest, and Mills was a major publicist and lobbyist behind the creation of forest preserves in the Lake Tahoe region. The next battle was the 1904 bill to rescind Yosemite Valley (still a state park, though surrounded by the new national park) to the United States as part of the national park, a measure which had to pass both the California legislature and Congress. Again, although Muir and the Sierra Club did their best, victory was due to the efforts of Southern Pacific lobbyists, Mills, and especially Muir's friend E. H. Harriman, Southern Pacific president since Huntington's death in 1901. Thus, thanks to the men of the Southern Pacific, two hundred miles of the Sierra crest came to rest permanently under federal protection.

Harriman and Muir had been friends ever since Harriman had transformed an 1899 vacation cruise to hunt Alaskan bear into a scientific expedition and invited Muir, Burroughs, and two dozen others to join him. Four years later, hearing of Muir's plans for a voyage around the world, Harriman put his steamship lines and agents at his disposal. A lover of hunting, fishing, and camping, Harriman had a lodge on Klamath Lake in Oregon. He invited Muir (and painter William Keith) there in 1907 and put at his disposal a stenographer. Normally a slow writer, Muir got a good start on several books, including his autobiography. Muir's repayment came in the form of a slim memorial volume, *Edward Henry Harriman*. Not surprisingly, Harriman left his own legacy in nature preservation. He accumulated a huge estate in New York for the purpose of bequeathing it as a park. As Harriman Park, it now constitutes a major portion of New York's series of Hudson River parks.[27]

In the second half of the nineteenth century, a small number of men of Calvinistic heritage rose to lead the capitalistic conquest of the American continent, winning profits, prestige, and pride in their contribution to civilization. Their attack on the wilderness was terribly hard on the natural environment. Forests were cut for ties, buildings, snow-sheds, and fuel. Coal mines opened across the country to stoke the steam engines. Iron and coal mines fed the steel mills which worked to fill the need for rails and rolling stock and polluted air and water. Construction crews leveled hills, filled in low spots, altered watersheds, and caused erosion and silting. Train smoke covered the landscape with ash and dust, and sparks caused forest and prairie fires. Garbage and sewage from passing trains went directly onto the tracks and rights-of-way. Railroads brought people, farms, towns, and mines to previously remote areas and fragile arid and mountain ecologies. And the railroad companies overoptimistically encouraged settlement in lands not suited to dry farming (and too far from other transportation to be farmed without rail transportation), an invitation to the ecological disaster of the Dust Bowl.

But as these men demonstrate, the transition from Calvinism to capitalism did not produce unmitigated environmental evil. Alongside that dreary record, the railroads left other monuments just as durable. Mixing self-interest with a genuine concern and even love for nature, railroadmen protected or set aside vast portions of the wilderness they had mastered. To their surprise and even chagrin, preservationists found themselves grateful to many "robber barons." Without their friendships with railroad leaders, the founders of the preservation movement would have had a far more difficult battle, whose outcome could easily have been more compromised.

SEVEN

Progressive Gospels of Nature

O beautiful for spacious skies,
For amber waves of grain,
For purple mountain majesties
Above the fruited plain!
America! America!
God shed his grace on thee
And crown thy good with brotherhood
From sea to shining sea!

O beautiful for pilgrim feet,
Whose stern, impassioned stress
A thoroughfare for freedom beat
Across the wilderness!
America! America!
God mend thine every flaw,
Confirm thy soul in self-control,
Thy liberty in law!

— KATHERINE LEE BATES (STANZAS 1 & 2; 1893)

In the summer of 1893, Katherine Lee Bates, professor of English at Welles-ley College, climbed Pike's Peak in Colorado. The view so inspired her that she penned the poem "America the Beautiful" and published it, fittingly, on July 4, 1895. By 1910 it had been set to the tune of Samuel Augustus Ward's *Materna* and since has become a sort of second national anthem. At the time, and still today, it expressed perfectly that combination of natural beauty, agrarian plenty, and divine mission that epitomized the American concep-tion of itself.

"America the Beautiful" also symbolized a look backward, an affirmation of tradition. In the decades before and after the turn of the century, urban growth, immigration, industrialization, and social change threatened nature, agrarianism, and mission. America needed to be saved from its own success. The varying strands of reform that appeared in response to these challenges in the last two decades of the nineteenth century intertwined to produce the Progressive movement and Party of the first two decades of the twentieth. Two of those responses created the forerunners of modern environmentalism: nature preservationism and conservation.

The environmental movements that began to coalesce around the leadership of John Muir, Gifford Pinchot, and others developed in a religious climate quite different from that of a generation or two earlier. In those earlier years the waves of religious and evangelical fervor that swept the English-speaking world had in Northern states produced millennialism, evangelism, and perfectionism, and inspired young men and women to seek and fight for purer churches, purer doctrine, purer lives, purer societies, a purer world. As time went on, evangelicalism triumphant lost its millennial urgency, even as it lapsed into the formulaic revivalism of evangelists like Dwight Moody. Many in generations succeeding the first revivals turned from the fervent severity of their elders toward a gentler Protestant spirituality that Romantics, Transcendentalists, and Unitarians had chiefly pioneered. A distinctive form of liberal Christianity emerged which dominated Protestant learning and theology by the early twentieth century, particularly in the North. Liberal churchmen accepted the advances in science and Biblical criticism and sought to accommodate belief to modern thought. They developed a theology which tended to dissolve the boundaries between God and man (the indwelling spirit), God and nature (the immanent spirit), and Jesus and man (the human potential), and to deemphasize the authority of the Bible and the centrality of Jesus.

Liberalism did not extinguish the moral fervor of the evangelical Calvinist tradition. For a time quiescent, following the end of Reconstruction, the movement for reform reignited during the 1880s. Some reformers emphasized moral reforms like temperance. Others concentrated on social reform, as in the settlement house and Social Gospel movements. Without rejecting civilization's material progress, these children of the revivals worried that the nation was straying from the proper path. They worried about divisive labor strikes, foreign immigration, rural migration to the cities, political corruption, powerful industrial monopolies, and what seemed a general growth of materialism and decline of morality.[1]

It was in this context that many Americans understood the disappearance of their forests and wildlife. The logic at the core of conservation grew from

anticipation of scarcity of natural resources and resulted in rational, puta-
tively scientific proposals. However clear and scientific, logic produces
nothing of itself and must shift with the affairs of humankind, from which it
is ever inseparable. "Scientific" conservation, blended with religious liberalism and moral reform, produced that unique mixture of the early environmental movement, a brew of science, neo-Platonism, natural theology,
moralism, militancy, higher law, evangelism, and millennialism. Progressive thought about nature brought together at once most of the main historical ingredients of Protestant nature doctrine and ethic.

Two Progressive prophets appeared with messages of salvation for a
people beset by change. The first, John Muir, preached a balm in mountain
and forest Gileads, where reason and faith returned to the weary urban
dweller. He made a moral cause of divine immanence in natural beauty.
The second, Gifford Pinchot, revealed the tablets of conservation and
prophesied a new future, a promised land of scientific harmony with nature.
In a faint echo of Baconian millennialism, he foresaw selfless technocrats
leading the way to the Kingdom of God. Muir and Pinchot were apostles of
differing versions of the same gospel whose devotees, in the early twentieth
century, made a test of faith of a dam in an obscure mountain valley—
Hetch Hetchy Valley in Yosemite National Park.

Paradise Lost: John Muir

Among the common denominators of Progressive religious liberals was
rebellion against the overstrict evangelical faith of their parents.[2] In large
measure, John Muir's wilderness gospel came out of a similar alienation.
When the wave of revivalism reached the shores of Scotland in the first
decades of the nineteenth century, a small merchant, Daniel Muir, rejected
the established Calvinist Presbyterian Church and embarked on a search
for the right combination of holiness and zeal. He finally found his church
home in the 1840s in a Scottish-American sect, the Campbellites, whose
rational and uncomplicated dogma and re-creation of the primitive church
appealed to him.[3] To the family of this strict and zealous man, John Muir
was born in 1838. Eleven years later, attracted by religious freedom and
cheap land, Daniel took his family to live in a Campbellite community in
frontier Wisconsin and became a locally known lay Campbellite preacher.[4]

As a teenager Muir's horizons broadened beyond his father's puritanical
zealotry when he avidly (and often secretly) began to read such books as the
poetry of Milton and the Romantics, the travels of Mungo Park and Alex-

ander von Humboldt, natural history, mathematics, and Thomas Dick's *Christian Philosopher*, a reconciliation of science and religion. Muir displayed a gift for inventiveness, but his father never praised him (for fear of engendering the sin of pride). However, the neighbors did, and Muir set off in 1860 to take his inventions to the state fair in Madison, which he hoped would get him a machine-shop job that would allow him to continue inventing.

Instead, Muir gravitated for a few years to the new University of Wisconsin at Madison, whose New England–trained professors taught him the inductive method of Bacon, the geology of Agassiz, and the literature of Wordsworth, Emerson, and Thoreau.[5] Muir's classics teacher was James Davie Butler, a follower of Emerson and afterward correspondent of Frederick Billings and instigator of Glacier National Park. Butler encouraged his students to keep journals, advice which Muir kept all his life, and he later first put Muir's writing into print.

A tendency toward dourness, preachiness, and general evangelical seriousness lingered in Muir's personality. He went down to the army encampment at the outbreak of war to give moral talks to soldiers, and served as president of the local Y.M.C.A., then an organization whose purpose was to promote Christian practice. Yet his religious beliefs were evolving. Through his science teacher's wife, Jeanne Carr, he learned of Unitarian William Ellery Channing's teachings of an immanent, loving God. (Mrs. Carr, a friend of Emerson and an intellectually frustrated academic wife, in time became a sort of mother–mentor for him.) From his readings of Dick, Agassiz, and others he learned of the harmony of the books of nature and revelation. From Darwin he accepted the idea of evolution but rejected its mechanistic, godless process in favor of a theistic indwelling process reminiscent of Lamarck.

Modern writers compare Muir's religion with Taoism or other Eastern religions, and indeed late in life he found much to admire in the Eastern point of view.[6] His changing beliefs elude exact definition, but paralleled the evolution of liberal Christianity. In the 1860s and '70s, in his letters to Mrs. Carr, he still mentioned the Fall, the divinity of Christ, and the harmony of the books of nature and revelation.[7] When in the 1890s it came time to give religious instruction to his two daughters, Muir taught them to revere God not as a person, but as a spirit who was loving and intelligent, an immanent creator ruling the universe — a move away from the God of the Old Testament and toward the God of the New Testament and of the Greeks. He had them learn the Lord's Prayer (although he did not generally like praying) and memorize portions of the Bible (including the sayings of Jesus), Milton's *Paradise Lost*, and Romantic poetry. Although he nowhere explicitly repudiated the divinity of Christ, he undoubtedly retreated from the Christocentrism of evangelical Protestantism and moved toward the theism of liberal Protestantism, which emphasized divine immanence in the processes of nature (evolution), history (progress), and life (salvation). As Muir matured, he tended to replace "God" or "the Lord" with the apparently synonymous "Nature" or "Beauty" (as Jefferson and Emerson had).

For a time, two impulses from his Calvinistic heritage, the utilitarian and the spiritual, warred within him. He apparently never lost an appreciation for the Protestant work ethic.[8] His aspirations as an inventor, an improver of lives through mechanical inventions, displayed the Protestant priority on leading a life useful to humanity. At one job, he improved productivity of a broomstick factory, and in a letter gave himself a tongue-in-cheek compliment on his usefulness to humanity, or at least to its cleanliness. In 1866 he moved to Indianapolis, an industrial center where he found success and rapid advancement in a major machine shop there.

Chance presented Muir anew with the choice between the virtue of industry and the study of the book of nature. An industrial accident injured one eye, causing both eyes to go into temporary blindness and Muir to enter a metaphoric darkness of despair. Experiencing something like a conversion, he arose from this death-in-life to dedicate his life to higher purposes. "God has to nearly kill us sometimes, to teach us lessons," he wrote Mrs. Carr.[9] As he later recalled that moment,

> As soon as I got out into Heaven's light I started on another long excursion, making haste with all my heart to store my mind with the Lord's beauty and thus be ready to any fate, light or dark. And it was from this time that my long continuous wanderings may be said to have fairly commenced. I bade adieu to all my mechanical inventions, determined to devote the rest of my life to the study of the inventions of God.[10]

After this brush with blindness, Muir, like Emerson, frequently referred to God and nature in terms of light, and later christened the Sierras the "Range of Light."

Muir immediately immersed himself in nature. After a farewell trip home and a final confrontation with his father, who regarded Muir's interest in geology and botany as devil-inspired, he set off on a walk to the Gulf of Mexico, determined to be a new Humboldt. He recorded in his journal his final break with the stern religion of his father. In those pages emerged the old neo-Platonic themes of the unity of life amidst its diversity, creation as the expression of a loving God, the divine design of creation in which each animal and plant plays its part, and becoming and change, even life and death, as part of the world's beauty. Muir's personal emphasis emerged as well, in a strong rejection of the notion that the world was made for man and in a powerful sense of nature's beauty spots as places of holiness.[11]

A letter from Mrs. Carr, now with her husband at the University of California in Berkeley, turned him toward California. He settled in Yosemite valley, from which he ranged up and down the mountains, botanizing and making his scientific notes. A family evangelical tendency now manifested itself in sermons of a new wilderness gospel equal to the gospel of Jesus. "Do behold the King in his glory, King Sequoia," he wrote Mrs. Carr.

> I never before knew the virtue of Sequoia juice. Seen with sunbeams in it, its color is the most royal of all royal purples. No wonder the Indians instinctively drink it for they know not what. I wish I were so drunk & Sequoical that I could preach the green brown woods to all the juiceless world, descending from this divine wilderness like a John the Baptist, eating Douglas squirrels & wild honey or wild anything, crying, Repent, for the Kingdom of Sequoia is at hand![12]

His letters mingled strains of neo-Platonism, natural theology, the book of nature, and Transcendentalism:

> I wish you could come here & rest a year in the simple unmingled Love fountains of God. You would then return to your scholars with fresh truth gathered & absorbed from pines & waters & deep singing winds, & you would find they all sang of fountain-Love, just as did Jesus Christ & all of pure God manifest in whatever form. . . . Rocks & waters, etc., are words of God & so are men. We all flow from one fountain Soul. All are expressions of one Love.[13]

In his journal from his first summer in the Sierras, Muir gave expression to the interconnectedness of nature in his oft-quoted remark that "when we try to pick out anything by itself, we find it hitched to everything else in the universe."[14]

The evangelism of the older generation of Baptists, Campbellites (today's Churches of Christ), and Methodists often transmuted in the younger generation into evangelism for other moral causes. Muir mixed the moral marginality of Transcendentalism with the Biblical marginality of the prophets. His religious and evangelical impulses transformed a retreat from American commerce and industry into a career of the righteous outsider decrying the sins of society. The protagonist of a wilderness *Pilgrim's Progress*, he left father, family, friends, and civilization behind and lived and communed with the trees and animals in the holy forests of California. He sloughed off his father's creed and utilitarian attitude toward nature. In the woods he found freedom from unrelenting paternal criticism and faith in a loving God. Liberated himself, he went on to preach deliverance to the captives of civilization. Here he applied, not denied, many lessons he learned from his father. Drawing on his Campbellite background and his father's example, he filled his life with holiness and zeal, evangelized for a saving cause, was an apostle of the true religion which civilization and the ages had lost or perverted, and was an interpreter of God's word, as read, however, from the Book of Nature rather than the Bible.[15]

Muir fit his role well. People compared him to an Old Testament prophet or John the Baptist, especially if they saw him striding down a mountain trail from a sojourn in the wilderness with his long beard flowing in the breeze. Although his stint as fruit rancher and friendship with a railroad tycoon made him more sympathetic to the use of nature for human benefit, his writings never lost their message of repentance from the sins of overcivilization, baptism in wilderness, and ejection of the money-changers from the mountain temples.

Muir's cause was feminized Nature—a moral resource of civilization like mother, home, and church—beset by base and corrupt exploiters. Although other mountaineers, like Clarence King, described their wilderness experience in masculine, adversarial terms of conquest, Muir used maternal and domestic nature imagery.[16] ". . . [G]oing to the mountains is going home. . . ." By too long an immersion in American commercial society, "tired, nerve-shaken, over-civilized people" fell under "the stupefying effects of the vice of over-industry and the deadly apathy of luxury"—his equivalent of the Fall and human depravity. Muir preached salvation through wilderness baptism, "washing off sins and cobweb cares of the devil's spinning," and "getting in touch with . . . Mother Earth."[17]

Those who entered the wilderness holy places from motives of profit or mere utilitarianism offended Muir. "Their arguments" he wrote, "are curiously like those of the devil, designed for the destruction of the first garden—so much of the very best Eden fruit going to waste. . . ." The worshippers of Mammon would desecrate the Yosemite, Hetch Hetchy, and the other great Sierra sanctuaries. He insisted that "mountain parks and reservations are useful not only as fountains of timber and irrigating rivers, but as fountains of life." Damming a great mountain canyon was like using a cathedral for a water tank.[18] Lumbering destroyed magnificent, irreplaceable Sequoia groves. "Any fool can destroy trees," Muir observed. "They cannot run away; and if they could, they would still be destroyed, — chased and hunted down as long as fun or a dollar could be got out of their bark hides, branching horns, or magnificent bole backbones."[19] Overgrazing by sheep ("hoofed locusts") devastated watersheds and fragile, high country meadows. Muir knew there was a place for reasonable use for natural resources. There must also be a place for urban people to come to "God's first temples," quoting William Cullen Bryant's poem, and worship.

For all Muir's insistence that animals and plants had a right to live for themselves and did not live for man,[20] he presented an anthropocentric rationale for preserving natural landscape. Parks were "the people's playgrounds."[21] To Muir, as to Emerson, nature had uses, one of which was as a source of new life and morality to the mass of humanity degraded by city living—the same sort of agrarian prejudice against cities that animated much of American thinking from the days of Jefferson. This clearly utilitarian argument described, however, an essentially passive use of nature producing as little man-made alteration of certain kinds of landscape as possible. Not unlike Emerson, Muir enticed people into the wilderness as tourists so that they might—passively—receive the moral and psychological benefits of proximity to the saving power of wildness.[22]

From 1869 to 1874 and off and on through 1879, Muir spent summers in the High Sierra reading "the glacial manuscripts of God."[23] His wonder-filled, ecstatic letters to Mrs. Carr prompted her to send a stream of important visitors his way. Visitors included Emerson, Clinton L. Merriman of the Smithsonian Institute, John Daniel Runkle of M.I.T., English geologist John Tyndall, botanist Sir Joseph Hooker, botanist Asa Gray, Gray's mentor John Torrey, State Superintendent of Schools John Swett, and landscape painter William Keith. Muir established long correspondences or friendships with most of them, received equipment from the scientists, and made connections that aided his rise to national voice and influence. He published his glacial research in articles that established a small niche for him in the history of science as the first theorist of the glacial origins of Yosemite Valley.[24] His regular natural history notes won him a nationwide popular audience.[25] When Muir began to lecture, his religion-infused natural history prompted one auditor to call him "the Hugh Miller of the Pacific Coast,"[26] an apt comparison to another religious Scottish scientist-author.

His writing career culminated with a series of books edited from his journals and published in the last two decades of his life.

In the mid-1870s, Muir turned his attention to an attempt to rescue Sierra forests, especially sequoias, from the wasteful harvest that was decimating them. George Perkins Marsh's *Man and Nature* taught him the importance of trees to watershed protection. Henry George's *Our Land and Land Policy* and *Progress and Poverty* increased his awareness of the problems of land ownership to be overcome to that goal. Muir's opening salvo for forest protection came in "God's First Temples. How Shall We Preserve Our Forests?" published in the Southern Pacific–owned *Sacramento Record-Union*. Although his intended target, the California legislature, took little notice, this and related articles published in the East helped establish him as a leader in California conservation.

Although temporarily stymied, a new era in wilderness protection was about to commence. A quiet decade on his new fruit ranch with wife and family ended in 1889 when publisher R. U. Johnson of *Century* magazine lured him back to his writing desk. The two hatched a publicity plan to create a national park to cover the abused and overused watershed of both Yosemite Valley and its neighboring, less accessible valley, Hetch Hetchy. With the help of the Southern Pacific lobby and railroad-supporting congressmen, the park bill passed in 1890.[27] Muir and Johnson also touted a Kings Canyon National Park to the south. Secretary of the Interior John W. Noble enthusiastically received the idea, had Muir draw up the boundaries, and submitted it to Congress — where it languished for decades.

Muir became a national spokesman for protected forests and mountains. The constant threat of development interests prompted Johnson to propose the Sierra Club, which John Muir as first president organized as part mountaineering club, part political watchdog. Its founding membership included many professors from the University of California and Stanford, future Progressives, and officials of the Southern Pacific. The club met its first test when it fended off demands to reduce the park's size.

In 1896 Muir accompanied the Forestry Commission of the National Academy of Sciences on its study tour of Western forests. On this trip Muir befriended a young member of the commission, Gifford Pinchot. The commission's report prompted President Cleveland in 1897 to add twenty-one million acres of forest reserves to President Harrison's original thirteen million of 1891, although under McKinley, Congress repudiated the commission's desire to preserve the forests and opened them to use.

A chance 1899 invitation opened more doors for Muir. The dynamic

president of the Union Pacific (and soon the Southern Pacific as well),
E. H. Harriman, decided to make a scientific expedition out of a pleasure
cruise to Alaska and invited Muir, John Burroughs, and other scientists,
artists, and photographers to accompany him. Overcoming worries that
this "robber baron" might want unnamed favors in return, Muir looked
forward to traveling farther along the Alaska coast than he had explored in
previous visits in 1879 and 1880.[28] Not only did he have a marvelous time,
but he acquired several valuable friendships and a powerful ally, for Harriman soon commanded the immense lobbying resources of the Southern
Pacific. When he and his Sierra Club allies could not get the Yosemite
recession passed through the California legislature, he penned a letter to
Harriman: the bill went through. When Speaker of the House of Representatives Joe Cannon refused to put the bill to accept the recession on
the House calendar, Muir wrote Harriman again: the bill was passed and
signed. Upon Harriman's death in 1909, Muir composed a slim volume of
tribute.[29] Moral purists could not understand how he could give his blessings to the enemy, but Muir had found good in unsuspected places.

Muir acquired more friends in high places. He camped in Yosemite for
three days with Theodore Roosevelt in 1903, and gave William Howard
Taft a Yosemite tour in 1909. A letter from Muir stirred Roosevelt to
establish the Petrified Forest National Monument. But his connections
failed him in the last and fiercest battle of his career: the issue of the Hetch
Hetchy dam. When earthquake and fire destroyed San Francisco, a city
with no natural water supply, pressure mounted to yield to the city's request
for a reservoir within the bounds of Yosemite National Park, in the Hetch
Hetchy Valley. Muir spent his last years in a fruitless attempt to stop the
dam, but finally, when the Democrats took Washington in 1913 and ousted
the administration conservationists who had opposed it, the dam was approved. Exhausted but relieved just to have the issue settled, Muir lived out
only another year, and died in December 1914.

John Muir has often been cited as the font of the American environmentalist movement.[30] His influence upon the whole gamut of environmental
organizations and opinion, from the Park Service to Earth First!, is unde-
niable. Muir formed a personal, direct link between the Calvinist ethic and
the striking spiritual and moral aspect in much of modern American environmentalism. For him, the wilderness and the mountains were a moral
cause. Moral causes rarely admit of compromise. If all the world is Eden, all
change is declension. For this reason, Muir could readily sound the trumpet
of alarm over the loss of forests, while allowing his friends to make the
back-room deals and do the arm-twisting in Sacramento and Washington

that achieved practical results. Muir had moved himself into the outsider status of a prophet, made his cause a morally uplifting nature, and defended her against amoral selfishness and greed. Among modern environmental organizations, such groups as Friends of the Earth and Earth First! adhere closest to the high standards of such moralism.

Muir ought to have learned some lessons from his friends in the Southern Pacific who got his favorite bills through the legislative process. If he had, he might not have lost the Hetch Hetchy dam battle. Since his only defense of the Valley was to take the moral high road, opponents could shove him aside as an obstacle to progress, scientific evidence, and the needs of civilization. The Sierra Club and its allies were better prepared in the 1940s and '50s. They defeated the Echo Park dam not by defending the canyon's spiritual value but by using scientific evidence that it was a bad dam. The larger environmental groups have used this approach ever since, strengthening their powerful moral defense of nature with scientific reasoning. This approach has broadened the movement's appeal and undermined the anti-"sentimental" mainstream ethic of economic progress.

Evangelical Science: Gifford Pinchot

On April 16, 1891, 26-year-old Gifford Pinchot saw the Grand Canyon for the first time. He struggled to put his reaction into words for his diary.

> Went at once to edge of cañon & looked & looked & cussed [his companion] for talking to me & looked & cussed. The cañon can not be adequately described. It is a vast hole full of air & full of mountains. It was so unexampled that I did not want to look at it as a whole at first, but stuck to the near bits & cañons. It stands alone, has its own character, own familiar atmosphere & is wholly without parallel or comparison. I could only strive to find a reference point, some way of measuring it. The whole made the effect of a picture & not of a real thing. God's hand is there most wonderfully. I thought & sang the Doxology.[31]

Any Northern American Protestant from Katherine Lee Bates to John Muir might have written these lines. Like Muir, Gifford Pinchot was something of an evangelist or even prophet, but his mission was of a different sort. Salvation came not from God of the mountains but from the moral regeneration of conservation. Pinchot grew up in a wealthy Eastern family, graduated from Yale, knew personally every President from Grant to Truman, and loved working close to the centers of political and economic power. He believed in a dignified, genteel religion, moralistic without Bible-thumping preachiness. His vision grew with his experience, from scientific forestry to conservation, from conservation to politics, from politics to a new political party, until he saw conservation and moral regeneration advancing hand in hand, led by scientific expertise to the Kingdom of God on earth. To Pinchot, conservation was a moral crusade to save the country and the world.

Born in 1865, Pinchot looked back to a long maternal line of Connecticut Yankees recently wealthy, and to a paternal lineage of successful Pennsylvania Huguenots (French Calvinists). Pinchot was very close to his mother. Always convinced her son had a mission to fulfill, she remained a force in his life until her death in 1914. To his father Pinchot was indebted for European connections, a love of hunting, fishing, and camping, and his life's career in forestry.[32] (This appreciation for the rugged life stood him in good stead in his close friendship with Theodore Roosevelt and endeared him to Muir when they camped out on the ground together at the Grand Canyon in 1896.)

Pinchot was quite religious, believing in an idiosyncratic mixture of his mother's Puritan heritage and his father's Swedenborgian spiritualism. While at Phillips Exeter he had attended meetings of the "Christian Fraternity" and joined the Presbyterian Church. When he entered Yale he intended a career in medicine or the ministry. For four years, he and two classmates were deacons of the class of '89, which meant they had responsibilities for the conduct of both Sunday and weekday prayer meetings for their class. He taught Sunday school. Like many liberal Protestants, Pinchot rebelled against formal creeds and denominations. He gave the prize oration at his Yale graduation, "The Quakers of the Seventeenth Century," in which he praised the Quaker reaction to Puritan "formalism and degeneracy" and called them martyrs to freedom and forerunners of modern reform, charity, beneficence, peace, and toleration. His admiration of their spiritual individualism helps explain why Pinchot was not a regular churchgoer as an adult, although nominally Episcopalian.[33]

While lacking strong denominational ties, Pinchot exhibited a strong streak of moralism and interest in evangelism. As a student of forestry in France, the moral laxity of his fellow students shocked and offended him. Pinchot always interested himself in spreading the faith. At Yale he worked for the Grand Street Mission. For most of his life, Pinchot was active in the Y.M.C.A., an organization which during his lifetime was focused on evangelism. Upon his graduation, the Yale Y.M.C.A. offered him the position of general secretary (equivalent to president), a job he seriously considered. Throughout his life, he continued to make contributions and sit on Y.M.C.A. boards and committees at local, state, national, and international levels. Similarly, moral earnestness and desire to spread the faith both manifested themselves in Pinchot's conservation "mission."[34]

Pinchot's private spirituality was, or became, quite unusual. In 1892 he fell in love with Laura Hoteling, who had tuberculosis. By the time she died two years later, they had convinced themselves they were spiritual mates. Pinchot did not grieve on her death, but continued to "talk" to his "spiritual wife" for the next twenty years at least. He read spiritualist books "together" with her, as well as Swedenborg (who had a theory of spiritual marriage), John and Revelation in the Bible, and even Emerson. He believed she had become one with God: when she was present so was God, and when God was present, she too was there. Using the language of Christian devotion and mysticism, his diary has notations that "she [or "she and God"] fills me." Pinchot rigidly divided his private and public lives: spirituality and mysticism had no part of his gospel of conservation.[35]

Instead of entering the ministry or the Y.M.C.A., at his father's urging and in the face of nearly unanimous discouragement from friends and experts, Pinchot decided to become the nation's first forester. He went to Europe, where the only forestry schools in the world were located, attended the French National Forestry School at Nancy, and toured forests in France, Switzerland, and Germany. He ceased his study after a single year and returned to the United States in 1890. Pinchot's big break in forestry came in 1892 from Frederick Law Olmsted. Advisor to George W. Vanderbilt on the planning of his North Carolina estate, Olmsted hired Pinchot to conduct the nation's first experiment in scientific forestry. After a year, Pinchot acclaimed the experiment a success (despite ambiguous results) and opened a New York office as a forestry consultant.

Pinchot's rising reputation in an up-and-coming field won him important new positions. First was appointment to the National Forest Commission in 1896, along with Muir and many botanical experts. The commission's recommendations included withdrawing forest preserves from any public use, but Pinchot argued for expert management of forests for public use. Appointed chief of the Division of Forestry in the Department of Agriculture in 1898, he continually and successfully worked to expand the size and effectiveness of his bureau. After 1901, he had the full support and sympathy of President Theodore Roosevelt. A great triumph came in 1905, when Congress passed a bill which reorganized his bureau into the Forest

Service and gave it control of federal forest reserves (now called "national forests"), previously under supervision of the General Land Office.

Forestry, in Pinchot's mind, was a rational solution to the problem of waste and inefficiency — science in the service of the Protestant ethic — but as his activities under Theodore Roosevelt's administration widened, so did his conception of his occupation. Pinchot served on the 1903 Committee on the Organization of Government Scientific Work and on the 1905 Committee on Department Methods (the Keep Committee), both of which promoted efficiency and coordination in governmental agencies (and, incidentally, held the Forest Bureau up as a model). He initiated and worked on the 1903 Public Lands Commission, which prompted a national classification of natural resources and land-law reform. In 1906 Pinchot began planning an Inland Waterways Commission to deal with competing requirements for water use, power, flood control, and navigation. He now began thinking about the diverse problems concerning the use and abuse of natural resources in national forests, including flood and erosion control, fish and wildlife, mining, grazing, and water power sites.

On a winter's day in 1907, Pinchot was out riding in Washington and mulling over these different problems, when he realized that they were all interconnected. "Seen in this light," he later remembered, "all these separate questions fitted into and made up the one great central problem of the use of the earth for the good of man." He added,

> It took time for me to appreciate that here were the makings of a new policy, not merely nationwide but world-wide in its scope — fundamentally important because it involved not only the welfare by the very existence of men on the earth.
>
> . . . As far as I knew then or have since been able to find out, it had occurred to nobody, in this country or abroad, that here was one question instead of many, one gigantic single problem that must be solved if the generations, as they came and went, were to live civilized, happy, useful lives in the lands which the Lord their God had given them.[36]

He thought this a perfect example of Roosevelt's doctrine of stewardship: the public servant as steward of the earth both for future generations and for God.

Now Pinchot had his cause and his mission but lacked a name and a program. He defined these in conversations with several friends and colleagues, especially Overton Price of the Forest Service and WJ McGee.

Former member of the Geological Survey and assistant to John Wesley Powell, former head of the Bureau of Ethnology, organizer of the National Geographical Society, instigator and member of Roosevelt's 1907 Inland Waterways Commission, McGee was the philosopher of the conservation movement.[37] They adopted the term "conservation" and defined it as the rational, scientific use of natural resources for the benefit of present and future generations. Like any good moral cause, this one needed a low-principled opponent. They found theirs in monopoly: "monopoly of natural resources was only less dangerous to the public welfare than their actual destruction."[38] Conservation quickly grew to be a central tenet of Roosevelt administration philosophy.

Pinchot's vision of the place of conservation in American life combined elements of Puritan values and virtues, Utilitarianism, Jeffersonian agrarianism, manifest destiny, and millennialism. Conservation's essential concern was that natural resources benefit all, not merely private interest, which echoed Puritan insistence on the common good above the private. Conservationists expressed this with a modified version of the familiar Utilitarian dictum: "Conservation means the greatest good to the greatest number for the longest time." Pursuit solely of private profit produced thoughtless "prodigal squandering" of the nation's heritage of natural resources. Conservation meant the application of the Protestant-ethic virtues of "foresight, prudence, thrift, and intelligence" to public matters, with the "inevitable result" of "national efficiency." Conservation thus was "far more than an economic question"; "in its essence and in every essential characteristic it is a moral question," "a question of a vastly higher duty," "a question of right and wrong," a struggle in the endless "war for righteousness."[39]

Conservation strengthened the Jeffersonian democratic republicanism that lay close to the heart of the American mission. Pinchot believed that the government must protect land from abuse until settlers could take possession of it. "The most valuable citizen of this or any other country is the man who owns the land from which he makes his living," because the virtues which his independent self-reliance put into him made him the "backbone of this Nation." Thus, it was in the national interest to promote equality of opportunity and not give privileges to rich special interests. Large holdings could only profit corporations or speculators and would make "the Western people . . . predominantly a people of tenants under the degrading tyranny of pecuniary and political vassalage," not "freeholders and free men."[40]

Unfortunately for the nation's agrarian wellsprings of virtue, every year thousands of farmers moved to the corrupting cities. To stem this flow,

Pinchot helped set up and contributed to the 1908 Country Life Commission, which concluded that it was necessary to make rural life more attractive and competitive with city life. Recommendations included more country churches and societies, better roads, country telephones, rural free delivery, parcel post, and anything which might enrich rural life.[41]

To Pinchot, strong country churches were critical to public virtue and to conservation. Between 1909 and 1919 he spent over $34,000 on the country church movement of the Federal Council of the Churches of Christ in America, mostly to fund studies by Reverend Charles O. Gill on the decline and current status of country churches in two counties in Vermont and New York, and throughout Ohio. He headed the Federal Council's Commission on Church and Country Life, which published the studies and sponsored a 1915 country church conference in Columbus, Ohio.

Pinchot saw the country church as an instrument for evangelism and conservation, indeed the most important "single factor in the advancement of righteousness and civilization." Country life without churches was "mean, hard, small, selfish, and covetous" and led directly to plummeting property values and pillaging of public lands. But when churches appeared in communities, morals rose, real estate values increased, and "public property, . . . once a source of graft and demoralization, became a public asset." (This applied only to "progressive" churches, not "excessively emotional type" churches like the Holy Rollers, whose "influence promotes immorality.") The moral influence of church was an essential partner with conservation.[42]

Pinchot proclaimed conservation a vital support for the American mission, for upon the nation's use of natural resources hung "the success or failure of this Nation in accomplishing its manifest destiny."

> . . . It is the manifest destiny of the United States to demonstrate that a democratic republic is the best form of government yet devised, and that the ideals and institutions of the great republic taken together must and do work out in a prosperous, contented, peaceful, and righteous people; and also to exercise, through precept and example, an influence for good among the nations of the world.[43]

Prosperity, contentment, peace, and righteousness could not thrive on a blighted, exhausted land.

Just as Edward Johnson and John Winthrop had done in their day, Pinchot decried how prosperity brought corruption both to the American moral fiber and to its democratic system. The alliance between politics and business had become a snake to be killed, since "a man in public life can no more serve both the special interests and the people than he can serve God and Mammon."[44]

Fortunately, with the rise of conservation and the Progressive movement, "morality has broken into politics" and would lead the way to the millennium. Public spirited moral activists had appeared who believed "in vision and in relentless loyalty to ideals — vision to see the great object, and relentless, unwavering, uninterrupted loyalty in its service." With the old Puritan virtues of "effort, self-denial, and endurance," dedicated to the higher causes of "to our country, to the brotherhood of man, and to the future," these men applied "Christianity to the commonwealth." Transforming America was the first step toward transforming the world because "the greatest human power for good, the most efficient earthly tool for the future uplifting of the nations, is without question the United States." At last, Progressivism would achieve the dream of mankind, "the Kingdom of God on earth."[45]

Pinchot now turned to evangelizing the nation with his new gospel. He and Roosevelt organized the successful 1908 White House Conference on the Conservation of Natural Resources, inviting all state governors and other leading figures (the first such governors' conference) and getting a unanimous statement for conservation out of them. That year, Pinchot also chaired the National Conservation Commission. In 1909 he founded the National Conservation Association to proselytize for conservation and headed it from 1910 until it dissolved in 1923.

Setbacks only increased Pinchot's determination. In 1909, Taft kept him in his administration but did not include him in his inner circle. Unused to such exclusion, Pinchot began to doubt the new President's commitment to the cause. That new Secretary of the Interior Richard A. Ballinger reversed conservation actions that the Roosevelt administration had taken alarmed him. He was quite ready to believe and encourage 1910 charges of corruption against Ballinger. The result was that Pinchot was dismissed, the press had a field day, Congress investigated, and a split in Republican ranks began. When Congress exonerated Ballinger but labeled him as hostile to conservation, Pinchot claimed a moral victory. Disillusioned and harassed, Ballinger resigned in 1911.

As Pinchot moved into politics he retained his commitments to moralism, scientific efficiency, conservation, opposition to monopolies (particularly utilities and power companies), and improvement of rural life. Author of Roosevelt's important "New Nationalism" speech of 1910, he helped form Roosevelt's Progressive Party in 1912 and led its radical wing. The Progressive Party convention and Roosevelt's battle for the presidency was the great culmination of the Progressive, Social Gospel, and conservationist battle for the creation of the Kingdom of God. The convention itself resembled a Methodist revival, with its pervasive religious rhetoric, the singing of "The Battle Hymn of the Republic" (several times), "Onward Christian Soldiers," and the Doxology, and Roosevelt's speech with its final line, "We stand at Armageddon, and we battle for the Lord." Indeed, at the close of 1912, the high water mark of Progressive optimism and power, Social Gospel leader Walter Rauschenbusch enthused, "We are having a revival of religion. There is a big camp-meeting going on from Maine to Oregon. . . . God is today writing a flaming message of social righteousness, and you and I must learn to read it." Conservation was a central tenet — and the least controversial tenet — of the Progressive faith.[46]

As Progressive fervor cooled after 1912, Pinchot kept his commitment to conservation and regulation of monopolies. He actively supported the passage of the Weeks Act of 1911, which allowed expansion of national forests by purchase, and the Waterpower Act of 1920, which regulated the power industry. In 1900, a grant from his father had created the Yale School of Forestry, and Pinchot continued to work there as lecturer and professor. He served successfully as forest commissioner for Pennsylvania from 1920 to 1922. His influence in the Forest Service declined, although his reputation among foresters remained strong. When in 1922 Pennsylvania elected him governor, he reorganized state government and finances to make them more efficient, and worked hard to extend regulation of utilities and power companies. A long and fruitless battle with utilities marred his second term, 1930–34, during which he combatted the Depression with construction of thousands of miles of rural roads, both helping the unemployed and improving rural life. Pinchot remained active in public affairs until his death in 1946.

Gifford Pinchot's version of conservation mixed rational science and moral crusade, and therein lay tension reminiscent of the division between the Victorian male and female spheres. Pinchot's allies in conservation did not necessarily share his moral intensity, but often approached the issues from a more strictly scientific or economic vantage point. At the same time, Pinchot's moral allies included urban reformers, but especially enthusiastic were women's clubs like the General Federation of Women's Clubs and the Daughters of the American Revolution (whose Conservation Committee chairman was Pinchot's mother). Pinchot welcomed women's participation in conservation. Because conservation was a moral issue, and Victorians as well as Progressives saw women as the moral influence on home and society, he was sure women would imbue their children and husbands with the moral integrity and patriotism to support conservation measures. Pinchot praised the effectiveness of women's organizations in getting government action in conservation.[47]

But the tension between the rational and the moral was difficult to contain. Pinchot became more and more identified with scientific approaches to natural resources, until after his death his name became emblematic of Progressive- and New Deal–style conservation. Today, the names of Pinchot and Muir stand for two different aspects of environmentalism. Environmentalism as a moral cause has eclipsed scientific conservationism and Pinchot's reputation, while Muir's moral purity has caused him to be looked upon as the source of the modern movement.[48] Modern environmentalism often purports to be based on the science of ecology and rational decision-making, but it is as a moral crusade that it attracts members.

Evangelical Science vs. Paradise Lost: Hetch Hetchy

Thus, two different religious views of nature, both tracing their genealogies to Puritanism and Calvinism, rested in uneasy partnership within the Progressive movement. The first, whose foremost representative was John Muir, derived its strength from the natural-theology and neo-Platonic search in nature for evidence of the attributes of God and in natural beauty for spiritual renewal. The second view, whose spokesman was Gifford Pinchot, combined such Puritan characteristics as moralism, hatred of waste, admiration of utility, denial of selfishness for the common good, and respect for rationality and science. Pinchot and fellow conservationists expected that scientific development of nature for the good of the people, not private interests, would help fulfill the American mission, make the country a true city upon a hill, and perhaps lead to the Kingdom of God. The issue that bitterly split these factions was a proposal for a dam in an obscure valley with a funny name — Hetch Hetchy.

At the eastern entrance to Hetch Hetchy Valley, just north of the Yosemite Valley, the Tuolumne River ceased its precipitous descent. For about seven miles the stream meandered through a flat canyon floor and across an oak-studded meadow a mile long and a quarter- to a half-mile wide. On either side, waterfalls crashed down over vertical granite walls thousands of feet high. At the end of the meadow, the river threaded through a narrow opening in the granite to rush once again down the mountainside. When it reached the edge of the arid San Joaquin Valley, it joined other waters flowing northwest, looking for an outlet to the sea. This granite-enclosed

meadowed valley possessed two outstanding qualities. First, it was one of
the world's most beautiful valleys. Second, it was a site perfectly suited for a
reservoir.

One hundred sixty miles to the west, the water and snowmelt of the
Sierras mixed with the Pacific Ocean in the San Francisco Bay. There, the
city of San Francisco, located at the end of a sandy peninsula, lacked any
major source of fresh water. A virtual monopoly named the Spring Valley
Water Company furnished water to the city. San Franciscans hated the
Spring Valley Water Company, one of many monopolies that made Califor-
nians feel victimized and powerless. While the San Francisco city government alternately fought and offered to buy the company, city engineers
searched for an alternate source. The place they located as the best alterna-
tive was Hetch Hetchy.[49]

San Francisco resolutely battled for twelve years for the right to dam the
valley. At first Secretary of the Interior E. A. Hitchcock denied a dam permit
because the dam would be within a national park. In the wake of the disas-
trous San Francisco earthquake and fire of 1906, which awakened sympathy
for the city's water plight, Hitchcock's successor, Pinchot ally James R.
Garfield, granted a permit in 1908 to dam nearby Lake Eleanor, and later,
when San Francisco outgrew Eleanor's capacity, Hetch Hetchy as well.

But San Francisco wanted not Lake Eleanor but the more cheaply
dammed Hetch Hetchy and its water-power potential. The city took its
case to Congress, where in 1909 Muir and his friends overwhelmed it with
testimony, lobbying, and telegrams. Park defenders convinced the Taft
administration in 1912 to drop Hetch Hetchy from Garfield's permit altogether. San Francisco had not yet given up. When, in 1913, the Democrats took Congress and Woodrow Wilson took the White House (and
appointed San Francisco attorney Franklin K. Lane secretary of the interior), California Representative John E. Raker introduced a bill allowing
construction of the dam. After months of bitter debate, Congress passed
the Raker Act and Wilson signed it on December 19, 1913.

Pinchot and Muir were intimately involved with the debate, and both
were frequently quoted and appealed to on their authority and reputation.
Pinchot had supported the Garfield permit, and in 1913 testified in the
Raker Act's favor. Muir vehemently opposed the bill all along and launched
a nationwide publicity campaign, even giving tours of Yosemite to Taft and
of Hetch Hetchy to Secretary of the Interior Richard A. Ballinger in 1909.
Muir rallied not only old friends like the Sierra Club and R. U. Johnson of
Century magazine, but representatives of the American Forestry Associa-
tion, the American Scenic and Historic Society, the Appalachian Club,

most newspapers outside the West, and many of Pinchot's usual allies as well, including the National Federation of Women's Clubs and the American Civic Association.

Many in Congress could not understand what all the fuss was over. Southern Senator James Reed of Missouri remarked,

> The Senate of the United States has devoted a full week of time to discussing the disposition of about 2 square miles of land, located at a point remote from civilization. . . . It is merely proposed to put water on these 2 square miles. Over that trivial matter the business of the country is halted, the Senate goes into profound debate, the country is thrown into a condition of hysteria, and one would imagine that chaos and old night were about to descend on the land. . . . The degree of opposition increases in direct proportion with the distance the objector lives from the ground to be taken. When we get as far east as New England the opposition has become a frenzy.[50]

Such Congressmen, remote from New England (and the Puritan tradition), did not realize that this great battle was not really over whether two square miles should be wet or dry. Hetch Hetchy became the proxy fight for a battle of moral visions. If the choice had simply been between wilderness or dams, the issue could not have survived twelve years, seesawing up and down the corridors of Washington and prompting editorials throughout the nation's press. The issues here were beauty and the public good versus materialism and private greed. Both sides naturally were for the first two and against the other two. What the opponents could not agree upon was what these terms meant and how they fitted into God's plan for mankind and creation.

Opponents and proponents agreed that beauty was an issue. Muir and his followers, devotees of the spiritualized beauty of Romanticism and Transcendentalism, regarded the valley as a temple of God, whose beauty inspired the moral faculties of the beholder and whose enemies were ensnared in the trap of mere material gain. Muir pleaded passionately,

> These temple destroyers, devotees of ravaging commercialism, seem to have a perfect contempt for Nature, and, instead of lifting their eyes to the God of the mountains, lift them to the Almighty Dollar. Dam Hetch-Hetchy! As well dam for water-tanks the people's cathedrals and churches, for no holier temple has ever been consecrated by the heart of man.[51]

If the money changers were not thrown from the temple, wrote Johnson, Hetch Hetchy's beauty could not help offset "the rampant materialism of today. . . . Without this touch of idealism, this sense of beauty, life would only be a race for the trough." Low motives threatened this work of God. "Public-spirited men" must protect parks from "the whim or advantage of local interests," whose true interest in the "production of power for use and for sale" was "commercialism pure and simple." Hetch Hetchy's advantage as a water source lay solely in its low cost, about $20,000,000 less than any other source; thus, San Francisco's desire to avoid paying a proper price for its water and to take the nation's "noblest pleasure ground" instead, became a "steal" or a "grab" — or worse: "The spectacle of thus parceling out the resources of one of God's most beautiful creations has had no counterpart since the casting of lots for the raiment of Jesus."[52]

These charges rankled with the dam supporters. If beauty is what you want, they said, the dam would do nothing more than create a beautiful mountain lake where there now lay a meadow that was covered with snow most of the year, infested with mosquitoes in spring, and too hot in summer. By the terms of the bill, San Francisco promised to build roads to and around the reservoir, carving them into the solid granite walls of the north wall, democratizing God's beauty so that "the poor can visit the park," not "only the rich and well-to-do people." To preserve the beauty of the entire park, Pinchot recommended an amendment prohibiting the cutting of timber — even dead or down timber — within its bounds.[53]

Both sides claimed to be acting in the best interests of the public good. To defenders of the undammed valley, its public purpose was simply the recreation and uplift of the people. Dam advocates on the other hand shifted their public-benefit rhetoric into high gear:

> To provide for the little children, men, and women of the 800,000 population who swarm the shores of San Francisco Bay is a matter of much greater importance than encouraging the few who, in solitary loneliness, will sit on the peak of the Sierra loafing around the throne of the God of Nature and singing his praise.[54]

Many dam proponents repeated the Pinchot definition of conservation as the greatest good for the greatest number. As Pinchot himself said, ". . . [T]he intermittent esthetic enjoyment of less than 1 per cent is being balanced against the daily comfort and welfare of 99 per cent." Hetch Hetchy's remoteness, allowing comparatively few to visit it, turned into a liability. Why should California lack water "in order that a few enthusiasts may go into this valley and be eaten up by mosquitoes while they are admiring some cliffs"? Such enthusiasts "would sooner save a rock than human life."[55]

The debate did not hinge upon whether the valley should be used; rather, the issue entailed the definition of Hetch Hetchy's *highest* use. Over against the preservationist claim that the highest use of the valley would be to allow people to experience it "in the condition fashioned by the hand of the Creator," proponents argued that "no higher purpose, no higher use, no higher conservation can ever be practiced than furnishing a municipality with clear, pure water to drink and to bathe in." It was a crime to let Sierra flood waters "flow idly, unsubdued, and unattended into the sea" (an appeal to both the Protestant ethic and Genesis 1:28). The choice was between "the sounds of nature on the floor of that valley" and "the cry of humanity all up and down the Pacific coast." There was much rhetorical hand-wringing over the cries of thirsty babies in San Francisco.[56]

God made earth for man, dam supporters said, who must use its resources for the good of all, not simply a supposed elite few. They resented that certain "nature lovers" who regarded themselves as "the direct agents of God Almighty" could take control of the federal government to circumvent the will of the people and even the will of God for their own private purposes. They argued that mankind had dominion over all the earth for "some useful purpose" and as earth's stewards humans must use it wisely, including God's great gift of water. The evident design of the world proved that

> the Almighty made Hetch Hetchy for some definite thing; he made it for the use of man above all other considerations, and if in forming the Sierras that gap was created designedly, it was not to be looked at through the centuries, but to use.[57]

Emerson and Muir's "uses" of nature were no uses at all. Many, especially states' rights Democrats, took a dim view of these versions of God's purposes and the common good. Both preservationists and conservationists believed the federal government should protect national interests against short-sighted local interests. States' righters insisted that San Francisco and California could best ascertain local needs and conditions and could best provide for its people. Representative Martin Dies of Texas attacked the very idea of conservation, which to him meant a group of "theorists" closing off "the great resources of this country." "God Almighty has located the resources of this country in such a form as that His children will not use them in disproportion," Dies proclaimed, "and your Pinchots will not be able to controvert and circumvent the laws of God Almighty."[58]

It was not Muir's forces but the hoary Jeffersonian vision of an agrarian republic drawing virtue from its contact with the earth that nearly derailed the Raker Act. Unlike the wet Sacramento Valley to the north, the arid San Joaquin depended totally on Sierra water to make the soil fruitful. Demanding that the cities of the San Francisco Bay take water from a northern California source, not from one of the few southern ones, San Joaquin Valley irrigators portrayed themselves as "home builders,"[59] a Pinchot–Roosevelt term which honored homesteaders as upholders of virtue who brought of civility and domesticity to the untamed wilderness. Dam proponents could only weakly counter that "the conservation of the people is more important than the conservation of agriculture."[60] (Conservation had become such a shibboleth that all sides to the controversy had to make it appear that they represented true "conservation.")

Yet these arguments about beauty, utility, the common good, and the use of God's earth did not determine the fate of the Raker Act as much as one provision which promised a housecleaning in the city upon a hill. This provision transformed the act from a water bill into a public-water-power bill. Progressives saw it as a landmark precedent for federally sponsored public utilities and a major blow against the evil of private monopoly. Senator George W. Norris later recalled that without this provision, the bill could not have passed Congress.[61] Representative William Kent of California had added it to ensure that Hetch Hetchy's public power station would never sell power wholesale to such power monopolies as Pacific Gas and Electric. As congressmen portrayed San Francisco as "in the grip" of power and water monopolies,[62] Progressives on both sides of the aisle joined the fight against the monopolies that had long burdened the state.

Unfortunately for the dam's opponents, they thus found themselves with very unpopular friends — the private power and water corporations fighting public power companies. Muir's stance as spokesman for moral uplift was now turned against him, for how could a moral position coincide with a venal, selfish one? The dam opponents' best arguments — that there were other viable water sources and that this violation of a national park, very few of which then existed, formed a precedent dangerous to all parks — faded from the debate. The dam forces used the preservationists' pose of moral superiority to business and politics to marginalize them and their arguments. Their coalition with the women's clubs worked against them as they became branded with that "womanish" trait, guidance by sentiment, not reason. Repeatedly, dam opponents characterized their adversaries as sentimentalists, tender esthetes, and misinformed women. How could "the tender sensibilities of the modern esthetician" compare with the "thoughtful brain of a common-sense, practical man"? Dam proponents' genderization of the Hetch Hetchy Valley debate reached astonishing extent in San Francisco newspapers and in the city's congressional lobby. Marsden Manson, San Francisco's chief lobbyist, belittled Muir's prose as "verbal lingerie and frills," replete with " 'networks,' 'veils,' 'fibers,' 'downy feathers,' 'fabrics,' 'textures,' 'patterns,' 'embroideries,' 'tissues,' 'plumes,' 'irised robes.' " Manson characterized dam opponents as "short-haired women and long-haired men."[63]

In vain did park defender Steenerson try to turn this marginalization of his position to his advantage (ironically, just as Pinchot had in his own writings):

> Now, you say that is all sentiment; that Mr. Muir and Dr. Johnson are sentimental. I grant it, and I am glad of it. You people in California, where woman suffrage prevails, will find out that you have got to pay some respect to sentiment hereafter. [Laughter.] One reason why I am opposing this bill is that the Woman's Club in Minnesota passed a resolution unanimously in favor of protecting this national park from vandalism and desecration. I have great respect for their sentiments. Such sentiments are the foundation of all noble and heroic deeds among men.[64]

Time and again, congressmen attacked dam opponents as "sentimentalists," uninformed as to the true facts, who consequently became unwitting pawns of the wily, nefarious trusts. "Generally speaking," said Senator Thomas of Colorado, "the crook has a natural affinity for the sentimentalist. He knows that he can utilize the sincerity of the latter's conviction and the simplicity of his nature by making it a commercial asset."[65] As a pro-dam editorial in *Harper's Weekly* put it,

> The forces in opposition are two — the water-power companies, who know exactly what they are doing, and the sentimental lovers of scenery, who do not know at all what they are doing. A very few of them, like John Muir, may know the facts and be out of perspective on the relative importance of things, but most of them are persons unaccustomed to studying exact conditions, who merely go up in the air, when somebody tells them that some scenery is going to be hurt somewhere.[66]

The very success of the effort to mobilize opinion against the bill became evidence to its supporters of tainted motives, for where had the money come from to finance this campaign, if not from the power companies?[67]

Pinchot's Progressive conservation program avoided such marginalization because it envisioned an active, economic relationship with nature. Unfortunately for defenders of the valley, to Progressives the great enemy of the public good was monopoly, in particular the power companies (which Pinchot later attacked as Pennsylvania governor). The supposed naïveté of femininized "nature lovers" in economic and practical matters made it easier to believe they were innocent dupes, out of their depth in the world of politics and public policy.

Progressive conservationists and national park defenders fought over issues that Puritans would have found familiar. For the Progressives, as for Edward Johnson, it was a fight for a Christian nation, and even for the kingdom of God on earth. To the Sierra Club and its allies, it was a battle to preserve the places of God where people could, like Anne Bradstreet, contemplate higher things. Both conservationist and preservationist agreed that greed and materialism were the snake in the Garden. Covetousness had no place in the New Jerusalem.

In many ways the rhetoric of the Hetch Hetchy debates encapsulated the history of Christian attitudes toward and ethical impact on nature. Dam supporters marshalled a variety of age-old religious arguments. God had made the earth for man's benefit and put it under his dominion; thus the Creator had intended that everything be put to good use. God had designed the earth; if a valley was perfectly fit for a dam, then the Great Artisan had planned it for that purpose. The highest use of anything is its use for the common good of mankind; a reservoir, not a remote valley, gave the greatest good to the greatest number, and public ownership would prevent the enrichment of selfish interests at public expense. The Puritan ethic had taught that usefulness was godly and idleness and waste were sins; water should be used, not flow idly and wastefully to the sea. To create a godly nation, society and nature must conform to religious and moral standards; rationalized use of resources would help perfect society. Pursuing that sparkling ideal which has always lured builders of the New Jerusalem, dam proponents believed that transformation of the landscape would produce prosperity, plenty, and peace.

Defenders of the undammed valley also appealed to ancient religious doctrines. To dam opponents, the world was an emanation of God's glory and power; a place like Hetch Hetchy was a temple designed to worship in. Earthly beauty mirrored the beauty of God; the government must preserve the valley for the moral and spiritual uplift it invoked. Periodic moral regeneration served best the public good; surrounded by the works of man, engaged in unholy commerce, urban dwellers needed places where they could rest and refresh both body and soul. As righteous prophets defending moral uplift, Muir and Johnson condemned holiness besmirched for base motives; money changers were in the temple, and the valley would be crucified while the interests cast lots for the profits. Like the Puritans, they had erected a Hedge to protect an Eden, yet here Satan had gained entrance.

Aside from the dam and reservoir, few things about the Hetch Hetchy dam came out as its proponents expected, and, of course, it did not help these Christian soldiers advance the Kingdom of God. Rather, all of Muir's direst predictions came true. San Francisco never completed its part of the bargain. Not surprisingly, the city never constructed the promised road through the solid granite cliffs of Hetch Hetchy's north wall. Moreover, there is no beautiful mountain lake at Hetch Hetchy. The annual rising and falling of the reservoir waters has left a bleached band on the granite walls and regularly exposes vast mud flats at the reservoir's shallow places. Far from being a beautiful playground of the public, the lake receives very few visitors. Despite an access road, it is still remote and has no place to stay and little to see.

What not even Muir foresaw was that this Progressive precedent in public power would be so compromised in execution. San Francisco flouted the Kent amendment and sold its electricity wholesale to Pacific Gas and Electric until Secretary of the Interior Harold Ickes stopped the practice in 1939. Nevertheless, even today, power travels from the dam on public lines only as far as Newark, on San Francisco's doorstep, and comes into the city on lines owned by Pacific Gas and Electric.

In the 1980s, when the reservoir had long since been superseded as San Francisco's water supply, Secretary of the Interior Donald Hodel proposed removal of the dam and restoration of Hetch Hetchy Valley. San Francisco objected because it would lose the income it receives from sale of electric power, money which lightens the burden of its taxpayers. After some discussion, the plan was dropped. Thus, as Muir might say, in the end it is the Almighty Dollar which keeps Hetch Hetchy dammed, and the choice between God and Mammon has been decided in favor of the latter.

The complicated battle over the Hetch Hetchy dam, too complex for easy identification of heroes and villains, symbolizes the ambiguity and ambivalence that have been expressed throughout history in religious doctrine and in people's lives. In America, the image of a renewed Eden, of humanity happy in abundant and harmonious nature, has created conflict between the ideals of capitalist plenty and nature preservation. Although both Puritans and Mormons sought to transform the wilderness for God, nevertheless worldly temptations transformed their saintly kingdoms for commerce and capitalism. William Gilpin expected industry and railroads to bring agrarian paradise, but they brought urbanized tartarus instead. Railroad leaders lived according to the work ethic, tirelessly conquering the wilderness, yet many like Jay Cooke, Frederick Billings, and James J. Hill found themselves working to preserve pieces of that wilderness or to repair the ecological damage their railroads had caused or made possible.

Ambivalence and unresolved contradictions find their way into every view of nature. Anne Hutchinson loved this world's beauty even as she longed for happiness in the next. Science and philosophy, seized by Cotton Mather to support orthodoxy, instead removed devils and angels from the world. Benjamin Franklin and Thomas Jefferson sought eternal truths in nature while endeavoring to make it an agent of reason. Emerson used natural beauty for mystical purposes, yet encouraged humanity to make nature an instrument of human will. A farmer, inventor, mechanic, sheep herder, sawyer, and fruit rancher, John Muir spent four decades of his life as a useful, practical man of the kind he often railed against. Gifford Pinchot's synthesis of scientific method and moral purpose faded with the Progressive movement which he helped lead. Even today, varieties of environmentalism contain seeds of their own contradiction.[68]

There is no better example of this ambiguity than the career of William Kent, sponsor of the public power amendment that turned a water-supply bill into a Progressive cause. Scion of a wealthy family of Yankee Calvinists, Kent had gone to Yale with Pinchot and later befriended Muir. He believed strongly in Progressivism, conservationism, and the Social Gospel. He earned his Progressive credentials as member of commissions which cleaned up corruption in Chicago and San Francisco.

Kent's active interest in conservation dated from 1900, when he bought a grove of redwood trees to save them from inundation by a water company. In 1908 he donated the grove to the United States and asked that it be named after Muir, and it is known today as Muir Woods National Monument. He fought for public ownership of the Marin County, California, water supply and for the creation of California's Mt. Tamalpais State Park. In 1909 he opposed the lowering of Lake Tahoe for the production of power and irrigation on the Truckee River in Nevada, basing his opposition upon the fact that the power would be in private hands.

The Truckee–Tahoe fight prepared Kent for Hetch Hetchy and his crucial amendment. Throughout the controversy, he staunchly supported the Raker Bill and ridiculed Muir as a man with an underdeveloped social sense whose position was, "it is me and God and the rock where God put it." Later, Kent, an independent Republican, became Wilson's main conservation advisor. In concert with Secretary of the Interior Franklin Lane, in 1916 he introduced the bill creating the National Park Service, a measure opposed by Pinchot, who wanted the parks in the care of the Forest Service. Upon its passage, Lane's friend Stephen Mather, a Sierra Club member, became its first director. Like many dam supporters, Kent's attitudes toward nature could not easily be pigeonholed. Progressive to the core, he aligned himself at times with Muir-style preservationism, at times with Pinchot conservation.[69]

While Muir's spiritualized nature had won a great following, especially in New England and areas of Yankee influence, and while it had very successfully popularized the national park ideal, it had done so against opponents who had no moral vision to defend, opponents whose sole apparent interest in mountains and forests was private gain. When the Sierra Club and its friends ran up against a conflicting moral vision, one moreover associated with a rationalist doctrine of economic use, they could not prevail. Ironically, Hetch Hetchy helped divest conservationism's moral from its scientific element. Women, "sentimentalists," and "aesthetes" seemed to fade from conservation's concerns. Perhaps a mid-twentieth-century world preoccupied with world wars and economic boom and bust could not afford the luxury of a Romantic relation with nature. For the next half century, government leaders developed a public policy entrusting scientists and experts with practical, common-sense issues like soil conservation, flood control, waterways, reservoirs, swamp drainage, and irrigation. So thoroughly had rational conservation eclipsed moral and mystical views that their dramatic revival during the last thirty years has appeared to most commentators as something radically new.

EIGHT

The Twentieth Century

> I came upon a child of God
> He was walking along the road
> And I asked him, where are you going
> And this he told me
> I'm going on down to Yasgurs' farm
> I'm going to join in a rock 'n' roll band
> I'm going to camp out on the land
> And try an' get my soul free
>> We are stardust
>> We are golden
>> And we've got to get ourselves
>> Back to the garden
>
> —JONI MITCHELL, "WOODSTOCK" (1969)

To put it mildly, there is something evangelical about [former Sierra Club President David] Brower. His approach is in some ways analogous to the Reverend Dr. Billy Graham's exhortations to sinners to come forward and be saved now because if you go away without making a decision for Christ coronary thrombosis may level you before you exit. Brower's crusade, like Graham's, began many years ago, and Brower's may have been more effective.... Brower is a visionary. He wants—literally—to save the world.... He thinks that conservation should be "an ethic and conscience in everything we do, whatever our field of endeavor"—in a word, a religion.

> —JOHN MCPHEE, ENCOUNTERS WITH THE ARCHDRUID (1971)

We were in ... a political and spiritual battle for the future of America.

> —LEILANI (MRS. JAMES G.) WATT,
> CAUGHT IN THE CROSSFIRE (1984)

At the onset of this century Americans were confident and self-assured. Protestants were confident and self-assured. Conservationists were confident and self-assured. The nation was strong and growing stronger. Its moral and political leaders pointed the way toward a better society, perhaps even to the Kingdom of God on earth. Its conservationists were restraining the plutocrats of self-interested monopoly and protecting America's natural heritage and resources.

At century's end, confidence and self-assurance are shaken. Protestants bicker among themselves over creed and doctrine. The old "mainline" churches dwindle, while upstarts like the Assembly of God or the Mormons or even the Roman Catholic Church flourish. Conservationists, now styled "environmentalists," have split into a dozen organizations with a dozen emphases, and all have been surprised by the increasing strength of their opponents.

The twentieth century transformed the nation. Protestant cultural dominance has been challenged and diminished by cultural diversity. Emerging from the background to which they had been pushed in the nineteenth century, Catholic, Jewish, and black Protestant voices contribute to public discourse. They have introduced new interests and arguments into conservationism. Their communal, social emphases have forced old issues like wilderness and the land ethic and the silent springs to share the spotlight with social problems such as "environmental racism."

Still, most Americans and, disproportionately, most articulate, well-educated, and affluent Americans are Protestant. The Calvinist tradition has yet a great deal of cultural power.

The polarization of Protestantism into evangelical and liberal camps that began in the seventeenth and eighteenth centuries has further crystallized in the twentieth century into recognizable conservative and liberal positions concerning nature. The conservative constellation of attitudes includes religious and political conservatism, empiricism tending toward Biblical literalism, the Protestant ethic, and laissez-faire anti-authoritarianism. Liberal religious attitudes tend to associate with political liberalism, theological eclecticism tending toward antinomianism and mysticism, humanitarianism, and trust in government action to protect the common good. Through these two traditions Protestant tenets survive in both religious and secular contexts.

The history of environmentalism in this century is one of dominance by Pinchot-style conservation followed by the curious gradual overshadowing of conservation by preservationism to form the modern environmental movement. Conservation's essential character as moral reform rather than science made this possible. Originally heavily Republican, conservationists joined the 1912 secession of the party's reform wing in the Progressive Party. When the Progressive Party melted away, the Republican Party received its members back as traitors, and reformers never regained their prominence in the party. With the Democrats the party of reform after 1933, conservationists found a new home. From the Square Deal to the New Deal to the Great Society, conservation and environmentalism have advanced in association with reform programs designed to realize visions of a better society. The stronger moral appeal of Muir-style preservation over Pinchot-type conservation, evident in the array of organizations which opposed the Hetch Hetchy dam, has caused Pinchot's reputation to go into eclipse.[1]

A momentous consequence has been to cut environmentalists off from government when the Democratic party falls from power and allow Republicans free rein to put the conservative constellation of attitudes into policy. Conservatives lack the *social* moral vision of liberals (although they strongly emphasize *personal* morality, particularly concerning values and behavior). Without that strong social role to play, their version of conservation tends to fall in line with their traditionally strong pro-business platform.

Protestant-linked economic attitudes remain prominent in Republican Party rhetoric. Its leaders still tout the Protestant work ethic and criticize those programs (especially concerning social welfare) which appear to undermine it. Convinced the public good depends directly upon prosperity, which in turn depends upon the free decisions of individuals in the marketplace (rather than a central government which might give error the force of law), the party is suspicious that government interference in the economy hobbles economic growth. Its business-mindedness thus has led it to concentrate on policies which lead to greater production and consumption and to weaken or eliminate policies, like environmental regulation, which seem to hinder economic growth.

The religious right continues the religious traditions disposed toward use and abuse of nature. Evangelicalism's heavy Biblicism incline it toward the Hebrew characteristics of the Christian God and away from the mystical Greek elements. Evangelicals recognize acts of Providence and God's power in nature (as when Republican televangelist Pat Robertson revealed in 1988 that his prayers had turned a hurricane away from Virginia), but they do not emphasize a reverent attitude toward nature and view non-Biblical, neo-Platonic theological tenets with mistrust.

Democrats also manifest connections with the Protestant heritage.

When the Democrats absorbed the Progressive program, they absorbed with it the New England reform tradition, outgrowth in turn of Puritan efforts to enlist the magistrate in the creation of a godly society. One element, for example, that Pinchot and Muir had in common was their reliance upon the central government to protect land for its proper purposes. Neither trusted the whims of private initiative or local or state governments. This dependence upon the federal government has increased with the strength of the environmental movement: from forest reserves, national parks and monuments, wildlife refuges, and wilderness areas, to the National Environmental Policy Act, the Environmental Protection Agency, and the Endangered Species Act, the federal government has gradually expanded its control in areas of environmental concern.

Liberal Protestantism forsakes literal Biblicism and shows an affinity for the neo-Platonic strain of Christian belief. The most striking current example is process theology. Developed by Alfred North Whitehead, Charles Hartshorne, John Cobb, Jr., and others, process theology teaches that the most basic building block of the universe is process, a conclusion drawn from modern physics and its supersession of Newtonian space and time. All elemental units are sentient (in that they react to other units), not unlike Leibniz's monads, and in a sense cooperate to construct larger units like rocks, plants, people, or planets. To process theologians, the universe itself is a process in which God is immanent — again, a renewed version of the World Soul of Plotinus and Hegel.

Upon this basis Cobb and others have founded an environmental ethic. Just as cooperation of the basic units of the body further the body's interest, humans' "rational interest" is not in "irrational," selfish self-aggrandizement, but in the society of which they are members, that is, in the common good. Their "enlightened interest" is thus in an altruism easily expanded to a system of ethics which includes all nature. This, in a roundabout way, returns to the Puritans' pointed insistence on each individual's usefulness to society, and rejects the "invisible hand" theory of self-interest as the best promotion of the common good. Hartshorne went on to elaborate a hierarchy of values based upon intelligence, creativity, and freedom, which makes humans most valuable — a clear echo of the Great Chain of Being.[2]

Due to its technical vocabulary and heavy intellectualization, process theology has not made its influence strongly felt outside seminaries and academia, but there are many popularized versions of neo-Platonic doctrines. The Gaia hypothesis, which considers the world as an organism, has undoubted neo-Platonic roots, although its formulator, J. E. Lovelock, disclaimed any mysticism.[3] Neo-Platonism's links with Indian thought have reappeared in the admiration environmentalists often have for Indian and Taoist philosophy. More common is simply a generalized feeling, evidenced by Thoreau's enduring popularity, for the earth's natural or rural beauty as a fount to refresh or renew the spirit far from the materialist concerns of American civilization. This feeling formed a major part of popular 1960s anti-materialist convictions, such as in the hippie and commune movements, and helped produce an explosion of interest in backpacking and outdoor activity during the 1970s.

The humanitarian tradition, which drives many aspects of the reform movement, has taken several forms in regard to nature. The extension of humanitarian feelings to animals is clear in the actions of animal-rights protesters, and also comes through in crusades to save wildlife such as the World Wildlife Fund's glossy campaigns on behalf of baby seals and pandas. The extremes which this impulse has reached appear in the Earth First! coalition, which places the earth first in any ethic, even ahead of people when necessary.

The old Calvinistic obedience to higher law continues to fuel civil disobedience among liberal activists (and, in a rare example of conservative civil disobedience, among anti-abortion groups). Earth First! is again the most extreme among environmental groups, eschewing all compromise and mere "reform" of American government and society. Earth First!ers might chain themselves to trees or take up residence in threatened caves, but their adherence to a law above the laws of society leads them to advocate, and occasionally practice, "the destruction of machines or property that are used to destroy the natural world."[4]

Ironically, the churches themselves, both conservative and liberal, have only slowly taken up the cause of the environment and ecological awareness. In the last decade, however, most churches have begun to explicitly discuss human responsibility to the natural world. The most common thread, and probably, therefore, the one with the strongest potential for influence in society, is the emphasis on stewardship. Stewardship derives from the idea that God has given earth to our care (which can leave moot the anthropocentric question whether the world was made for man). However, for all its potency, the concept suffers from its vague implications, which could range from the open-use intent in former Secretary of the Interior James G. Watt's adoption of the term to its selfless representation in the creed of the National Wildlife Federation.[5]

Both conservatives and liberals have drawn upon the American evangelical heritage. The foremost conservative exemplar has been Watt, who believed himself fulfilling a mission from God. He consciously preached his message to the country, using the first year of his two and a half-year term as secretary of the interior to proselytize (with rather negative results).[6] The environmental movement has been full of evangelists for the cause, beginning with Muir. Howard Zahniser of the Wilderness Society, son of a Methodist minister, supposed it was his father's evangelicalism that propelled him in his defense of wilderness and untiring lobbying for the Wilderness Act from 1956 to his death in 1964, three months before its final passage.[7] Wes Jackson, another son of the Methodist Church, speaks with the cadence and metaphors of a preacher as he proselytizes for sustainable agriculture and the Land Institute of Salina, Kansas, which he founded in 1976.[8] Powerful evangelists for the environmental gospel also include David Brower (raised Baptist), past president of the Sierra Club and founder of the Friends of the Earth, and Dave Foreman (raised Churches of Christ), co-founder of Earth First!.

Periodically, environmental evangelism rides a crest of optimism and exhilaration that carries it into hopes that the millennium lies within its grasp—if only the evil forces of society could be vanquished and the message gotten out to convert the world. Liberal Protestantism shows a greater tendency in this direction because liberals often prefer less-apocalyptic post-millennialism, in which Christ returns after a Kingdom for which believers have prepared the earth. In contrast, conservatives incline less optimistically toward pre-millennialism, the belief that Christ will return amidst divine vengeance before the thousand-year Kingdom of God. (Of course, although environmentalists have often enough indulged in apocalyptic end-of-the-world prophesying to get the world to change its ways before it's too late.) Premillennialists might, like early Mormons, prepare a refuge for the imminent last days, but postmillennialists believe that their own efforts might prepare the earth for the Second Coming and that, to that end, reform and evangelism must move forward with haste.

This enthusiasm captured Progressive conservationists like Pinchot and again burst forth in the environmentalist flowering of the late 1960s and early 1970s. Along with hopes at the time that in a transformed world, peace would guide the planets and love steer the stars, many cultural dissidents looked forward to restored harmony with nature. This desire expressed itself in both the rise of the subsistence communal movement and predictions that technology could solve our pollution problems and bring back Edenic harmony.[9]

In the late 1990s Protestantism and its spirit still lie close to the heart of America. It shows itself in the business and conscience of the Rockefellers.

A Lutheran variation influenced the popular "land ethic" of Aldo Leopold. Evangelicalism and self-righteousness drove the policies of James Watt. "Lapsed Presbyterian" Annie Dillard searches nature for signs of God. Dave Foreman takes up the wilderness gospel and preaches. The plant that the *Arbella* had brought to New England in 1630 flourishes yet on the American soil.

The Protestant Ethic: The Rockefellers

The Rockefeller story could only have been foreshadowed had Cotton Mather been a merchant or Ben Franklin been religious. Eliza Davison Rockefeller was a fervent believer who joined the Baptist Church in the "burnt-over district" (so-called from its frequent revivals) of antebellum New York State. Her son, John Davison Rockefeller, remained stubbornly Baptist as he grew inconceivably rich, and once told a reporter, "God gave me my money." With the demeanor more of a minister than a businessman, John D. Rockefeller, Jr. made the family name synonymous with modern corporate philanthropy, which the family invented, while a pillar of the foremost liberal church in America. Junior's sons dutifully and successfully carried on the family traditions of business, philanthropy, and religion. Most of the brothers' baby-boomer-era children left business and the church, and many embraced liberal and even radical causes. The Rockefeller fortune naturally makes the family story far from typical, yet from generation to generation the trajectory of its attitudes toward religion and the Protestant ethic and toward nature has closely followed that of the American middle class.

The tale begins with Eliza Davison, born in 1813, who invested her children with intense Scottish–Puritan Calvinistic piety and morality. Dour, severe, stern, full of moral maxims like "Willful waste makes woeful want," she brought up her children in the Congregational and later the Baptist Church in the heavily New England communities of western New York and Cleveland. Serious Scots and Scots-Irish Sunday school teachers and headmasters schooled her sons. Perhaps in a moment of weakness, she had married a colorful scoundrel, William Avery Rockefeller, who instructed his sons in his business methods: strict attention to business and contracts, and little regard for morality. He once remarked to a neighbor, "I trade with the boys and skin 'em and I just beat 'em every time I can. I want to make 'em sharp." William went on long mysterious trips from which he returned with abundant money, much of which was earned selling herbal cancer "cures." Into this familial mix of piety, diligence, and rapacity, John Davison Rockefeller was born in 1839.[10]

An earnest, reserved, and business-minded young man, called "the Deacon" by high school classmates, John D. began his steady climb to wealth as a clerk in a prosperous firm. Exemplar of his mother's maxims, paragon of the Protestant ethic, he saved his money compulsively, never wasted time or money if he could help it, punctually paid debts, and exemplified sobriety and industry. By 1865 he was senior partner in an oil refining business serving the recently opened, booming oil fields of Pennsylvania. By shrewd and ruthless moves that soon made his name infamous, he began to absorb or destroy any competitors, first in Cleveland, then elsewhere. In 1870 he formed Standard Oil; a decade later it refined 95 percent of the nation's oil production. In 1882 he formed the Standard Oil Trust, his ultimate weapon of control of oil refining. His fortune was worth about $900,000,000 by 1913.[11]

All was not business, however. Rockefeller regularly attended the Baptist Church throughout his life, despite its lower-class congregation. Beginning with his first paycheck, Rockefeller gave a tithe of his income (10 percent) to church and charity, including mission societies, the Y.M.C.A., and donations to the poor. He gave of his time as well, and taught Sunday school, where he reportedly expounded on a favorite quotation, "Seest thou a man diligent in his business? He shall stand before kings." Laura Spelman Rockefeller, whom he married in 1864, became his partner in piety. Congregationalist daughter of abolition and temperance activists, Laura's religion was broader than her husband's; before marriage, she had attended lectures by liberal minister Henry Ward Beecher, abolitionist Wendell Phillips, and Emerson. After their marriage, she taught Sunday school (marking "C" — for "Christian" — beside the names in her roll book of children she thought saved), helped organize the Cleveland Y.W.C.A., and was active in temperance and other causes. Both mothers-in-law joined the household while the children were young, giving it a powerful atmosphere of feminine religious and moral influence. Clergymen and missionaries were frequent visitors, and various religious and reform groups met in the house. As John D., Jr. (usually called "Junior") remembered it, "Everything centered around the home and the church, and there was nothing else. We had no childhood friends, no school friends." In spite of money evident all around the family, they were frugal: the children shared a single bicycle, and Junior wore hand-me-downs recut from his elder sisters' clothes.[12]

John D., Sr.'s charitable donations increased with his wealth, mainly to

Baptist churches, colleges (especially the University of Chicago), mission work, schools, hospitals, libraries, Y.M.C.A.'s, and temperance organizations. By 1891 requests for money and investigation into their worthiness took large amounts of his time, so he hired a Baptist minister, Frederick T. Gates, to manage them for him. Gates began to systematize Rockefeller's philanthropy, which now branched into black education and medical research. The result was the Rockefeller Foundation, a path-breaking trust fund devoted to philanthropy, education, science, and religion, chartered in 1913.

Due to his father's advanced age by then, Junior was the man who made Rockefeller the leading family in philanthropy. Serious, shy, and moralistic as a young man, temperamentally better fit for the ministry than business, Junior slowly learned under his father's tutelage to make his way in the business world. With many of his generation, and perhaps as due to the influence of his less-sectarian mother, he moved in a religiously more liberal direction. At Brown University he was an officer in the Y.M.C.A. and taught boys' Bible classes, but in the 1920s he backed the liberals in the heated fundamentalist controversy. He gave $26 million to build the famous inter-denominational Riverside Church in New York and convinced prominent anti-fundamentalist minister Harry Emerson Fosdick to take its pulpit. Religiously broad minded, Junior supported the ecumenical movement, including the Federal (later National) Council of Churches and World Council of Churches. Moreover, while he gave millions to Protestant seminaries, he also donated to secular, Catholic, and Jewish organizations.[13]

Junior's heart was more in philanthropy than business, both as part of the duty to the world that came with the Rockefeller millions, and as part of a campaign to clear perhaps the most vilified name in the country. Perhaps because he was of the generation of the Progressive Era, he steered the Rockefeller Foundation's donations into conservation, an area untouched by Gates or Senior. Like many a lonely, or loner, child, Junior had drawn pleasure from nature and its beauty which continued into adulthood. Rockefeller largesse created or contributed to Forest Hill Park in Cleveland and Fort Tryon Park in New York, the Palisades Park in New York (with help from Mrs. E. H. Harriman), a Hudson interstate park (on whose first commission sat one Rockefeller and two Harriman sons), Arcadia National Park, Shenandoah National Park, Great Smoky Mountains National Park, additional land for Yosemite, interpretive museums at Mesa Verde, the Grand Canyon, Yellowstone, and Yosemite, Virgin Islands National Park, Redwoods National Park, and the saving of bald cypresses in Florida and the South Calaveras Grove of sequoias in California. In 1943 he op-

posed dams on the upper Rio Grande that imperiled pueblos and land of
the Pueblo Indians. Junior's greatest effort and perhaps greatest achievement, considering the local political opposition, was the addition of Jackson
Hole to Grand Tetons National Park. During all this activity, Junior carried on voluminous correspondence with conservation leader Horace M.
Albright, head of the National Park Service from 1929 to 1933, and relied
constantly on his advice and counsel. Considering the appalling environmental degradation in the Pennsylvania oil fields from which the Rockefeller wealth was extracted, it is ironic if fitting that so many millions of that
fortune should preserve so much beauty.[14]

Junior's children inherited the Rockefeller fortune and the sense of duty
that went with it, but they did not receive the traditional strict Baptist
religious training. Junior's wife, Abby Aldrich Rockefeller (incidentally,
sister-in-law to Charles Crocker's granddaughter), was descended from Puritans on both sides of the family but had cast off Puritan seriousness. Active
in New York's cultural and social life, she was one of the founders of the
Museum of Modern Art in 1929. It was not Abby but Junior who took their
five children to church every Sunday and gave them religious instruction.

Junior's daughter and five sons were less devout than he but were still
affected by the family's moral intensity and Protestant-ethic values. While
at Princeton, John D. III (or JDR3) volunteered at the Y.M.C.A. David
took over the Rockefeller role in Riverside Church. As a teenager, Laurence doubted the existence of God, but retained a keen sensitivity to moral
issues and majored in philosophy at Princeton, where he entitled his bachelor's thesis "The Concept of Value and its Relation to Ethics." As for the
Protestant ethic, David's Ph.D. thesis at the University of Chicago, "Unused Resources and Economic Want," criticized inefficiency, waste, and
idleness ("willful waste make woeful want," in great-grandma's words).

All of the brothers involved themselves in philanthropy and public service. Of the siblings, Laurence had the greatest interest in conservation,
which dated to a 1924 family trip to Yellowstone during which then–Park
Superintendent Horace Albright had given them a tour. Laurence married
Mary French, a descendant of Frederick Billings and very religious, and
later bought the Billings–Marsh estate in Vermont. Although no real outdoorsman, he yearly took his family to his ranch in the Tetons. "Close to
nature," he remarked, "people find a mystical, almost physical kind of
rapport. It is uplifting and creative."[15]

Calling himself an apprentice to his father in conservation, after World
War II Laurence took over Jackson Hole Preserve, Inc., the organization
through which the Grand Teton land purchases had been funded, and other

Rockefeller conservation interests. He helped Fairfield Osborn, author of the influential *Our Plundered Planet*, start the Conservation Foundation in 1947 and served as a trustee, and a decade later created an organization, the American Conservation Association, which he hoped would become the leading conservation organization. By that time, he was also a commissioner of the Palisades Park, a director of the Hudson River Conservation Society, a trustee of the New York Zoological Society, and head of President Eisenhower's Outdoor Recreation Resources and Review Commission. This latter work led President Kennedy to appoint Laurence head of the Advisory Council on Recreation. His influence peaked during the Johnson administration, when he served in succession on the Task Force on Natural Beauty, as head of the White House Conference on Natural Beauty, as chairman of the Citizens' Advisory Committee on Recreation and Natural Beauty, and as White House advisor on environmental matters. Lady Bird Johnson worked closely with him and became a trustee of Jackson Hole Preserve, Inc.

Laurence Rockefeller, however, leaned to the Pinchot tradition; while he supported the creation of parks, he was just as concerned with the conscientious development of American resources, especially during the darkest days of the Cold War, when it seemed that every resource must be mobilized to save the free world. Thus, Resources for the Future, a sort of conservation think tank, in 1958 invited him to join its board, which also at times included Osborn and Albright. Laurence's conservation interest also often had a business angle. In 1951, at an associate's urging, he studied the Livingston estate in Puerto Rico, which the University of Puerto Rico wanted as a botanical garden, and constructed an elegant hotel there. He bought an exclusive resort in the Virgin Islands, had the Jackson Hole Preserve, Inc., buy much of the rest of the island, and gave the property (except the resort) to the government as the Virgin Islands National Park. His construction of the Mauna Kea Hotel spurred development of the little-used Kohala coast in Hawaii. At its opening he noted, "This is an uplifting, creative environment, and my hotels are designed to keep people as close to nature as possible."[16]

That attitude meant that the environmental movement would leave Laurence Rockefeller behind after the mid-1960s. The turning point was his support of Consolidated Edison's plan to transform the dramatic Hudson granite bluff Storm King into a huge hydroelectric pumping station, and a plan to place along the Hudson an interstate highway (which deliberately ran along the water to avoid the Rockefeller Pocantico estate). The public outcry was immediate and powerful, and both plans eventually died in the courts. Laurence's sensitive negotiations with interested groups in drawing up boundaries for Redwood National Park resulted in a smaller, less spectacular park because of his friendship with and sympathy with Weyerhaeuser Timber Company's management. Although his power in government conservation circles continued in the 1970s, his business interests often compromised his effectiveness as an environmental spokesman.

The motive power of Rockefeller duty and purpose inevitably waned among Junior's two dozen grandchildren, brought up in six different families and born over a span of a quarter century. In his family, Nelson laid heavy emphasis on duty and ethics and continued Junior's practice of Bible readings and Sunday devotions. David took his family to church; the other brothers let lapse the stricter Rockefeller moral traditions. For most of the brothers' children, then, nineteenth-century Protestant fire from the burnt-over district survived in embers of varying heat. Only Nelson's son Rodman, the eldest male cousin, took up traditional Rockefeller interests, from business (in his father's company, International Basic Economy Corporation) to membership in Riverside Church. Some of the female cousins, however, moved in a radical direction. Outsiders in a patriarchal family, they had no expected role to fill in business or philanthropy. Laurence's daughter Laura joined the SDS in the 1960s, and David's daughter Abby was a 1960s Marxist and feminist. Yet, in a curiously New Age twist to Rockefeller tradition, Abby combined business and environmental activism when in 1974 she set up a company, Clivus Multrum, USA, to manufacture a Swedish composting toilet.

Laurence, Jr. (Larry) and Nelson's son Steven have been most involved in conservation. Larry donated to the Sierra Club Legal Defense while it was opposing his father over the Redwood National Park. A lawyer with the Natural Resources Defense Council, he has stepped into his father's shoes in conservation organizations and is president of the Palisades Interstate Park Commission and the American Conservation Association, a trustee of Jackson Hole Preserve, Inc., and active in the Alaska Coalition and the Barrier Island Coalition. The Beaverkill Mountain Corporation, of which he is also president, is a pet enterprise, his "weekend conservation project" since 1976. Having bought a farmhouse in a beautiful valley of the Catskills, half of which was state forest, he worked with hunting and fishing clubs and like-minded landowners to buy up valley land threatened with subdivision and then sell high-priced fifteen-acre lots to buyers willing to put their land into conservation easements. Such a combination of business and conservation recalls his father's projects.[17]

In Laurence Rockefeller, Sr., youthful interest in values and ethics had preceded a career interest in conservation. The pattern repeated itself in Nelson's son Steven, the cousins' "conscience" and leading environmental activist, although his interest in nature had a far more spiritual tendency. A trustee of Jackson Hole Preserve, Inc., and the American Conservation Association, Steven opposed his father Nelson and Laurence over Storm King. Steven's reading in Paul Tillich and theology led him to spend three years at Union Theological Seminary, although he was not a believing Christian, followed by a doctorate in philosophy at Columbia University with a thesis on the ethical grounds of John Dewey's thought. Steven quit the boards of his uncle's foundations and took a job as professor of religion at Middlebury College in Vermont. In 1990 he organized a symposium and art exhibition at Middlebury called "Spirit and Nature" which treated all religious traditions equally and which he hoped might "contribute to a transformation of awareness and values that will save the Earth and make possible the unfolding of spirit and nature that is yet to be." (The symposium was featured in the PBS special "Spirit & Nature with Bill Moyers.")[18] Steven's non-denominational spiritual interest in nature was quite in tune with the baby-boomer generations' "New Age" spiritual tendencies and what Catherine Albanese calls "nature religion."[19]

In a land without primogeniture, it is striking that the Rockefeller "dynasty" lasted three generations before splintering. In large measure, the family's staying power in business and philanthropy while other families of great wealth rose and fell resulted from its strong Protestant tradition, which also began to fade with the third generation. It was the faith that bound together work and wealth, creed and conservation. Out of this faith came a great business empire, built on resource exploitation, memorialized in monuments in natural beauty from Acadia to the Redwoods and from the Virgin Islands to the Grand Tetons. Yet this faith, this business, these monuments have changed as the nation changed. The family moved, each generation, in a more liberal religious direction. It has taught an ever milder version of the religious duty to work and save. And it shifted from shameless resource exploitation, to conservation and parks, and thence to modern environmental activism.

The Lutheran Ethic: Aldo Leopold

Separated by ninety-nine years, the lives of the mature Aldo Leopold and the young John Muir had many points in common. Eleven-year-old John Muir settled in frontier Wisconsin in May 1849, while in April 1948, shortly before his death, Leopold discussed making Muir's homestead a park. Muir's first American home had been a cabin on the wilderness plot that his father began turning into a farm, but not many miles away Leopold spent weekends in a cabin transforming the worn-out farmland into wilderness. Muir studied and Leopold taught at the University of Wisconsin.

Religiously, there was also a sense of God-in-nature that linked the two men, although, for Leopold, attenuated for the more secular early twentieth century and held so privately that even his daughter, a year before his death, asked him if he believed in God.

> He replied that he believed there was a mystical supreme power that guided the Universe. But to him this power was not a personalized God. It was more akin to the laws of nature. He thought organized religion was all right for many people, but he did not partake of it himself, having left that behind him a long time ago. His religion came from nature, he said.[20]

According to his son Luna, Leopold "was kind of pantheistic. The organization of the universe was enough to take the place of God, if you like. . . . The wonders of nature were, of course, objects of admiration and satisfaction to him."[21]

The fact that his religious beliefs were so private that biographers must glean them from his children declares that Leopold, whatever his admiration for Muir, was quite another man. Indeed, he began his career not in Muir's camp but in Pinchot's. He attended Yale's forestry school, founded with Pinchot money. His first summer as a forester he spent on the Pinchot Pennsylvania estate, located adjacent to the Pinchot family seat and donated to the forestry school. Leopold's influential ideas on wilderness preservation and wildlife conservation grew out of a philosophy of making the best use of America's forests.

At heart, Leopold was neither of Muir nor of Pinchot, and his book, *A Sand County Almanac and Sketches Here and There*, a cornerstone of modern environmental thought, is neither an exposition of the Book of Nature nor a chapter in the Gospel of Efficiency. Leopold's blood was German, his heritage Lutheran. He lacked the Calvinistic intensity that made others evangelists for their cause, reformers of the world, or millennialists preparing the way for the Kingdom of God. Martin Luther had quailed at the revolutionary implications of radical Protestantism and reined them in. The world he firmly divided into the "two kingdoms," the realm of spiritual concerns and the realm of earthly endeavors. Governments were divinely instituted to restrain sin and should not be challenged. Lutherans focused on personal salvation. To Calvinists righteous action indicated salvation, but for Lutherans those who trusted in God received saving grace. Embracing Old Testament Law, Luther's church emphasized personal morality. Lacking the Calvinist emphasis on action in this world and forging the godly society through reform or revolution, Lutherans concentrated on individual piety and adherence to a personal ethic.[22]

The great differences between the Lutheran ethic and the "Protestant" ethic of Calvinism and Pietism have left their imprint on American society. More Americans claim German ancestry than any other ethnic group, yet German Lutherans have rarely become leading capitalists, social reformers, or conservationists. Great Lutheran moral exemplars have tended to be people who follow codes of personal morality. Albert Schweitzer, perhaps the most inspirational Lutheran of this century (whom Leopold admired), left a career in Germany to practice medicine in a remote part of Africa. He hoped his books and life would inspire others to similar moral acts, but he did not fight to change society, colonialism, or government. Similarly, Aldo Leopold's study of the Book of Nature inspired him not to stride down the mountainside with the tablets of a new Law, but to write a quiet little book urging the adoption, by a sort of individual conversion, of an ethic of respect for the earth as a living organism.

Leopold was born in Burlington, Iowa, in 1887, the grandson of German immigrants and son of a prosperous furniture manufacturer. His family environment was mildly Lutheran and heavily German — typical for Germans of his class, to whom German culture was superior to American. German language as well as German culture and philosophy (with its Romantic neo-Platonism) were staples of his boyhood and youth. The abundance of the nineteenth-century Mississippi Valley landscape left its mark on him in two ways. First, his father was an avid hunter and Leopold acquired from him his lifelong love of hunting. Second, quiet and intellectual, Leopold spent time alone in the fields, forests, and marshes, giving him a deep love of nature and birdwatching. Perhaps it was only natural that a teenager with these interests would look for a career in the outdoors, and Leopold entered the newly endowed school of forestry at Yale in 1905.

Leopold's private religious views make it difficult to trace his religious and spiritual thinking. James I. McClintock supposes a youthful bout with doubt and atheism, based on this passage from Leopold's posthumously published "Goose Music":

What value has wildlife from the standpoint of morals and religion? I heard of a boy once who was brought up an atheist. He changed his mind when he saw that there was a hundred-odd species of warblers, each bedecked like to the rainbow, and each performing yearly sundry thousands of miles of migration about which scientists wrote wisely but did not understand.

Denying that such beings could be the product of blind chance, Leopold concluded, "There are yet many boys to be born who, like Isaiah, 'may see, and know, and consider, and understand together, that the hand of the Lord hath done this.' "[23] Whether or not this is autobiographical, as McClintock believes, the passage, along with his children's memories, indicate that natural theology lay at the base of Leopold's beliefs.

In college, anyway, Leopold was a believing Christian. One Easter he wrote a sustained analogy of the Resurrection of Christ with the miraculous beauty of the resurrection of nature in spring. Throughout his Yale years, he worked at the Y.M.C.A., sometimes to the detriment of his classwork, and attended Bible study classes or studied the Bible on his own. Leopold's study of the Bible continued into the 1920s. Evidence of this interest appears in his frequent Biblical allusions in his writings and especially in his 1920 article in the *Journal of Forestry*, "The Forestry of the Prophets." This article explored the conservation consciousness of various prophets, calling Isaiah "the Roosevelt of the Holy Land" and Job "the John Muir of Judah."[24]

After graduation in 1909 from the Forestry School, Leopold took his first job in New Mexico, where the semi-arid climate magnified the human impact on the environment and sensitized Leopold to recent and ongoing artificial ecological disasters. In Iowa, he and his father watched as year after year marshes and wild areas turned into farmland and wildlife disappeared. Never very interested in harvesting trees, Leopold on his own initiative pushed successfully for Forest Service establishment of game preserves and management of game and wildlife. A nearly fatal illness in 1913 took him out of the field. After a long recuperation, he returned to the Forest Service a more thoughtful man, having spent many hours reading the Bible, literature and philosophy like Thoreau and Emerson, and works like William Temple Hornaday's *Our Vanishing Wildlife*.

Leopold seemed galvanized to action. He gradually focused his energies on two issues: game management and wilderness. He was prominent in regional and national game protective associations and lobbied state government for responsible conservation and game management laws and agencies. In pursuit of wildlife protection, he resigned in 1928 from an uncongenial assignment in the Forest Service's Forest Products Laboratory to conduct a game survey of the north central states for the Sporting Arms and Ammunitions Manufacturers' Institute, published in 1931. Two years later he published his path-breaking *Game Management*. That summer the University of Wisconsin appointed him the nation's first Professor of Game Management, a position he held until his death in 1948. After 1943 he sat on Wisconsin's Conservation Commission, where he led a long, public battle to reduce the overpopulation of Wisconsin's deer.

By 1920 he had joined other like-minded men in the Forest Service to push for wilderness areas in national forests large enough for two-week hunting and fishing trips. The most articulate advocate of national forest wilderness areas, he saw his efforts repaid with the 1924 creation of the Gila Wilderness Area. His interest in wilderness led him to be a founding member of the Wilderness Society in 1935.

Throughout his forty-year career, Leopold looked at conservation problems in terms of spirituality and personal ethic. His father had responded to declining wildlife populations by adopting a personal code restricting himself regarding the season and animals he hunted, and supported Iowa's first game laws. As early as 1913 Leopold himself was emphasizing to fellow Forest Service personnel "the moral and aesthetic arguments" on the question of game management. In his speech accepting a Permanent Wildlife Fund medal, he remarked, "It is our task to educate the moral nature of each and every one of New Mexico's half million citizens to look upon our beneficial birds and animals, not as so much gun fodder to satisfy his instinctive love of killing, but as irreplaceable works of art, drawn by the Great Artist."[25]

Leopold's spiritual understanding of nature peaked after he read the 1922 translation of P. D. Ouspensky's *Tertium Organum*, which along with Thoreau was among his library's most marked-up books.[26] The vigorous neo-Platonism of Ouspensky's view of the earth as a living organism impressed him and for a time became the new basis for his view of "Conservation as a Moral Issue," the title for a section for an unpublished Ouspensky-inspired piece, "Conservation in the Southwest." This brief Ouspensky enthusiasm faded but left behind the idea of the land as organism. Some enlightening hunting trips to the untouched Mexican wilderness of the Gavilan, along with problems in America with deer overpopulation due to extermination of predators, left him with a new metaphor of the land, in America, as a sick organism.

During the 1920s and '30s Leopold secularized the basis for his ethic by drawing on concepts of the developing science of ecology. The ecological concepts he used in describing the organic unity of the earth had their neo-Platonic analogs. The food chain and biotic pyramid resembled the Great Chain of Being, with matter at the bottom and man (now with a few predators) at the top. Instead of the world as emanation of the divine like light from the sun, the land was "a fountain of energy" flowing upward through the food chain. The interconnectedness of life implied that humankind was part of the plant and animal community. Leopold made this insight the basis for the ethic he published in his famous essay, "The Land Ethic," in *The Sand County Almanac*: "When we see land as a community to which we belong, we may begin to use it with love and respect. . . . That land is a community is the basic concept of ecology, but that land is to be loved and respected is an extension of ethics."[27] Unethical conduct he defined as abuse of the land for economic gain.

The upshot of the Lutheran ethic in Leopold's life and work was that he steadfastly believed that government had a role through conservation and game laws to restrain sinners against the land ethic, but that the adoption of a personal land ethic, not government action, would ultimately save the individual and the land. The basis for this ethic shifted throughout his life from Christianity to ecological neo-Platonism (what his son called "pantheism") — but a twentieth-century neo-Platonism much diluted from the days of the Romantics, Transcendentalists, and John Muir. Foreshadowing Lynn White, Jr.'s argument a generation later, Leopold after World War II attacked the technological domination of nature as a product of the "Abrahamic" view of the land as made for man.[28] *The Sand County Almanac*, his mature thoughts on the conservation ethic, sold steadily throughout the 1950s, but after the paperback edition of 1966 took off, it became the classic it is now regarded. The time had come for the nation to heed the Lutheranistic and Calvinistic calls for personal and national regeneration.

Evangelical Stewardship: James G. Watt

In the May 1981 issue of *Audubon* magazine, Leilani Watt read an article about her husband, the secretary of the interior, entitled, "God, James Watt, and the Public Land." In it, author Ron Wolf asserted a variation of the Lynn White thesis, then at the peak of its influence. Wolf traced the environmental movement to the religious tradition of Emerson, "in which a person's spiritual, physical, and even economic well-being are considered to derive from his rapport with all of creation." He put Watt in a "more imperious, totally contradictory tradition," in which "the earth was put here by the Lord for His people to subdue and to use for profitable purposes on their way to the hereafter."[29]

After reading this article, Leilani Watt said to her husband, "You worship the Creator; your opponents worship the creation." She recalled,

> James' job was that of a steward, caring for the land and managing its resources for this and future generation. The goal of environmentalists was to preserve as much of the environment as possible, preferably totally undisturbed. People's needs were not part of their equation. When James saw that this difference was irreconcilable, he accepted it and stopped worrying about trying to please this special-interest group.[30]

To a large degree, the conflict surrounding James Watt, perhaps history's most controversial secretary of the interior, stemmed from the breakup of the Christian Hebrew-Greek synthesis into "irreconcilable" fundamentalist God-of-creation and liberal God-in-creation. At the same time, the terms of the debate had not changed much since the Hetch Hetchy dam debate, when proponents had compared the needs of thirsty babies in San Francisco to the rights of an elite few to loaf around the throne of God. Watt would have completely agreed with Martin Dies's argument that God created the earth for man's use.

Watt represented quite well the viewpoint of the average conservative Christian, if not conservative theologians, about religion, economics, and nature. As a son of the Methodist tradition, he inherited the Wesleyan disinclination to social reform, predilection for evangelism, and emphasis on personal salvation. A member of the charismatic Assembly of God church, his sectarian beliefs also increased his confidence he was doing the Lord's work as well as his expectations he would have to battle the unsaved to do it. His book, for example, *The Courage of a Conservative*, repeatedly conveys the sense that the wagons are circled in the battle for the Lord.[31]

Watt was born in 1938 in Lusk, Wyoming. His grandparents had homesteaded the family ranch, and his father ranched on his own homestead while practicing law in Lusk. His parents were conservative Protestants who disciplined strictly, practiced personal piety, and voted against the New Deal. His middle name, Gaius, which he shared with his father and passed on to his two children, was taken not from pagan Rome, but from the Third Epistle of John, verse 1. The harsh climate and semi-arid land gave young Watt the conviction that nature was an opponent to be conquered, the same impression it has given to such fellow sons of the arid West brought up in strict religious homes as the dam-building Commissioner of Reclamation Floyd Dominy.[32]

The family moved to Wheatland, where Watt attended high school, an overachiever as is common in strict families. He attended the College of Commerce and Industry and law school at the University of Wyoming, racking up a series of academic awards and honors. In 1957 he and his high school sweetheart, Leilani, married, and produced two children, Erin Gaia and Eric Gaius, before completing his law degree in 1962. He immediately involved himself in politics and came to Washington that year as an aide to new Wyoming Senator Milward Simpson. When Simpson retired in 1966, Watt spent the next three years as advisor and spokesman on resources and the environment for the U.S. Chamber of Commerce. The Nixon and Ford administrations appointed him to a series of posts as deputy assistant secretary for water and power resources and director of the Bureau of Outdoor Recreation in the Interior Department, and member of the Federal Power Commission. During the Carter years Watt headed the Mountain States Legal Foundation, newly formed with the money of the National Legal Center for the Public Interest and with money from archconservative and evangelical Joseph Coors, the Colorado brewery heir. Under Watt, the foundation opposed, often successfully, federal regulation and conservation policies, such as policies to control overgrazing on federal lands and to promote occupational safety.

At a meeting in late 1980, five Western senators picked James Watt as Ronald Reagan's nominee for Secretary of the Interior. Environmental organizations of all stripes lined up to oppose him at his well-publicized confirmation hearings, but the Republican Senate confirmed him easily on January 22, 1981. Interestingly, Watt's remark that caused the first storm of criticism was one made during his answers to a House Interior and Insular Affairs Committee meeting two weeks later: "I do not know how many future generations we can count on before the Lord returns. . . ." Although this statement meant that we must be good stewards because the Christ might not come again for a long while, his opponents instantly made Watt into the personification of everything Lynn White had warned against: the traditional Christian who believed God gave earth to man to use up before the Second Coming. The image would dog him for the rest of his two-year term in office.

This image was exaggerated but not inapt, for Watt had become a "born-again" charismatic Christian. Under the influence of the devout and devoted Leilani, Watt had moved steadily toward more conservative belief, from Congregationalist, Presbyterian, Methodist, and Southern Baptist to Assembly of God. At her urging, he attended Full Gospel Businessman's prayer meetings, at one of which in February 1964 he had had a classic nineteenth-century-style conversion experience. The leader had stopped the music and said, "Just a minute. There is someone in this crowd who wants to know Jesus." Watt told his wife, "When he said that, my heart felt like someone had gripped it tight. My thought was, 'Do *I* know Jesus?'" At that moment, he said, "I committed my life to Jesus Christ." At Sunday evening church meetings, he heard evidence of the power of prayer that moved him to begin frequent and fervent praying. As Secretary of the Interior, he began each morning with a Bible reading and prayer, often using homemade banners set in front of the fireplace. The banners had messages like, "The Lord shall fight for you and you shall hold your peace," and "I have called you into righteousness and I will hold your hand."[33]

Several elements of his religious belief would lead him into conflict with the environmental community. As a member of the Assembly of God, he not only believed that God guided his life but that the Holy Spirit spoke directly to the believer (who may respond by speaking in tongues). In a sect-type denomination like this one, believers concern themselves primarily with their own salvation and holiness and feel no responsibility for creation of a godly society. They expect that the worldly will oppose them, and that the saved must fight for truth and righteousness. The Watts' religion was a militant nineteenth-century-style Protestantism. For example, Leilani saw it as her duty to submit to her husband and to make their home a "refuge" in a way reminiscent of the doctrine of the spheres. Her autobiography, *Caught in the Crossfire*, repeatedly stressed submission, both to God and to her husband, an American religious theme that goes back to Anne Bradstreet, although Leilani expressed it with less poetry and more anxiety.[34]

Watt's view of God and nature also came from nineteenth-century frontier Protestantism. Many times he clearly stated that the earth was given to man for his use. His most common description of his role was as "steward" of the earth, a concept he took very seriously. Stewardship is a very broad concept, and for conservative Christians has economic connotations of making the most out of what has been given to mankind's care. The "good and faithful servant" of Christ's parable (Matt. 25:14–30 and Luke 19:11–27) was the man who invested the money entrusted to him and showed his master a good return on his money. Watt called national parks "cathedrals to the wonder of nature and to the glory of the Creator" and wanted to pre-serve "the best that remains in God's creation," yet he clearly felt enough had been preserved already and the rest rightly ought to be put to use.[35]

Consequently, Watt put a moratorium on buying new parkland and facil-itated development of the other lands under his jurisdiction. His arguments were generally economic but at base rested on his religious convictions. His sudden reversal of twenty years of environmental progress raised storm after storm. The certitude he was doing the Lord's work insulated him from criticism and doubts. Ironically, it was not conservation issues but an appar-ent preference for Wayne Newton over the Beach Boys and an unfortunate remark about the diverse makeup of a commission that caused even his staunchest supporters to desert him and occasioned his resignation. Trou-ble has continued to follow him, first as a board member for PTL, the organization of jailed and defrocked televangelist Jim Bakker, and than as a Washington consultant, as which he was indicted in 1995. The "Wise Use" anti-environmentalist movement of the last few years, which has important support in parts of the West, carries on Watt's advocacy of government-assisted development of public land.[36]

The continued strengthening of the religious right that James Watt rep-resented may continue to put public and private environmental organiza-tions on the defensive. Since World War II the growth of cities and suburbs has sparked the growth of giant fundamentalist churches. Southern Bap-tists, Mormons, and charismatics like the Assembly of God have seen their denominations surge forward, while Episcopalians, Presbyterians, Con-gregationalists, and members of other "mainline" churches have seen their numbers shrink. But this may also hold a promise for future generations, because Protestant revivals also generate fiery apostates like John Muir and gentle conservationists like John D. Rockefeller, Jr.

Post-Protestant Theology: Annie Dillard

The closest thing to Henry David Thoreau that the twentieth century has produced is Annie Dillard. In 1972 Dillard lived for a year in a "hermitage" or "anchor-hold" near Tinker Creek in Virginia's Blue Ridge, kept a jour-nal like Emerson or Thoreau or Muir, and mined it for a book, *Pilgrim at Tinker Creek*, which won a Pulitzer Prize in 1975. But this century is not a Transcendental century where the surface of Walden Pond mirrors the smiling face of God. Dillard quotes Pascal: "Every religion / which does not affirm that God is hidden / is not true." She also cites Pascal's notion of God as *deus absconditus*. For an age of trench-warfare, depression, blitzkrieg and holocaust and atom bomb, nuclear arms race, terrorism, and ecological crisis, God is at the very least hidden, if not dead. After Walden Pond, Thoreau climbed Mount Katahdin in Maine and saw true wildness face to face, and he wondered at his former optimism. In the darker moments of this century, so do we.[37]

Dillard has continued the Protestant search for God in nature, although the results of her search are more ambiguous than former seekers found. Though she is not a theologian, her *Pilgrim at Tinker Creek* is the most celebrated and most widely read theological musing on the troubling problem that "we wake, if we ever wake at all, to mystery, rumors of death, beauty, violence."[38] Academic theologians have not written as well, as popularly, or as powerfully of the darkness present in God's beauty. Stung by criticism begun by Lynn White, Jr., that Christianity was partly to blame for environmental damage, Protestant theologians responded with theologies that created a basis for a Christian environmentalism. Some like Francis A. Schaeffer and Calvin De Witt decry materialism and call for a responsible exercise of stewardship and dominion. Others like Susan Power Bratton, H. Paul Santmire, and Max Oelschlaeger use new readings of Christian doctrine and Biblical passages to construct an ethic of "caring for creation." A few of the most liberal, like Sallie McFague and John Cobb, Jr., embrace neo-Platonic panentheism to create an ethic of respect for all God's creation.[39] For many Americans from the Protestant tradition, the devising of an environmental theology a decade or two after the first Earth Day demonstrates how little leadership and creativity are left in Protestant theology. Like Dillard, they now pass church doors by to go confront directly the mystery of why God's creation encompasses a "nature, red in tooth and claw."

Born in 1945 in Pittsburgh, Pennsylvania, Dillard had an affluent childhood. Her paternal grandfather was a strict Scots-Irish Presbyterian and her father, though lapsed, dropped his children off at Sunday school and church and sent them to church camp. Dillard was quite pious. She remembers, "I had a head for religious ideas. They were the first ideas I ever encountered. They made other ideas seem mean." Teenage doubts began to bother, and she briefly quit church at age 16 to be lured back when the minister loaned her works by C. S. Lewis. In high school she loved poetry and Emerson, and took English literature and theology in college. She wrote a master's thesis entitled "Walden Pond and Thoreau." At some point, she left orthodoxy behind to become, in her words, "spiritually promiscuous," attending any church that is nearby and accepting of any religion, whether Christianity, Judaism, or Islam. She once considered converting to Roman Catholicism, and recently has grown interested in Hasidism. Religious concerns remain the focus of her thoughts and inform the themes as well as titles of much of her prose and poetry — *Pilgrim at Tinker Creek*, *Tickets for a Prayer Wheel*, *Holy the Firm*, and *Teaching a Stone to Talk* — and the frequent Biblical allusions and quotations they contain.[40]

The most significant of Dillard's many books, poems, and essays remains *Pilgrim at Tinker Creek*. Here she states most clearly and beautifully the contradictions of nature. She is not the first to see them, of course. Philosophers of the late Enlightenment understood that nature taught nothing of goodness or divinity. John Burroughs, Muir's contemporary and the most popular naturalist of his day, wrote an essay denying that anything of God could be learned from the study of nature. At times she seems like Muir, drunk with the evidence of God in the leaves on a tree, the song of a bird, the web of a spider. The world is intricate, abundant, and beautiful beyond all reason. Yet, beneath this surface of beauty and mystery runs a current that by the second half of the book scatters the shimmering reflections of divinity with the disturbing, insistent signs of death. Creatures eat each other in various horrible ways. Parasites attach to all life, and have parasites themselves. "The wonder is," Dillard writes, ". . . that all forms are not monsters, that there is beauty at all, grace gratuitous. . . . Beauty itself is the fruit of the creator's exuberance that grew such a tangle, and the grotesques and horrors bloom from that same free growth, that intricate scramble and twine up and down the conditions of time."[41]

The central question is the one God asks in the Koran, "The heaven and the earth and all in between, thinkest thou I made them *in jest*?" "The question from agnosticism is, Who turned on the lights?" Dillard says. "The question from faith is, Whatever for?" Her answer is not a comfortable one: "Divinity is not playful. The universe was not made in jest but in solemn incomprehensible earnest. By a power that is unfathomably secret, and holy, and fleet. There is nothing to be done about it, but ignore it, or see." Yet Dillard finds the needs of her spirit have been met, and her response to this mysterious life and world are to give thanks, and she concludes with the memorable lines,

> . . . I go my way, and my left foot says "Glory," and my right foot says "Amen": in and out of Shadow Creek, upstream and down, exultant, in a daze, dancing, to the twin silver trumpets of praise.[42]

Many contemporary children of the Protestant tradition have left the church, wandered into Transcendentalistic wonder, and gone through it and out the other side into the maze of appealing and interesting religious and ethical traditions from the world over. A few, like Gary Snyder, have found satisfaction and meaning in Buddhism, or Taoism, or Hinduism. Many others, like Dillard and Steven Rockefeller, hold onto the Christian God while reaching out to other religious traditions, hoping that together they will form the strands that link God, humanity, and nature into a meaningful web. Their efforts are symptomatic of the fact that Reformation theology has failed to provide convincing and comforting answers to a disturbing and threatening world of environmental crisis, war, oppression, genocide, and disorder.

Paradise Lost: Dave Foreman

Shortly after James Watt was sworn in as Secretary of the Interior, on March 21, 1981 an unknown organization called Earth First! enacted a bit of guerrilla theater that captured headlines across the United States. The site was Glen Canyon Dam on the Arizona–Utah border, whose reservoir covers one of the world's most beautiful canyons and whose name moves almost any environmentalist to emotions from wistfulness to rage. Carrying signs that read "Damn Watt, Not Rivers," "Free the Colorado," and "Let it Flow," seventy-five Earth First!ers cheered as five others unfurled a three-hundred-foot, black plastic "crack" down the front of the dam.[43] Founded the previous year by a small group of disgruntled activists from the Wilderness Society, Friends of the Earth, and Sierra Club, Earth First!'s most prominent leader has always been Dave Foreman.

If Leopold's land ethic were to have converts, it needed missionary-preachers, and Foreman has stepped into that role with a passion. In the words of journalist Susan Zakin, "Dave Foreman's rabble rousing, foot-stomping fundamentalist-preacher speechifying" fired people up to throw "a monkeywrench into the works of Demonic Progress." Foreman proclaimed,

Why shouldn't I be emotional, angry, passionate? Madmen and madwomen are wrecking this beautiful, blue-green, living Earth. Fiends who hold nothing of value but a greasy dollar bill are tearing down the pillars of evolution a-building for nearly four thousand million years.[44]

Foreman had been in training for this role since boyhood. He had grown up dreaming of becoming a preacher, although his original cause was the fundamentalist Churches of Christ, known as "Campbellites" in the days when John Muir's father preached for them. The principles of the Churches of Christ emphasize common sense, evangelism, individual conversion and piety, pure doctrine, exacting faithfulness to the source of truth and inspiration, and uncompromising militance of the faithful against the evil forces of the worldly. These principles Dave Foreman has never forsaken, though he dropped church doctrine long ago. It was the deft substitution of "wilderness" for "God" that made of him a man who could make a believer out of anybody.

Foreman's roots are in New Mexico, where his Scots-Irish Churches of Christ maternal grandparents homesteaded in the territory days. His father was a career military man. Born in 1946, Foreman moved more than a dozen times while growing up. His father's stern discipline, his close relationship with his mother, his intense fundamentalist church, all produced in him the classic "Protestant temperament": uncompromising, self-righteous, bold, and angry.[45]

Foreman is, in short, Watt's wilderness twin. Foreman took the path Watt left untrod, beginning with his University of New Mexico years when Foreman's increasing rebelliousness led him to loss of faith and libertarianism. The final act of rebellion and break with his father came with his dishonorable discharge from the Marines, followed by a period of drift. In the early 1970s, backpacking and interest in wilderness (both in Aldo Leopold's old stomping grounds) prompted him to become active in various environmental organizations, culminating in a job in the Wilderness Society's Washington, D.C., office during the Carter administration. The Forest Service's major concessions of wilderness to industry at the conclusion of the second Roadless Area Review and Evaluation (RARE II) in 1979 disillusioned Foreman with the political process and mainstream environmental organizations, and back to New Mexico he went.

With a group of like-minded friends, inspired by Edward Abbey's books, especially *Desert Solitaire* and *The Monkey Wrench Gang* (a novel of environmental sabotage), Foreman organized Earth First! to be the radical wing of the environmental movement. With no ideology except to promote a "biocentric" world view, it was intended to embody enthusiasm and good humor and to inspire people to civil disobedience and sabotage of development of wilderness areas.

Foreman found his scripture text in the Book of Nature (rechristened Wilderness), the central gospel of salvation for humankind.

> In a true Earth-radical group, concern for wilderness preservation must be the keystone. . . . Wilderness says: Human beings are not paramount, Earth is not for *Homo sapiens* alone, human life is but one life form on the planet and has no right to take exclusive possession. Yes, wilderness for its own sake, without any need to justify it for human benefit. Wilderness for wilderness. For bears and whales and titmice and rattlesnakes and stink bugs. And . . . wilderness for human beings. Because it is the laboratory for human evolution, and because it is home.
>
> It is not enough to protect our few remaining bits of wilderness. The only hope for Earth (including humanity) is to withdraw huge areas as inviolate natural sanctuaries from the depredations of modern industry and technology.[46]

Foreman possesses that Calvinist emphasis on activity in society to reform a too-worldly nation, that Campbellite desire to simplify theology on the basis of a simple creed. He has, too, the righteous anger of the prophets against the faithful who turned to worship Baal or Mammon.

> Action is the key. Action is more important than philosophical hair-splitting or endless refining of dogma. . . . All that would be required to join Earth First! . . . was a belief in Earth first. . . . It's time to get angry, to cry, to let rage flow at what the human cancer is doing to Earth, to be uncompromising.[47]

For several years Foreman rode high on a crest of enthusiasm, crossing the country and giving his speeches in "The Road Show" with Bart Koehler singing "green" songs, and participating in civil disobedience. But Earth First!, an informal association without organization or officers, grew fast and got out of control. Press coverage increased. Earth First!ers themselves became targets for violent right-wingers. The FBI infiltrated with *agents provocateurs*, one of whom convinced Foreman to agree to a plot to blow up a power line. Foreman was tried but escaped with no jail time. Yet he also decided that Earth First! had evolved in directions different from the original purpose, and quit in 1989. He continues his "speechifying" and "rabble-rousing" for the same cause but for different people and organizations.

Foreman is a type. He comes from the tradition of fiery, uncompromising defenders of nature like John Muir and David Brower. Like them he grew up in a fundamentalist-style church (Baptist for Brower) and found youthful solace and security in nature or animals. He and they transformed alienation from church and fathers into anger against business, "the vandals looting the riches of this Earth" in Foreman's phrase, and into defense of our wilderness "home."[48] By assuming the Protestant prophetic tradition, they have inspired three separate generations to the cause of nature against capitalism.

From Anne Bradstreet and Edward Johnson to Annie Dillard and Dave Foreman, poet-theologians and crusader-Jeremiahs, we have come full circle.

"We are involved," said Foreman, "in the most sacred crusade ever waged on earth."[49] He is neither the first, nor, doubtless, the last American from the Protestant tradition to make that claim. The American character, with its strong streak of evangelical Protestantism, has established across the continent both a vigorous entrepreneurial capitalism and the world's foremost environmental organizations. Capitalism and environmentalism are in each other's grip, which sometimes tightens in contention or relaxes in embrace but never loosens. Americans love economic success, yet their idealism never lets them entirely enjoy it. The Puritan legacy yields both a sense of sin and a sense of possibility, that we have failed to live up to moral standards yet we can build the city upon a hill. It blesses an urge for worldly success which it then seeks to control. It sometimes seems a contradiction that Americans want a growing economy along with an improving natural environment preserved from corruption. Yet this is emblematic of the American belief that we can accept the wealth providence sends our way, yet we will not let it tempt us from the path of our mission. As long as nature in the American mind forms the spiritual counterweight to material civilization, the environmental movement will continue to be refreshed with strength and vitality.

Notes

INTRODUCTION

1. See White, "The Historical Roots of Our Ecologic Crisis," *Science* 155 (1967): 1203–7, reprinted with a reply to critics in Ian G. Barbour, ed., *Western Man and Environmental Ethics: Attitudes Toward Nature and Technology* (Reading, Mass.: Addison–Wesley, 1973); William Leiss, *The Domination of Nature* (New York: George Braziller, 1972); Frederick Turner, *Beyond Geography: The Western Spirit Against the Wilderness* (New York: Viking Press, 1980); and Peter Marshall, *Nature's Web: Rethinking Our Place on Earth* (New York: Paragon House, 1994).

2. Those who have maintained that environmentalists have been forced to go outside the Christian tradition to find a spirituality that values nature include Stephen Fox, *The American Conservation Movement: John Muir and His Legacy* (1981; reprint, Madison: University of Wisconsin Press, 1985), chapter 11; and Roderick Nash, *Wilderness and the American Mind*, 3rd rev. ed. (New Haven: Yale University Press, 1982), chapter 1. This sort of thinking forms a part of the current fashion that denigrates Western and romanticizes non-Western intellectual heritage. See Donald Worster, *Dust Bowl: The Southern Plains in the 1930s* (Oxford: Oxford University Press, 1979), Introduction, in which he blames capitalism for ecological crisis; Donald Worster, "The Vulnerable Earth: Toward a Planetary History," in *The Ends of the Earth: Perspectives on Modern Environmental History*, ed. Donald Worster (Cambridge: Cambridge University Pres, 1988), in which he blames overpopulation, capitalism, and science; and Carolyn Merchant, *The Death of Nature: Women, Ecology, and the Scientific Revolution* (San Francisco: Harper & Row, 1980), and *Ecological Revolutions: Nature, Gender, and Science in New England* (Chapel Hill: University of North Carolina Press, 1989), in which she blames science, patriarchy, and capitalism. Martin W. Lewis has examined such "eco-radicalism" in *Green Delusions: An Environmentalist Critique of Radical Environmentalism* (Durham: Duke University Press, 1992).

Environmental ethicist Eugene C. Hargrove found no promise for a positive view of nature in the Western philosophical tradition. *Foundations of Environmental Ethics*

(Englewood Cliffs, N.J.: Prentice-Hall, 1989), chapter 1. In a critique of Hargrove, Robin Attfield asserted that there were positive attitudes to nature in the Western tradition, but he could not identify their roots. "Has the History of Philosophy Ruined the Environment?" *Environmental Ethics* 13 (1991): 127–37.

3. On the general subject of human ecological impact, see Erik P. Eckholm, *Losing Ground: Environmental Stress and World Food Prospects* (New York: Norton, 1976), especially chapter 2. See also Lewis G. Regenstein, *Replenish the Earth: A History of Organized Religious Treatment of Animals and Nature — Including the Bible's Message of Conservation and Kindness toward Animals* (New York: Crossroads, 1991), part 3; and Yi-Fu Tuan, "Discrepancies between Environmental Attitude and Behavior: Examples from Europe and China," in *Ecology and Religion in History*, ed. David Spring and Eileen Spring (New York: Harper & Row, 1974). I am indebted to T. P. Ramamoorthy for recalling the forest fire in the *Mahabharata*.

4. See I. G. Simmons, *Changing the Face of the Earth: Culture, Environment, History* (Oxford: Blackwell, 1989), chapters 2 and 3, esp. table 3.1.

5. See Richard H. Grove, "Origins of Western Environmentalism," *Scientific American* 267 (1992): 42–47.

6. On medieval agriculture, see Georges Duby, *The Early Growth of the European Economy: Warriors and Peasants from the Seventh to the Twelfth Century*, trans. Howard B. Clarke (Ithaca: Cornell University Press, 1974), chapters 1 and 7; Keith Thomas, *Man and the Natural World: A History of the Modern Sensibility* (New York: Pantheon Books, 1983), chapter II.ii; and Clarence Glacken, *Traces on the Rhodian Shore: Nature and Culture in Western Thought from Ancient Times to the End of the Eighteenth Century* (Berkeley: University of California Press, 1967), 291, 318–20. On the escalation of environmental effects, see L. Harrison Matthews, *Man and Wildlife* (London: Croom Helm, 1975), esp. chapter 6.

CHAPTER ONE

1. See Keith Thomas, *Religion and the Decline of Magic: Studies in Popular Beliefs in Sixteenth and Seventeenth Century England* (London: Weidenfeld and Nicolson, 1971), esp. chapters 2 and 3.

2. For discussions of the classical authors and their impact on Christian thought, see William Lane Craig, *The Cosmological Argument from Plato to Leibniz* (New York: Barnes & Noble, 1980), chapters 1 and 2; Clarence Glacken, *Traces on the Rhodian Shore: Nature and Culture in Western Thought from Ancient Times to the End of the Eighteenth Century* (Berkeley: University of California Press, 1967), part 1; David Knowles, *The Evolution of Medieval Thought* (London: Longmans, 1962), chapters 1–4; and Jaroslav Pelikan, *The Christian Tradition: A History of the Development of Doctrine*, vol. 1, *The Emergence of the Catholic Tradition (100–600)* (Chicago: University of Chicago Press, 1971), 44–55. A good example is St. Ambrose, *Hexameron, Paradise, and Cain and Abel*, trans. John J. Savage (New York: Fathers of the Church, 1961); see Savage, vii–viii.

3. Wisdom 11:21 in the Vulgate. All Biblical quotations come from the Authorized, or King James, Version because its phrases are most familiar to English speakers and because it reflects the common understanding of Biblical texts before this century. Note that the Catholic Vulgate sometimes numbers verses differently, and that because it combines Psalms 9 and 10, it numbers the Psalms differently from other versions. Other translations differ as well. Throughout, all numbering agrees with the King James version. Cp. Psalms 47:7 and 50; and Isaiah 45:9, Ecclesiasticus 33:13, and Romans 9:20. In Colossians 1:15–17, St. Paul Christianized this theme. He transferred lordship of the earth to Jesus, the first of God's creatures, who created the world for himself.

4. Cp. Psalm 65 and 145:15–17. In Wisdom 11:21–12:1, God's love for all his creatures is shown by his creation and sustenance of them. See David Winston, *The Wisdom of Solomon*, vol. 43 of *The Anchor Bible* (Garden City, N.Y.: Doubleday, 1979), 20–58. On ecological interconnectedness, cp. Psalm 74:12–17, and Job 36: 27–37:18 and 38–39.

5. Wisdom of Solomon will hereafter be called Wisdom.

6. Cp. Hebrews 11:1, 3.

7. See Douglas A. Knight, "Cosmogony and Order in the Hebrew Tradition," in *Cosmogony and Ethical Order: New Studies in Comparative Ethics*, ed. Robin W. Lovin and Frank E. Reynolds (Chicago: University of Chicago Press, 1985), 134–35; *Paradise Lost*, 5:153–59.

8. See *Timaeus*, esp. 27C–33B. See also Arthur O. Lovejoy, *The Great Chain of Being: A Study of the History of an Idea* (1936; reprint, Cambridge: Harvard University Press, 1964), 46–51; Glacken, *Traces*, chapters 1.2 and 4, and part 1, Introductory Essay, section 1; and Frank Egleston Robbins, *The Hexaemeral Literature: A Study of the Greek and Latin Commentaries on Genesis* (Chicago: University of Chicago Press, 1912), 2–10. For a discussion of Plato's *Laws*, see Clement C. J. Webb, *Studies in the History of Natural Theology* (Oxford: Clarendon Press, 1915), 84–136. See also Raymond Klibansky, *The Continuity of the Platonic Tradition during the Middle Ages* (Munich: Kraus International, 1981), 28–29. For examples of Christian design arguments, see Ambrose, *Hexameron*, 93, 119; and St. Augustine, *The Literal Meaning of Genesis*, trans. John Hammond Taylor (New York: Newman Press, 1982), 5.22.43, vol. 1, 173–74.

On lack of scientific curiosity, cp. St. Ambrose, *Hexameron*, 22, 259; St. John Chrysostom, *Homilies on Genesis 1–17*, trans. Robert C. Hill (Washington, D.C.: Catholic University of America Press, 1986), 41, 71; and see Robbins, *Hexameral Literature*, chapter 4.

9. See Lovejoy, *Great Chain of Being*, for the classic study of the idea of the chain of being.

10. Plotinus's philosophy is contained in his *The Enneads*, 2nd rev. ed., trans. Stephen MacKenna (London: Faber and Faber, 1956). See relevant sections, esp. V.1; on conversion, I.3 and I.6; on the world's beauty, II.9; on nature's contemplation of the One, III.8; also MacKenna's discussion of terminology, xxii–xxxii. Quotation

is in I.6.8, p. 63. For a useful introduction to and extracts from Plotinus, see A. H. Armstrong, *Plotinus* (London: George Allen & Unwin, 1953).

11. See Paul Henry, *Plotin et l'Occident: Firmicus Maternus, Marius Victorinus, Saint Augustine et Macrobe* (Louvain: Spicilegium Sacrum Lovaniense, 1934), esp. chapters 3 and 4 on Augustine; Etienne Gilson, *The Christian Philosophy of Saint Augustine*, trans. L. E. M. Lynch (New York: Random House, 1960), 232–35; Pelikan, *Christian Tradition*, 33–35, 295–97, 343–49; Dominic J. O'Meara, "Introduction" and "The Neoplatonism of Saint Augustine," in *Neoplatonism and Christian Thought*, ed. Dominic J. O'Meara (Albany: State University of New York Press, 1982); also Mary T. Clark, "Augustine the Christian Thinker," and Robert J. O'Connell, "Porphyrianism in the Early Augustine: Oliver DuRoy's Contribution," both in F. X. Martin and J. A. Richmond, eds., *From Augustine to Eriugena: Essays on Neoplatonism and Christianity in Honor of John O'Meara* (Washington, D.C.: Catholic University of American Press, 1991). On the neo-Platonic origins of Western mysticism, see Andrew Louth, *The Origins of the Christian Mystical Tradition: From Plato to Denys* (Oxford: Clarendon Press, 1981).

For examples of neo-Platonic Patristic emphasis on the goodness, beauty, providence, the design of the universe, and conversion, see Augustine, *Literal Meaning*, 1.8.14, 2.8.17, 4.12.22, 4.32.22, 5.20.41, and 7.14; *Confessions*, XI.iv (6); *City of God*, 11.4; Chrysostom, *Genesis*, 33, 58, and 88–89; and Ambrose, *Hexameron*, 16–17.

On the contradictions in the neo-Platonic legacy to Christianity, see Lovejoy, *Great Chain of Being*, chapter 3.

12. On the influence of neo-Platonism generally, see Thomas Whittaker, *The Neo-Platonists: A Study in the History of Hellenism*, 4th ed. (1928; reprint, Hildesheim: Georg Olms, 1961), chapter 10; and R. T. Wallis, *Neo-Platonism* (London: Duckworth, 1972), chapter 6. On Renaissance neo-Platonism, see Nesca A. Robb, *Neoplatonism of the Italian Renaissance* (1935; reprint, New York: Octagon Books, 1968). J. E. Lovelock presented the scientific Gaia hypothesis in *Gaia: A New Look at Life on Earth* (Oxford: Oxford University Press, 1979); for a theistic Gaia vision, see Herman E. Daly and John B. Cobb, Jr., *For the Common Good: Redirecting the Economy toward Community, the Environment, and a Sustainable Future* (Boston: Beacon Press, 1989), chapter 20.

On Hegel and the German idealists, see Werner Beierwaltes, *Platonismus und Idealismus* (Frankfurt: Vittorio Klostermann, 1972); more briefly, Werner Beierwaltes, "Image and Counterimage? Reflections on Neoplatonic Thought with Respect to Its Place Today," in H. J. Blumenthal and R. A. Markus, eds., *Neoplatonism and Early Christian Thought* (London: Variorum, 1981), 241–42, 244–45; and Jost Hermand, *Grüne Utopien in Deutschland: Zur Geschichte des ökologischen Bewußseins* (Frankfurt am Main: Fischer Taschenbuch Verlag, 1991), 50–59, 70–75. On theistic evolution, see Peter J. Bowler, *The Eclipse of Darwinism: Anti-Darwinian Evolution Theories in the Decades around 1900* (Baltimore: John Hopkins University Press, 1983), chapters 3 and 6; and J. R. Moore, *The Post-Darwinian Controversies* (Cambridge: Cambridge University Press, 1979), chapter 6. On process philosophy, see George R. Lucas Jr., *The Rehabilitation of Whitehead: An Analytic and Historic Assessment of Process Philosophy* (Albany: State University of New York Press, 1989); Victor Lowe, "Whitehead's Metaphysical System," esp. 3 and 12–14, and Gene Reeves and Delwin Brown, "The Development of Process Theology," both in Delwin Brown, Ralph E. James, Jr., and Gene Reeves, eds., *Process Philosophy and Christian Thought* (Indianapolis: Bobbs–Merrill, 1971).

For Augustine on art and beauty, see Emmanuel Chapman, *Saint Augustine's Philosophy of Beauty* (New York: Sheed & Ward, 1939); Robert J. O'Connell, *Art and the Christian Intelligence in St. Augustine* (Cambridge: Harvard University Press, 1978); Carol Harrison, *Beauty and Revelation in the Thought of Saint Augustine* (Oxford: Clarendon Press, 1992); and, for example, Augustine's *Confessions*, X.xxxiv (53). On Bonaventure, the Franciscans, Edwards, and Emerson, see discussions below.

For a contemporary attempt to revive neo-Platonic speculation in Christianity, see the Gifford lectures of Stephen R. L. Clark, expanded in *From Athens to Jerusalem: The Love of Wisdom and the Love of God* (Oxford: Clarendon Press, 1984); chapter 8 develops a defense of nature and animal rights.

13. Natural theology has also been known as physical or physico-theology. "Natural theology" differs from "natural religion"; the latter was the name that Enlightenment thinkers and Deists gave to the idea that the specific forms of religion were contingent on local and historical circumstances, whereas there existed a core group of religious ideas common to all religions that were "natural" to all nations at all times and constituted religious truth. On natural theology's Greek origins and Christian adaptation, see Webb, *Natural Theory*, 10–22.

14. Discussed in Ian G. Barbour, *Religion in an Age of Science: The Gifford Lectures, 1989–1991*, vol. 1 (San Francisco: Harper & Row, 1990), 25.

15. Cp. Augustine's commentary on Psalm 145, in *Expositions on the Book of Psalms*, Psalm CXLV.4, 9, 10, Oxford Translation, ed. A. Cleveland Coxe, in *A Select Library of the Nicene and Post-Nicene Fathers of the Christian Church*, ed. Philip Schaff (New York: The Christian Literature Company, 1905), vol. VIII, pp. 657, 659. On Augustine and nature, see Glacken, *Traces*, chapter 5.5; and H. Paul Santmire, *The Travail of Nature: The Ambiguous Ecological Promise of Christian Theology* (Philadelphia: Fortress Press, 1985), chapter 4.

16. Chysostomum, "The Homilies on the Statues. To the People of Antioch," IX.5, Oxford Translation, rev. ed., ed. W.R.W. Stephens, in *A Select Library of the Nicene and Post-Nicene Fathers of the Christian Church*, ed. Philip Schaff (New York: Charles Scribner's Sons, 1903), 9:401–2.

17. See Edward Grant, "Science and Theology in the Middle Ages," in David C. Lindberg and Ronald L. Numbers, eds., *God and Nature: Historical Essays on the Encounter between Christianity and Science* (Berkeley: University of California Press, 1986), 51–52.

18. See Webb, *Natural Theology*, 5; and Glacken, *Traces*, 238–40.

19. Cp., for example, William Ames, in *The Marrow of Theology* (1629), trans. and ed. John D. Eusden (Boston: Pilgrim Press, 1968), chapter 8.

20. *An Antidote Against Atheism*, Book II, chapter headings, in *Philosophical Writings of Henry More*, ed. Flor Isabel Mackinnon (New York: Oxford University Press, 1925), 42–46.

21. Mackinnon, "Notes," p. 301, in More, *Philosophical Writings of Henry Moree*. For the Cambridge Platonists, see G. R. Cragg, *From Puritanism to the Age of Reason: A Study of Changes in Religious Thought Within the Church of England, 1660 to 1700* (Cambridge: Cambridge University Press, 1966), chapter 3, esp. 52–57. This neo-Platonist revival included others like Spinoza and Leibniz.

22. William Paley, *Natural Theology* (New York: American Tract Society, n.d.), 9–10, 15–16. See also Charles Coulston Gillispie, *Genesis and Geology: A Study in the Relations of Scientific Thought, Natural Theology, and Social Opinion in Great Britain, 1790–1850* (1951; reprint, New York: Harper & Brothers, 1959).

23. St. Bonaventure, *The Mind's Road to God*, trans. George Boas (Indianapolis: Bobbs-Merrill Educational Publishing, 1953); see xiv–xvii.

24. See Tess Cosslet, ed., *Science and Religion in the Nineteenth Century* (Cambridge: Cambridge University Press, 1984), 46–47; and Gillispie, *Genesis and Geology*, 149–59.

25. Hugh Miller, *Footprints of the Creator; or The Asterolepis of Stromness* (Edinburgh: Nimmo, Hay, and Mitchell, 1860), 13–14, 290–95. On Miller, see Gillispie, *Genesis and Geology*, 170–81.

26. See Moore, *Post-Darwinian Controversies*, chapter 6; and Kenneth Cauthen, *The Impact of American Religious Liberalism*, 2nd ed. (Washington, D.C.: University Press of America, 1983), 9ff.

27. Evidence for Jeanne Kay's thesis that God gave nature dominion over man is weak. God did, however, use natural means to express his anger or pleasure with mankind. See her "Concepts of Nature in the Hebrew Bible," *Environmental Ethics* 10 (1988): 309–27.

28. Cp. Deuteronomy 28:15–68; Isaiah 13:9–10 and 50:2–3; and Amos 1:2.

29. Cp. Augustine, *Literal Meaning*, 3.15.24, vol. 1, p. 91, 3.18.28, vol. 1, p. 94; Ambrose, *Hexameron*, 3, 128–29; Origen, *Homilies on Genesis and Exodus*, trans. Ronald E. Heine (Washington, D.C.: Catholic University of America Press, 1982), 59–60.

30. Cp. English Calvinist William Ames, *The Marrow of Theology*, chapter 15; and Calvin, *Commentaries on the First Book of Moses called Genesis*, trans. John King (Grand Rapids: Eerdmans, 1948), 1:96, 290–91 (on dominion); 1:97–98 (on multiply and subdue); 1:104, 116, 173 (on fallen nature); 1:105 (on God the artificer); 1:125 (on stewardship); and Calvin, *Commentaries on the Epistle of Paul the Apostle to the Romans*, trans. John Owens (Grand Rapids: Eerdmans, 1948), on Romans 1:19–21 (natural theology), pp. 69–71; on Romans 8:20–22 (the fall and redemption of creation), pp. 304–6; and Calvin, *The Epistle of Paul the Apostle to the Hebrews*, trans.

William B. Johnston (Grand Rapids: Eerdmans, 1963), on Hebrews 2:5–9 (loss of dominion), p. 21. Further similar commentary appears in Calvin, *Commentary on the Book of Psalms*, trans. James Anderson (Grand Rapids: Eerdmans, 1949), for example, on Psalm 104, v. 4, and on Psalm 148, v. 5.

31. Cp. 66:22, 2 Peter 3:13, and Revelation 21:1.

32. Chrysostom, *Genesis*, p. 122; cp. p. 190; but see Augustine's dissent, *Literal Meaning*, 9.12.20, vol. 2, p. 84.

33. See also the elaboration in Ecclesiasticus 17:1–4, 6–9.

34. On the soul and dominion, cp. Ambrose, *Hexameron*, 256; and Augustine, *Literal Meaning*, 6.12.21, 1:193; and 7.22.32, 2:23. On image and dominion, cp. Chrysostom, *Genesis*, 110; and Augustine, *Literal Meaning*, 9.14.25, 2:87–88. On chain of being, Augustine, *City of God*, 11.16; cp. *Tractates on the Gospel of John*, 18:7 (2). On superiority to animals, see Origen, *Genesis and Exodus*, 62–63; Ambrose, *Hexameron*, 233; and Augustine, *City of God*, Book 12, p. 406; *Literal Meaning*, 2.8.17, 1:57; and *Literal Meaning*, 3.16.25, 1:92. See Keith Thomas, *Man and the Natural World: A History of the Modern Sensibility* (New York: Pantheon Books, 1983), chapter I.iv.

35. On God's purpose for the world, see Chrysostom, *Genesis*, 100.

36. The classic statement of this principle is Aristotle, *Politics* I.viii.11–12.

37. Francis Bacon, "Announcement of the Author," xi; *Novum Organum; or True Suggestions for the Interpretation of Nature*, I.65, p. 328; *The Dignity and Advancement of Learning*, p. 5; and *Novum Organum*, I.89, p. 346, I.93, pp. 348–49, and II.52, p. 470 (quotation); all in *Advancement of Learning and Novum Organum*, rev. ed. (New York: The Colonial Press, 1900).

38. See Charles Webster, *The Great Instauration: Science, Medicine and Reform, 1626–1660* (London: Duckworth, 1975), introduction, chapters 1 and 4, and conclusion. See also Herbert Hovenkamp, *Science and Religion in America, 1800–1860* (Philadelphia: University of Pennsylvania Press, 1978), chapter 2.

39. See Thomas, *Man and the Natural World*, chapter 1; for countervailing views, see Lovejoy, *Great Chain of Being*, 186–89. Cp. Ambrose, *Hexameron*, 99; Origen, *Genesis and Exodus*, 62; and Chrysostom, *Genesis*, 101.

40. Calvin, *Commentaries on . . . Genesis*, 1:125.

41. Matthew 21:33–41, Mark 12:1–9, and Luke 20:9–16; Matthew 24:43–51 and Luke 12:42–48; and Matthew 25:14–30 and Luke 19:12–27.

42. Cp. Peter Marshall, *Nature's Web: Rethinking Our Place on Earth* (New York: Paragon House, 1994), 119 ff.

43. Both "wilderness" and "desert" translate Hebrew and Greek words with greatly different connotations than modern English word. Moreover, "desert" in the King James Version simply meant a place without human habitation (a sense retained today only in the phrase "desert island" — which is usually depicted as lush and tropical, not arid — and in the word "deserted"). See "wilderness" and "desert" in James Strong, *The Exhaustive Concordance of the Bible* (New York: Abingdon Press,

1890); see also "wilderness" in *The Eerdmans Bible Dictionary*, ed. Allen C. Myers (Grand Rapids: William B. Eerdmans, 1987).

44. Isaiah 32:15–16, 35:1–2, 6–10, 41:18–20, 51:3; cp. Ezekiel 34:25.

CHAPTER TWO

1. On Protestantism's affinity with industrial capitalism, especially in religiously pluralistic areas, see Rex A. Lucas, "A Specification of the Weber Thesis: Plymouth Colony," *History and Theory* 10 (1971): 318–46. On similarities between American and German industrialization, see Hubert Kiesewetter, *Industrielle Revolution in Deutschland* (Frankfurt: Suhrkamp, 1989), Introduction, esp. "Die Rolle des Staates," 18 ff.

2. Anna Bramwell analyzed the American, British, and German Protestant roots of "ecologism" in *Ecology in the 20th Century* (New Haven: Yale University Press, 1989).

3. Max Weber, *The Protestant Ethic and the Spirit of Capitalism*, trans. Talcott Parsons (New York: C. Scribner's Sons, 1930), 60–75; R. H. Tawney, *Religion and the Rise of Capitalism: A Historical Study* (1926; reprint, New York: Pelican Books, 1947), chapter 1; and Christopher Hill, *Society and Puritanism in Pre-Revolutionary England*, 2nd ed. (New York: Schocken Books, 1967), chapter 3.

4. See Weber, *Protestant Ethic*, 95–115; Tawney, *Religion and the Rise of Capitalism*, chapter 2; Ernst Troeltsch, "The Economic Ethic of Calvinism," and Albert Hyma, "The Economic Views of the Protestant Reformers," both in *Protestantism and Capitalism: The Weber Thesis and Its Critics*, ed. Robert Green (Boston: D.C. Heath, 1959).

5. Arnold Williams, *The Common Expositor: An Account of the Commentaries on Genesis, 1527–1633* (Chapel Hill: University of North Carolina Press, 1948), 110.

6. Quoted in William J. Bouwsma, *John Calvin: A Sixteenth-Century Portrait* (New York: Oxford University Press, 1988), 198, 199.

7. William Perkins, *A Golden Chain or the Description of Theology*, in *The Work of William Perkins*, ed. Ian Breward (Appleford, England: Sutton Courtenay Press, 1970), 187–88.

8. John Cotton, *Commentary on I John*, quoted in Karl H. Hertz, "Max Weber and American Puritanism," *Journal for the Scientific Study of Religion* 1 (1962): 194.

9. The classic study of the connection between the calling and the work ethic is Max Weber, *The Protestant Ethic and the Spirit of Capitalism*. Previously, a medieval notion of the calling (*vocatio*) predominated, as in Aquinas (see H. M. Robertson, "A Criticism of Max Weber and His School," in Green, *Protestantism and Capitalism*, 69) and Calvin (see *Institutes of the Christian Religion*, 7th rev. ed., trans. John Allen [Philadelphia: Presbyterian Board of Christian Education, 1936], III.X.VI, 1:790–91). On the relationship between "vocation" and "calling," see Weber, *Protestant Ethic*, 79 f.; Tawney, *Religion and the Rise of Capitalism*, 8; Winthrop S. Hudson,

"Puritanism and the Spirit of Capitalism," in Green, *Protestantism and Capitalism*, 58; and Robertson, "Criticism," 68.

10. Arnold Eisen, "Called to Order: The Role of the Puritan Berufsmensch in Weberian Sociology," *Sociology* 13 (1979): 204–8; Perkins quoted (from *Treatise of the Vocations, or Callings of Men, with the sorts and kinds and the right use thereof*), 205.

11. See *Saints' Everlasting Rest*, esp. the exhortation in Part III, chapter 6, in *The Practical Works of the Late Reverend and Pious Mr. Richard Baxter* (London: 1707), vol. 3; and *The Christian Directory*, in Baxter, *Practical Works*, vol. 1, p. 358; cp. pp. 356, 444, and 492. See also *The Whole Treatise of the Cases of Conscience*, in *William Perkins, 1558–1602, English Puritanist*, ed. Thomas F. Merrill (Niewkoop, Netherlands: B. de Graaf, 1966), 190, 191, 196–97; Calvin in Bouwsma, *Calvin*, 202; and Weber, *Protestant Ethic*, 156–64.

12. See, for example, Benton Johnson, "Do Holiness Sects Socialize in Dominant Values?" *Social Forces* 39 (1961): 309–16; and Richard Higgins, "Analysts say Americans Fail to Turn Interest in Religion into Commitment," Knight-Ridder Tribune News Service, in *Austin (Texas) American-Statesman*, 5 May 1991, p. F6. On the fate of the calling in eighteenth-century America, see J. E. Crowley, *This Sheba, Self: The Conceptualization of Economic Life in Eighteenth-Century America* (Baltimore: Johns Hopkins University Press, 1974), chapter 2.

13. Cp. Yale president Timothy Dwight in 1821, in A. Whitney Griswald, "Three Puritans on Prosperity," *The New England Quarterly* 7 (1934): 492.

14. Baxter, *Practical Works*, vol. 3, *A Treatise of Self-Denial*, 432; and vol. 1, *Christian Directory*, 106; cp. 356 and 493.

15. When a newspaper columnist recently vented his anger at the proliferation of disposable articles, he made environmentalism's reliance on the "old-fashioned" (Puritan) virtues explicit. See Jonathan Yardley, "On Diapers and Other Disposables," *Washington Post*, 26 June 1989, p. B2.

16. See Charles E. Hambrick-Stowe, *The Practice of Piety: Puritan Devotional Disciplines in Seventeenth-Century New England* (Chapel Hill: University of North Carolina Press, 1982).

17. See Crowley, *This Sheba, Self*, 67 ff.

18. For example, in regulations regarding just price and usury. See Tawney, *Religion and the Rise of Capitalism*, 1.

19. See Ellen Frankel Paul, *Moral Revolution and Economic Science: The Demise of Laissez-Faire in Nineteenth-Century British Political Economy* (Westport, Conn.: Greenwood Press, 1979).

20. *Spiritual Exercises*, in Antonio T. de Nicolas, *Ignatius de Loyola: Powers of Imagining: A Philosophical Hermeneutic of Imagining through the Collected Works of Ignatius de Loyola* (Albany: State University of New York Press, 1986), 172; cp. 303–4.

21. See R. Hooykaas, "Science and Reformation," in *The Protestant Ethic and Modernization: A Comparative View*, ed. S. N. Eisenstadt (New York: Basic Books, 1968); Charles Webster, "Puritanism, Separatism, and Science," in *God and Nature:*

Historical Essays on the Encounter between Christianity and Science, ed. David C. Lindberg and Ronald L. Numbers (Berkeley: University of California Press, 1986); and Charles Webster, "Puritanism and Science: The Anatomy of a Controversy," *Journal of the History of Ideas* 30 (1969): 345–68.

22. For more on this point see Herman Israel, "Some Influences of Hebraic Culture on Modern Social Organization," *American Journal of Sociology* 71 (1966): 384–94.

23. See Herman Israel, "Some Religious Factors in the Emergence of Industrial Society in England," *American Sociological Review* 31 (1966): 589–99, esp. 590–93.

24. For Revolutionary references to the Solemn League and Covenant of the English Civil War, see Catherine L. Albanese, *Sons of the Fathers: The Civil Religion of the American Revolution* (Philadelphia: Temple University Press, 1976), 43, 200. Much of the ideology of the Revolution derived from Whig justifications of the Glorious Revolution of 1688. See Bernard Bailyn, *Ideological Origins of the American Revolution* (Cambridge: Harvard University Press, 1967).

25. Roderick Nash, *Wilderness and the American Mind*, 3rd rev. ed. (New Haven: Yale University Press, 1982), 113–15.

26. One of the recent arguments against environmentalists is that they are "druids"—they sacrifice people and worship trees. See John McPhee, *Encounter with the Archdruid: Narratives about a Conservationist and Three of his Natural Enemies* (New York: Farrar, Straus and Giroux, 1971), part 2, esp. p. 95.

27. Wolfgang Schluchter, *The Rise of Western Rationalism: Max Weber's Developmental History*, trans. Guenther Roth (Berkeley: University of California Press, 1981), 170–71.

28. Protestantism of course has had no monopoly on rational thought. See William B. Ashworth, Jr., "Catholicism and Early Modern Science," Jacques Roger, "The Mechanistic Conception of Life," and Richard S. Westfall, "The Rise of Science and the Decline of Orthodox Christianity: A Study of Kepler, Descartes, and Newton," all in Lindberg and Numbers, *God and Nature*; and Joseph M. Bryant, "From Myth to Theology: Intellectuals and the Rationalization of Religion in Ancient Greece," and Donald A. Nielsen, "The Inquisition, Rationalization, and Sociocultural Change in Medieval Europe," both in *Time, Place, and Circumstance: Neo-Weberian Studies in Comparative Religious History*, ed. William W. Swatos (New York: Greenwood Press, 1990).

29. Max Weber, *General Economic History*, trans. Frank H. Knight (Glencoe, Ill.: The Free Press, 1927), 312–14; and Schluchter, *Western Rationalism*, 171–73.

30. See Bouwsma, *Calvin*, chapters 2 and 5.

31. S. N. Eisenstadt, "The Protestant Ethic in the Framework of Sociological Theory and of Weber's Work," in *The Protestant Ethic and Modernization: A Comparative View*, ed. S. N. Eisenstadt (New York: Basic Books, 1968), 8–13; and Bryan S. Turner, "The Rationalization of the Body: Reflections of Modernity and Discipline," in Scott Lasch and Sam Whimster, eds., *Max Weber, Rationality and Modernity* (London: Allen & Unwin, 1987), 223. A good discussion and historiography of

Weber and rationalization is in G. H. Mueller, "The Notion of Rationality in the Work of Max Weber," *Archives Européennes de Sociologie* 20 (1979): 149–71. See also Max Weber, "Science as a Vocation," in H. H. Gerth and C. Wright Mills, trans. and eds., *From Max Weber: Essays in Sociology* (New York: Oxford University Press, 1946); Guenter Roth and Wolfgang Schluchter, *Max Weber's Vision of History: Ethics and Methods* (Berkeley: University of California Press, 1979); Rogers Brubaker, *The Limits of Rationality: An Essay on the Social and Moral Thought of Max Weber* (London: Allen & Unwin, 1984); Niles M. Hansen, "On the Sources of Economic Rationality," *Zeitschrift für Nationalökonomie* 24 (1962): 445–55; Niles M. Hansen, "The Protestant Ethic as a General Precondition for Economic Development," *Canadian Journal of Economics and Political Science* 29 (1963): 462–74; and Herbert Lüthy, "Once Again: Calvinism and Capitalism," and David Little, "Calvinism and Law," both in Eisenstadt, *Protestant Ethic and Modernization*. On the effects of rationalization, see Keith Thomas, *Religion and the Decline of Magic* (New York: Scribner, 1971); and Carolyn Merchant, *The Death of Nature: Women, Ecology, and the Scientific Revolution* (San Francisco: Harper & Row, 1980).

32. Peter N. Carroll, *Puritanism and the Wilderness: The Intellectual Significance of the New England Frontier, 1629–1700* (New York: Columbia University Press, 1969), 17, 22, 87–92, 104–6, 109–12, and *passim*.

33. Samuel P. Hays attributed the geographic distribution of environmental sentiment to the rise of urbanization. Because he ignored cultural and religious factors, he could not explain aberrations like environmentalism's strength in rural Vermont and Maine and its weakness in urban Pennsylvania. It is true that urbanism has given rise to sentimentalization of the countryside since Roman times, yet clearly American environmentalism sprang up along paths of nineteenth-century Yankee migration. See Hays's *Beauty, Health, and Permanence: Environmental Politics in the United States, 1955–1985* (Cambridge: Cambridge University Press, 1987), 40–52.

34. See G. R. Cragg, *From Puritanism to the Age of Reason: A Study of Changes in Religious Thought within the Church of England* (Cambridge: University Press, 1966); Margaret C. Jacob, "Christianity and the Newtonian Worldview," in Lindberg and Numbers, *God and Nature*; Margaret C. Jacob, *The Newtonians and the English Revolution, 1689–1720* (Ithaca, N.Y.: Cornell University Press, 1976); and Colin Campbell, *The Romantic Ethic and the Spirit of Modern Consumerism* (Oxford: B. Blackwell, 1987), chapter 6. On Mather and Franklin, see below.

35. This status could be achieved either by adopting negative religious symbols or taboos (abstinence from sex or fasting, for example) or exhibiting positive religious characteristics, like charisma, to an extraordinary degree. See Emile Durkheim, *The Elementary Forms of the Religious Life*, trans. Joseph Ward Swain (1915; reprint, New York: Free Press, 1965), book 3; and Max Weber, *The Sociology of Religion*, trans. Ephraim Fischoff (1922; reprint, Boston: Beacon Press, 1963), chapters 4 and 11.

36. See "Celibacy, History of," "Eunuch," and "Peter, Apostle, St." in *New Catholic Encyclopedia* (New York: McGraw-Hill, 1967).

37. Moral marginality lay at the heart of the early anti-slavery movement of the

eighteenth century. As long as slaves could be seen as victims of innate characteristics—that is, they were slaves because they were heathen, or by nature morally, spiritually, and intellectually inferior to whites—Europeans and Americans could justify slavery. But when slaves came to be seen as feminized victims—"unmanned," in the characteristic phrase of anti-slavery, with their masculinity stolen from them, and helpless before the unholy passions of any ungodly white man—slaves became legitimate objects of humanitarian concern.

After emancipation, moral concern for blacks waned, and racial assumptions caused whites to see their condition as a natural and just result of their inferior racial characteristics. The Reverend Martin Luther King, Jr., refeminized black marginality by using explicitly Christian rhetoric and passive tactics. He could then effectively make the black condition once again a moral cause.

38. Quoted in Carl N. Degler, *At Odds: Women and the Family in America from the Revolution to the Present* (New York: Oxford University Press, 1980), 351. For a general discussion of nineteenth-century sex roles, see chapters 2 and 13. On the nineteenth-century doctrine of the "spheres," see Nancy F. Cott, *The Bonds of Womanhood: "Women's Sphere" in New England, 1780–1835* (New Haven: Yale University Press, 1977). On Puritan gradual separation of masculine and feminine spheres of piety, see Gerald F. Moran, *Religion, Family, and the Life Course: Explorations in the Social History of Early America* (Ann Arbor: University of Michigan Press, 1992), chapter 3.

39. On the genderization of science and of landscape in Victorian America, see Michael L. Smith, *Pacific Visions: California Scientists and the Environment, 1850–1915* (New Haven: Yale University Press, 1987), 77 ff. On the feminization of American religion, see Ann Douglas, *The Feminization of American Culture* (New York: Knopf, 1977); and on American intellectuals, see Christopher Lasch, *The New Radicalism in America, 1889–1963: The Intellectual as a Social Type* (New York: Knopf, 1965), chapters 2 and 5.

40. Current examples are sympathy for minorities, non-Western culture, women, the handicapped, the aged, and homosexuals, all groups that were originally marginal to public life, and all transformed into moral causes.

41. Cp. Leo Marx, *The Machine in the Garden: Technology and the Pastoral Ideal in America* (New York: Oxford University Press, 1964), 28, 29.

42. See esp. Philip Greven, *Spare the Child: The Religious Roots of Punishment and the Psychological Impact of Physical Abuse* (New York: Knopf, 1991), 46–96 and part 4, and *The Protestant Temperament: Patterns of Child-Rearing, Religious Experience, and the Self in Early America* (Chicago: University of Chicago Press, 1977), part 2; also Merlin B. Brinkerhoff, Elaine Grandin, and Eugen Lupri, "Religious Involvement and Spousal Violence: The Canadian Case," *Journal for the Scientific Study of Religion* 31 (1992): 15–31; Donald Capps, "Religion and Child Abuse: Perfect Together," *Journal for the Scientific Study of Religion* 31 (1992): 1–14; Alice Miller, *For Your Own Good: Hidden Cruelty in Child-Rearing and the Roots of Violence*, trans. Hildegarde Hannum and Hunter Hannum (New York: Farrar, Straus, Giroux, 1983); Linda A. Pollock, *Forgotten Children: Parent–Child Relations from 1500 to 1900* (Cambridge: Cambridge

University Press, 1983), chapter 5 (on Greven, see pp. 103 and 155); and Murray A. Straus, with Denise A. Donnelly, *Beating the Devil Out of Them: Corporal Punishment in American Families* (New York: Lexington Books, 1994). Cp. Carl N. Degler, *At Odds*, chapters 4 and 5. See also John Nash, "Historical and Social Changes in the Perception of the Role of the Father," in *The Role of the Father in Child Development*, ed. Michael E. Lamb (New York: John Wiley & Sons, 1976); Edmund S. Morgan, *The Puritan Family: Religion and Domestic Relations in Seventeenth-Century New England*, rev. and enl. ed. (New York: Harper & Row, 1966); and Steven Ozment, *When Fathers Ruled: Family Life in Reformation Europe* (Cambridge: Harvard University Press, 1983), 144–50. On the rise of the evangelical family and child punishment, see Moran, *Religion, Family, and the Life Course*, 110–18. Karl A. Menninger connected animal abuse and sport hunting to corporal punishment and displaced resentment toward parents, in "Totemic Aspects of Contemporary Attitudes Toward Animals," in George B. Wilbur and Werner Muensterberger, eds., *Psychoanalysis and Culture* (New York: International Universities Press, 1951), 44–45.

43. Ted Ownby, *Subduing Satan: Religion, Recreation, and Manhood in the Rural South, 1865–1920* (Chapel Hill: University of North Carolina Press, 1990), chapters 1 and 9, esp. 34–37, 177–82.

44. Campbell, *The Romantic Ethic*, 222–25.

45. Bouwsma, *Calvin*, 49, 173–76.

46. *Institutes of the Christian Religion*, 7th rev. ed., trans. John Allen (Philadelphia: Presbyterian Board of Christian Education, 1936), IV.XX.XXX, 2:803–4.

47. *Institutes*, IV.XX.XXXII, 2:805–6.

48. See Israel, "Hebraic Culture."

49. See Michael Walzer, *The Revolution of the Saints: A Study in the Origins of Radical Politics* (London: Weidenfeld & Nicolson, 1966); and Christopher Hill, *The World Turned Upside Down: Radical Ideas during the English Revolution* (New York: Viking Press, 1973).

50. Henry David Thoreau, "On the Duty of Civil Disobedience," in *Walden: or Life in the Woods, and On the Duty of Civil Disobedience* (1849; reprint, New York: New American Library, 1960), 223, 239.

51. Quoted in "Last Words: A Question of Moment," *Sierra: The Magazine of the Sierra Club*, September/October 1991, 138.

52. McPhee, *Archdruid*, 83, 84.

53. For the evangelical motif in environmentalism, see Robert G. Athearn, *The Mythic West in Twentieth-Century America* (Lawrence: University of Kansas Press, 1986), chapter 9.

CHAPTER THREE

1. Quoted in Hans Huth, *Nature and the American: Three Centuries of Changing Attitudes* (Berkeley: University of California Press, 1957), 6.

2. Chapter 2 of Roderick Nash, *Wilderness and the American Mind*, 3rd rev. ed.

(New Haven: Yale University Press, 1982), best typifies this view of Puritan hostility to nature. See also Alan Heimert, "Puritanism, the Wilderness, and the Frontier," *New England Quarterly* 26 (1953): 361–82; George H. Williams, *Wilderness and Paradise in Christian Thought: The Biblical Experience of the Desert in the History of Christianity and the Paradise Theme in the Theological Idea of the University* (New York: Harper, 1962), 97 ff.; Leo Marx, *The Machine in the Garden: Technology and the Pastoral Ideal in America* (New York: Oxford University Press, 1964), 41–43; Peter N. Carroll, *Puritanism and the Wilderness: The Intellectual Significance of the New England Frontier, 1629–1700* (New York: Columbia University Press, 1969); and J. Vasmar Dalton, "Ministers, Metaphors, and the New England Wilderness, 1650–1700" (Ph.D. diss., University of New Hampshire, 1981). Cp. Keith Thomas, *Man and the Natural World: A History of the Modern Sensibility* (New York: Pantheon Books, 1983), chapter 1.

3. On Puritan theology, see esp. Perry Miller, *The New England Mind: The Seventeenth Century* (1939; reprint, Cambridge: Harvard University Press, 1967), chapter 8; on Calvinism, see H. Paul Santmire, *The Travail of Nature: The Ambiguous Ecological Promise of Christian Theology* (Philadelphia: Fortress Press, 1985), chapter 7; on the relation of Puritans to the landscape, see Belden C. Lane, *Landscapes of the Sacred: Geography and Narrative in American Spirituality* (New York: Paulist Press, 1988), chapter 4.

4. "To my Dear Children," in *The Complete Works of Anne Bradstreet*, ed. Joseph R. McElrath, Jr. and Allan P. Robb (Boston: Twayne, 1981), 216. McElrath and Robb's otherwise excellent edition lacks line numbers. Any inquiry into Bradstreet's life and work should begin with Ann Stanford, *Ann Bradstreet: The Worldly Puritan* (New York: Burt Franklin & Co., 1974), and Pattie Cowell and Ann Stanford, eds., *Critical Essays on Anne Bradstreet* (Boston: G. K. Hall & Co., 1983). See also Robert Daly, *God's Altar: The World and the Flesh in Puritan Poetry* (Berkeley: University of California Press, 1978), chapter 3; Jeffrey A. Hammond, *Sinful Self, Saintly Self: The Puritan Experience of Poetry* (Athens: University of Georgia Press, 1993); Rosamond R. Rosenmeier, *Anne Bradstreet Revisited* (Boston: Twayne, 1991); Rosamond R. Rosenmeier, "The Wounds Upon Bathsheba: Anne Bradstreet's Prophetic Art," in *Puritan Poets and Poetics: Seventeenth-Century American Poetry in Theory and Practice*, ed. Peter White (University Park: Pennsylvania State University Press, 1985); William J. Scheick, *Design in Puritan American Literature* (Lexington: University Press of Kentucky, 1992), 35–45; Ivy Schweitzer, *The Work of Self-Representation: Lyric Poetry in Colonial New England* (Chapel Hill: University of North Carolina Press, 1991), chapter 4; and Elizabeth Wade White, *Anne Bradstreet: "The Tenth Muse"* (New York: Oxford University Press, 1971). For more general background, see Barbara Kiefer Lewalski, *Protestant Poetics and the Seventeenth-Century Religious Lyric* (Princeton: Princeton University Press, 1979).

Compare Bradstreet's memory that her heart "rose" on arrival in the New World with that of William Bradford, who gave the impression that his heart sank. William

Bradford, *Of Plymouth Plantation*, ed. Harvey Wish (New York: Capricorn Books, n.d.), 60.

5. The works of Guillaume de Saluste du Bartas, a sixteenth-century French Protestant and the last and greatest of the hexameral writers, were admired by Protestant and Catholic alike and often translated. "Introduction," in *The Works of Anne Bradstreet*, ed. John Harvard Ellis (1867; reprint, New York: Peter Smith, 1932), p. li, note. A hexameron is an exposition of the six days of creation based upon and illustrated by the best science of the day. On Du Bartas, see Arnold Williams, *The Common Expositor: An Account of the Commentaries on Genesis 1527–1633* (Chapel Hill: University of North Carolina Press, 1948), 27 ff.

6. I rely on the chronology of Bradstreet's works in Stanford, 125–27.

7. McElrath and Robb, *Complete Works of Anne Bradstreet*, 49. On the vogue for pastoral poetry, see James Sambrook, *English Pastoral Poetry* (Boston: Twayne Publishers, 1983), 59.

8. "Water," in McElrath and Robb, *Complete Works of Anne Bradstreet*, 17.

9. A second "Letter to her Husband," in McElrath and Robb, *Complete Works of Anne Bradstreet*, 181–82.

10. A third "Letter to her Husband," in McElrath and Robb, *Complete Works of Anne Bradstreet*, 182–83.

11. Although many critics have taken these poems to mean that Bradstreet covertly rebelled against Puritan dogma, they show instead that in spite of her pain caused by death and loss, she found continuing solace in the doctrine of the vanity of worldly creatures.

12. Such meditation was important enough to Bradstreet to place it first in her "Meditations Diuine and morall." McElrath and Robb, *Complete Works of Anne Bradstreet*, 195. See Lewalski, *Protestant Politics*, 151 ff., 162–65.

13. For example, Josephine K. Piercy, *Anne Bradstreet* (New York: Twayne, 1965), 100–101; Alvin H. Rosenfeld, "Anne Bradstreet's 'Contemplations': Patterns of Form and Meaning," in Cowell and Stanford, *Critical Essays*; Cecil Eby, Jr. and Richard Crowder, cited in Rosenfeld, "Anne Bradstreet's 'Contemplations'," 125; and Adrienne Rich and Percy Boynton, cited in Rosenmeier, "Wounds Upon Bathsheba," in White, *Puritan Poets and Politics*, 143, n. 15.

14. Retold in Nash, *Wilderness and the American Mind*, 19–20.

15. See Louis L. Martz, *The Paradise Within: Studies in Vaughan, Traherne, and Milton*, New Haven: Yale University Press, 1964, 122.

16. "To my Dear Children," in McElrath and Robb, *Complete Works of Anne Bradstreet*, 217–18. Anne Bradstreet's phrase, "hovshold vpon yᵉ Earth," foreshadows the concept of ecology (or "economy of nature" in the older phrase): "ecology" (and "economy") derive from the Greek word *oikos*, "house," implying that God or nature manages creation the way a steward manages a household. See Donald Worster, *Nature's Economy: A History of Ecological Ideas* (1977; reprint, Cambridge: Cambridge University Press, 1985), 191–93.

17. "In honour of Du Bartas, 1641," in McElrath and Robb, *Complete Works of Anne Bradstreet*, 353–56.

18. The one exception was Bradstreet's use of natural imagery to describe the dangers that beset the pilgrim, a common Puritan metaphor for the Christian's life (as in Bunyan's *Pilgrim's Progress*). The lines of the very late poem "As weary pilgrim, now at rest" (McElrath and Robb, *Complete Works of Anne Bradstreet*, 210–11) describe someone exhausted by an arduous journey through the wilderness. This passage is reminiscent of other Puritan accounts of being lost in early New England. Cp. Bradford, *Of Plymouth Plantation*, 63; and Edward Johnson, *Wonder-working Providence of Sions Saviour, in New England*, in *Wonder-Working Providence of Sions Saviour in New-England (1654) and Good News From New England (1648)* (Delmar, New York: Scholars' Facsimiles & Reprints, 1974), 81.

19. For Anne Bradstreet's popularity, see JoElla Doggett, "Another Eighteenth-Century Instance of Anne Bradstreet's Continuing Appeal," and Pattie Cowell, "The Early Distribution of Anne Bradstreet's Poems," both in Cowell and Stanford, *Critical Essays*.

20. These included Thomas Shepard and John Allin's *A Defence of the Answer*, Thomas Hooker's *Survey of the Summe of Church Discipline*, and John Cotton's *The Way of Congregational Churches Cleared*.

21. On Johnson, see Samuel Eliot Morison's entry in the *Dictionary of American Biography*, and Edward J. Gallagher's introduction to Johnson's *Wonder-working Providence of Sions Saviour in New-England* (1654; reprint, Delmar, N.Y.: Scholars' Facsimiles & Reprints, 1974) (hereafter cited as *WWP*). Sacvan Bercovitch's "The Historiography of Johnson's *Wonder-Working Providence*," *Essex Institute Historical Collections* 104 (1968): 138–61, is a superb key to the meaning of Johnson's work. See also Alan Heimert, "Puritanism, the Wilderness, and the Frontier," *The New England Quarterly* 26 (1953): 361–82; John C. Kilman, "A Joiner Looks at Colonial New England: Edward Johnson's Special Providences," *Southern Folklore Quarterly* 45 (1981): 135–44; and Philip F. Gura, *A Glimpse of Sion's Glory: Puritan Radicalism in New England, 1620–1660* (Middletown, Conn.: Wesleyan University Press, 1984), 214, 229–32. For the colonial transformation of New England ecology, see William Cronon, *Changes in the Land: Indians, Colonists, and the Ecology of New England* (New York: Hill and Wang, 1983). Although her treatment of Johnson and Mather are ahistorical, Cecelia Tichi correctly sees millennialism as the basis for an American ideology of ecological transformation. Cecilia Tichi, *New World, New Earth: Environmental Reform in American Literature from the Puritans through Whitman* (New Haven: Yale University Press, 1979).

22. *WWP*, A2 recto. On the original Puritan purpose, see Theodore Dwight Bozeman, *To Live Ancient Lives: The Primitivist Dimension in Puritanism* (Chapel Hill: University of North Carolina Press, 1988), chapter 3; John Winthrop, "Arguments for the Plantation of New England," and "A Model of Christian Charity," in *Winthrop Papers* (Massachusetts Historical Society, 1931), 2:111–45, and 282–95;

and John Cotton, "Gods Promise To His Plantations" (London, 1630), in *Old South Leaflets* (New York: Burt Franklin, n.d.), vol. 3, no. 53.

23. *WWP*, 3. Cp. 6, 34, 121, and the prophecies of Isaiah 65:17 and Revelation 21:1.

24. *WWP*, 25, 70.

25. *WWP*, 54, 216. On testing, see 30–32. On typology, see Bercovitch, "Historiography," and more concisely, Gallagher, *WWP*, vii–viii.

26. *WWP*, 16, 17, 57, 120.

27. *WWP*, 119, 53, 113, 117, 110; see Exodus 16:3–4. P. 49 recalls as well the miracle of the loaves and fishes.

28. *WWP*, 110–11; cp. p. 200 and Psalms 2:8–9 and 24:1.

29. *WWP*, 123, 122, 47; cp. Revelations 14:8. On "living stones," cp. I Peter 2:4–6, *WWP*, 47. On building the new Jerusalem, see Revelation 21. On Nehemiah, cp. 26, 190.

30. *WWP*, 90, 108, 112, 113. The fall of Babylon also had eschatological meaning; see Revelation 21:3. On the devil and the Indians, cp. 114, 225.

31. *WWP*, 7, and again 107; Isaiah 11:9.

32. *WWP*, 189. Cp. Matthew 20:1–16, Psalm 80, Isaiah 5:1–7.

33. *WWP*, 46, 77. 126, 100. See John 10 and 21:15–18. Cp. Ezekiel 35.

34. *WWP*, 40, 44, 43; cp. 78.

35. *WWP*, 173, 209–10. Cp. 172–73.

36. *WWP*, 208. Book III, chapter VI, praised the state of manufactures in New England.

37. *WWP*, 46, 40, 75–76, 112, 197, 215.

38. *WWP*, 214; cp. 200 and Genesis 32:10. See his prayer, 220–21.

39. Ursula Brumm, " 'What Went You Out into the Wilderness to See?' Nonconformity and Wilderness in Cotton Mather's *Magnalia Christi Americana*," *Prospects: The Annals of American Cultural Studies* 6 (1981): 1–15.

40. See Winthrop, "Arguments for the Plantation of New England," and "A Modell of Christian Charity," in *Works*. Cp. Cotton, 6, 7, 10, 14–15; on trade and covetousness, see, for example Winthrop, *The History of New England from 1630 to 1649*, ed. James Savage (Boston: 1825–1826), 1:116, 313–17; 2:71, 94, 312.

41. The best account of Cotton Mather's life is Kenneth Silverman, *The Life and Times of Cotton Mather* (New York: Harper & Row, 1984), which is particularly good on his religious life. More intellectually oriented is Robert Middlekauff, *The Mathers: Three Generations of Puritan Intellectuals, 1596–1728* (New York: Oxford University Press, 1971). See also Babette M. Levy, *Cotton Mather* (Boston: Twayne Publishers, 1979).

42. *The Short History of New-England. . . .* (Boston, 1694), in *Cotton Mather: Historical Writings* (New York: AMS Press, 1991) (hereafter cited as *History*), 3 ff., 26, 30, 33, 37, 41, 47, 52, and on Nehemiah, 18, 53, 56, 61.

43. Vineyard metaphor, *History*, 17, 33, 34, 60, 65 (see Psalm 80:12–13); flock

metaphor, 22, 55; churches as gardens, 23 (cp. Song of Solomon 6;2); ministers, 20; seminary, 21; moving outside the Hedge, 45. On the seminary, see George H. Williams, "The Idea of the Wilderness of the New World in Cotton Mather's *Magnalia Christi Americana*," in Cotton Mather, *Magnalia Christi Americana Books I and II*, ed. Kenneth B. Murdock (Cambridge, Massachusetts: Belknap Press, 1977), 55–57; also Williams, *Wilderness and Paradise in Christian Thought*.

44. *History*, 64; cp. *Magnalia Christi Americana: or the Ecclesiastical History of New-England, from its first planting in the year 1620, unto the year of our Lord, 1698*, 2nd ed. (Hartford: Silas Andrus, 1820) (hereafter cited as *Magnalia*), 1:25; *Magnalia*, 1:44, 25–26.

45. *History*, 1:12, 15, 28, 31–32; *Magnalia*, 1:72, 78. Book VI of *Magnalia Christi Americana* detailed God's providences in New England.

46. *Magnalia*, 2:74.

47. *Magnalia*, 2:45.

48. See Middlekauff, *The Mathers*, 211; Mason I. Lowance, Jr., "Cotton Mather's *Magnalia* and the Metaphors of Biblical History," in *Typology and Early American Literature*, ed. Sacvan Bercovitch ([Amherst]: University of Massachusetts Press, 1972); and Mason I. Lowance, Jr., *The Language of Canaan: Metaphor and Symbol in New England from the Puritans to the Transcendentalists* (Cambridge: Harvard University Press, 1980), chapter 7.

49. *Magnalia*, 1:104, 109–10. Mather broke the rules of typology by including not one but two Moseses (and later added John Cotton as a third) and broke them again when he applied a second type to Winthrop, "Nehemias Americanus." *Magnalia*, 1:103.

50. On Mather's millennialism, see Middlekauff, *The Mathers*, chapter 18, and Lowance, *Language of Canaan*, 154.

51. *Magnalia*, 1:44–45; Cotton Mather, preface to *Manuductio ad Ministerium. Directions for a Candidate of the Ministry . . .*, ed. Thomas J. Holmes and Kenneth Murdock (1726; reprint, New York: Published for the Facsimile Text Society by Columbia University Press, 1938), viii. Cp. Romans 8:18–22. See also Middlekauff, *The Mathers*, 322.

52. Described in an advertisement for subscribers appended to *Bonifacius. Bonifacius: An Essay . . . to Do Good . . .*, ed. Josephine K. Piercy (1710; reprint, Gainesville, Fla.: Scholars' Facsimiles & Reprints, 1967), 204.

53. Raymond Phineas Stearns, *Science in the British Colonies of America* (Urbana: University of Illinois Press, 1970), 159–61.

54. Cotton Mather, *The Christian Philosopher: A Collection of the Best Discoveries in Nature, with Religious Improvements*, ed. Josephine K. Piercy (1720, post-dated 1721 on the title page; reprint, Gainesville, Fla.: Scholars' Facsimiles & Reprints, 1968) (hereafter cited as *CP*), 2. On Mather and science, see Pershing Vartanian, "Cotton Mather and the Puritan Transition into the Enlightenment," *Early American Literature* 7 (1973): 213–24; Jeffrey Jeske, "Cotton Mather: Physico-Theologian," *Journal of the History of Ideas* 47 (1986): 583–95; Winton U. Solberg, "Cotton Mather, *The*

Christian Philosopher, and the Classics," *Proceedings of the American Antiquarian Society* 96 (1987): 323–65; Winton U. Solberg, "Science and Religion in Early America: Cotton Mather's *Christian Philosopher*," *Church History* 56 (1987): 73–92; and David Levin, "Giants in the Earth: Science and the Occult in Cotton Mather's Letters to the Royal Society," *William and Mary Quarterly* 3rd Ser., 45 (1988): 751–70.

55. *CP*, 1–9, 13. Cp. Mather, *Manuductio*, 47–52.

56. *CP*, 23–25, 25, 52–53, 72, 154, 225 ff., 293.

57. *CP*, 81, 88, 103, 194 ff., 211, 215.

58. *CP*, 292–93. See also Arthur O. Lovejoy, *The Great Chain of Being: A Study of the History of an Idea* (1936; reprint, Cambridge: Harvard University Press, 1964), esp. chapter 6.

59. On the new temper of the times, see Thomas, *Religion and the Decline of Magic*, chapter 22, esp. 657–58.

CHAPTER FOUR

1. For a short biography of Edwards, see Wallace E. Anderson, "Editor's Introduction," in *The Works of Jonathan Edwards* (hereafter cited as *Works*), v. 6, *Scientific and Philosophical Writings* (New Haven: Yale University Press, 1980), 3–37. Perry Miller's thesis about the significance of Locke in Edwards's thought is generally agreed to be overstated; see his *Jonathan Edwards* (New York: W. Sloane Associates, 1949); see Anderson, "Editor's Introduction," in *Works*, v. 6, *Scientific and Philosophical Writings*, 52–136. Of the immense literature on Edwards, the following are helpful: Stephen H. Daniel, "Introduction," in *The Philosophy of Jonathan Edwards: A Study in Divine Semiotics* (Bloomington: Indiana University Press, 1994); Norman Fiering, *Jonathan Edwards's Moral Thought and Its British Context* (Chapel Hill: University of North Carolina Press, 1981); Clyde A. Holbrook, *Jonathan Edwards, the Valley and Nature: An Interpretive Essay* (Lewisburg: Bucknell University Press, 1987); William Sparkes Morris, *The Young Jonathan Edwards: A Reconstruction* (Brooklyn, N.Y.: Carlson Publishing, 1991).

2. "Personal Narrative," in *The Works of President Edwards*, 8th ed. (New York, 1856), 14, 16, 16–17, 18, 19, 20, 22.

3. Pierpont quote in C. C. Goen, "Editor's Introduction," in *Works*, v. 4, *The Great Awakening* (New Haven: Yale University Press, 1972), 68; *Works*, v. 7, *The Life of David Brainerd*, ed. Norman Petit (New Haven: Yale University Press, 1985), 138–39, 144.

4. "Personal Narrative," in *The Works of President Edwards*, 21–22.

5. "Wisdom in the Contrivance of the World"; "Of Being," 204; both in *Works*, v. 6, *Scientific and Philosophical Writings*.

6. Anderson, "Editor's Introduction," in *Works*, v. 6, *Scientific and Philosophical Writings*, 37–52.

7. "Things to be Considered and Written fully about," LS 14, 231, and "The Mind," 353–54, both in *Works*, v. 6, *Scientific and Philosophical Writings*; *An Humble*

Attempt . . . , in *Works*, v. 5, *Apocalyptic Writings*, ed. Stephen J. Stein (New Haven: Yale University Press, 1977), 346.

8. *Some Thoughts Concerning the present Revival of Religion in New England*, in *Works*, v. 4, *The Great Awakening*, 353–58.

9. Edwards, *Apocalypse Series, Apocalyptic Writings*, no. 41, 140–42; cp. nos. 59, 62, 64, 73a, 85; cp. also *Works*, v. 9, *A History of the Work of Redemption*, ed. John F. Wilson (New Haven: Yale University Press, 1989), 348–50; *The Philosophy of Jonathan Edwards From His Private Notebooks*, ed. Harvey G. Townsend (1955; reprint, Westport, Ct.: Greenwood Press, 1972), nos. 725, 867, 990, 263–65.

10. See Daniel Walker Howe, "The Cambridge Platonists of Old England and the Cambridge Platonists of New England," in Conrad Edick Wright, ed., *American Unitarianism, 1805–1865* (Boston: Northeastern University Press, 1989).

11. "Of Being," 204; "The Mind," 353–54, 339, both in *Works*, v. 6, *Scientific and Philosophical Writings*. See Anderson, "Editor's Introduction," also in *Works*, v. 6, *Scientific and Philosophical Writings*, 52–136.

12. *Works*, v. 3, *Original Sin*, ed. Clyde A. Holbrook (New Haven: Yale University Press, 1970), 404; Great Chain of Being, in *Works*, v. 13, *Miscellanies*, ed. Thomas A. Schafer (New Haven: Yale University Press, 1994), no. 103, 271–72.

13. *Dissertation I. Concerning the End for which God Created the World*, 432–43, 491, 513–35 (quote on p. 531), and "Unpublished letter on assurance and participating in the divine nature," 640, both in *Works*, v. 8, *Ethical Writings*, ed. Paul Ramsey (New Haven: Yale University Press, 1989). Cp. "God's Excellencies," *Works*, v. 10, *Sermons and Discourses, 1720–1723*, ed. Wilson H. Kimnach (New Haven: Yale University Press, 1992), and *Works*, v. 13, *Miscellanies*, nos. 104, 106, 107a–b, 108, 182–87, etc.

14. *Miscellanies*, no. 362, p. 435 (quotation), in *Works*, v. 13, *Miscellanies*; *Types*, pp. 150–52, and *Images of Divine Things*, esp. nos. 8 and 57, pp. 53, 67, both in *Works*, v. 11, *Typological Writings*, ed. Wallace E. Anderson and Mason I. Lowance, Jr. (New Haven: Yale University Press, 1993); *Miscellanies*, no. 108, pp. 278–80 (quotation), in *Works*, v. 13, *Miscellanies*; *Images*, no. 156, p. 106, in *Works*, v. 11, *Typological Writings*; and Daniel, *The Philosophy of Jonathan Edwards*, nos. 986, 1170, 1297, pp. 212–18.

15. Winton U. Solberg, "Science and Religion in Early America: Cotton Mather's *Christian Philosopher*," *Church History* 56 (1987): 77.

16. See G. R. Cragg, *From Puritanism to the Age of Reason: A Study of Changes in Religious Thought Within the Church of England, 1660 to 1700* (Cambridge: Cambridge University Press, 1966), esp. chapters 3, 5, 6, and 7.

17. See William H. Goetzmann, *New Lands, New Men: America and the Second Great Age of Discovery* (New York: Viking, 1986).

18. *Autobiography*, 1317; and letter to Samuel Mather, 12 May 1784, 1092, both in Benjamin Franklin, *Writings*, ed. J. A. Leo Lemay (New York: Library of America, 1987) (hereafter cited as *Writings*). For recent biographies of Franklin, see David Freeman Hawke, *Franklin* (New York: Harper & Row, 1976); Esmond Wright,

Franklin of Philadelphia (Cambridge: Belknap Press of Harvard University Press, 1986); and Ronald Clark, *Benjamin Franklin: A Biography* (New York: Random House, 1983).

19. Autobiography, in *Writings*, 1317, 1359.

20. *Writings*, 57–71. Cp. Heinz Otto Sibum, "The Bookkeeper of Nature: Benjamin Franklin's Electrical Research and the Development of Experimental Natural Philosophy in the Eighteenth Century," in *Reappraising Benjamin Franklin: A Bicentennial Perspective*, ed. J. A. Leo Lemay (Newark: University of Delaware Press, 1993), 226.

21. *Autobiography*, in *Writings*, 83.

22. *Writings*, 84.

23. *Writings*, 164–65; cp. "Proposals Relating to the Education of Youth in Pensilvania," *Writings*, 340.

24. *Writings*, 83–90; quote on p. 88. For parallels with Newton, see I. Bernard Cohen, *Franklin and Newton* (Philadelphia: American Philosophical Society, 1956), 209. On ambiguous evidence, Alfred Owen Aldridge concluded that Franklin never discarded his polytheism. See *Benjamin Franklin and Nature's God* (Durham: Duke University Press, 1967), 31–33.

25. On Franklin's beliefs, see Aldridge, *Benjamin Franklin and Nature's God*, and Donald H. Meyer, "Franklin's Religion," in *Critical Essays on Benjamin Franklin*, ed. Melvin H. Buxbaum (Boston: G. K. Hall, 1987).

26. See Aldridge, *Benjamin Franklin and Nature's God*, 62–63; and Wright, *Franklin of Philadelphia*, 25, 37.

27. See Samuel J. Edgerton, Jr., "The Franklin Stove," in *Benjamin Franklin's Science*, ed. I. Bernard Cohen (Cambridge: Harvard University Press, 1990).

28. Cohen, *Franklin and Newton*, 207.

29. Cohen, *Franklin and Newton*, 295–97.

30. See Cohen, *Franklin's Science*, chapter 2; and Cohen, *Franklin and Newton*, chapters 5 and 6.

31. See Cohen, *Franklin and Newton*, chapter 8. See also J. L. Heilbron, "Franklin as an Enlightened Natural Philosopher," and Sibum, "Bookkeeper of Nature," both in Lemay, *Reappraising Benjamin Franklin*.

32. Cohen, *Franklin's Science*, chapter 6; and Hawke, *Franklin*, chapter 10.

33. Cohen, *Franklin's Science*, 6.

34. "Advice to a Young Tradesman, Written by an Old One" (1748), in *Writings*, 320, 321; "Father Abraham's Speech," in *Writings*, 1294–1303. See Tracy Mott and George W. Zink, "Benjamin Franklin's Economic Thought: A Twentieth Century Appraisal," in Buxbaum, *Critical Essays*.

35. Letter to Peter Collinson, 9 May 1753, in *Writings*, 469.

36. *Writings*, 295–97; cp. letter to Mary Stevenson, 11 June 1760, in *Writings*, 768–70.

37. "Positions To Be Examined," 4 April 1769, in *Writings*, 645; cp. "On the Price of Corn, and Management of the Poor," 29 November 1766, in *Writings*, 585–88.

38. See Timothy Breen, *Tobacco Culture: The Mentality of the Great Tidewater Planters on the Eve of the Revolution* (Princeton: Princeton University, 1985). Rhys Isaac explored the relationship between Virginia church and society in *The Transformation of Virginia, 1740–1790* (Chapel Hill: University of North Carolina Press, 1982), chapter 4. On Jefferson's Anglicanism, see Charles B. Sanford, *The Religious Life of Thomas Jefferson* (Charlottesville: University Press of Virginia, 1984), 93. On Jefferson's religious development, see Paul K. Conkin, "The Religious Pilgrimage of Thomas Jefferson," in *Jeffersonian Legacies*, ed. Peter S. Onuf (Charlottesville: University Press of Virginia, 1993).

39. See Albert E. Cowdrey, *This Land, This South: An Environmental History* (n.p.: University Press of Kentucky, 1983), 44–50, 65, 83; Edmund S. Morgan, *American Slavery, American Freedom: The Ordeal of Colonial Virginia* (New York: Norton, 1975), esp. chapter 18; and Timothy Breen, *Puritans and Adventurers: Change and Persistence in Early America* (New York: Oxford University Press, 1980), chapter 6 (quotation, p. 109).

40. TJ to Dr. Thomas Cooper (10 February 1814), in *The Writings of Thomas Jefferson*, ed. Albert Ellery Bergh (Washington, D.C.: Thomas Jefferson Memorial Association, 1905), 14:85. Laws establishing religion were "tyrannical laws." See *Notes on the State of Virginia* (hereafter cited as *Notes*), in *Writings*, 2:219–24 (quotation on p. 224); and "Second Inaugural Address, March 4, 1805," in *Writings*, 3:378. On free enterprise and low taxes, see "First Inaugural Address, March 4, 1801," in *Writings*, 3:321; and "First Annual Message, December 8, 1801," in *Writings*, 3:337. On philosophy and science, see *Notes*, 222; TJ to John Dickinson (6 March 1801), in *Writings*, 10:217–18; and TJ to Joseph Willard, in *The Papers of Thomas Jefferson*, ed. Julian P. Boyd (Princeton: Princeton University Press, 1950–) (hereafter cited as *Papers*), 14:699. On duty, see A. J. Beitzinger, "Political Theorist," in *Thomas Jefferson: A Reference Biography*, ed. Merrill D. Peterson (New York: Charles Scribner's Sons, 1986), 86–87. See also Breen, *Puritans and Adventurers*, chapter 9, esp. 193 ff.

41. TJ to Peter Carr (10 August 1787), in *Papers*, 12:14–15; TJ to John Adams (22 August 1813), in *The Adams-Jefferson Letters: The Complete Correspondence Between Thomas Jefferson and Abigail and John Adams*, ed. Lester J. Cappon (Chapel Hill: University of North Carolina Press, 1959) (hereafter cited as *A.-J. Letters*), 2:368. See Garry Wills, *Inventing America: Jefferson's Declaration of Independence* (Garden City, N.Y.: Doubleday, 1978), chapter 13.

42. TJ to Dr. Benjamin Waterhouse (19 July 1822), in *Writings*, 15:392; *Notes*, in *Writings*, 221; TJ to John Adams (15 August 1820 and 11 April 1823), in *A.-J. Letters*, 2:567–69, 593. See also "Second Inaugural Address," in *Writings*, 3:381–82; TJ to Carr (10 August 1787), in *Papers*, 12:15–17, 18–19; TJ to John Adams (22 August 1813), in *A.-J. Letters*, 2:369. On the writers who influenced Jefferson's religious thinking, see E. S. Gaustad, "Religion," in Peterson, *Thomas Jefferson*, 279, 283, 287; and Sanford, *Religious Life*, 12, 85.

43. Sanford, *Religious Life*, 48–52; Daniel J. Boorstin, *The Lost World of Thomas Jefferson* (Boston: Beacon Press, 1948), 166, 171.

44. TJ to John Adams (11 August 1823 and 12 October 1813), in *A.–J. Letters*, 2:594, 384; TJ to Dr. Benjamin Waterhouse (19 July 1822), in *Writings*, 15:391.

45. TJ to Adams (11 May 1823), in *A.–J. Letters*, 2:592. Cp. TJ to Charles Thomson (17 December 1786), in *Papers*, 10:608.

46. TJ to Adams (11 April 1823), in *A.–J. Letters*, 2:591–92.

47. See Charles A. Miller, *Jefferson and Nature: An Interpretation* (Baltimore: Johns Hopkins University Press, 1988), chapter 1; also Joyce Appleby, "Jefferson and His Complex Legacy," in Onuf, *Jeffersonian Legacies*, 3–7.

48. See TJ to Adams (11 April 1823), in *A.–J. Letters*, 2:593.

49. See Donald Worster, *Nature's Economy: A History of Ecological Ideas* (1977; reprint, Cambridge: Cambridge University Press, 1985), part 1; and Arthur O. Lovejoy, *The Great Chain of Being: A Study of the History of an Idea* (1936; reprint, Cambridge: Harvard University, 1964), chapters 6–8; TJ to David Rittenhouse (19 July 1778), in *Papers*, 2:203; *Notes*, in *Writings*, 71, 60; cp. "Memoranda taken on a Journey from Paris into the Southern Parts of France, and Northern of Italy, in the year 1787," in *Writings*, 17:234; TJ to Colonel John Stuart (10 November 1776), in *Writings*, 9:350; TJ to Adams (11 April 1823), in *A.–J. Letters*, 2:592.

50. TJ to Dr. Benjamin Rush (16 January 1811), in *Writings*, 7:4.

51. On Jefferson and science, see Edwin T. Martin, *Thomas Jefferson: Scientist* (New York: Henry Schuman, 1952), 9 ("zealous amateur"), 32–48. See also Henry F. May, "The Enlightenment," 54, and Silvio A. Bedini, "Man of Science," both in Peterson, *Thomas Jefferson*. On *Notes on Virginia* and the Buffon controversy, see esp. Antonello Gerbi, *The Dispute of the New World: The History of a Polemic, 1750–1900*, rev. and enl. ed., tr. Jeremy Moyle (Pittsburgh: University of Pittsburgh Press, 1973), 252–68.

52. See Robert E. Shalhope, "Agriculture," in Peterson, *Thomas Jefferson*, 309.

53. TJ to Adams (11 April 1823, 12 October 1813), in *A.–J. Letters*, 2:592, 385; "First Inaugural Address, March 4, 1801," in *Writings*, 3:320. Cp. "First Annual Message, December 8, 1801," in *Writings*, 3:327; and "Second Annual Message, December 15, 1802," in *Writings*, 3:340. *Notes*, in *Writings*, 227. On God's purposes in evil events and war, see TJ to Dr. Benjamin Rush (23 September 1800), in *Writings*, 10:173; and TJ to William Short (20 August 1814), in *Writings*, 18:283.

54. "Second Inaugural Address, March 4, 1805," in *Writings*, 3:383; Beitzinger, "Political Theorist," 98.

55. *Notes*, in *Writings*, 229. Jefferson's suspicions of mercantile activity accorded closely with Edward Johnson's and Franklin's; cp. *Encyclopedie Methodique*, "I. Answers to Démeunier's First Queries, January 24, 1786," in *Papers*, 10:16.

56. "First Inaugural Address, March 4, 1801," in *Writings*, 3:320.

57. "Second Inaugural Address, March 4, 1805," in *Writings*, 3:379; cp. "First Annual Message, December 8, 1801," in *Writings*, 3:328.

58. Cp. "First Annual Message, December 8, 1801," in *Writings*, 3:330. TJ to Archibald Stuart (25 January 1786), in *Papers*, 9:218. TJ to Charles Thomson (17 December 1786), in *Papers*, 10:609.

59. See E. Brooks Holifield, *The Gentlemen Theologians: American Theology in Southern Culture, 1795–1860* (Durham: Duke University Press, 1978), esp. chapters 3, 4, and 5. On Emerson, cp. antebellum minister John Holmes Bocock, "Emerson on History," in *All Clever Men, Who Make Their Way: Critical Discourse in the Old South*, ed. Michael O'Brien (Fayetteville: University of Arkansas Press, 1982). On conservation, see Ted Ownby, *Subduing Satan: Religion, Recreation, and Manhood in the Rural South, 1865–1920* (Chapel Hill: University of North Carolina Press, 1990), 177–82.

60. See Cowdrey, *This Land, This South*, 73–80, 154–55.

CHAPTER FIVE

1. Oliver Wendell Holmes, *Ralph Waldo Emerson* (Boston: Houghton Mifflin, 1885), 115.

2. See Wesley T. Mott, "Emerson and Antinomianism: The Legacy of the Sermons," *American Literature* 50 (1978): 369–97; and Edmund S. Morgan, *The Puritan Dilemma: The Story of John Winthrop* (Boston: Little, Brown, 1958).

3. Among the best books on Emerson's life and work are Gay Wilson Allen, *Waldo Emerson: A Biography* (New York: Viking, 1981); Evelyn Barish, *Emerson: The Roots of Prophecy* (Princeton: Princeton University Press, 1989); Joel Porte, *Representative Man: Ralph Waldo Emerson in His Time* (New York: Oxford University Press, 1979); Robert D. Richardson, Jr., *Emerson: The Mind on Fire* (Berkeley: University of California Press, 1995); Ralph L. Rusk, *The Life of Ralph Waldo Emerson* (New York: Charles Scribner's Sons, 1949); and Stephen E. Whicher, *Freedom and Fate: An Inner Life of Ralph Waldo Emerson* (Philadelphia: University of Pennsylvania Press, 1953).

4. See Whicher, *Freedom and Fate*, 26, 103.

5. See Daniel Walker Howe, "The Cambridge Platonists of Old England and the Cambridge Platonists of New England," in *American Unitarianism, 1805–1865*, ed. Conrad Edick Wright (Boston: Northeastern University Press, 1989); *Nature*, in *The Collected Works of Ralph Waldo Emerson*, ed. Ralph E. Spiller, Alfred R. Ferguson, et al. (Cambridge: The Belknap Press of Harvard University Press, 1971–) (hereafter *CW*), 1:37. On English Romanticism, see Marjorie Hope Nicolson, *Mountain Gloom and Mountain Glory: The Development of the Aesthetics of the Infinite* (Ithaca: Cornell University Press, 1959), esp. chapter 3. On Emerson's readings in idealism, see Allen, *Waldo Emerson*, 160–76, 269–81, 375–76, 381, 386, 455; cp. Emerson's comments on Plato and the neo-Platonists in "Books," *CW*, 2:198 ff., 202–3.

For the neo-Platonic revival in England and Germany, see Mary T. Clark, "Neoplatonism," in *The Encyclopedia of Religion*, ed. Mircea Eliade (New York: Macmillan, 1987), 366; R. T. Wallis, *Neo-Platonism* (London: Duckworth, 1972), 173; and Werner Beierwaltes, "Plotin im deutschen Idealismus," *Platonismus und Idealismus*

(Frankfurt: Vittorio Klostermann, 1972). For the German influence on Transcendentalism, see Henry A. Pochmann, *German Culture in America 1600–1900: Philosophical and Literary Influence* (Madison: University of Wisconsin Press, 1957), 79–152; on Emerson, 153–207.

On Emerson's idealism, see *Centenary Edition: The Complete Works of Ralph Waldo Emerson*, ed. Edward Waldo Emerson (Boston: Houghton Mifflin, 1903), 1:427n. (hereafter *CE*); Barish, *Emerson*, chapter 10; Pochmann, *German Culture in America*, 156.

6. *Nature*, in *CW,* 1:37. Cp. "Beauty," in *CE*, 6:322; and "The Transcendentalist," in *CW,* 1:211.

7. "Man the Reformer," in *CW,* 1:148, 153; "The American Scholar," in *CW,* 1:62; "Heroism," in *CW,* 2:151; "Beauty," in *CE*, 6:279; "The Poet," in *CW,* 3:3; "Art," in *CW,* 2:218. Cp. "The Transcendentalist," in *CW,* 1:207, 211; "Culture," in *CE*. 6:155 ff.; "Domestic Life," in *CW,* 7:115 ff., 120–21; "Intellect," in *CW,* 2:202; *Nature*, in *CW,* 1:20, 36, 39; "Success," in *CW,* 7:208; "Literary Ethics," in *CW,* 1:115, 110, 109.

On the doctrine of the "spheres," see Nancy F. Cott, *The Bonds of Womanhood: "Women's Sphere" in New England, 1780–1835* (New Haven: Yale University Press, 1977); on genderization of landscape and the sciences, see Michael L. Smith, *Pacific Visions: California Scientists and the Environment, 1850–1915* (New Haven: Yale University Press, 1987), 77 ff.; and on the feminization of American religion, see Ann Douglas, *The Feminization of American Culture* (New York: Knopf, 1977).

Barish, *Emerson*, chapter 1; Allen, *Waldo Emerson*, 3–5, 10, 86; David Leverenz, "The Politics of Emerson's Man-Making Words," in David Leverenz, *Manhood and the American Renaissance* (Ithaca: Cornell University Press, 1989); "The American Scholar," in *CW,* 1:59, 64. Cp. "The Transcendentalist," in *CW,* 1:202, 206; "Prudence," in *CW,* 2:131; "Domestic Life," in *CW,* 7:129, 132; "Power," in *CE*, 6:57; "Civilization," in *CE*, 7:24. On his alienation from fathers and his father, see *CW,* 1:184–85; *CW,* 1:232–33; *CW,* 2:188; *CW,* 2:202.

8. *Nature*, in *CW,* 1:7, 36; "The Divinity School Address," in *CW,* 1:84.

9. *Nature*, in *CW,* 1:8–10, 21, 36; cp. "Astronomy," "Summer," in *Young Emerson Speaks*, ed. (Boston: Houghton Mifflin, 1938) (hereafter *YES*), 40; *Nature*, in *CW,* 1:42; "Self-Reliance," in *CW,* 1:28; "History," in *CW,* 2:8, 15, 23; "The Over-Soul," in *CW,* 2:163; "Beauty," in *CE*, 6:322; "Civilization," in *CE*, 7:20–21; "Self-Reliance," in *CW,* 1:39–40. Cp. Richardson, *Emerson*, 228.

See Harry Hayden Clark, "Emerson and Science," *Philological Quarterly* 10 (1931): 225–60, esp. 234–39, 254–55; Wesley T. Mott, "From Natural Religion to Transcendentalism: An Edition of Emerson's Sermon No. 43," *Studies in the American Renaissance* (1985): 1–27; and Gay Wilson Allen, "A New Look at Emerson and Science," and David Robinson, "Emerson's Natural Theology and the Paris Naturalists: Toward a Theory of Animated Nature," both in *Critical Essays on Ralph Waldo Emerson*, ed. Robert E. Burkholder and Joel Myerson (Boston: G. K. Hall, 1983).

10. *Nature*, in *CW,* 1:36; "Wealth," in *CE*, 6:83; "Love," in *CW,* 2:106; "Pru-

dence," in *CW,* 2:132; *Nature,* in *CW,* 1:11, 12; "Wealth," in *CE,* 6:85, 99; "Civilization," in *CE,* 7:23; "Domestic Life," in *CW,* 7:116 ff. Cp. *Nature,* in *CW,* 1:7; "Spiritual Laws," in *CW,* 2:86; "Beauty," in *CE,* 6:286.

11. *Nature,* in *CW,* 1:12, 17; cp. "Beauty" and "Summer," in *YES,* 43.

12. *Nature,* in *CW,* 1:17–22; cp. "The Poet," in *CW,* 3:8. Cp. "The Poet," in *CW,* 3:9. On Edwards's influence on Emerson, see Richardson, *Emerson,* 24, 54, and 54n.

13. "Works and Days," in *CW,* 7:172 ff.; *Nature,* in *CW,* 1:23, 34; cp. "Summer," in *YES,* 40–42; "Astronomy," in *YES,* 178. *Nature,* in *CW,* 1:17–23; cp. 38; also "Summer," in *YES,* 44. The chapter in *Nature* on language parallels Schelling. See Henry Clarke Goddard, *Studies in New England Transcendentalism* (1908; reprint, New York: Hillary House, 1960), 80–81; cp. 104–12. But see Pochmann, *German Culture in America,* 188.

14. *Nature,* in *CW,* 1:23; cp. "Summer," in *YES,* 44–45; "History," in *CW,* 2:5.

15. *Nature,* in *CW,* 1:25. Cp. "Compensation," in *CW,* 2:61; "Works and Days," in *CW,* 7:158.

16. "The Young American," in *CW,* 1:226–29; "Farming," in *CW,* 7:135, 150; "Works and Days," in *CW,* 7:162; cp. "Fate," in *CE,* 6:43.

17. *Nature,* in *CW,* 1:25, 27, 40; "Beauty," in *CE,* 6:281–84; "The American Scholar," in *CW,* 1:54. Cp. nature's moral effect on the farmer, "The Young American," in *CW,* 1:227; "Farming," in *CW,* 7:137, 153–54. Cp. also "History," in *CW,* 2:8; "Compensation," in *CW,* 2:60; "The Over-Soul," in *CW,* 2:159; "Circles," in *CW,* 2:179. A Bacon-inspired ideology of empirical science as a support of religion dominated American thinking about science through much of the nineteenth century. See Theodore Dwight Bozeman, *Protestants in an Age of Science: The Baconian Ideal and Ante-Bellum Religious Thought* (Chapel Hill: University of North Carolina Press, 1977); and Herbert Hovenkamp, *Science and Religion in America, 1800–1860* (Philadelphia: University of Pennsylvania Press, 1978), chapter 2. On Romantic neo-Platonism, see M. H. Abrams, *Natural Supernaturalism: Tradition and Revolution in Romantic Literature* (New York: W. W. Norton & Co., 1971), 146–54.

18. *Nature,* in *CW,* 1:39; "Nature," in *CW,* 3:104; "Beauty," in *CE,* 6:298; "Heroism," in *CW,* 2:147–48. Cp. "The Poet," in *CW,* 3:11.; *Nature,* in *CW,* 1:42, 43. On Milton, see Richardson, *Emerson,* 16, 520; and Abrams, *Natural Supernaturalism,* 33, 95.

19. "The Divinity School Address," in *CW,* 1:76, 80, 77. *Nature,* in *CW,* 1:43, 44, 45. Cp. "The Divinity School Address," in *CW,* 84; "Man the Reformer," in *CW,* 1:159, Luke 17:20 ff. On the role and method of the "Artist," see "Art," in Emerson, *Essays: First Series* and *Society and Solitude.*

20. *CW,* 2:270n; "The Young American," in *CW,* 1:227, 229; "The Miracle of Our Being," in *YES,* 204; "Self-Reliance," in *CW* 1:44. Cp. "Art," in *CW,* 7:50; "History," in *CW,* 2:18. See also Merrill D. Peterson, "The American Scholar: Emerson and Jefferson," in *Thomas Jefferson and the World of Books: A symposium held at the Library of Congress September 21, 1976* (Washington: Library of Congress, 1977).

21. See William O. Douglas, *Go East, Young Man: The Early Years* (New York:

Random House, 1974), chapter 14; and particularly Gary Snyder's younger poems. Cp. Stephen Fox, *The American Conservation Movement: John Muir and His Legacy* (1981; reprint, Madison: University of Wisconsin Press, 1985), chapter 11.

C. L. Tripathi, "The Influence of Indian Philosophy on Neoplatonism," and Albert M. Wolters, "A Survey of Modern Scholarly Opinion on Plotinus and Indian Thought," both in *Neoplatonism and Indian Thought*, ed. R. Baine Harris (Norfolk, Va.: International Society for Neoplatonic Studies, 1982). Modern scholars have taken note of the similarities between Eastern and ecological thought, although none has discerned the neo-Platonic link; see William Irwin Thompson, "Pacific Shift," in *Nature in Asian Traditions of Thought: Essays in Environmental Philosophy*, ed. J. Baird Callicott and Roger T. Ames (Albany: State University of New York Press, 1989).

22. Klaus J. Hansen, *Mormonism and the American Experience* (Chicago: University of Chicago Press, 1981), 67.

23. For relevant descriptions of this world, see Gordon S. Wood, "Evangelical America and Early Mormonism," *New York History* 61 (1980): 359–86; and Nathan O. Hatch, *The Democratization of American Christianity* (New Haven: Yale University Press, 1989), esp. the introduction and p. 35. On outsiderness, see R. Laurence Moore, *Religious Outsiders and the Making of Americans* (New York: Oxford University Press, 1986), chapter 1. Mary Douglas and Aaron Wildavsky, *Risk and Culture: An Essay on the Selection of Technical and Environmental Dangers* (Berkeley: University of California Press, 1982), esp. chapters 5 and 6, contains insightful and provocative comments on sects and churches, outsiderness and insiderness.

David Brion Davis identified in Mormonism the Puritan ideals of theocratic church government, affirmation of a close and personal God, a providential view of history, and a gospel of works. "The New England Origins of Mormonism," in *Mormonism and American Culture*, ed. Marvin S. Hill and James B. Allen (New York: Harper & Row, 1972). But see John L. Brooke, *The Refiner's Fire: The Making of Mormon Cosmology, 1644–1844* (Cambridge: Cambridge University Press, 1994), chapter 3.

24. On Mormonism's New England roots, see Leonard J. Arrington, *Great Basin Kingdom: An Economic History of the Latter-day Saints, 1830–1900* (Cambridge: Harvard University Press, 1958), 3; on its appeal to the lower classes, see Hill and Allen, *Mormonism and American Culture*, xvii–xviii and chapter 1. The Book of Mormon is filled with condemnations of the rich, the "carnal," the proud, and the learned. For a good selection of examples, see Alma 1:6, 1:16, 4:6 and 12, 11:21–25, 31:24–25, 38:1, and 39:14; on vain learning: 2 Nephi 9:28. (Hereafter, books from the Book of Mormon will be cited by their names alone.)

Earth made for man: cp. 1 Nephi 17:36; *Doctrine and Covenants* (hereafter *DC*) 49:16–17, 61:17.

Power and providence in natural events: cp. Helaman 14:20–24, and 3 Nephi 8; Mosiah 1:17 and 12:6, and Alma 10:22–23, Helaman 11:4–15, and Ether 9:28–34; and Helaman 11:16, Ether 9:35; and Jacob 4:9, Helaman 12:8–17, and Ether 4:9.

"Mother earth" Mosiah 2:26; *Pearl of Great Price* (hereafter *PGP*), and Moses 7:48.

25. See *DC*, 45:63–71; Alma 16:2–8 (which reads like a Puritan Indian captivity narrative), and *DC*, 3:17–20, 10:48, 19:27, 49:24; *DC* 49:24–25; Jacob 5:41 and 6:2, 2 Nephi 15:7, Alma 25:12, and 3 Nephi 15:17; and *DC*, 117:7. Ironically, Puritans evinced much greater concern to respect Indians' title to their land than Mormons. See Eugene E. Campbell, *Establishing Zion: The Mormon Church in the American West, 1847–1869* (Salt Lake City: n.p., 1988), chapter 6.

26. Joseph Smith's story has been told many times. Perhaps the best account of his early life is Richard L. Bushman, *Joseph Smith and the Beginnings of Mormonism* (Urbana: University of Illinois Press, 1984). For the best one-volume account of Mormonism, see Hansen, *Mormonism and the American Experience*. Other valuable studies are Leonard Arrington and Davis Bitton, *The Mormon Experience: A History of the Latter-day Saints* (New York: Alfred A. Knopf, 1979); and Jan Shipps, *Mormonism: The Story of a New Religious Tradition* (Urbana: University of Illinois Press, 1985).

27. "Autobiographical Sketch," in *An American Prophet's Record: The Diaries and Journals of Joseph Smith*, ed. Scott H. Faulring (Salt Lake City: Signature Books, 1989), 5; cp. Book of Mormon, Alma 30:44.

28. The significance of this vision changed as Smith's career unfolded. His earliest description appeared in his "Autobiographical Sketch" (pp. 5–6). For an official account, see *PGP, Joseph Smith* 2:11 ff., which is an edited version of his history reprinted in *The Personal Writings of Joseph Smith*, ed. Dean C. Jessee (Salt Lake City: Deseret Books, 1984), 196 ff.

29. *DC*, 107:53 and 116; *DC*, 133:23–24; 1 Nephi 12:4; *PGP*, "Articles of Faith," 10; *DC*, 49:23. Cp. *DC*, 109:74, 133:22 and 133:29.

Smith's additions were later collected in *The Doctrine and Covenants of the Church of Jesus Christ of Latter-day Saints* and *The Pearl of Great Price*. As for the status of the Bible, "The Articles of Faith" in *PGP* stated, "We believe the Bible to be the word of God as far as it is translated correctly. . . ." By means of revelation, Smith ventured to "correct" a number of sections of the Bible. For a succinct and clear summary of Mormon doctrine, see Hansen, *Mormonism and the American Experience*, chapter 2.

On the older view of mountains and valleys as products of God's curse, see Nicolson, *Mountain Gloom and Mountain Glory*, chapters 1 and 2. On Adam's fall, see "How God Came to Be God" (or "King Follett Sermon"), in *Joseph Smith: Selected Sermons & Writings*, ed. Robert L. Millet (New York: Paulist Press, 1989), 138–39; *PGP*, Moses 4:3 and 7:32, and Abraham 3:26–28; *DC*, 30:36–39.

30. *DC*, 130:22 and 131:7–8; and "Lecture on Faith #4," in *Selected Sermons*, 123–24 and note.

31. *PGP*, Abraham 4; "How God Came to Be God," in *Selected Sermons*, 136; *DC*, 132:20, 49, 63; *PGP*, Moses 2:33–37 and Abraham 3:16–22; *DC*, 130:7 and *PGP*, Abraham 3:2–3.

32. *DC*, 128; *DC*, 132; Alma 40:13. See Marvin S. Hill, *Quest for Refuge: The Mormon Flight from American Pluralism* (Salt Lake City: Signature Books, 1989), 48.

33. *DC*, 133. See Davis, "New England Origins of Mormonism." For economic equality, see *DC*, 49:20. On Mormon millennialism, see Grant Underwood, *The Millenarian World of Early Mormonism* (Urbana: University of Illinois, 1993), chapter 3.

34. Brigham Young's address of 1846, on the eve of the trek to Utah, paralleled those of the Puritans upon their reluctant departure from England, although notably more bitter and vengeful. Hill, *Quest for Refuge*, 179.

35. On the Mormon re-creation of the Puritan community, see Arrington, *Great Basin Kingdom*, 24; Hansen, *Mormonism and the American Experience*, 123–30; Hill, *Quest for Refuge*, xii–xiii and chapter 3; and John W. Reps, *Cities of the American West: A History of Frontier Urban Planning* (Princeton: Princeton University Press, 1979), chapters 16 and 9. See also Richard V. Francaviglia, *The Mormon Landscape: Existence, Creation, and Perception of a Unique Image in the American West* (New York: AMS Press, 1978); Charles S. Peterson, "Imprint of Agricultural Systems on the Utah Landscape," in *The Mormon Role in the Settlement of the West*, ed. Richard H. Jackson (Provo: Brigham Young University Press, 1978), 94–95; Arrington, *Great Basin Kingdom*, 4, 24–28, 52–54; and Hansen, *Mormonism and the American Experience*, 109–10. On the work ethic, cp. Jacob 6:3, Mosiah 9:12, Alma 36:24 and 38:12.

36. See Arrington, *Great Basin Kingdom*, 161; and Mark P. Leone, *Roots of Modern Mormonism* (Cambridge: Harvard University Press, 1979), chapter 4.

37. Arrington, *Great Basin Kingdom*, 64–66, 204–5, 255. Leonard Arrington, Feramorz Y. Fox, and Dean L. May examined the powerful, long-lived Mormon communitarian impulse, even now not totally extinct, in *Building the City of God: Community and Cooperation among the Mormons*, 2nd ed. (Urbana: University of Illinois Press, 1992). For a view of the Mormon church as a totalitarian institution using irrigation to preserve and expand its power, see Donald Worster, *Rivers of Empire: Water, Aridity, and the Growth of the American West* (New York: Pantheon Books, 1985), 74–83.

38. Arrington, *Great Basin Kingdom*, 323; and Peterson, "Imprint of Agricultural Systems," 97–103.

39. Jackson, *Mormon Role*, 37–38; Leone, *Roots of Modern Mormonism*, chapter 4; and Peterson, "Imprint of Agricultural Systems," 97.

40. *DC*, 49:19–21.

41. On Manifest Destiny, see Norman A. Graebner on commercial considerations in *Empire on the Pacific: A Study in American Continental Expansion* (New York: Ronald Press, 1955); on intellectual elements, Frederick Merk, *Manifest Destiny and Mission in American History* (New York: Knopf, 1963); on foreign policy implications, Frederick Merk, *The Monroe Doctrine and American Expansionism, 1843–1849* (New York: Knopf, 1966).

42. Merk, *Manifest Destiny*, chapters 1 and 2. For the events of Gilpin's life this chapter relies primarily upon Thomas L. Karnes, *William Gilpin: Western Nationalist* (Austin: University of Texas Press, 1970). On Gilpin's commercial vision, see Henry Nash Smith, *Virgin Land: The American West as Symbol and Myth* (1950; reprint, Cambridge: Harvard University Press, 1970), chapter 3.

43. Karnes, *Gilpin*, 13; Merk, *Manifest Destiny*, 27. On Joshua Gilpin, see G. E. Bentley, Jr., "The Way of a Papermaker with a Poet: Joshua G. Gilpin, William Blake, and the Arts in 1796," *Notes and Queries* 33 (1986): 80–84, 525; and John Bidwell, "Joshua Gilpin and Lord Stanhope's Improvements in Printing," *Papers of the Bibliographical Society of America* 76 (1982): 143–58.

44. On slaves, see "Ordered Out of Missouri," *St. Louis Globe-Democrat*, 2 February 1888, p. 12, clipping in Gilpin file, Missouri Historical Society, St. Louis, Mo. Karnes neglected this clipping and never mentioned Gilpin's slaves.

45. Bound volume of Gilpin's letters entitled "Dragoon Letters from the Western Frontier," Missouri Historical Society, St. Louis, Mo. The journal from Joshua Gilpin's 1809 trip into western Pennsylvania showed the same three preoccupations, although with rather more sophistication. See Joshua Gilpin, *Pleasure and Business in Western Pennsylvania: The Journal of Joshua Gilpin, 1809*, ed. Joseph E. Walker (Harrisburg: Pennsylvania Historical and Museum Commission, 1975).

46. Joshua Gilpin, *Mission of the North American People, Geographical, Social, and Political*, 2nd rev. ed. (Philadelphia: Lippincott, 1874) (hereafter *Mission*), 40.

47. *Mission*, 33. "Aboriginal cattle" means buffalo and deer.

48. *Mission*, 17, 49, 71, 70; cp. 22.

49. *Mission*, 74, 61, 15, 81, 69. "Calcareous," another favorite Gilpinism, meant limestone-based and hence naturally fertile.

50. *Mission*, 114, 53. Gilpin described his theory in chapters 11–13.

51. *Mission*, 43, 61, 41.

52. *Mission*, 105, 115.

53. *Mission*, 104. On the British empire, see pp. 100–101. On Anglophobia in Manifest Destiny, see Merk, *The Monroe Doctrine*.

54. *Mission*, 99, 7, 142, 95, 99.

55. "Speech of Col. William Gilpin on the subject of the Pacific railway. . . . November 5, 1849," in *Mission*, 143. For an extended metaphor of this war upon the wilderness, see pp. 142 ff.

56. *Mission*, 90, 116. "The Cities of Missouri," *The Western Journal and Civilian* 11 (October 1853): 37. Richard Slotkin had a less sympathetic opinion of Gilpin's prophecy in *The Fatal Environment: The Myth of the Frontier in the Age of Industrialization* (New York: Atheneum, 1985), 219–24.

Gilpin may have engaged personally in a bit of blending of the races. In 1888, when asked whether he had had any family in Missouri when he lived in Independence, he replied, "I had no white family." The interviewer did not extract from Gilpin whether that meant he had a non-white family, but he did ascertain later that Gilpin's slaves included "an old woman and two children," leaving the question of their paternity moot. On the other hand, perhaps he simply regarded his slaves as "family." See "Ordered Out of Missouri," Gilpin file, Missouri Historical Society.

57. *Mission*, 8 (cp. 33, 45); 102–103; 116 (cp. 95); and "Cities of Missouri," 38. Eastern cities conspired to hold back the "pioneer army"; see "Pacific Railway," in *Mission*, 149 ff.; and "Cities of Missouri," 38.

58. *Mission*, 70, 91.

59. *Mission*, 43.

60. Cp. John Quincy Adams, in Merk, *Manifest Destiny*, 31; Thomas Hart Benton, *Thirty Years' View; or, A History of the Working of the American Government for Thirty Years, from 1820 to 1850* (New York: Appleton, 1886), 2:474; and Daniel S. Dickinson, in Merk, *Manifest Destiny*, 29.

61. Smith, *Virgin Land*, 37.

62. Karnes discussed Whitman's possible debts to Gilpin in *Gilpin*, 345–47.

63. *Mission*, 67. On abundance and the American mission, see David M. Potter, *People of Plenty: Economic Abundance and the American Character* (Chicago: University of Chicago Press, 1954), esp. chapter 6. See Lee Clark Mitchell, *Witnesses to a Vanishing America: The Nineteenth-Century Response* (Princeton: Princeton University Press, 1981).

CHAPTER SIX

1. The most complete modern history of American railroads is Albro Martin, *Railroads Triumphant: the Growth, Rejection, and Rebirth of a Vital American Force* (New York: Oxford University Press, 1992); esp. relevant are chapters 10 and 11. On the role of railroads in the opening of land to white settlement and development, see Martin, *Railroads Triumphant*, chapter 7; and Robert G. Athearn, *High Country Empire: The High Plains and Rockies* (New York: McGraw-Hill, 1960), chapter 7.

2. E. H. Harriman, quoted in George Kennan, *E. H. Harriman: A Biography* (Boston: Houghton Mifflin, 1922), 1:415.

3. Thomas C. Cochran, *Railroad Leaders, 1845–1890: The Business Mind in Action* (Cambridge: Harvard University Press, 1953), 53, 158; Stewart H. Holbrook, *The Age of the Moguls* (Garden City, N.Y.: Doubleday, 1953), viii; Robin W. Winks, *Frederick Billings: A Life* (New York: Oxford University Press, 1991), 229; cp. 188–89, 193; and Billings to General Rosser, 3 November 1879, in Cochran, *Railroad Leaders*, 253.

4. See Cochran, *Railroad Leaders*, 202–11.

5. Quoted in Oscar Lewis, *The Big Four: The Story of Huntington, Stanford, Hopkins, and Crocker, and of the Building of the Central Pacific* (1938; reprint, New York: Knopf, 1955), 6. For Judah's biography, see "Judah," in Lewis, *The Big Four*.

6. Quoted in Lewis, *The Big Four*, 53.

7. On Huntington, see "Huntington," in Lewis, *The Big Four* (quotation on p. 212); and Cerinda W. Evans, *Collis Potter Huntington* (Newport News, Va.: Mariners' Museum, 1954), 2 vols. On Gould, see Julius Grodinsky, *Jay Gould: His Business Career, 1867–1892* (Philadelphia: University of Pennsylvania Press, 1957), esp. chs. I and XXX; and also Maury Klein, *The Life and Legend of Jay Gould* (Baltimore: Johns Hopkins University Press, 1986).

8. Lewis's "Hopkins," in *The Big Four*, contains the standard version of Hopkins's life. There was considerable evidence of fraud in the distribution of his estate after

his death intestate. The details of his life became the subject of great controversy when an entirely different Hopkins family in North Carolina claimed kinship, and claimed the Hopkinses from New York who inherited much of the estate were non-relatives who conspired with the depression-strapped Southern Pacific to divide Hopkins's money. The North Carolinians' version appeared in Estelle Latta, *Controversial Mark Hopkins* (New York: Greenberg, 1953). Latta's story of deceit, subterfuge, and altered and destroyed documents was compelling, yet left nearly as many questions unanswered as it answered. Mark Hopkins remains a man of much mystery. See Lewis's book review, "One of the Most Picturesque of the Celebrated Legal Wrangles," *San Francisco Chronicle*, 24 May 1953, "This World," p. 22.

9. Evans, *Huntington*, 2:659.

10. "Commerce," in James J. Hill, *Highways of Progress* (Garden City, N.Y.: Doubleday, Page, 1912), 101.

11. Richard J. Orsi, " 'Wilderness Saint' and 'Robber Baron': The Anomalous Partnership of John Muir and the Southern Pacific Company for Preservation of Yosemite National Park," *Pacific Historian* 29 (1985): 142.

12. Lewis, *The Big Four*, 278; Evans, *Huntington*, 2:653; Lewis, *The Big Four*, 280, and Evans, *Huntington*, 2:651; Lewis, *The Big Four*, 214.

13. "The Natural Wealth of the Land and Its Conservation," address before the Conference of Governors, 1907, in Hill, *Highways of Progress*, 309; Joseph Gilpin Pyle, *The Life of James J. Hill* (Garden City, N.Y.: Doubleday, Page, 1917), 387; cp. 390–92. See "The Nation's Future," in Hill, *Highways of Progress*; Pyle, *Hill*, vol. II, chapters 32 and 36; Stewart H. Holbrook, *James J. Hill: A Great Life in Brief* (New York: Knopf, 1955), 165–83; and Albro Martin, *James J. Hill and the Opening of the Northwest* (New York: Oxford University Press, 1976), 309–14, 548–55.

14. On Stanford, see "Stanford," in Lewis, *The Big Four*; George T. Clark, *Leland Stanford: War Governor of California, Railroad Builder, and Founder of Stanford University* (Stanford University: Stanford University Press, 1931); and Norman E. Tutorow, *Leland Stanford: Man of Many Careers* (Menlo Park: Pacific Coast, 1971).

15. Address to the opening exercises of Stanford University, 1 October 1891, quoted in Clark, *Stanford*, 409.

16. Quoted in H. Brett Melandy and Benjamin F. Gilbert, *The Governors of California: Peter H. Burnett to Edmund G. Brown* (Georgetown, Cal.: Talisman, 1965), 124. On laissez faire, see Leland Stanford, "Interstate commerce speech of Hon. Leland Stanford of California in the United States Senate, Jan. 10, 1887," in U.S. Congress, *Interstate Commerce Speeches* (Washington, D.C., 1887).

17. Melandy and Gilbert, *Governors of California*, 119, 124. The first was "An Act for the Protection of Growing Timber on all . . . Private Property . . . and on or along Public Streets or Highways, and on Public Grounds," which prohibited unauthorized cutting but exempted (perhaps due to legislators' objections) twenty-one forest counties from Del Norte to San Bernardino! *The Statutes of California passed at the Thirteenth Session of the Legislature, 1862* (Sacramento: Avery, 1862), chapter 273, p. 307. The second punished cutting of timber on specific public lands — "Swamp

and Overflowed, Tide, or Marsh, or School Lands." *The Statutes of California passed at the Fourteenth Session of the Legislature, 1863* (Sacramento: Avery, 1863), chapter 467, p. 739.

18. Quoted in Ellis Paxson Oberholtzer, *Jay Cooke: Financier of the Civil War* (Philadelphia: George W. Jacobs, 1907), 1:5.

19. Oberholtzer, *Cooke*, 1:15; Henrietta M. Larson, *Jay Cooke: Private Banker* (New York: Greenwood, 1968), 356.

20. Quoted in Larson, *Cooke*, 47.

21. For Cooke's personal and religious qualities, see Larson, *Cooke*, 190–97; also Oberholtzer, *Cooke*, 2:482–502.

22. Quoted in Oberholtzer, *Cooke*, 2:540.

23. On the Northern Pacific and Yellowstone and Mt. Rainier, see Richard A. Bartlett, *Nature's Yellowstone* (Albuquerque: University of New Mexico Press, 1974), 206–8; Richard A. Bartlett, *Yellowstone: A Wilderness Besieged* (Tucson: University of Arizona Press, 1985), chapter 4; and Alfred Runte, *Trains of Discovery: Western Railroads and the National Parks* (Flagstaff: Northland, 1984), chapter 1.

24. Coincidentally, their path crossed Huntington's, who had taken a different ship but crossed Panama at exactly the same time. Cp. Lewis, *The Big Four,* 223 and Winks, *Billings,* 30, 32. For Billings's life, see Winks.

25. See Carroll Van West, *Capitalism on the Frontier: Billings and the Yellowstone Valley in the Nineteenth Century* (Lincoln: University of Nebraska Press, 1993). See John W. Reps, *Cities of the American West: A History of Frontier Urban Planning* (Princeton: Princeton University Press, 1979), chapter 16.

26. Winks discussed Billings's ideas and actions in conservation in *Billings*, chapters 25 and 26; see also 117, 130, 147, 156, 168, 172, 228.

27. See Orsi for the story of the Southern Pacific and environmentalism. John Muir, *Edward Henry Harriman* (Garden City, N.Y.: Doubleday, Page, 1912); Kennan, *Harriman,* 2:339–44. See also William H. Goetzmann and Kay Sloan, *Looking Far North* (New York: Viking Press, 1982); and Kennan, *Harriman,* vol. I, chapter 7.

CHAPTER SEVEN

1. On American liberal Protestantism, see Kenneth Cauthen, *The Impact of American Religious Liberalism,* 2nd ed. (Washington, D.C.: University Press of America, 1983); and William R. Hutchison, *The Modernist Impulse in American Protestantism* (Cambridge: Harvard University Press, 1976). See also Henry F. May, *Protestant Churches and Industrial America,* 2nd ed. (1967; reprint, New York: Octagon Books, 1977); and Ferenc Morton Szasz, *The Divided Mind of Protestant America, 1880–1930* (University: University of Alabama Press, 1982).

2. See, for example, Susan Curtis, *A Consuming Faith: The Social Gospel and Modern American Culture* (Baltimore: Johns Hopkins University Press, 1991), chapter 3, which relates strict evangelical family background to support for the Social Gospel. Robert M. Crunden pursued the general theme of the Progressives and their moral-

ist, evangelical spirit in *Ministers of Reform: The Progressives' Achievement in American Civilization, 1889–1920* (New York: Basic Books, 1982).

3. For the Campbellites, see Andrew L. Drummond and James Bullock, *The Church in Victorian Scotland, 1843–1874* (Edinburgh: Saint Andrew Press, 1975), 55 ff.; and Sydney E. Ahlstrom, *A Religious History of the American People* (New Haven: Yale University Press, 1972), 447–49. For the religious atmosphere in Scotland at the time, see A. C. Cheyne, *The Transforming of the Kirk: Victorian Scotland's Religious Revolution* (Edinburgh: Saint Andrew Press, 1983), 88.

4. John Muir has been the subject of many good biographies, which however emphasize the discontinuities of his religious life rather than the continuities, leading to distortion both of his place in the context of American religion and of the relationship of American religion to nature. See his autobiography, *The Story of My Boyhood and Youth* (Boston: Houghton-Mifflin, 1913); William Frederic Badè, *The Life and Letters of John Muir*, 2 vols. (Boston: Houghton-Mifflin, 1924); Linnie Marsh Wolfe, *Son of the Wilderness: The Life of John Muir* (New York: Knopf, 1945); Stephen Fox, *The American Conservation Movement: John Muir and His Legacy* (1981; reprint, Madison: University of Wisconsin Press, 1985); Frederick Turner, *Rediscovering America: John Muir in His Time and Ours* (New York: Viking, 1985); and Michael P. Cohen, *The Pathless Way: John Muir and American Wilderness* (Madison: University of Wisconsin Press, 1984).

5. See his notebook, "Principles of Physics or Natural Philosophy," 1861, in *The John Muir Papers*, ed. Ronald H. Limbaugh and Kirsten E. Lewis (Cambridge: Chadwyck-Healy, 1986, microfilm) (hereafter cited as *Papers*), esp. 00040. For Muir's long and influential relationship with New Englanders, see Edmund A. Schofield, "John Muir's Yankee Friends and Mentors: The New England Connection," *Pacific Historian* 29 (1985): 65–89.

6. See Fox, *American Conservation*, chapter 11; and Cohen, *Pathless Way*, 120–21.

7. January 21, 1866, in *Papers*, 00407.

8. See his list of Harriman's Protestant-ethic virtues in *Edward Henry Harriman* (Garden City, N.Y.: Doubleday, Page, 1912), 3 ff.

9. Quoted in Wolf, *Son of the Wilderness*, 105.

10. Quoted in Badè, *Life and Letters*, 1:155.

11. See, for example, Journal, "John Muir, Earth-planet, Universe," in *Papers*, 00020, 00034, 00078. Muir later substantially revised this journal for publication, released posthumously as *A Thousand Mile Walk to the Gulf*, ed. William F. Badè (1916; reprint, Boston: Doubleday, 1975).

12. Quoted in Badè, *Life and Letters*, 1:270–71.

13. Quoted in Badè, *Life and Letters*, 1:332–33.

14. Quoted in Wolf, *Son of the Wilderness*, 123.

15. The significance of Muir's relationship with his father in determining his career is explored in Mark Stoll, "God and John Muir: A Psychological Interpretation of Muir's Life and Religion," in *John Muir: Life and Work*, ed. Sally M. Miller (Albuquerque: University of New Mexico Press, 1993).

16. See Michael L. Smith, *Pacific Visions: California Scientists and the Environment, 1850–1915* (New Haven: Yale University Press, 1987), chapter 4.

17. John Muir, *Our National Parks* (Boston: Houghton Mifflin, 1901), 1–2. For various contemporary religious responses to "nervousness" and similar new maladies of late-nineteenth-century urban America, see Donald B. Meyer, *The Positive Thinkers: Popular Religious Psychology from Mary Baker Eddy to Normal Vincent Peale and Ronald Reagan*, rev. ed. (Middletown, Conn.: Wesleyan University Press, 1988).

18. John Muir, *The Yosemite* (1914; reprint, San Francisco: Sierra Club Books, 1988), 195, 196–97; Muir, *Our National Parks*, 1.

19. Muir, *Our National Parks*, 364.

20. An oft-cited example of this point is in "Wild Wool," in *Steep Trails*, ed . William Frederic Badè (1919; reprint, Dunwoody, Georgia: Norman S. Berg, 1970), 11–12.

21. John Muir, *My First Summer in the Sierra* (Boston: Houghton Mifflin, 1911), dedication.

22. Although at other times Muir stated nature was not made for man or his use. Cp. "Wild Wool," in *Steep Trails*, 11.

23. Quoted in Badè, *Life and Letters*, 1:358.

24. These have been republished in *John Muir's Studies in the Sierra*, rev. ed., ed. William E. Colby (San Francisco: Sierra Club, 1960). On Muir's scientific contributions, see Bart O'Brien, "Earthquakes or Snowflowers: The Controversy Over the Formation of Yosemite Valley," *Pacific Historian* 29 (1985): 31–41.

25. Robert Engberg collected the first fifteen of these in *John Muir Summering in the Sierra* (Madison: University of Wisconsin Press, 1984).

26. Quoted in Wolf, *Son of the Wilderness*, 203.

27. For an account of Muir's relationship with the Southern Pacific, see Richard J. Orsi, " 'Wilderness Saint' and 'Robber Baron': The Anomalous Partnership of John Muir and the Southern Pacific Company for Preservation of Yosemite National Park," *Pacific Historian* 29 (1985): 136–56.

28. See John Muir, *Travels in Alaska* (Boston: Houghton Mifflin, 1915). For the "Harriman Alaska Expedition," see William H. Goetzmann and Kay Sloan, *Looking Far North: The Harriman Expedition to Alaska, 1899* (New York: Viking Press, 1982).

As suspicious of railroad management as other reformers of the day, Muir had nothing against railroads or tourism in themselves, and had lent his articles for use in railroad promotional brochures. See items 166 and 184 in William F. Kimes and Maymie B. Kimes, *John Muir: A Reading Bibliography* (Fresno: Panorama West Books, 1986).

29. John Muir, *Edward Henry Harriman* (Garden City, N.Y.: Doubleday, Page, 1912). Muir went so far as to praise Harriman's railroads' changes of the landscape. See pp. 3–5.

30. See esp. Fox, *American Conservation*.

31. Pinchot Diary, Gifford Pinchot Papers, Library of Congress, Washington,

D.C. (hereafter cited as Pinchot Papers). I am indebted to Char Miller for this quotation.

32. The best biography of Pinchot is M. Nelson McGeary, *Gifford Pinchot: Forester-Politician* (Princeton: Princeton University Press, 1960). See also his autobiography, *Breaking New Ground* (New York: Harcourt, Brace, 1947); Martin L. Fausold, *Gifford Pinchot: Bull Moose Progressive* (Syracuse: Syracuse University Press, 1961); James Penick, Jr., *Progressive Politics and Conservation: The Ballinger–Pinchot Affair* (Chicago: University of Chicago Press, 1968); and Harold T. Pinkett, *Gifford Pinchot: Private and Public Forester* (Urbana: University of Illinois Press, 1970). I have found McGeary and Pinchot most valuable. None of these biographies or the accounts of conservation's beginnings that I know brings out Pinchot's religious motivation.

33. Conversation with Ed Brannon, director, Grey Towers National Historical Landmark, Milford, Penn., July 27, 1995; "The Quakers of the Seventeenth Century," DeForest Prize Oration, 1889, in container 949, Pinchot Papers; Henry W. Shoemaker, *The Man Who Made Good: Gifford Pinchot* (Altoona, Pa.: n.p., n.d. [1923?]), 3.

34. On Pinchot's Y.M.C.A. activities, see Pinchot Papers, containers 79, 83, 86, 90, 94, 99, 105, 127, and 432. Pinchot once referred to his work as "to a certain extent missionary work." Letter to S. W. Woodward, 15 December 1905, Pinchot Papers, container 99.

35. Conversation with Jim Bradley, 28 July 1995.

36. Pinchot, *Breaking New Ground*, 322, 323. Of course, there was nothing new about the idea of the interconnectedness of things.

37. On McGee, see Samuel Hays, *Conservation and the Gospel of Efficiency: The Progressive Conservation Movement, 1890–1920* (Cambridge: Harvard University Press, 1959), 102–6.

38. Pinchot, *Breaking New Ground*, 326.

39. Pinchot laid out his program in *The Fight for Conservation* (1910; reprint, Seattle: University of Washington Press, 1967). See pp. 42–44. Quotations on pp. 48, 8, 48, 50, 69, 77, 88, 92.

40. Pinchot, *Fight*, 11, 21, 22, 24, 12, 93.

41. See Pinchot, *Breaking New Ground*, 340–44; cp. Pinchot, *Fight*, 38–39.

42. Charles Otis Gill and Gifford Pinchot, *The Country Church: The Decline of Its Influence and the Remedy* (New York: Macmillan, 1913), vii, x; Charles Otis Gill and Gifford Pinchot, *Six Thousand Country Churches* (New York: Macmillan, 1920), 21, 23. Pinchot's expenditure in container 707, Pinchot Papers.

43. Pinchot, *Fight*, 121.

44. *Fight*, 133, 115.

45. *Fight*, 141, 99, 96, 95.

46. Rauschenbusch quoted in Donald K. Gorrell, *The Age of Social Responsibility: The Social Gospel in the Progressive Era, 1900–1920* (Macon, Ga.: Mercer University Press, 1988), 194. On the Progressive movement, see John Allen Gable, *The Bull*

Moose Years: Theodore Roosevelt and the Progressive Party (Port Washington, N.Y.: Kennikat Press, 1978), esp. ix–x, 39–40, 75, 96–98. See also Roosevelt, "Confession of Faith," in *Progressive Principles*, ed. Elmer H. Youngman (New York: Progressive National Service, 1913); conservation, 166–68; quote on p. 173.

47. On conservation as a "scientific movement," see Hays, *Conservation*, 2. On moral conservationism, which Hays viewed as a distraction from real issues, see p. 142. Hays asserted (without documentation, 145–46) that Pinchot and other Progressive leaders were forced to cultivate the moral angle of conservation to broaden its appeal. This view ignores the powerful Protestant component of Progressivism and of Pinchot's own background.

48. Cp. the title of Stephen Fox's book, *The American Conservation Movement: John Muir and His Legacy*. Just twenty-two years earlier, Samuel Hays's history of Progressive conservation had disregarded Muir, mentioning him on only two pages.

49. The most complete account of the battle for the Hetch Hetchy dam is in Holway R. Jones, *John Muir and the Sierra Club: The Battle for Yosemite* (San Francisco: Sierra Club, 1965).

A variety of interpretations may be found in: Robert Underwood Johnson, *Remembered Yesterdays* (Boston: Little, Brown, 1923), 307–13; George W. Norris, *Fighting Liberal* (New York: Macmillan, 1945), chapter 18; Judson King, *The Conservation Fight: From Theodore Roosevelt to the Tennessee Valley Authority* (Washington, D.C.: Public Affairs Press, 1959), 40–44; John Ise, *Our National Park Policy: A Critical History* (Baltimore: Johns Hopkins Press, 1961), 85–96; Elmo R. Richardson, *The Politics of Conservation: Crusades and Controversies, 1897–1913* (Berkeley: University of California Press, 1962), which put the issue in its political context; Frank E. Smith, *The Politics of Conservation* (New York: Pantheon Books, 1966), 134–38; Roderick Nash, *Wilderness and the American Mind*, 3rd rev. ed. (New Haven: Yale University Press, 1982), chapter 10; Alfred Runte, *National Parks: The American Experience*, 2nd rev. ed. (Lincoln: University of Nebraska Press, 1987), 77–81; Fox, *American Conservation*, 139–46; Craig W. Allin, *The Politics of Wilderness Preservation* (Westport, Conn.: Greenwood Press, 1982), 44–48; and Michael P. Cohen, *The History of the Sierra Club, 1892–1970* (San Francisco: Sierra Club Books, 1988), 22–33.

Of these authors, only Norris and King defended the dam. The rest of them (and especially Nash's influential account) tended to portray the fight as utilitarianism against the value of wilderness. The arguments in the *Congressional Record* belie this interpretation. Few debaters defended bald utilitarianism and "wilderness" was rarely even mentioned. The battle, as will be shown, was between the values of a publicly owned power source versus natural beauty as a moral resource. Monopolyphobia killed the Hetch Hetchy Valley.

50. *Congressional Record* (hereinafter *CR*) 51, 6 December 1913, 362.

51. Muir, *The Yosemite*, 196–97.

52. "The Hetch Hetchy Scheme — Why It Should Not Be Rushed Through the Extra Session — An Open Letter to the American People," press release, in *CR* 50,

29 August 1913, 3898, 3899; *Hearing before the Committee on the Public Lands on H.R. 6281*, 63rd Cong., 1st Sess., 1913, 236, 237. Cp. Representative Steenerson's remarks, *CR* 50, 30 August 1913, 3973–75; and John Muir, "The Hetch Hetchy Valley in the Yosemite National Park: What It is and the Dangers Threatening Its Destruction," in *CR* 50, 3 November 1913, 5904–5.

53. *CR* 50, 29 August 1913, 3894. *Hearing . . . on H.R. 6281*, 26–27. Pinchot's proposal clearly astonished Raker. Pinchot intended the amendment as something of a sop to "the nature lover."

54. *CR* 50, 30 August 1913, 3909.

55. Letter in *CR* 50, 3 November 1913, 5846; 30 August 1913, 3979, 3980.

56. Hitchcock, in *CR* 50, 10 November 1913, 5876; *CR* 50, 29 August 1913, 3895; *CR* 50, 3 November 1913, 5473.

57. *CR* 51, 1 December 1913, 19, 17, 19; 3 December 1913, 117.

58. *CR* 50, 30 August 1913, 4004. Cp. North Dakota Senator McCumber's argument, *CR* 51, 1 December 1913, 12.

59. Telegram in *CR* 50, 3 November 1913, 5487.

60. Representative Edward T. Taylor, Colorado, *Hearing . . . on H.R. 6281*, 26–27.

61. Norris, *Fighting Liberal*, 164.

62. *CR* 51, 3 December 1913, 126.

63. *CR* 51, 6 December 1913, 362; *CR* 50, 29 August 1913, 3895. For a detailed discussion of genderization of the debate, see Smith, *Pacific Visions*, chapter 8; quote, p. 178.

64. *CR* 50, 30 August 1913, 3974.

65. *CR* 51, 3 December 1913, 130.

66. Norman Hapgood, "The Hetch Hetchy Controversy," *Harper's Weekly*, 6 December 1913, in *CR* 51, 4 December 1913, 182.

67. *CR* 51, 5 December 1913, 273, 274. Cp. 6 December, 363. No one has published a history of the Hetch Hetchy controversy that discusses the actions of the power companies. Jones implicitly refuted the charges that they financed the dam opposition; see Jones, *John Muir and the Sierra Club*, 156, 160, 162.

68. See Martin W. Lewis, *Green Delusions: An Environmentalist Critique of Radical Environmentalism* (Durham: Duke University Press, 1992).

69. Robert L. Woodbury, *William Kent: Progressive Gadfly, 1864–1928* (Ph.D. diss., Yale University, 1967).

CHAPTER EIGHT

1. Within the Forest Service and the forestry profession, Pinchot's perspective remained dominant.

2. See John Cobb, Jr., and David Ray Griffin, *Process Theology: An Introductory Exposition* (Philadelphia: Westminster Press, 1976); Charles Birch and John Cobb, Jr., *The Liberation of Life: From the Cell to the Community* (Cambridge: Cambridge University Press, 1981); Steven Keffer, Sallie King, and Steven Kraft, "Process

Metaphysics and Minimalism: Implications for Public Policy," *Environmental Ethics* 13 (1991): 23–47; Ian G. Barbour, *Religion in an Age of Science: The Gifford Lectures, 1989–1991* (San Francisco: Harper & Row, 1990), vol. 1, chapters 8 and 9; and on neo-Platonism, David F. T. Rodier, "The Problem of Ordered Chaos in Whitehead and Plotinus," in *The Significance of Neoplatonism*, ed. R. Baine Harris (Norfolk, Va.: International Society for Neoplatonic Studies, 1976).

3. J. E. Lovelock, *Gaia: A New Look at Earth* (Oxford: Oxford University Press, 1979).

4. Dave Foreman, *Confessions of an Eco-Warrior* (New York: Harmony Books, 1991), 118.

5. Thomas B. Allen, *Guardian of the Wild: The Story of the National Wildlife Federation, 1936–1986* (Bloomington: Indiana University Press, 1987), 190.

6. C. Brant Short, *Ronald Reagan and the Public Lands: America's Conservation Debate, 1979–1984* (College Station: Texas A&M University Press, 1989), 55–59.

7. See Stephen Fox, *The American Conservation Movement: John Muir and his Legacy* (1981; reprint, Madison: University of Wisconsin Press, 1985), 269–70.

8. Wes Jackson, *New Roots for Agriculture* (San Francisco: Friends of the Earth, 1980); Wes Jackson, *Altars of Unhewn Stone: Science and the Earth* (San Francisco: North Point Press, 1987); and "Statement by Dr. Wes Jackson," in *Christian Ecology: Building an Environmental Ethic for the Twenty-First Century*, ed. Frederick W. Krueger (San Francisco: North American Conference on Christianity and Ecology, 1988).

9. Cp. Ernest Callenbach's popular novel, *Ecotopia: The Notebooks and Reports of William Weston* (Berkeley, Cal.: Banyan Tree Books, 1975).

10. Among the many biographies of John D. Rockefeller, the most reliable and least partisan include Peter Collier and David Horowitz, *The Rockefellers: An American Dynasty* (New York: Holt, Reinhart and Winston, 1976), which is also good on Rockefeller's descendants; and Allan Nevins, *Study in Power: John D. Rockefeller: Industrialist and Philanthropist*, 2 vols. (New York: Charles Scribner's Sons, 1953). Collier, *Rockefellers*, 41; Nevins, *Rockefeller*, 1:7, 10. On the Rockefellers and the Protestant ethic, see John Ensor Harr and Peter J. Johnson, *The Rockefeller Century* (New York: Charles Scribner's Sons, 1988), 23–26.

11. Collier, *Rockefellers*, 11, 29, 69–72; Nevins, *Rockefeller*, 2:405.

12. Collier, *Rockefellers*, 12, 80.

13. On John D. Rockefeller, Jr., see also Raymond B. Fosdick, *John D. Rockefeller, Jr.: A Portrait* (New York: Harper & Bros., 1956); and Albert F. Schenkel, *The Rich Man and the Kingdom: John D. Rockefeller, Jr., and the Protestant Establishment* (Minneapolis: Fortress Press, 1995). See also Joseph W. Ernst, ed., *"Dear Father"/"Dear Son": Correspondence of John D. Rockefeller and John D. Rockefeller, Jr.* (New York: Fordham University Press, 1994), 123–25.

14. On Junior's conservation achievements, see Nancy Newhall, *A Contribution to the Heritage of Every American: The Conservation Activities of John D. Rockefeller, Jr.* (New York: Alfred A. Knopf, 1957); and Joseph W. Ernst, ed., *Worthwhile Places:*

Correspondence of John D. Rockefeller, Jr. and Horace M. Albright (New York: Fordham University Press, 1991), esp. "An Overview" and "Epilogue," which also discusses the conservation activities of Laurence S. and Laurence Rockefeller.

15. Collier, *Rockefellers*, 307.

16. Collier, *Rockefellers*, 398.

17. Patricia Beard, "A Chip Off the Old Rock," *Town & Country*, 1 January 1994, 60–67.

18. Collier, *Rockefellers*, 614; Steven C. Rockefeller and John C. Elder, *Spirit and Nature: Visions of Interdependence* (Middlebury, Vt.: Christian A. Johnson Memorial Gallery, Middlebury College, 1990), 22; "Spirit & Nature with Bill Moyers," transcript (New York: Journal Graphics, 1991).

19. Catherine L. Albanese, *Nature Religion in America: From the Algonkian Indians to the New Age* (Chicago: University of Chicago Press, 1990).

20. In Curt Meine, *Aldo Leopold: His Life and Work* (Madison: University of Wisconsin Press, 1988), 506. Although Meine is the best biographical source for Leopold, see also Susan L. Flader, *Thinking Like a Mountain: Aldo Leopold and the Evolution of an Ecological Attitude toward Deer, Wolves, and Forests* (Lincoln: University of Nebraska Press, 1974); Roderick Nash, *Wilderness and the American Mind*, 3rd rev. ed. (New Haven: Yale University Press, 1982), chapter 11.

21. Meine, *Aldo Leopold*, 506–7.

22. Lawrence K. Kersten, *The Lutheran Ethic: The Impact of Religion on Laymen and Clergy* (Detroit: Wayne State University Press, 1970), chapter 1.

23. *Round River: From the Journals of Aldo Leopold*, ed. Luna B. Leopold (1953; reprint, Oxford: Oxford University Press, 1993), 171; James I. McClintock, *Nature's Kindred Spirits: Aldo Leopold, Joseph Wood Krutch, Edward Abbey, Annie Dillard, and Gary Snyder* (Madison: University of Wisconsin Press, 1994), 33.

24. Aldo Leopold, "The Forestry of the Prophets," in *The River of the Mother of God and Other Essays*, ed. Susan L. Flader and J. Baird Callicott (Madison: University of Wisconsin Press, 1991), 71, 72.

25. Meine, *Aldo Leopold*, 129, 161.

26. Thomas Tanner, ed., *Aldo Leopold: The Man and His Legacy* (Ankeny, Iowa: Soil Conservation Society of America, 1987), 168.

27. Aldo Leopold, *A Sand County Almanac and Sketches Here and There* (1949; reprint, New York: Oxford University Press, 1987), 216, viii–ix.

28. Leopold, *Sand County Almanac*, viii, 204–5.

29. Ron Wolf, "God, James Watt, and the Public Land," *Audubon* 83 (May 1981): 65.

30. Leilani Watt and Al Janssen, *Caught in the Conflict: My Life with James Watt* (Eugene, Ore.: Harvest House Publishers, 1984), 82–83.

31. James G. Watt with Doug Wead, *The Courage of a Conservative* (New York: Simon and Schuster, 1985).

32. The only available biography of Watt is the partisan Ron Arnold, *At the Eye of*

the *Storm: James Watt and the Environmentalists* (Chicago: Regnery Gateway, 1982). On Dominy, see Marc Reisner, *Cadillac Desert: The American West and Its Disappearing Water* (New York: Penguin Books, 1986), chapter 7.

33. Watt, *Courage of a Conservative*, 94–97.

34. Watt, *Courage of a Conservative*, e.g., 59, 158.

35. James Watt, "Ours is the Earth," *Saturday Evening Post*, Jan./Feb. 1982, 104; quote in Arnold, *Eye of the Storm*, 60. See also Susan Power Bratton, "The Ecotheology of James Watt," *Environmental Ethics* 5 (1983): 225–36.

36. Short, *Reagan and the Public Lands*, chapter 5. On "Wise Use," see Christopher McGrory Klyza, "Framing the Debate in Public Lands Politics," *Policy Studies Journal* 19 (1991): 577–85; and Alan M. Gottlieb, ed., *The Wise Use Agenda: The Citizen's Guide to Environmental Resource Issues* (Bellevue, Wash.: Free Enterprise Press, 1989).

37. Annie Dillard, *Pilgrim at Tinker Creek* (New York: Harper's Magazine Press, 1974), 2, 7; "Tickets for a Prayer Wheel," in Annie Dillard, *Tickets for a Prayer Wheel* (New York: Harper & Row, 1974), 111. See also Annie Dillard, *Holy the Firm* (New York: Harper & Row, 1977); and Annie Dillard, *Teaching a Stone to Talk: Expeditions and Encounters* (New York: Harper & Row, 1982), which make similar points.

38. Dillard, *Pilgrim*, 4.

39. Francis A. Schaeffer, *Pollution and the Death of Man: The Christian View of Ecology* (Wheaton, Ill.: Tyndale House, 1970); Calvin De Witt et al., *Earthkeeping in the Nineties: Stewardship of Creation*, rev. ed. (Grand Rapids, Mich.: William B. Eerdmans, 1991); Susan Power Bratton, *Christianity, Wilderness, and Wildlife: The Original Desert Solitaire* (Scranton, Pa.: University of Scranton Press, 1993); H. Paul Santmire, *The Travail of Nature: The Ambiguous Ecological Promise of Christian Theology* (Philadelphia: Fortress Press, 1985); Max Oelschlaeger, *Caring for Creation: An Ecumenical Approach to the Environmental Crisis* (New Haven: Yale University Press, 1994); Cobb and Birch, *Liberation of Life*; Cobb and Griffin, *Process Theology*; Sallie McFague, *Models of God: Theology for an Ecological, Nuclear Age* (Philadelphia: Fortress Press, 1987), and her *The Body of God: an Ecological Theology* (Minneapolis: Fortress Press, 1993). On the theological response to the environmental crisis, see Roderick Frazier Nash, *The Rights of Nature: A History of Environmental Ethics* (Madison: University of Wisconsin Press, 1989), chapter 4.

40. Dillard, *An American Childhood* (New York: Harper & Row, 1987), 8, 61, 132–35, 191–99, 226–28 (quotation on p. 133); Linda L. Smith, "Annie Dillard" (Ph.D. diss., University of Toledo, 1992), chapter 1 (quotation on p. 24).

41. John Burroughs, "The Gospel of Nature," in John Burroughs, *Time and Change* (Boston: Houghton Mifflin, 1912); Dillard, *Pilgrim*, 146.

42. Dillard, *Pilgrim*, 7, 144, 270, 271.

43. Susan Zakin, *Coyotes and Town Dogs: Earth First! and the Environmental Movement* (New York: Viking, 1993), 147 ff.; Dave Foreman, *Confessions of an Eco-Warrior* (New York: Harmony Books, 1991), 21–22.

44. Zakin, *Coyotes*, 9; Foreman, *Confessions*, 5. Zakin is the best biographical source available on Foreman. Foreman's book is little more than a print version of his speeches. Cp. his speeches recorded in Zakin, pp. 291–94, 397–400.

45. Foreman's psychology is analyzed in Zakin, *Coyotes*, 288–91.

46. Foreman, *Confessions*, 19; ellipsis in the original.

47. Foreman, *Confessions*, 20.

48. Foreman, *Confessions*, 219. On Brower, see John McPhee's *Encounter with the Archdruid: Narratives about a Conservationist and Three of His Natural Enemies* (New York: Farrar, Straus and Giroux, 1971), esp. 28–29, 83–87.

49. Zakin, *Coyotes*, 398.

Bibliography

PRIMARY SOURCES

Ambrose, Saint. *Hexameron, Paradise, and Cain and Abel.* Translated by John J. Savage. New York: Fathers of the Church, 1961.

Ames, William. *The Marrow of Theology.* Translated and edited by John D. Eusden. Boston: Pilgrim Press, 1968.

Aristotle. *Politics.*

Augustine, Saint. *City of God.*

———. *Confessions.*

———. *Expositions on the Book of Psalms.* Oxford translation edited by A. Cleveland Coxe. Vol. 8 of *A Select Library of the Nicene and Post-Nicene Fathers of the Christian Church*, edited by Philip Schaff. New York: The Christian Literature Company, 1905.

———. *The Literal Meaning of Genesis.* Translated by John Hammond Taylor. New York: Newman Press, 1982.

Bacon, Francis. "Announcement of the Author." In *Advancement of Learning and Novum Organum.* Rev. ed. New York: The Colonial Press, 1900.

———. *Novum Organum; or True Suggestions for the Interpretation of Nature.* In *Advancement of Learning and Novum Organum.* Rev. ed. New York: The Colonial Press, 1900.

———. *The Dignity and Advancement of Learning.* In *Advancement of Learning and Novum Organum.* Rev. ed. New York: The Colonial Press, 1900.

Baxter, Richard. *The Christian Directory.* In vol. 1 of *The Practical Works of the Late Reverend and Pious Mr. Richard Baxter.* London, 1707.

———. *Saints' Everlasting Rest.* In vol. 3 of *The Practical Works of the Late Reverend and Pious Mr. Richard Baxter.* London, 1707.

———. *A Treatise of Self-Denial.* In vol. 3 of *The Practical Works of the Late Reverend and Pious Mr. Richard Baxter.* London, 1707.

Bonaventure, Saint. *The Mind's Road to God*. Translated by George Boas. Indianapolis: Bobbs-Merrill Educational Publishing, 1953.

Bradford, William. *Of Plymouth Plantation*. Edited by Harvey Wish. New York: Capricorn Books, n.d.

Bradstreet, Anne. *The Complete Works of Anne Bradstreet*. Edited by Joseph R. McElrath, Jr. and Allan P. Robb. Boston: Twayne, 1981.

———. *The Works of Anne Bradstreet*. Edited by John Harvard Ellis. 1867. Reprint, New York: Peter Smith, 1932.

Burroughs, John. "The Gospel of Nature." In *Time and Change*. Boston: Houghton Mifflin, 1912.

Callenbach, Ernest. *Ecotopia: The Notebooks and Reports of William Weston*. Berkeley, Calif.: Banyan Tree Books, 1975.

Calvin, John. *Commentaries on the Epistle of Paul the Apostle to the Romans*. Translated by John Owens. Grand Rapids: Eerdmans, 1948.

———. *Commentaries on the First Book of Moses called Genesis*. Translated by John King. Grand Rapids: Eerdmans, 1948.

———. *Commentary on the Book of Psalms*. Translated by James Anderson. Grand Rapids: Eerdmans, 1949.

———. *The Epistle of Paul the Apostle to the Hebrews*. Translated by William B. Johnston. Grand Rapids: Eerdmans, 1963.

———. *Institutes of the Christian Religion*. Translated by John Allen. 7th rev. ed. Philadelphia: Presbyterian Board of Christian Education, 1936.

Chrysostom, Saint John. *Homilies on Genesis 1–17*. Translated by Robert C. Hill. Washington, D.C.: Catholic University of America Press, 1986.

———. "The Homilies on the Statues. To the People of Antioch." Oxford translation revised by W. R. W. Stephens. Vol. 9 of *A Select Library of the Nicene and Post-Nicene Fathers of the Christian Church*. Edited by Philip Schaff. New York: Charles Scribner's Sons, 1903.

Cotton, John. "Gods Promise To His Plantations." In *Old South Leaflets*. Vol. 3, no. 53. 1630. Reprint, New York: Burt Franklin, n.d.

Dillard, Annie. *An American Childhood*. New York: Harper & Row, 1987.

———. *Holy the Firm*. New York: Harper & Row, 1977.

———. *Pilgrim at Tinker Creek*. New York: Harper's Magazine Press, 1974.

———. *Teaching a Stone to Talk: Expeditions and Encounters*. New York: Harper & Row, 1982.

———. *Tickets for a Prayer Wheel*. New York: Harper & Row, 1974.

Edwards, Jonathan. *The Works of Jonathan Edwards*. 13 vols. to date. Edited by Perry Miller et al. New Haven: Yale University Press, 1957–.

———. "Personal Narrative." In *The Works of President Edwards*. New York, 1856.

———. *The Philosophy of Jonathan Edwards From His Private Notebooks*. Edited by Harvey G. Townsend. 1955. Reprint, Westport, Ct.: Greenwood Press, 1972.

Emerson, Ralph Waldo. *Centenary Edition: The Complete Works of Ralph Waldo*

Emerson. 12 vols. Edited by Edward Waldo Emerson. Boston: Houghton Mifflin, 1903–4.

——. *The Collected Works of Ralph Waldo Emerson.* 4 vols. Edited by Ralph E. Spiller, Alfred R. Ferguson, et al. Cambridge: The Belknap Press of Harvard University Press, 1971–.

——. *Young Emerson Speaks.* Edited by Arthur Cushman McGiffert, Jr. Boston: Houghton Mifflin, 1938.

Foreman, Dave. *Confessions of an Eco-Warrior.* New York: Harmony Books, 1991.

Franklin, Benjamin. *Writings.* Edited by J. A. Leo Lemay. New York: Library of America, 1987.

Gill, Charles Otis, and Gifford Pinchot. *Six Thousand Country Churches.* New York: Macmillan, 1920.

——. *The Country Church: The Decline of Its Influence and the Remedy.* New York: Macmillan, 1913.

Gilpin, Joshua. *Pleasure and Business in Western Pennsylvania: The Journal of Joshua Gilpin, 1809.* Edited by Joseph E. Walker. Harrisburg: Pennsylvania Historical and Museum Commission, 1975.

Gilpin, William. "Dragoon Letters from the Western Frontier." Gilpin file. Missouri Historical Society, St. Louis, Missouri.

——. "The Cities of Missouri." *The Western Journal and Civilian* 11 (October 1853) p. 37.

——. *Mission of the North American People, Geographical, Social, and Political.* 2nd rev. ed. Philadelphia: Lippincott, 1874.

Hill, James J. *Highways of Progress.* Garden City, N.Y.: Doubleday, Page, 1912.

Jefferson, Thomas, and Abigail and John Adams. *The Adams-Jefferson Letters: The Complete Correspondence Between Thomas Jefferson and Abigail and John Adams.* 2 vols. Edited by Lester J. Cappon. Chapel Hill: University of North Carolina Press, 1959.

——. *The Papers of Thomas Jefferson.* 24 vols. Edited by Julian P. Boyd. Princeton: Princeton University Press, 1950.

——. *The Writings of Thomas Jefferson.* 20 vols. Edited by Albert Ellery Bergh. Washington, D.C.: Thomas Jefferson Memorial Association, 1905.

Johnson, Edward. *Wonder-working Providence of Sions Saviour, in New England.* In *Wonder-Working Providence of Sions Saviour in New-England (1654) and Good News From New England (1648).* Delmar, N.Y.: Scholars' Facsimiles & Reprints, 1974.

Leopold, Aldo. *The River of the Mother of God and Other Essays.* Edited by Susan L. Flader and J. Baird Callicott. Madison: University of Wisconsin Press, 1991.

——. *Round River: From the Journals of Aldo Leopold.* Edited by Luna B. Leopold. 1953. Reprint, Oxford: Oxford University Press, 1987.

——. *A Sand County Almanac and Sketches Here and There.* 1949. Reprint, London: Oxford University Press, 1968.

Loyola, Saint Ignatius de. *Spiritual Exercises.* In Antonio T. de Nicolas, *Ignatius de Loyola: Powers of Imagining: A Philosophical Hermeneutic of Imagining through the Collected Works of Ignatius de Loyola.* Albany: State University of New York Press, 1986.

Mather, Cotton. *Bonifacius: An Essay . . . to Do Good. . . .* Edited by Josephine K. Piercy. 1710. Reprint, Gainesville, Florida: Scholars' Facsimiles & Reprints, 1967.

———. *The Christian Philosopher: A Collection of the Best Discoveries in Nature, with Religious Improvements.* Edited by Josephine K. Piercy. 1720, post-dated 1721 on the title page. Reprint, Gainesville, Florida: Scholars' Facsimiles & Reprints, 1968.

———. *Magnalia Christi Americana: or the Ecclesiastical History of New-England, from its first planting in the year 1620, unto the year of our Lord, 1698.* 2 vols. 2nd ed. Reprint, Hartford: Silas Andrus, 1820.

———. *Manuductio ad Ministerium. Directions for a Candidate of the Ministry. . . .* Edited by Thomas J. Holmes and Kenneth Murdock. 1726. Reprint, New York: published for the Facsimile Text Society by Columbia University Press, 1938.

———. *The Short History of New-England. A Recapitulation of Wonderful Passages Which have Occurr'd, First in the Protections, and then in the Afflictions, of New-England. . . .* In *Cotton Mather: Historical Writings.* 1694. Reprint, New York: AMS Press, 1991.

Miller, Hugh. *Footprints of the Creator; or The Asterolepis of Stromness.* Edinburgh: Nimmo, Hay, and Mitchell, 1860.

Milton, John. *Paradise Lost.*

More, Henry. *An Antidote Against Atheism.* In *Philosophical Writings of Henry More,* edited by Flor Isabel Mackinnon. New York: Oxford University Press, 1925.

Muir, John. *Edward Henry Harriman.* Garden City, N.Y.: Doubleday, Page, 1912.

———. "The Hetch Hetchy Valley in the Yosemite National Park: What It is and the Dangers Threatening Its Destruction." In *Congressional Record,* vol. 50, 3 November 1913, pp. 5904–5.

———. *The John Muir Papers.* Edited by Ronald H. Limbaugh and Kirsten E. Lewis. Cambridge: Chadwyck-Healy, 1986. Microfilm.

———. *John Muir Summering in the Sierra.* Edited by Robert Engberg. Madison: University of Wisconsin Press, 1984.

———. *John Muir's Studies in the Sierra.* Edited by William E. Colby. Rev. ed. San Francisco: Sierra Club Books, 1960.

———. *My First Summer in the Sierra.* Boston: Houghton Mifflin, 1911.

———. *Our National Parks.* Boston: Houghton Mifflin, 1901.

———. *The Story of My Boyhood and Youth.* Boston: Houghton-Mifflin, 1913.

———. *A Thousand Mile Walk to the Gulf.* Edited by William F. Badè. 1916. Reprint, Boston: Doubleday, 1975.

———. *Travels in Alaska.* Boston: Houghton Mifflin, 1915.

———. "Wild Wool." In *Steep Trails,* edited by William Frederic Badè. 1919. Reprint, Dunwoody, Ga.: Norman S. Berg, 1970.

——. *The Yosemite.* 1914. Reprint, San Francisco: Sierra Club Books, 1988.

Origen. *Homilies on Genesis and Exodus.* Translated by Ronald E. Heine. Washington, D.C.: Catholic University of America Press, 1982.

Paley, William. *Natural Theology.* New York: American Tract Society, n.d.

Perkins, William. *A Golden Chain or the Description of Theology.* In *The Work of William Perkins,* edited by Ian Breward. Appleford, England: Sutton Courtenay Press, 1970.

——. *The Whole Treatise of the Cases of Conscience.* In *William Perkins, 1558–1602, English Puritanist,* edited by Thomas F. Merrill. Niewkoop, Netherlands: B. de Graaf, 1966.

Pinchot, Gifford. *Breaking New Ground.* New York: Harcourt, Brace, 1947.

——. Papers. Library of Congress, Washington, D.C.

——. *The Fight for Conservation.* 1910. Reprint, Seattle: University of Washington Press, 1967.

Plato. *Laws.*

——. *Timaeus.*

Plotinus. *The Enneads.* Translated by Stephen MacKenna. 2nd rev. ed. London: Faber and Faber, 1956.

Rockefeller, John D., and John D. Rockefeller, Jr. *"Dear Father"/"Dear Son": Correspondence of John D. Rockefeller and John D. Rockefeller, Jr.* Edited by Joseph W. Ernst. New York: Fordham University Press, 1994.

Rockefeller, John D., Jr., and Horace M. Albright. *Worthwhile Places: Correspondence of John D. Rockefeller, Jr. and Horace M. Albright.* New York: Fordham University Press, 1991.

Rockefeller, Steven C., and John C. Elder. *Spirit and Nature: Visions of Interdependence.* Middlebury, Vt.: Christian A. Johnson Memorial Gallery, Middlebury College, 1990.

Roosevelt, Theodore. *Progressive Principles.* Edited by Elmer H. Youngman. New York: Progressive National Service, 1913.

Smith, Joseph. *An American Prophet's Record: The Diaries and Journals of Joseph Smith.* Edited by Scott H. Faulring. Salt Lake City: Signature Books, 1989.

[Smith, Joseph.] *Book of Mormon.*

[——.] *The Doctrine and Covenants of the Church of Jesus Christ of Latter-day Saints.*

——. *Joseph Smith: Selected Sermons & Writings.* Edited by Robert L. Millet. New York: Paulist Press, 1989.

[——.] *Pearl of Great Price.*

——. *The Personal Writings of Joseph Smith.* Edited by Dean C. Jessee. Salt Lake City: Deseret Books, 1984.

Thoreau, Henry David. "On the Duty of Civil Disobedience." In *Walden: or Life in the Woods, and On the Duty of Civil Disobedience.* 1849. Reprint, New York: New American Library, 1960.

Watt, James G. "Ours is the Earth." *Saturday Evening Post,* 245 (January/February 1982): 75–75+.

Watt, James G., with Doug Wead. *The Courage of a Conservative*. New York: Simon and Schuster, 1985.

Watt, Leilani, and Al Janssen. *Caught in the Conflict: My Life with James Watt*. Eugene, Ore.: Harvest House Publishers, 1984.

DOCUMENTS

Congressional Record. 1913. Washington, D.C.

The Statutes of California passed at the Fourteenth Session of the Legislature, 1863. Sacramento, 1863.

The Statutes of California passed at the Thirteenth Session of the Legislature, 1862. Sacramento, 1862.

U.S. Congress. House. *Hearing before the Committee on the Public Lands on H.R. 6281*. 63rd Congress, 1st Session, 1913.

The Westminster Confession of Faith. In S. W. Carruthers, *The Westminster Confession of Faith*. Manchester, England: R. Aikman and Son, n.d.

SECONDARY SOURCES

Abrams, M. H. *Natural Supernaturalism: Tradition and Revolution in Romantic Literature*. New York: W. W. Norton & Co., 1971.

Ahlstrom, Sydney E. *A Religious History of the American People*. New Haven: Yale University Press, 1972.

Albanese, Catherine L. *Nature Religion in America: From the Algonkian Indians to the New Age*. Chicago: University of Chicago Press, 1990.

———. *Sons of the Fathers: The Civil Religion of the American Revolution*. Philadelphia: Temple University Press, 1976.

Aldridge, Alfred Owen. *Benjamin Franklin and Nature's God*. Durham: Duke University Press, 1967.

Allen, Gay Wilson. "A New Look at Emerson and Science." In *Critical Essays on Ralph Waldo Emerson*, edited by Robert E. Burkholder and Joel Myerson. Boston: G. K. Hall, 1983.

———. *Waldo Emerson: A Biography*. New York: Viking, 1981.

Allen, Thomas B. *Guardian of the Wild: The Story of the National Wildlife Federation, 1936–1986*. Bloomington: Indiana University Press, 1987.

Allin, Craig W. *The Politics of Wilderness Preservation*. Westport, Conn.: Greenwood Press, 1982.

Anderson, Wallace E. "Editor's Introduction." In *The Works of Jonathan Edwards*, vol 6, *Scientific and Philosophical Writings*. New Haven: Yale University Press, 1980.

Appleby, Joyce. "Jefferson and His Complex Legacy." In *Jeffersonian Legacies*, edited by Peter S. Onuf. Charlottesville: University Press of Virginia, 1993.

Armstrong, A. H. *Plotinus*. London: George Allen & Unwin, 1953.

Arnold, Ron. *At the Eye of the Storm: James Watt and the Environmentalists*. Chicago: Regnery Gateway, 1982.

Arrington, Leonard J. *Great Basin Kingdom: An Economic History of the Latter-day Saints, 1830–1900*. Cambridge: Harvard University Press, 1958.

Arrington, Leonard J., and Davis Bitton. *The Mormon Experience: A History of the Latter-day Saints*. New York: Alfred A. Knopf, 1979.

Arrington, Leonard J., Feramorz Y. Fox, and Dean L. May. *Building the City of God: Community and Cooperation among the Mormons*. 2nd ed. Urbana: University of Illinois Press, 1992.

Ashworth, William B., Jr. "Catholicism and Early Modern Science." In *God and Nature: Historical Essays on the Encounter between Christianity and Science*, edited by David C. Lindberg and Ronald L. Numbers. Berkeley: University of California Press, 1986.

Athearn, Robert G. *High Country Empire: The High Plains and Rockies*. New York: McGraw-Hill, 1960.

———. *The Mythic West in Twentieth-Century America*. Lawrence: University of Kansas Press, 1986.

Attfield, Robin. "Has the History of Philosophy Ruined the Environment?" *Environmental Ethics* 13 (1991): 127–137.

Badè, William Frederic. *The Life and Letters of John Muir*. 2 vols. Boston: Houghton-Mifflin, 1924.

Bailyn, Bernard. *Ideological Origins of the American Revolution*. Cambridge: Harvard University Press, 1967.

Barbour, Ian G. *Religion in an Age of Science: The Gifford Lectures, 1989–1991*. Vol. 1. San Francisco: Harper & Row, 1990.

———, ed. *Western Man and Environmental Ethics: Attitudes Toward Nature and Technology*. Reading, Mass.: Addison-Wesley, 1973.

Barish, Evelyn. *Emerson: The Roots of Prophecy*. Princeton: Princeton University Press, 1989.

Bartlett, Richard A. *Nature's Yellowstone*. Albuquerque: University of New Mexico Press, 1974.

———. *Yellowstone: A Wilderness Besieged*. Tuscon: University of Arizona Press, 1985.

Beard, Patricia. "A Chip Off the Old Rock." *Town & Country*, January 1994, 60–67.

Bedini, Silvio A. "Man of Science." In *Thomas Jefferson: A Reference Biography*, edited by Merrill D. Peterson. New York: Charles Scribner's Sons, 1986.

Beierwaltes, Werner. "Image and Counterimage? Reflections on Neoplatonic Thought with Respect to Its Place Today." In *Neoplatonism and Early Christian Thought*, edited by H. J. Blumenthal and R. A. Markus. London: Variorum, 1981.

———. "Plotin im deutschen Idealismus." In *Platonismus und Idealismus*. Frankfurt: Vittorio Klostermann, 1972.

———. *Platonismus und Idealismus*. Frankfurt: Vittorio Klostermann, 1972.

Beitzinger, A. J. "Political Theorist." In *Thomas Jefferson: A Reference Biography*, edited by Merrill D. Peterson. New York: Charles Scribner's Sons, 1986.

Bentley, G. E., Jr. "The Way of a Papermaker with a Poet: Joshua G. Gilpin, William Blake, and the Arts in 1796." *Notes and Queries* 33 (1986): 80–84 and 33 (1986): 525.

Benton, Thomas Hart. *Thirty Years' View; or, A History of the Working of the American Government for Thirty Years, from 1820 to 1850*. 2 vols. New York: Appleton, 1886.

Bercovitch, Sacvan. "The Historiography of Johnson's *Wonder-Working Providence*." *Essex Institute Historical Collections* 104 (1968): 138–61.

Bidwell, John. "Joshua Gilpin and Lord Stanhope's Improvements in Printing." *Papers of the Bibliographical Society of America* 76 (1982): 143–58.

Birch, Charles, and John Cobb, Jr. *The Liberation of Life: From the Cell to the Community*. Cambridge: Cambridge University Press, 1981.

Bocock, John Holmes. "Emerson on History." In *All Clever Men, Who Make Their Way: Critical Discourse in the Old South*, edited by Michael O'Brien. Fayetteville: University of Arkansas Press, 1982.

Boorstin, Daniel J. *The Lost World of Thomas Jefferson*. Boston: Beacon Press, 1948.

Bouwsma, William J. *John Calvin: A Sixteenth-Century Portrait*. New York: Oxford University Press, 1988.

Bowler, Peter J. *The Eclipse of Darwinism: Anti-Darwinian Evolution Theories in the Decades around 1900*. Baltimore: John Hopkins University Press, 1983.

Bozeman, Theodore Dwight. *Protestants in an Age of Science: The Baconian Ideal and Ante-Bellum Religious Thought*. Chapel Hill: University of North Carolina Press, 1977.

———. *To Live Ancient Lives: The Primitivist Dimension in Puritanism*. Chapel Hill: University of North Carolina Press, 1988.

Bramwell, Anna. *Ecology in the 20th Century*. New Haven: Yale University Press, 1989.

Bratton, Susan Power. *Christianity, Wilderness, and Wildfire: The Original Desert Solitaire*. Scranton, Pa.: University of Scranton Press, 1993.

———. "The Ecotheology of James Watt." *Environmental Ethics* 5 (1983): 225–36.

Breen, Timothy. *Puritans and Adventurers: Change and Persistence in Early America*. New York: Oxford University Press, 1980.

———. *Tobacco Culture: The Mentality of the Great Tidewater Planters on the Eve of the Revolution*. Princeton: Princeton University, 1985.

Brinkerhoff, Merlin B., Elaine Grandin, and Eugen Lupri. "Religious Involvement and Spousal Violence: The Canadian Case." *Journal for the Scientific Study of Religion* 31 (1992): 15–31.

Brooke, John L. *The Refiner's Fire: The Making of Mormon Cosmology, 1644–1844*. Cambridge: Cambridge University Press, 1994.

Brubaker, Rogers. *The Limits of Rationality: An Essay on the Social and Moral Thought of Max Weber*. London: Allen & Unwin, 1984.

Brumm, Ursula. " 'What Went You Out into the Wilderness to See?' Nonconformity and Wilderness in Cotton Mather's *Magnalia Christi Americana.*" *Prospects: The Annals of American Cultural Studies* 6 (1981): 1–15.

Bryant, Joseph M. "From Myth to Theology: Intellectuals and the Rationalization of Religion in Ancient Greece." In *Time, Place, and Circumstance: Neo-Weberian Studies in Comparative Religious History,* edited by William H. Swatos. New York: Greenwood Press, 1990.

Bushman, Richard L. *Joseph Smith and the Beginnings of Mormonism.* Urbana: University of Illinois Press, 1984.

Campbell, Colin. *The Romantic Ethic and the Spirit of Modern Consumerism.* Oxford: B. Blackwell, 1987.

Campbell, Eugene E. *Establishing Zion: The Mormon Church in the American West, 1847–1869.* Salt Lake City: n.p., 1988.

Capps, Donald. "Religion and Child Abuse: Perfect Together." *Journal for the Scientific Study of Religion* 31 (1992): 1–14.

Carroll, Peter N. *Puritanism and the Wilderness: The Intellectual Significance of the New England Frontier, 1629–1700.* New York: Columbia University Press, 1969.

Cauthen, Kenneth. *The Impact of American Religious Liberalism.* 2nd ed. Washington, D.C.: University Press of America, 1983.

Chapman, Emmanuel. *Saint Augustine's Philosophy of Beauty.* New York: Sheed & Ward, 1939.

Cheyne, A. C. *The Transforming of the Kirk: Victorian Scotland's Religious Revolution.* Edinburgh: Saint Andrew Press, 1983.

Clark, George T. *Leland Stanford: War Governor of California, Railroad Builder, and Founder of Stanford University.* Stanford University: Stanford University Press, 1931.

Clark, Harry Hayden. "Emerson and Science." *Philological Quarterly* 10 (1931): 225–60.

Clark, Mary T. "Augustine the Christian Thinker." In *From Augustine to Eriugena: Essays on Neoplatonism and Christianity in Honor of John O'Meara,* edited by F. X. Martin and J. A. Richmond. Washington, D.C.: Catholic University of American Press, 1991.

———. "Neoplatonism." In *The Encyclopedia of Religion,* edited by Mircea Eliade. New York: Macmillan, 1987.

Clark, Ronald. *Benjamin Franklin: A Biography.* New York: Random House, 1983.

Clark, Stephen R. L. *From Athens to Jerusalem: The Love of Wisdom and the Love of God.* Oxford: Clarendon Press, 1984.

Cobb, John, Jr., and David Ray Griffin. *Process Theology: An Introductory Exposition.* Philadelphia: Westminster Press, 1976.

Cochran, Thomas C. *Railroad Leaders, 1845–1890: The Business Mind in Action.* Cambridge: Harvard University Press, 1953.

Cohen, I. Bernard. *Franklin and Newton.* Philadelphia: American Philosophical Society, 1956.

———, ed. *Benjamin Franklin's Science*. Cambridge: Harvard University Press, 1990.

Cohen, Michael P. *The History of the Sierra Club, 1892–1970*. San Francisco: Sierra Club Books, 1988.

———. *The Pathless Way: John Muir and American Wilderness*. Madison: University of Wisconsin Press, 1984.

Collier, Peter, and David Horowitz. *The Rockefellers: An American Dynasty*. New York: Holt, Reinhart, and Winston, 1976.

Conkin, Paul. K. "The Religious Pilgrimage of Thomas Jefferson." In *Jeffersonian Legacies*, edited by Peter S. Onuf. Charlottesville: University Press of Virginia, 1993.

Cosslet, Tess, ed. *Science and Religion in the Nineteenth Century*. Cambridge: Cambridge University Press, 1984.

Cott, Nancy F. *The Bonds of Womanhood: "Women's Sphere" in New England, 1780–1835*. New Haven: Yale University Press, 1977.

Cowdrey, Albert E. *This Land, This South: An Environmental History*. Lexington: University Press of Kentucky, 1983.

Cowell, Pattie, and Ann Stanford, eds. *Critical Essays on Anne Bradstreet*. Boston: G. K. Hall & Co., 1983.

Cowell, Pattie. "The Early Distribution of Anne Bradstreet's Poems." In *Critical Essays on Anne Bradstreet*, edited by Pattie Cowell and Ann Stanford. Boston: G. K. Hall & Co., 1983.

Cragg, G. R. *From Puritanism to the Age of Reason: A Study of Changes in Religious Thought Within the Church of England, 1660 to 1700*. Cambridge: Cambridge University Press, 1966.

Craig, William Lane. *The Cosmological Argument from Plato to Leibniz*. New York: Barnes & Noble, 1980.

Cronon, William. *Changes in the Land: Indians, Colonists, and the Ecology of New England*. New York: Hill and Wang, 1983.

Crowley, J. E. *This Sheba, Self: The Conceptualization of Economic Life in Eighteenth-Century America*. Baltimore: Johns Hopkins University Press, 1974.

Crunden, Robert M. *Ministers of Reform: The Progressives' Achievement in American Civilization, 1889–1920*. New York: Basic Books, 1982.

Curtis, Susan. *A Consuming Faith: The Social Gospel and Modern American Culture*. Baltimore: Johns Hopkins University Press, 1991.

Dalton, J. Vasmar. "Ministers, Metaphors, and the New England Wilderness, 1650–1700." Ph.D. diss., University of New Hampshire, 1981.

Daly, Herman E., and John B. Cobb, Jr. *For the Common Good: Redirecting the Economy toward Community, the Environment, and a Sustainable Future*. Boston: Beacon Press, 1989.

Daly, Robert. *God's Altar: The World and the Flesh in Puritan Poetry*. Berkeley: University of California Press, 1978.

Daniel, Stephen H. *The Philosophy of Jonathan Edwards: A Study in Divine Semiotics*. Bloomington: Indiana University Press, 1994.

Davis, David Brion. "The New England Origins of Mormonism." In *Mormonism and American Culture*, edited by Marvin S. Hill and James B. Allen. New York: Harper & Row, 1972.

Degler, Carl N. *At Odds: Women and the Family in America from the Revolution to the Present*. New York: Oxford University Press, 1980.

De Witt, Calvin, et al. *Earthkeeping in the Nineties: Stewardship of Creation*. Rev. ed. Grand Rapids, Mich.: William B. Eerdmans, 1991.

Doggett, JoElla. "Another Eighteenth-Century Instance of Anne Bradstreet's Continuing Appeal." In *Critical Essays on Anne Bradstreet*, edited by Pattie Cowell and Ann Stanford. Boston: G. K. Hall & Co., 1983.

Douglas, Ann. *The Feminization of American Culture*. New York: Alfred A. Knopf, 1977.

Douglas, Mary, and Aaron Wildavsky. *Risk and Culture: An Essay on the Selection of Technical and Environmental Dangers*. Berkeley: University of California Press, 1982.

Douglas, William O. *Go East, Young Man: The Early Years*. New York: Random House, 1974.

Drummond, Andrew L., and James Bullock. *The Church in Victorian Scotland, 1843–1874*. Edinburgh: Saint Andrew Press, 1975.

Duby, Georges. *The Early Growth of the European Economy: Warriors and Peasants from the Seventh to the Twelfth Century*. Translated by Howard B. Clarke. Ithaca: Cornell University Press, 1974.

Durkheim, Emile. *The Elementary Forms of the Religious Life*. Translated by Joseph Ward Swain. New York: Free Press, 1965.

Eckholm, Erik P. *Losing Ground: Environmental Stress and World Food Prospects*. New York: Norton, 1976.

Edgerton, Samuel J., Jr. "The Franklin Stove." In *Benjamin Franklin's Science*, edited by I. Bernard Cohen. Cambridge: Harvard University Press, 1990.

Eisen, Arnold. "Called to Order: The Role of the Puritan Berufsmensch in Weberian Sociology." *Sociology* 13 (1979): 204–8.

Eisenstadt, S. N. "The Protestant Ethic in the Framework of Sociological Theory and of Weber's Work." In *The Protestant Ethic and Modernization: A Comparative View*, edited by S. N. Eisenstadt. New York: Basic Books, 1968.

Evans, Cerinda W. *Collis Potter Huntington*. 2 vols. Newport News, Va.: Mariners' Museum, 1954.

Fausold, Martin L. *Gifford Pinchot: Bull Moose Progressive*. Syracuse: Syracuse University Press, 1961.

Fiering, Norman. *Jonathan Edwards's Moral Thought and Its British Context*. Chapel Hill: University of North Carolina Press, 1981.

Flader, Susan L. *Thinking Like a Mountain: Aldo Leopold and the Evolution of an Ecological Attitude toward Deer, Wolves, and Forests*. Lincoln: University of Nebraska Press, 1974.

Fosdick, Ramond B. *John D. Rockefeller, Jr.: A Portrait*. New York: Harper & Bros., 1956.

Fox, Stephen. *The American Conservation Movement: John Muir and His Legacy*. 1981. Reprint, Madison: University of Wisconsin Press, 1985.

Francaviglia, Richard V. *The Mormon Landscape: Existence, Creation, and Perception of a Unique Image in the American West*. New York: AMS Press, 1978.

Gable, John Allen. *The Bull Moose Years: Theodore Roosevelt and the Progressive Party*. Port Washington, N.Y.: Kennikat Press, 1978.

Gallagher, Edward J. Introduction to *Wonder-working Providence of Sions Saviour, in New England*, by Edward Johnson. In *Wonder-Working Providence of Sions Saviour in New-England (1654) and Good News From New England (1648)*. Delmar, N.Y.: Scholars' Facsimiles & Reprints, 1974.

Gaustad, E. S. "Religion." In *Thomas Jefferson: A Reference Biography*, edited by Merrill D. Peterson. New York: Charles Scribner's Sons, 1986.

Gerbi, Antonello. *The Dispute of the New World: The History of a Polemic, 1750–1900*. Rev. and enl. ed. Translated by Jeremy Moyle. Pittsburgh: University of Pittsburgh Press, 1973.

Gillispie, Charles Coulston. *Genesis and Geology: A Study in the Relations of Scientific Thought, Natural Theology, and Social Opinion in Great Britain, 1790–1850*. 1951. Reprint, New York: Harper & Brothers, 1959.

Gilson, Etienne. *The Christian Philosophy of Saint Augustine*. Translated by L. E. M. Lynch. New York: Random House, 1960.

Glacken, Clarence. *Traces on the Rhodian Shore: Nature and Culture in Western Thought from Ancient Times to the End of the Eighteenth Century*. Berkeley: University of California Press, 1967.

Goddard, Henry Clarke. *Studies in New England Transcendentalism*. 1908. Reprint, New York: Hillary House, 1960.

Goen, C. C. "Editor's Introduction." In *The Works of Jonathan Edwards*, vol. 4, *The Great Awakening*. New Haven: Yale University Press, 1972.

Goetzmann, William H. *New Lands, New Men: America and the Second Great Age of Discovery*. New York: Viking, 1986.

Goetzmann, William H., and Kay Sloan. *Looking Far North*. New York: Viking Press, 1982.

Gorrell, Donald K. *The Age of Social Responsibility: The Social Gospel in the Progressive Era, 1900–1920*. Macon, Ga.: Mercer University Press, 1988.

Gottlieb, Alan M., ed. *The Wise Use Agenda: The Citizen's Guide to Environmental Resource Issues*. Bellevue, Wash.: Free Enterprise Press, 1989.

Graebner, Norman A. *Empire on the Pacific: A Study in American Continental Expansion*. New York: Ronald Press, 1955.

Grant, Edward. "Science and Theology in the Middle Ages." In *God and Nature: Historical Essays on the Encounter between Christianity and Science*, edited by David C. Lindberg and Ronald L. Numbers. Berkeley: University of California Press, 1986.

Greven, Philip. *Spare the Child: The Religious Roots of Punishment and the Psychological Impact of Physical Abuse*. New York: Alfred A. Knopf, 1991.

———. *The Protestant Temperament: Patterns of Child-Rearing, Religious Experience, and the Self in Early America*. Chicago: University of Chicago Press, 1977.

Griswald, A. Whitney. "Three Puritans on Prosperity." *The New England Quarterly* 7 (1934) p. 492.

Grodinsky, Julius. *Jay Gould: His Business Career, 1867–1892*. Philadelphia: University of Pennsylvania Press, 1957.

Grove, Richard H. "Origins of Western Environmentalism." *Scientific American* 267 (1992): 42–47.

Gura, Philip F. *A Glimpse of Sion's Glory: Puritan Radicalism in New England, 1620–1660*. Middletown, Conn.: Wesleyan University Press, 1984.

Hambrick-Stowe, Charles E. *The Practice of Piety: Puritan Devotional Disciplines in Seventeenth-Century New England*. Chapel Hill: University of North Carolina Press, 1982.

Hammond, Jeffrey A. *Sinful Self, Saintly Self: The Puritan Experience of Poetry*. Athens: University of Georgia Press, 1993.

Hansen, Klaus J. *Mormonism and the American Experience*. Chicago: University of Chicago Press, 1981.

Hansen, Niles M. "On the Sources of Economic Rationality." *Zeitschrift für Nationalökonomie* 24 (1962): 445–55.

———. "The Protestant Ethic as a General Precondition for Economic Development." *Canadian Journal of Economics and Political Science* 29 (1963): 462–74.

Hapgood, Norman. "The Hetch Hetchy Controversy." *Harper's Weekly*, December 6, 1913. In *Congressional Record*, vol. 51, 4 December 1913, p. 182.

Hargrove, Eugene C. *Foundations of Environmental Ethics*. Englewood Cliffs, N.J.: Prentice-Hall, 1989.

Harr, John Ensor, and Peter J. Johnson. *The Rockefeller Century*. New York: Charles Scribner's Sons, 1988.

Harrison, Carol. *Beauty and Revelation in the Thought of Saint Augustine*. Oxford: Clarendon Press, 1992.

Hatch, Nathan O. *The Democratization of American Christianity*. New Haven: Yale University Press, 1989.

Hawke, David Freeman. *Franklin*. New York: Harper & Row, 1976.

Hays, Samuel. *Beauty, Health, and Permanence: Environmental Politics in the United States, 1955–1985*. Cambridge: Cambridge University Press, 1987.

———. *Conservation and the Gospel of Efficiency: The Progressive Conservation Movement, 1890–1920*. Cambridge: Harvard University Press, 1959.

Heilbron, J. L. "Franklin as an Enlightened Natural Philosopher." In *Reappraising Benjamin Franklin: A Bicentennial Perspective*, edited by J. A. Leo Lemay. Newark: University of Delaware Press, 1993.

Heimert, Alan. "Puritanism, the Wilderness, and the Frontier." *The New England Quarterly* 26 (1953): 361–82.

Henry, Paul. *Plotin et l'Occident: Firmicus Maternus, Marius Victorinus, Saint Augustine et Macrobe*. Louvain: Spicilegium Sacrum Lovaniense, 1934.

Hermann, Jost. *Grüne Utopien in Deutschland: Zur Geschichte des ökologischen Bewußtseins.* Frankfurt am Main: Fischer Taschenbuch Verlag, 1991.

Hertz, Karl H. "Max Weber and American Puritanism." *Journal for the Scientific Study of Religion* 1 (1962): 189–197.

Higgins, Richard. "Analysts say Americans fail to turn interest in religion into commitment." Knight-Ridder Tribune New Service. In *Austin (Texas) American-Statesman,* 5 May 1991, p. F6.

Hill, Christopher. *Society and Puritanism in Pre-Revolutionary England.* 2nd ed. New York: Schocken Books, 1967.

———. *The World Turned Upside Down: Radical Ideas during the English Revolution.* New York: Viking Press, 1973.

Hill, Marvin S. *Quest for Refuge: The Mormon Flight from American Pluralism.* Salt Lake City: Signature Books, 1989.

Holbrook, Clyde A. *Jonathan Edwards, the Valley and Nature: An Interpretive Essay.* Lewisburg: Bucknell University Press, 1987.

Holbrook, Stewart H. *James J. Hill: A Great Life in Brief.* New York: Alfred A. Knopf, 1955.

———. *The Age of the Moguls.* Garden City, N.Y.: Doubleday, 1953.

Holifield, E. Brooks. *The Gentlemen Theologians: American Theology in Southern Culture, 1795–1860.* Durham: Duke University Press, 1978.

Holmes, Oliver Wendell. *Ralph Waldo Emerson.* Boston: Houghton Mifflin, 1885.

Hooykaas, R. "Science and Reformation." In *The Protestant Ethic and Modernization: A Comparative View,* edited by S. N. Eisenstadt. New York: Basic Books, 1968.

Hovenkamp, Herbert. *Science and Religion in America, 1800–1860.* Philadelphia: University of Pennsylvania Press, 1978.

Howe, Daniel Walker. "The Cambridge Platonists of Old England and the Cambridge Platonists of New England." In *American Unitarianism, 1805–1865,* edited by Conrad Edick Wright. Boston: Northeastern University Press, 1989.

Hudson, Winthrop S. "Puritanism and the Spirit of Capitalism." In *Protestantism and Capitalism: The Weber Thesis and Its Critics,* edited by Robert Green. Boston: D. C. Heath, 1959.

Hutchison, William R. *The Modernist Impulse in American Protestantism.* Cambridge: Harvard University Press, 1976.

Huth, Hans. *Nature and the American: Three Centuries of Changing Attitudes.* Berkeley: University of California Press, 1957.

Hyma, Albert. "The Economic Views of the Protestant Reformers." In *Protestantism and Capitalism: The Weber Thesis and Its Critics,* edited by Robert Green. Boston: D. C. Heath, 1959.

Isaac, Rhys. *The Transformation of Virginia, 1740–1790.* Chapel Hill: University of North Carolina Press, 1982.

Ise, John. *Our National Park Policy: A Critical History.* Baltimore: Johns Hopkins Press, 1961.

Israel, Herman. "Some Influences of Hebraic Culture on Modern Social Organization." *American Journal of Sociology* 71 (1966): 384–94.

———. "Some Religious Factors in the Emergence of Industrial Society in England." *American Sociological Review* 31 (1966): 589–99.

Jackson, Richard H., ed. *The Mormon Role in the Settlement of the West.* Provo: Brigham Young University Press, 1978.

Jackson, Wes. *Altars of Unhewn Stone: Science and the Earth.* San Francisco: North Point Press, 1987.

———. *New Roots for Agriculture.* San Francisco: Friends of the Earth, 1980.

———. "Statement by Dr. Wes Jackson." In *Christian Ecology: Building an Environmental Ethic for the Twenty-First Century,* edited by Frederick W. Krueger. San Francisco: North American Conference on Christianity and Ecology, 1988.

Jacob, Margaret C. "Christianity and the Newtonian Worldview." In *God and Nature: Historical Essays on the Encounter between Christianity and Science,* edited by David C. Lindberg and Ronald L. Numbers. Berkeley: University of California Press, 1986.

———. *The Newtonians and the English Revolution, 1689–1720.* Ithaca, N.Y.: Cornell University Press, 1976.

Jeske, Jeffrey. "Cotton Mather: Physico-Theologian." *Journal of the History of Ideas* 47 (1986): 583–95.

Johnson, Benton. "Do Holiness Sects Socialize in Dominant Values?" *Social Forces* 39 (1961): 309–16.

Johnson, Robert Underwood. *Remembered Yesterdays.* Boston: Little, Brown, 1923.

Jones, Holway R. *John Muir and the Sierra Club: The Battle for Yosemite.* San Francisco: Sierra Club Books, 1965.

Karnes, Thomas L. *William Gilpin: Western Nationalist.* Austin: University of Texas Press, 1970.

Kay, Jeanne. "Concepts of Nature in the Hebrew Bible." *Environmental Ethics* 10 (1988): 309–27.

Keffer, Steven, Sallie King, and Steven Kraft. "Process Metaphysics and Minimalism: Implications for Public Policy." *Environmental Ethics* 13 (1991): 23–47.

Kennan, George. *E. H. Harriman: A Biography.* 2 vols. Boston: Houghton Mifflin, 1922.

Kersten, Lawrence K. *The Lutheran Ethic: The Impact of Religion on Laymen and Clergy.* Detroit: Wayne State University Press, 1970.

Kiesewetter, Hubert. *Industrielle Revolution in Deutschland.* Frankfurt: Suhrkamp, 1989.

Kilman, John C. "A Joiner Looks at Colonial New England: Edward Johnson's *Special Providences.*" *Southern Folklore Quarterly* 45 (1981): 135–44.

Kimes, William F., and Maymie B. Kimes. *John Muir: A Reading Bibliography.* Fresno, Calif.: Panorama West Books, 1986.

King, Judson. *The Conservation Fight: From Theodore Roosevelt to the Tennessee Valley Authority*. Washington, D.C.: Public Affairs Press, 1959.

Klein, Maury. *The Life and Legend of Jay Gould*. Baltimore: Johns Hopkins University Press, 1986.

Klibansky, Raymond. *The Continuity of the Platonic Tradition during the Middle Ages*. Munich: Kraus International, 1981.

Klyza, Christopher McGrory. "Framing the Debate in Public Lands Politics." *Policy Studies Journal* 19 (1991): 577–85.

Knight, Douglas A. "Cosmogony and Order in the Hebrew Tradition." In *Cosmogony and Ethical Order: New Studies in Comparative Ethics*, edited by Robin W. Lovin and Frank E. Reynolds. Chicago: University of Chicago Press, 1985.

Knowles, David. *The Evolution of Medieval Thought*. London: Longmans, 1962.

Lane, Belden C. *Landscapes of the Sacred: Geography and Narrative in American Spirituality*. New York: Paulist Press, 1988.

Larson, Henrietta M. *Jay Cooke: Private Banker*. New York: Greenwood, 1968.

Lasch, Christopher. *The New Radicalism in America, 1889–1963: The Intellectual as a Social Type*. New York: Alfred A. Knopf, 1965.

"Last Words: A Question of the Moment." *Sierra: The Magazine of the Sierra Club* 76 (September/October 1991): 138.

Latta, Estelle. *Controversial Mark Hopkins*. New York: Greenberg Press, 1953.

Leiss, William. *The Domination of Nature*. New York: George Braziller, 1972.

Leone, Mark P. *Roots of Modern Mormonism*. Cambridge: Harvard University Press, 1979.

Leverenz, David. "The Politics of Emerson's Man-Making Words." In *Manhood and the American Renaissance*. Ithaca: Cornell University Press, 1989.

Levin, David. "Giants in the Earth: Science and the Occult in Cotton Mather's Letters to the Royal Society." *William and Mary Quarterly* 3rd Ser., 45 (1988): 751–70.

Levy, Babette M. *Cotton Mather*. Boston: Twayne Publishers, 1979.

Lewalski, Barbara Kiefer. *Protestant Poetics and the Seventeenth-Century Religious Lyric*. Princeton: Princeton University Press, 1979.

Lewis, Martin W. *Green Delusions: An Environmentalist Critique of Radical Environmentalism*. Durham: Duke University Press, 1992.

Lewis, Oscar. "One of the Most Picturesque of the Celebrated Legal Wrangles." *San Francisco Chronicle*, 24 May 1953, "This World" section, p. 22.

———. *The Big Four: The Story of Huntington, Stanford, Hopkins, and Crocker, and of the Building of the Central Pacific*. 1938. Reprint, New York: Alfred A. Knopf, 1955.

Little, David. "Calvinism and Law." In *The Protestant Ethic and Modernization: A Comparative View*, edited by S. N. Eisenstadt. New York: Basic Books, 1968.

Louth, Andrew. *The Origins of the Christian Mystical Tradition: From Plato to Denys*. Oxford: Clarendon Press, 1981.

Lovejoy, Arthur O. *The Great Chain of Being: A Study of the History of an Idea*. 1936. Reprint, Cambridge: Harvard University Press, 1964.

Lovelock, J. E. *Gaia: A New Look at Life on Earth*. Oxford: Oxford University Press, 1979.

Lowance, Mason I., Jr. "Cotton Mather's *Magnalia* and the Metaphors of Biblical History." In *Typology and Early American Literature*, edited by Sacvan Bercovitch. [Amherst]: University of Massachusetts Press, 1972.

———. *The Language of Canaan: Metaphor and Symbol in New England from the Puritans to the Transcendentalists*. Cambridge: Harvard University Press, 1980.

Lowe, Victor. "Whitehead's Metaphysical System." In *Process Philosophy and Christian Thought*, edited by Delwin Brown, Ralph E. James, Jr., and Gene Reeves. Indianapolis: Bobbs-Merrill, 1971.

Lucas, George R., Jr. *The Rehabilitation of Whitehead: An Analytic and Historic Assessment of Process Philosophy*. Albany: State University of New York Press, 1989.

Lucas, Rex A. "A Specification of the Weber Thesis: Plymouth Colony." *History and Theory* 10 (1971): 318–46.

Lüthy, Herbert. "Once Again: Calvinism and Capitalism." In *The Protestant Ethic and Modernization: A Comparative View*, edited by S. N. Eisenstadt. New York: Basic Books, 1968.

Mackinnon, Flor Isabel. "Notes." In *Philosophical Writings of Henry More*, edited by Flor Isabel Mackinnon. New York: Oxford University Press, 1925.

Marshall, Peter. *Nature's Web. Rethinking Our Place on Earth*. New York: Paragon House, 1994.

Martin, Albro. *James J. Hill and the Opening of the Northwest*. New York: Oxford University Press, 1976.

———. *Railroads Triumphant: The Growth, Rejection, and Rebirth of a Vital American Force*. New York: Oxford University Press, 1992.

Martin, Edwin T. *Thomas Jefferson: Scientist*. New York: Henry Schuman, 1952.

Martz, Louis L. *The Paradise Within: Studies in Vaughan, Traherne, and Milton*. New Haven: Yale University Press, 1964.

Marx, Leo. *The Machine in the Garden: Technology and the Pastoral Ideal in America*. New York: Oxford University Press, 1964.

Matthews, L. Harrison. *Man and Wildlife*. London: Croom Helm, 1975.

May, Henry F. "The Enlightenment." In *Thomas Jefferson: A Reference Biography*, edited by Merrill D. Peterson. New York: Charles Scribner's Sons, 1986.

———. *Protestant Churches and Industrial America*. 2nd ed. 1967. Reprint, New York: Octagon Books, 1977.

McClintock, James I. *Nature's Kindred Spirits: Aldo Leopold, Joseph Wood Krutch, Edward Abbey, Annie Dillard, and Gary Snyder*. Madison: University of Wisconsin Press, 1994.

McFague, Sallie. *The Body of God: An Ecological Theology*. Minneapolis: Fortress Press, 1993.

——. *Models of God: Theology for an Ecological, Nuclear Age*. Philadelphia: Fortress Press, 1987.

McGeary, M. Nelson. *Gifford Pinchot: Forester-Politician*. Princeton: Princeton University Press, 1960.

McPhee, John. *Encounter with the Archdruid: Narratives about a Conservationist and Three of his Natural Enemies*. New York: Farrar, Straus and Giroux, 1971.

Meine, Curt. *Aldo Leopold: His Life and Work*. Madison: University of Wisconsin Press, 1988.

Melandy, H. Brett, and Benjamin F. Gilbert. *The Governors of California: Peter H. Burnett to Edmund G. Brown*. Georgetown, Calif.: Talisman Press, 1965.

Menninger, Karl A. "Totemic Aspects of Contemporary Attitudes Toward Animals." In George B. Wilbur and Werner Meunsterberger, eds. *Psychoanalysis and Culture*. New York: International Universities Press, 1951.

Merchant, Carolyn. *Ecological Revolutions: Nature, Gender, and Science in New England*. Chapel Hill: University of North Carolina Press, 1989.

——. *The Death of Nature: Women, Ecology, and the Scientific Revolution*. San Francisco: Harper & Row, 1980.

Merk, Frederick. *Manifest Destiny and Mission in American History*. New York: Alfred A. Knopf, 1963.

——. *The Monroe Doctrine and American Expansionism, 1843–1849*. New York: Alfred A. Knopf, 1966.

Meyer, Donald B. *The Positive Thinkers: Popular Religious Psychology from Mary Baker Eddy to Normal Vincent Peale and Ronald Reagan*. Rev. ed. Middletown, Conn.: Wesleyan University Press, 1988.

Meyer, Donald H. "Franklin's Religion." In *Critical Essays on Benjamin Franklin*, edited by Melvin H. Buxbaum. Boston: G. K. Hall, 1987.

Middlekauff, Robert. *The Mathers: Three Generations of Puritan Intellectuals, 1596–1728*. New York: Oxford University Press, 1971.

Miller, Alice. *For Your Own Good: Hidden Cruelty in Child-Rearing and the Roots of Violence*. Translated by Hildegarde Hannum and Hunter Hannum. New York: Farrar, Straus, Giroux, 1983.

Miller, Charles A. *Jefferson and Nature: An Interpretation*. Baltimore: Johns Hopkins University Press, 1988.

Miller, Perry. *Jonathan Edwards*. New York: W. Sloane Associates, 1949.

——. *The New England Mind: The Seventeenth Century*. 1939. Reprint, Cambridge: Harvard University Press, 1967.

Mitchell, Lee Clark. *Witnesses to a Vanishing America: The Nineteenth-Century Response*. Princeton: Princeton University Press, 1981.

Moore, J. R. *The Post-Darwinian Controversies*. Cambridge: Cambridge University Press, 1979.

Moore, R. Laurence. *Religious Outsiders and the Making of Americans*. New York: Oxford University Press, 1986.

Moran, Gerald F. *Religion, Family, and the Life Course: Explorations in the Social History of Early America*. Ann Arbor: University of Michigan Press, 1992.

Morgan, Edmund S. *American Slavery, American Freedom: The Ordeal of Colonial Virginia*. New York: Norton, 1975.

———. *The Puritan Dilemma: The Story of John Winthrop*. Boston: Little, Brown, 1958.

———. *The Puritan Family: Religion and Domestic Relations in Seventeenth-Century New England*. Rev. and enl. ed. New York: Harper & Row, 1966.

Morison, Samuel Eliot. "Edward Johnson." *Dictionary of American Biography*. New York: Scribner, 1932.

Morris, William Sparkes. *The Young Jonathan Edwards: A Reconstruction*. Brooklyn, N.Y.: Carlson Publishing, 1991.

Mott, Tracy, and George W. Zink. "Benjamin Franklin's Economic Thought: A Twentieth Century Appraisal." In *Critical Essays on Benjamin Franklin*, edited by Melvin H. Buxbaum. Boston: G. K. Hall, 1987.

Mott, Wesley T. "Emerson and Antinomianism: The Legacy of the Sermons." *American Literature* 50 (1978): 369–97.

———. "From Natural Religion to Transcendentalism: An Edition of Emerson's Sermon No. 43." *Studies in the American Renaissance* 1985: 1–27.

Mueller, G. H. "The Notion of Rationality in the Work of Max Weber." *Archives Européennes de Sociologie* 20 (1979): 149–71.

Myers, Allen C. *The Eerdmans Bible Dictionary*. Rev. ed. Grand Rapids: William B. Eerdmans, 1987.

Nash, John. "Historical and Social Changes in the Perception of the Role of the Father." In Michael E. Lamb, ed., *The Role of the Father in Child Development*. New York: John Wiley & Sons, 1976.

Nash, Roderick Frazier. *The Rights of Nature: A History of Environmental Ethics*. Madison: University of Wisconsin Press, 1989.

———. *Wilderness and the American Mind*. 3rd rev. ed. New Haven: Yale University Press, 1982.

Nevins, Allan. *Study in Power: John D. Rockefeller: Industrialist and Philanthropist*. 2 vols. New York: Charles Scribner's Sons, 1953.

New Catholic Encyclopedia. New York: McGraw-Hill, 1967.

Newhall, Nancy. *A Contribution to the Heritage of Every American: The Conservation Activities of John D. Rockefeller, Jr*. New York: Alfred A Knopf, 1957.

Nicolson, Marjorie Hope. *Mountain Gloom and Mountain Glory: The Development of the Aesthetics of the Infinite*. Ithaca: Cornell University Press, 1959.

Nielsen, Donald A. "The Inquisition, Rationalization, and Sociocultural Change in Medieval Europe." In *Time, Place, and Circumstance: Neo-Weberian Studies in Comparative Religious History*, edited by William H. Swatos. New York: Greenwood Press, 1990.

Norris, George W. *Fighting Liberal*. New York: Macmillan, 1945.

Oberholtzer, Ellis Paxson. *Jay Cooke: Financier of the Civil War*. Philadelphia: George W. Jacobs, 1907.

O'Brien, Bart. "Earthquakes or Snowflowers: The Controversy Over the Formation of Yosemite Valley." *Pacific Historian* 29 (1985): 31–41.

O'Connell, Robert J. "Porphyrianism in the Early Augustine: Oliver DuRoy's Contribution." In *From Augustine to Eriugena: Essays on Neoplatonism and Christianity in Honor of John O'Meara*, edited by F. X. Martin and J. A. Richmond. Washington, D.C.: Catholic University of American Press, 1991.

———. *Art and the Christian Intelligence in St. Augustine*. Cambridge: Harvard University Press, 1978.

O'Meara, Dominic J. "Introduction" and "The Neoplatonism of Saint Augustine." In *Neoplatonism and Christian Thought*, edited by Dominic J. O'Meara. Albany: State University of New York Press, 1982.

Oelschlaeger, Max. *Caring for Creation: An Ecumenical Approach to the Environmental Crisis*. New Haven: Yale University Press, 1994.

"Ordered Out of Missouri." *St. Louis Globe-Democrat*, 2 February 1888, p. 12. Gilpin file. Missouri Historical Society, St. Louis, Missouri.

Orsi, Richard J. " 'Wilderness Saint' and 'Robber Baron': The Anomalous Partnership of John Muir and the Southern Pacific Company for Preservation of Yosemite National Park." *Pacific Historian* 29 (1985): 136–56.

Ownby, Ted. *Subduing Satan: Religion, Recreation, and Manhood in the Rural South, 1865–1920*. Chapel Hill: University of North Carolina Press, 1990.

Ozment, Steven. *When Fathers Ruled: Family Life in Reformation Europe*. Cambridge: Harvard University Press, 1983.

Paul, Ellen Frankel. *Moral Revolution and Economic Science: The Demise of Laissez-Faire in Nineteenth-Century British Political Economy*. Westport, Conn.: Greenwood Press, 1979.

Pelikan, Jaroslav. *The Christian Tradition: A History of the Development of Doctrine*. Vol. 1, *The Emergence of the Catholic Tradition (100–600)*. Chicago: University of Chicago Press, 1971.

Penick, James, Jr. *Progressive Politics and Conservation: The Ballinger-Pinchot Affair*. Chicago: University of Chicago Press, 1968.

Peterson, Charles S. "Imprint of Agricultural Systems on the Utah Landscape." In *The Mormon Role in the Settlement of the West*, edited by Richard H. Jackson. Provo: Brigham Young University Press, 1978.

Peterson, Merrill D. "The American Scholar: Emerson and Jefferson." In *Thomas Jefferson and the World of Books: A symposium held at the Library of Congress September 21, 1976*. Washington: Library of Congress, 1977.

Piercy, Josephine K. *Anne Bradstreet*. New York: Twayne, 1965.

Pinkett, Harold T. *Gifford Pinchot: Private and Public Forester*. Urbana: University of Illinois Press, 1970.

Pochmann, Henry A. *German Culture in America 1600–1900: Philosophical and Literary Influence*. Madison: University of Wisconsin Press, 1957.

Pollack, Linda A. *Forgotten Children: Parent-Child Relations from 1500 to 1900.* (Cambridge: Cambridge University Press, 1983).

Porte, Joel. *Representative Man: Ralph Waldo Emerson in His Time.* New York: Oxford University Press, 1979.

Potter, David M. *People of Plenty: Economic Abundance and the American Character.* Chicago: University of Chicago Press, 1954.

Pyle, Joseph Gilpin. *The Life of James J. Hill.* 2 vols. Garden City, N.Y.: Doubleday, Page, 1917.

Reeves, Gene, and Delwin Brown. "The Development of Process Theology." In *Process Philosophy and Christian Thought,* edited by Delwin Brown, Ralph E. James, Jr., and Gene Reeves. Indianapolis: Bobbs-Merrill, 1971.

Regenstein, Lewis G. *Replenish the Earth: A History of Organized Religious Treatment of Animals and Nature — Including the Bible's Message of Conservation and Kindness toward Animals.* New York: Crossroads, 1991.

Reisner, Marc. *Cadillac Desert: The American West and Its Disappearing Water.* New York: Penguin Books, 1986.

Reps, John W. *Cities of the American West: A History of Frontier Urban Planning.* Princeton: Princeton University Press, 1979.

Richardson, Elmo R. *The Politics of Conservation: Crusades and Controversies, 1897–1913.* Berkeley: University of California Press, 1962.

Richardson, Robert D., Jr. *Emerson: The Mind on Fire.* Berkeley: University of California Press, 1995.

Robb, Nesca A. *Neoplatonism of the Italian Renaissance.* 1935. Reprint, New York: Octagon Books, 1968.

Robbins, Frank Egleston. *The Hexaemeral Literature: A Study of the Greek and Latin Commentaries on Genesis.* Chicago: University of Chicago Press, 1912.

Robertson, H. M. "A Criticism of Max Weber and His School." In *Protestantism and Capitalism: The Weber Thesis and Its Critics,* edited by Robert Green. Boston: D. C. Heath, 1959.

Robinson, David. "Emerson's Natural Theology and the Paris Naturalists: Toward a Theory of Animated Nature." In *Critical Essays on Ralph Waldo Emerson,* edited by Robert E. Burkholder and Joel Myerson. Boston: G. K. Hall, 1983.

Rodier, David F. T. "The Problem of Ordered Chaos in Whitehead and Plotinus." In *The Significance of Neoplatonism,* edited by R. Baine Harris. Norfolk, Va.: International Society for Neoplatonic Studies, 1976.

Roger, Jacques. "The Mechanistic Conception of Life." In *God and Nature: Historical Essays on the Encounter between Christianity and Science,* edited by David C. Lindberg and Ronald L. Numbers. Berkeley: University of California Press, 1986.

Rosenfeld, Alvin H. "Anne Bradstreet's 'Contemplations': Patterns of Form and Meaning." In *Critical Essays on Anne Bradstreet,* edited by Pattie Cowell and Ann Stanford. Boston: G. K. Hall & Co., 1983.

Rosenmeier, Rosamond R. *Anne Bradstreet Revisited.* Boston: Twayne, 1991.

———. "The Wounds Upon Bathsheba: Anne Bradstreet's Prophetic Art." In *Puritan Poets and Poetics: Seventeenth-Century American Poetry in Theory and Practice*, edited by Peter White. University Park: Pennsylvania State University Press, 1985.

Roth, Guenter, and Wolfgang Schluchter. *Max Weber's Vision of History: Ethics and Methods*. Berkeley: University of California Press, 1979.

Runte, Alfred. *National Parks: The American Experience*. 2nd rev. ed. Lincoln: University of Nebraska Press, 1987.

———. *Trains of Discovery: Western Railroads and the National Parks*. Flagstaff: Northland, 1984.

Rusk, Ralph L. *The Life of Ralph Waldo Emerson*. New York: Charles Scribner's Sons, 1949.

Sambrook, James. *English Pastoral Poetry*. Boston: Twayne, 1983.

Sanford, Charles B. *The Religious Life of Thomas Jefferson*. Charlottesville: University Press of Virginia, 1984.

Santmire, H. Paul. *The Travail of Nature: The Ambiguous Ecological Promise of Christian Theology*. Philadelphia: Fortress Press, 1985.

Schaeffer, Francis A. *Pollution and the Death of Man: The Christian View of Ecology*. Wheaton, Ill.: Tyndale House, 1970.

Scheick, William J. *Design in Puritan American Literature*. Lexington: University Press of Kentucky, 1992.

Schenkel, Albert F. *The Rich Man and the Kingdom: John D. Rockefeller, Jr., and the Protestant Establishment*. Minneapolis: Fortress Press, 1995.

Schluchter, Wolfgang. *The Rise of Western Rationalism: Max Weber's Developmental History*. Translated by Guenther Roth. Berkeley: University of California Press, 1981.

Schofield, Edmund A. "John Muir's Yankee Friends and Mentors: The New England Connection." *Pacific Historian* 29 (1985): 65–89.

Schweitzer, Ivy. *The Work of Self-Representation: Lyric Poetry in Colonial New England*. Chapel Hill: University of North Carolina Press, 1991.

Shalhope, Robert E. "Agriculture." In *Thomas Jefferson: A Reference Biography*, edited by Merrill D. Peterson. New York: Charles Scribner's Sons, 1986.

Shipps, Jan. *Mormonism: The Story of a New Religious Tradition*. Urbana: University of Illinois Press, 1985.

Shoemaker, Henry W. *The Man Who Made Good: Gifford Pinchot*. Altoona, Pa.: n.p., n.d. [1923?].

Short, C. Brant. *Ronald Reagan and the Public Lands: America's Conservation Debate, 1979–1984*. College Station: Texas A&M University Press, 1989.

Sibum, Heinz Otto. "The Bookkeeper of Nature: Benjamin Franklin's Electrical Research and the Development of Experimental Natural Philosophy in the Eighteenth Century." In *Reappraising Benjamin Franklin: A Bicentennial Perspective*, edited by J. A. Leo Lemay. Newark: University of Delaware Press, 1993.

Silverman, Kenneth. *The Life and Times of Cotton Mather*. New York: Harper & Row, 1984.

Simmons, I. G. *Changing the Face of the Earth: Culture, Environment, History*. Oxford: Blackwell, 1989.

Slotkin, Richard. *The Fatal Environment: The Myth of the Frontier in the Age of Industrialization*. New York: Atheneum, 1985.

Smith, Frank E. *The Politics of Conservation*. New York: Pantheon Books, 1966.

Smith, Henry Nash. *Virgin Land: The American West as Symbol and Myth*. 1950. Reprint, Cambridge: Harvard University Press, 1970.

Smith, Linda L. "Annie Dillard." Ph.D. diss., University of Toledo, 1992.

Smith, Michael L. *Pacific Visions: California Scientists and the Environment, 1850–1915*. New Haven: Yale University Press, 1987.

Solberg, Winton U. "Cotton Mather, *The Christian Philosopher*, and the Classics." *Proceedings of the American Antiquarian Society* 96 (1987): 323–65.

———. "Science and Religion in Early America: Cotton Mather's *Christian Philosopher*." *Church History* 56 (1987): 73–92.

"Spirit and Nature with Bill Moyers." Transcript. New York: Journal Graphics, 1991.

Stanford, Ann. *Ann Bradstreet: The Worldly Puritan*. New York: Burt Franklin & Co., 1974.

Stanford, Leland. "Interstate commerce speech of Hon. Leland Stanford of California in the United States Senate, Jan. 10, 1887." In *Interstate Commerce Speeches*, published by U.S. Congress. Washington, D.C., 1887.

Stearns, Raymond Phineas. *Science in the British Colonies of America*. Urbana: University of Illinois Press, 1970.

Stoeffler, F. Ernest. *The Rise of Evangelical Pietism*. Leiden: Brill, 1965.

Stoll, Mark. "God and John Muir: A Psychological Interpretation of Muir's Life and Religion." In *John Muir: Life and Work*, edited by Sally M. Miller. Albuquerque: University of New Mexico Press, 1993.

Straus, Murray A., with Denise A. Donnelly. *Beating the Devil Out of Them: Corporal Punishment in American Families*. New York: Lexington Books, 1994.

Strong, James. *The Exhaustive Concordance of the Bible*. New York: Abingdon Press, 1890.

Szasz, Ferenc Morton. *The Divided Mind of Protestant America, 1880–1930*. University: University of Alabama Press, 1982.

Tanner, Thomas, ed. *Aldo Leopold: The Man and His Legacy*. Ankeny, Iowa: Soil Conservation Society of America, 1987.

Tawney, R. H. *Religion and the Rise of Capitalism: A Historical Study*. 1926. Reprint, New York: Pelican Books, 1947.

Thomas, Keith. *Man and the Natural World: A History of the Modern Sensibility*. New York: Pantheon Books, 1983.

———. *Religion and the Decline of Magic: Studies in Popular Beliefs in Sixteenth and Seventeenth Century England*. London: Weidenfeld and Nicolson, 1971.

Thompson, William Irwin. "Pacific Shift." In *Nature in Asian Traditions of Thought: Essays in Environmental Philosophy*, edited by J. Baird Callicott and Roger T. Ames. Albany: State University of New York Press, 1989.

Tichi, Cecilia. *New World, New Earth: Environmental Reform in American Literature from the Puritans through Whitman*. New Haven: Yale University Press, 1979.

Tripathi, C. L. "The Influence of Indian Philosophy on Neoplatonism." In *Neoplatonism and Indian Thought*, edited by R. Baine Harris. Norfolk, Va.: International Society for Neoplatonic Studies, 1982.

Troeltsch, Ernst. "The Economic Ethic of Calvinism." In *Protestantism and Capitalism: The Weber Thesis and Its Critics*, edited by Robert Green. Boston: D. C. Heath, 1959.

Tuan, Yi-Fu. "Discrepancies between Environmental Attitudes and Behavior: Examples from Europe and China." In *Ecology and Religion in History*, edited by David and Eileen Spring. New York: Harper & Row, 1974.

Turner, Bryan S. "The Rationalization of the Body: Reflections of Modernity and Discipline." In *Max Weber, Rationality and Modernity*, edited by Scott Lasch and Sam Whimster. London: Allen & Unwin, 1987.

Turner, Frederick. *Beyond Geography: The Western Spirit Against the Wilderness*. New York: Viking Press, 1980.

———. *Rediscovering America: John Muir in His Time and Ours*. New York: Viking, 1985.

Tutorow, Norman E. *Leland Stanford: Man of Many Careers*. Menlo Park: Pacific Coast, 1971.

Vartanian, Pershing. "Cotton Mather and the Puritan Transition into the Enlightenment." *Early American Literature* 7 (1973): 213–24.

Wallis, R. T. *Neo-Platonism*. London: Duckworth, 1972.

Walzer, Michael. *The Revolution of the Saints: A Study in the Origins of Radical Politics*. London: Weidenfeld & Nicolson, 1966.

Webb, Clement C. J. *Studies in the History of Natural Theology*. Oxford: Clarendon Press, 1915.

Weber, Max. *General Economic History*. Translated by Frank H. Knight. Glencoe, Ill.: The Free Press, 1927.

———. *The Protestant Ethic and the Spirit of Capitalism*. Translated by Talcott Parsons. New York: C. Scribner's Sons, 1930.

———. "Science as a Vocation." In *From Max Weber: Essays in Sociology*, translated and edited by H. H. Gerth and C. Wright Mills. New York: Oxford University Press, 1946.

———. *The Sociology of Religion*. Translated by Ephraim Fischoff. Boston: Beacon Press, 1963.

Webster, Charles. "Puritanism and Science: The Anatomy of a Controversy." *Journal of the History of Ideas* 30 (1969): 345–68.

———. "Puritanism, Separatism, and Science." In *God and Nature: Historical Essays* on the Encounter between Christianity and Science, edited by David C. Lindberg and Ronald L. Numbers. Berkeley: University of California Press, 1986.

———. *The Great Instauration: Science, Medicine and Reform, 1626–1660*. London: Duckworth, 1975.

West, Carroll Van. *Capitalism on the Frontier: Billings and the Yellowstone Valley in the Nineteenth Century*. Lincoln: University of Nebraska Press, 1993.

Westfall, Richard S. "The Rise of Science and the Decline of Orthodox Christianity: A Study of Kepler, Descartes, and Newton." In *God and Nature: Historical Essays on the Encounter between Christianity and Science*, edited by David C. Lindberg and Ronald L. Numbers. Berkeley: University of California Press, 1986.

Whicher, Stephen E. *Freedom and Fate: An Inner Life of Ralph Waldo Emerson*. Philadelphia: University of Pennsylvania Press, 1953.

White, Elizabeth Wade. *Anne Bradstreet: "The Tenth Muse."* New York: Oxford University Press, 1971.

White, Lynn, Jr. "The Historical Roots of Our Ecologic Crisis." *Science* 155 (1967): 1203–7.

Whittaker, Thomas. *The Neo-Platonists: A Study in the History of Hellenism*. 4th ed. 1928. Reprint, Hildesheim: Georg Olms, 1961.

Williams, Arnold. *The Common Expositor: An Account of the Commentaries on Genesis, 1527–1633*. Chapel Hill: University of North Carolina Press, 1948.

Williams, George H. "The Idea of the Wilderness of the New World in Cotton Mather's *Magnalia Christi Americana*." In Cotton Mather, *Magnalia Christi Americana Books I and II*, edited by Kenneth B. Murdock. Cambridge, Mass.: Belknap Press, 1977.

———. *Wilderness and Paradise in Christian Thought: The Biblical Experience of the Desert in the History of Christianity and the Paradise Theme in the Theological Idea of the University*. New York: Harper & Brothers, 1962.

Wills, Garry. *Inventing America: Jefferson's Declaration of Independence*. Garden City, N.Y.: Doubleday, 1978.

Winks, Robin W. *Frederick Billings: A Life*. New York: Oxford University Press, 1991.

Winston, David. *The Anchor Bible*. Vol. 43, *The Wisdom of Solomon*. Garden City, N.Y.: Doubleday, 1979.

Winthrop, John. "Arguments for the Plantation of New England," and "A Model of Christian Charity." In *Winthrop Papers*. 2 vols. Massachusetts Historical Society, 1931.

———. *The History of New England from 1630 to 1649*. 2 vols. Edited by James Savage. Boston: 1825–26.

Wolf, Ron. "God, James Watt, and the Public Land." *Audubon*, May 1981, 58–61+.

Wolfe, Linnie Marsh. *Son of the Wilderness: The Life of John Muir*. New York: Alfred A. Knopf, 1945.

Wolters, Albert M. "A Survey of Modern Scholarly Opinion on Plotinus and Indian Thought." In *Neoplatonism and Indian Thought*, edited by R. Baine Harris. Norfolk, Va.: International Society for Neoplatonic Studies, 1982.

Wood, Gordon S. "Evangelical America and Early Mormonism." *New York History* 61 (1980): 359–86.

Woodbury, Robert L. *William Kent: Progressive Gadfly, 1864–1928*. Ph.D. diss., Yale University, 1967.

Worster, Donald. *Dust Bowl: The Southern Plains in the 1930s*. Oxford: Oxford University Press, 1979.

——. *Nature's Economy: A History of Ecological Ideas*. 1977. Reprint, Cambridge: Cambridge University Press, 1985.

——. *Rivers of Empire: Water, Aridity, and the Growth of the American West*. New York: Pantheon Books, 1985.

——. "The Vulnerable Earth: Toward a Planetary History." In *The Ends of the Earth: Perspectives on Modern Environmental History*, edited by Donald Worster. Cambridge: Cambridge University Press, 1988.

Wright, Esmond. *Franklin of Philadelphia*. Cambridge: Belknap Press of Harvard University Press, 1986.

Yardley, Jonathan. "On Diapers and Other Disposables." *Washington Post*, 26 June 1989, p. B2.

Zakin, Susan. *Coyotes and Town Dogs: Earth First! and the Environmental Movement*. New York: Viking, 1993.

Index